T0290460

Inside the Global Economy

Inside the Global Economy

A Practical Guide

Andrew Vonnegut

ROWMAN & LITTLEFIELD
Lanham • Boulder • New York • London

Published by Rowman & Littlefield
A wholly owned subsidiary of The Rowman & Littlefield Publishing Group, Inc.
4501 Forbes Boulevard, Suite 200, Lanham, Maryland 20706
www.rowman.com

Unit A, Whitacre Mews, 26-34 Stannary Street, London SE11 4AB, United Kingdom

British Library Cataloguing in Publication Information Available

Library of Congress Cataloging-in-Publication Data

Names: Vonnegut, Andrew, 1966– author.
Title: Inside the global economy : a practical guide / Andrew Vonnegut.
Description: Lanham : Rowman & Littlefield, [2017] | Includes bibliographical references and index.
Identifiers: LCCN 2017018439 (print) | LCCN 2017020094 (ebook) | ISBN 9781442277304 (electronic) | ISBN 9781442277281 (cloth : alk. paper) | ISBN 9781442281608 (pbk. : alk. paper)
Subjects: LCSH: International trade—Econometric models. | International economic relations—Econometric models. | Competition, International—Econometric models.
Classification: LCC HF1379 (ebook) | LCC HF1379 .V66 2017 (print) | DDC 337—dc23
LC record available at https://lccn.loc.gov/2017018439

∞™ The paper used in this publication meets the minimum requirements of American National Standard for Information Sciences—Permanence of Paper for Printed Library Materials, ANSI/NISO Z39.48-1992.

Printed in the United States of America

Contents

Preface

Returning to California after sixteen years working abroad in emerging markets finance and economic policy advisory, I found myself the owner of a small manufacturing company in the metal industry. To balance days spent squinting at drawings and dealing with machine maintenance, I picked up an evening class teaching global economics at the University of California Santa Barbara. It was a great chance to keep in touch with topics I loved, and honestly knew more about than my new day job.

What frustrated me was the state of the materials available to teach the course. Most of my students were older and heading for professional careers in international companies and organizations. The books I found mainly served up a light version of standard economic theory at the expense of fleshing out the complex realities on the ground. I struggled with the relevance of the material for my students, in the same way I had struggled at the beginning of my own nonacademic career with much of the economic theory in my PhD program.

Sitting near an avocado tree in my yard late one evening, I had a Newton moment as an avocado came crashing to the ground, followed soon thereafter by a swarm of skunks, raccoons, rats, and who knows what else. The feeding frenzy and chaos that ensued became the foundation for how I wanted to write and teach about the global economy. It's not neat and tidy, and though it follows few patterns for very long, it is driven by basic and not always pretty instincts and behaviors. This book represents much of what I learned in my career to date and what I think people should know as they prepare to live in, work in, invest in, or write about the global economy.

Acknowledgments

This book was the effort of many people from different stages of my life who contributed in many and various ways. A few managed to read all or most of the manuscript. Kim Kotnik slogged through every word at least once, and sometimes multiple times. If it turns out to be an economics book that is intelligible to non-economists, as intended, then it is much to her credit. Murat Ucer and William Infante, two lifelong friends and accomplished economists, also managed to get through the bulk of it at different stages, sometimes in painfully early ones. If the book turns out to be anything but a rambling bunch of nonsense, it is to their credit.

Others commented on different parts of the book, mainly as subject matter experts and members of the potential target audience. These include Adam Karson, Riad Al Khoury, Jelena Sevo, Cullen Roche, John Mennel, Garret Tankosic-Kelly, Lawrence Groo, Timothy Collins, Dusan Kovacevic, Matt Adams, Milica Popovic, Przemek Wozniak, Aashish Mehta, Gillette Hall, and Dan Engel. I also owe a debt to Ana Trbovic, Gregory Mitrovic, Norb Vonnegut, and Rowman & Littlefield acquisitions editors Susan McEachern and Rebeccah Shumaker, who helped guide me through the publication process and encouraged me along the way. My students over the last three years get much credit for patiently allowing me to test various versions of the materials on them. They were the underserved target audience that inspired me to write the book in the first place. Finally, I thank Katerina Kotnik Vonnegut for granting me some time in between making the mermaids talk to work on the book.

Introduction

In case there was any doubt before, the 2008 crisis called the great recession laid bare the interconnectedness of the global economy. It was not the first global financial crisis by any means, but it was nearly comprehensive in its reach. What started as a handful of bad mortgages in the United States blew across the globe into a major conflagration.

As the crisis unfolded, from small Norwegian towns to the largest banks in the world, those that invested in US mortgage bonds found the value of their holdings plummeting. As the crisis deepened, almost no asset class or country was left untouched, as weaknesses in US markets exposed risks across the ocean in Europe. Stock, bond, and currency markets all over the world were decimated as investors tried to stem losses or just raise money to pay their obligations. Property, share, and bond markets were hit especially hard in the indebted countries of Ireland, Spain, Portugal, Italy, and Greece. Banks refused to clear accounts with each other, seizing up global money and trade markets.

The 2008 crisis was indeed a major historical event that remains etched in recent memory, but the broader global story is even more complex and interesting. It reveals the 2008 crisis as just an extreme example of what are nearly everyday global events. Cycles of global market turbulence started long before 2008 and continue after the main effects of the great recession fade. In past decades, not to mention centuries, booms and busts have resonated through the global economy in much of Asia, Russia, Southern and Eastern Europe, Mexico, Argentina, and Brazil, among others.

Global economic turbulence is not just about clearly overpriced mortgage-backed assets doomed to an eventual fall. Why did a crisis in US mortgage markets spread to Greek government bonds? Why did major emerging markets initially escape the worst effects, only to be decimated by what was actually another country's cure for the crisis? How could a Russian default contribute to a Brazilian default a year later?

Why did the value of the US dollar actually go up in 2008, when the United States was the apparent source of the crisis? Why have many emerging markets been lousy medium- to long-term investments despite high overall growth? In the last fifty years, why have only an infinitesimal group of countries joined the ranks of the rich, developed nations?

This book was written to provide a foundation for understanding these sorts of questions. It starts with as clear and accurate a *description* of the workings of the real global economy as I can manage. This is hard, since the economy is always in flux. However, certain trends, participants, institutions, incentives and behaviors, rules, and money flows are either fairly readily identifiable and/or stable over at least the medium term. A lot of good data is available if you look for it, understand its limitations, and maintain the flexibility to update points of view.

The description leads to *analysis*. The analysis begins with concepts from standard economics texts, but then moves to a broader range of sources and disciplines, including investment finance, decision theory, economic history, behavioral psychology and finance, and accounting. The approach embraces the sometimes humbling recognition that humans often simply do not understand things for sure, or even very well at all. The world is uncertain, but using all the data, models, analysis, logic, and creative and critical thinking we can muster can bring a bit more order to it.

This sort of broad, hybrid approach is not new or original. It's only unusual in classrooms. Such an approach fills the pages of the top news outlets for global finance, such as *The Economist* and the *Financial Times*. Analysts of the global economy use it all the time in their strategic outlooks. The glimpse into the world of top global-macro hedge fund managers in Steven Drobny's "House of Money" series shows similar thinking. Bits and pieces of the approach are also scattered across numerous books, articles, and blogs on specific global economic topics. Many of those are documented here. This book consolidates the main lessons from many of these sources into a basic foundation that can be used to better understand and make decisions in the global economy.

Trying to understand the workings of the global economy is not just a hobby for geeks. Anyone who invests, has money invested for them, makes strategic business decisions, or has a career that is touched by the global economy should be interested. In the modern world, that is nearly everyone. Those that do manage to benefit from and limit their risks in the global economy, by and large rely not only on luck but on the kind of extensive, holistic approach put forth here. They acknowledge, but then go beyond, the basics such as volatility in terms of bell curves, correlation of single asset classes, the omnipotence of central bank policy levers, and the rationality of markets.

In this book, the real global economy is ultimately about people moving massive and increasing amounts of money, making the best decisions they can, buying, selling, investing, and moving goods, money, and themselves from place to place. These global flows result from purposeful, but often imperfect human behavior and decision making. That behavior is shaped by the incentives that people feel, and the establishment and evolution of those incentives within the global economic system. The money moved by these millions of decisions runs increasingly freely and capriciously around the globe, often swamping officially controlled flows and the intentions of policy makers everywhere.[1] These flows lift, wreck, and redeem economies around the world.

This book covers who in the global economy has money now, who moves it, who makes the rules, and how what is happening now is constantly changing and could change even more dramatically in the future. Economic activity around the globe is not referred to as "international economics," because what is happening is not "between nations" in any meaningful way. It is between individuals and the banks, companies, governments, funds, and other institutions that people are making decisions in and for.

Formal economics tells the tale as a systematic, top-down story with aggregated accounts, and theories and equations describing why and how goods and money move from country to country. It's a good start, but too often sits above the grit of how the economy actually works, and pays only passing service to the real, human drivers of the economy. The explanation here builds from the more rigid concepts and moves toward shedding light on the bottom-up chaos of multiple levels of participants, rules, pools of global capital, and human incentives and behaviors.

Central to the approach is analysis of the participants in the global economy and why they behave the way they do—i.e., what their incentives are. Doing so requires defining and understanding the rules that frame the global economy and govern the exchange of money and products across borders, as well as how those rules are created, implemented, and changed. A knowledge of economic history and a comparative analysis of past, similar cases then lend an understanding of what may or may not be different this time and why. The approach is broad, interdisciplinary, and holistic.

The exposition does not rely on formal mathematical models, but contrary to popular opinion that does not make it simplistic. Math as used in economics is actually a simplifier, with the world more complex than what even the most detailed mathematical model can capture.[2] Many of the concepts used in this book have been formalized into mathematical form in other places, and their legacy and lessons are leaned on heavily here. However, to embrace the chaos that is the global economy, the approach relies on those legacies and then steps when required outside the constraints that mathematical models place on analysis.

In describing and analyzing the global economic system, this book merges together two divisions that are often explicitly or implicitly present in many analyses of the global economy.

First, lines between global and domestic economics are merged together. Domestic policy affects and is affected by what happens in the global economy. How individual governments choose to subsidize industries and population groups, set trade and investment policies, tax, regulate, manage money supply and interest rates, borrow, and invest all can have big effects—if not the biggest effects—on the international flow of money. If global economic decisions are driven by incentives (a central theme of this book), domestic policy in individual countries is a huge creator and changer of the incentives felt by people all over the world. In turn, the reality of what is going on in the global economy can limit, influence, and/or enhance domestic policy, in both small and large economies.

The second division merged is between global economics and finance. Global economics is about flows that happen when people trade, invest, borrow, or do anything else. In doing that they are making financial decisions using financial instruments through financial channels. Economic stocks and flows are by and large financial stocks and flows, aggregated. Economic crises are mainly financial crises driven or at least triggered by financial decisions on the parts of people and their governments. Economic growth is influenced and even defined by financing flows and vice versa. Domestic and global money supply is essentially the result of financial decisions, mainly lending decisions by banks. Central bank monetary policy is driven by a desire to influence financial decisions. Financial incentives are what drive people to try to change the rules of the global economy to suit them better.

The book is about identifying and following the participants in the global economy and their behaviors, the rules and rule makers, the incentives and incentive makers, and the stocks and flows of money that the participants move around the global economy. Along the way, the approach tries to make sense of some global economic events that more traditional methods alone struggle to describe. As a bonus, global economics turns out to be more interesting and relevant than it often seems.

Finally, this book is about starting to understand how and why the global economy could undergo more radical changes in the future. Almost by definition, major events in global economic history represent discontinuities or departures from past trends. Booms, busts, and large changes in prices consistently catch us by surprise because we are not good at anticipating discontinuities. But this is where fortunes and careers are won and lost.

Sadly, but realistically, the goal is not to try to predict the future. However, it is to work to think more clearly about how discontinuities form and what some of the future directions, opportunities, and risks might be in the global economy. Trends are developing both inside and outside the field of economics that could sharply change the current composition and direction of the global economy. In the second section of the book, five such trends are highlighted: demographic change, ecological change, increasing inequality, information technology advances, and emerging markets wealth. Designated the five "big shifts," using the tools developed in the first half of the book each of these is analyzed along with scenarios of how they might change the world.

Expanding liberally and apparently nonanalytically on the traditional textbook methods of describing the global economy might seem radical. It is not. It is how pretty much everyone outside of economics departments thinks about and interacts with the economy. Companies, banks, buyers and sellers of goods and services, portfolio managers, and successful fund managers of all kinds rarely if ever use a strictly formal approach, but instead opt for the more nuanced, multidisciplinary, and humble approach used here.

ORGANIZATION OF THE BOOK

There are two more short parts to this introduction. The first is a brief overview of the tools of economic analysis, and why economists struggle to reach solid conclusions on even some of the most basic questions in economics. The section concludes that economists need to be more comfortable with economics' working in a gray area of knowledge and develop flexible ways of thinking to account for that.

The last part of the introduction briefly covers five "big shifts" that have the potential to disrupt the current path of the global economy: demographic shifts, ecological change, changes in wealth and income distribution, advances in technology, and shifts in emerging markets wealth. The second section of the book is dedicated to examining these in greater detail.

Chapter 1 is an exposition of annotated data on a range of different countries in the global economy. The overview includes data and explanatory text on where wealth in the global economy is now, how economies are measured, how countries are categorized economically, how certain economies are composed in terms of their debt levels, reserves, and how equally money is distributed between and within them. Think of it as a series of detailed snapshots giving an understanding of where the wealth is now—the starting point for the future.

Chapter 2 is an overview of the main national, multilateral, and private participants in the global economy. The chapter describes who and what they are and their incentives to act, covering both those participants who set the rules and incentives, and those who move the money. At the end of this chapter is the story of how many of the participants in the global economy worked together to contribute to the economic crisis called the **great recession** that started in 2008.[3] The conclusion is that the crisis was **incentive compatible**, in that the participants pretty much all did what they would be expected to do. The case illustrates how a more behavioral approach could improve insights into economic events.

Chapter 3 covers central banking and monetary policy. One of the great ironies of central banking is that policies may have a more limited effect on the domestic economy where the central bank is located, than on other countries and money flows through the global economy. Changes in interest rates in the main reserve currencies may have limited impact at home, but they definitely can affect where and how money moves around the planet. Topics include money creation, central bank policy, and impacts on global interest and exchange rates.

Chapter 4 looks at how the setting of policies meant to affect a domestic economy actually creates and changes major incentives in the global economy. Spending, taxing, borrowing, and regulatory decisions all drive money in and out of economies, sometimes in predictable ways and sometimes as the result of "unintended consequences." Extensive mini case studies and examples are given to illustrate the points.

Chapter 5 covers trade and trade policy. The main focus is on current and historical trade flows, and how these have and will likely evolve. Topics include movements toward freer trade, what the barriers are, how they have changed over time, and who agrees or doesn't with freer trade and why. Though difficult to measure precisely, there is an overview of the impact of freer trade on economies and how this can vary considerably depending on the conditions that exist in a country at a particular time.

Chapter 6 considers international payments and exchange rates. It starts with an overview of the main accounts, what comprises them, and how and why they balance. Exchange rates, the extreme risks in foreign exchange exposure, and actions meant to mitigate or profit from that risk, all drive decisions and money flows in the global economy. The final part of the chapter covers the global shocks and contagion effects that can both drive and result from problems in payments accounts and foreign exchange exposure.

Chapter 7 is about global investors and managers, and their decisions. In some ways this is the most important chapter, but it had to be left for later so that background information could be filled in first. The chapter delves more deeply into the main categories of money that make up the balance of payments, then goes into brief overviews of the different instruments that are traded, how they are valued, and some of the basic strategies used by investors moving money around the planet. The chapter also includes a discussion of investor behavior and some of the insights from the field of behavioral finance.

Chapter 8 covers economic growth and consolidates a lot of ideas about why some countries grow, others don't, which ones have, and what we can expect in the future. It also examines the paradox as to why many emerging markets countries, despite higher than average growth rates, have often been poor medium- to long-term investment holds.

Chapter 8 concludes section I of the book on the structure of the global economy.

Section II focuses on the five previously mentioned "big shifts" that can greatly influence the global economy going forward. Each chapter is divided into two parts. The first identifies the shift, the data behind it, and its likely persistence and direction. The second presents a series of speculative but analytic scenarios that highlight how each shift may change the direction of the global economy. The scenarios are developed using the tools from the first section of the book and are designed to provoke ongoing thinking about probabilities, impacts, and ways to benefit from or mitigate negative effects from the shifts.

ECONOMICS AND METHODOLOGY

Economists are notorious for never agreeing with each other. There are a lot of pretty dumb jokes about that, like figure 0.1.

Figure 0.1.

Source: Signe Wilkinson Editorial Cartoon used with the permission of Signe Wilkinson, the Washington Post Writers Group, and the Cartoonist Group. All rights reserved. Used with permission.

They disagree because in fact it is nearly impossible to apply economics methodologies to reach definitive conclusions on anything but the simplest of points. This is not the case in biology, chemistry, physics, or other "hard" sciences where a considerable body of knowledge is established and continually evolving. What is going on?

The truth is that regardless of what many economists want to believe and the often-used term "economic sciences," despite all the math used in the field, economics is not really a science in the traditional definition of the word.

Economics falls short because the always-evolving, chaotic, and noisy economic environment does not allow for the use of sound scientific method to test and definitively validate through clear results and replication even the most important of economic hypotheses.[4] Because of this, it is also usually not possible to use the results of hypothesis tests to go to the next step and definitively prove or disprove broader theories. As economist Danik Rodrik notes, economics "does not presume that there are fixed laws of nature waiting to be discovered."[5] Consequently, answers to many of even the most basic and important economic questions are not well supported by a proven body of theory or reinforcing evidence. You might never know that listening to economists, but it is true and it leads inexorably to disagreement and bad jokes.[6] A short exposition on the challenges of applying scientific method to economics is contained in the appendix. If interested, please take a look there.

For now, it is sufficient to say that few if any actual practitioners in the global economy (i.e., investment managers, company CEOs, economics journalists, central bank staff, and traders) use theoretical economic models or their conclusions as the sole or even primary resource for decision making. Such models are mainly confined between the covers of textbooks and economics journals. Former US Federal Reserve Chairman Alan Greenspan in his introspective book on the future of forecasting notes, "We will forever need to reach beyond our equations to apply economic judgement."[7]

What do these "practitioners" do to find the answers they need and what does Greenspan have in mind when he talks about applying "economic judgement"? There is no formal methodology, but a fluid framework of relevant information and steps, combined to shed light on the current position of the global economy, why it is that way, and what might happen and why. This more robust understanding of global economic events can evolve from researching and analyzing a combination of the following:

- Use of economic research and theory as appropriate. Formal economics can hold answers to important questions. There are many conditional and partial conclusions that can be used judiciously to understand what is going on and what may happen. It is critical to understand the presence, strengths, limitations, and conditions of this research.[8]
- Cataloguing who is doing what, who has the money and power, what decisions are being made by whom, and what incentives are at play. These are the policy makers, investors, traders, and others.
- Collecting and organizing the relevant qualitative and quantitative data. Where the money is currently, where it was before, where it might go, and what has happened in the past. These are the stocks and flows of money, commodities, goods, whatever matters in the particular case.
- Analyzing the supply and demand conditions. Supply and demand are pretty much the only rules that always hold, and they are almost always useful. From commodities, to housing, to exchange rates, to trade prices and volumes, shifts in supply and demand are ignored at peril.
- How liquid and volatile the related markets are and why, taking some but not too much account of historical volatility.
- The presence and strength of rules in place that govern the relevant transactions.
- What happened in similar cases before, and what has changed. Similarly, what other events and trends are important inside and outside of economics that might make things turn out the same or differently.
- What is connected to the event that might affect or be affected by it, both to analyze the event and to understand what related events might occur.

As a short example of this type of analysis, most economics textbooks say that if a country's exchange rate drops against another country's currency, exports will increase and imports will decrease. It makes perfect sense, and it can be shown mathematically why this should happen. But it might not happen that way, and there are lots of reasons for that which are hard to model.

There may be other events happening in the economy at the same time. A falling exchange rate may be a sign of a weak or crisis-ridden economy where credit, human capital, and/or resources are scarce and managers cannot manage a supply response and increase production. It may be that the exchange rate was and still is overvalued, so local companies are still not competitive. The infrastructure may not support more exports, or exporting may be too costly bureaucratically for the products that have become more competitive. The goods made in the country may not be exact or even close enough substitutes for other goods that are in demand internationally. Or, in response to the dropping exchange rate, the central bank of the country may increase interest rates to combat expected inflation as imports get more expensive. That may increase the cost of financing production for export.

Other reasons may be behavioral and linked to individuals and their incentives. Buyers may be already locked into contracts with sellers in other countries, and/or are comfortable with those relationships. Or sellers in other countries may accept a lower profit to ensure ongoing business. Or buyers or sellers may have anticipated exchange rate changes and hedged against them in the financial markets. Governments might introduce subsidy programs so markets are not lost. The drop might be seen as temporary, depending on local monetary conditions, so producers and traders may not bother to react.[9]

Logically, it makes sense that what the textbooks and formulas say should happen. But when you think about how real people making decisions might respond and why, the picture that emerges is often more complex. In principle, all this could be captured in a mathematical model, but the number of unknowns would make the model unsolvable.

Academic economists might dismiss the approach as "nonrigorous," where rigor means the exposition must be expressed mathematically. But math usually only gives the illusion of rigor. In academic economics, equations made up of concave functions and normal probability distributions would be considered good, rigorous economics even when they are only vaguely related to how the economy works. Most functional forms are chosen because they allow the model to solve, not because they reflect reality. The point is not to dismiss these models, but to recognize their limitations and supplement and bring them to life with additional data and analysis.

There is no formulaic or strict way to carry out this analysis. The approach does not even have a real methodology. It cannot be summarized in a matrix on a PowerPoint slide. Its application changes as the situations change. That does not mean analysis should not be carried out as carefully and systematically, and with as much humility, as possible. Many successful global business and investment fund managers use similar methods of analysis when analyzing company strategy or looking for trading opportunities, developing trades, and managing risk.[10] The successful ones have developed their methodology a lot more for their particular portfolios, but still follow such a systematic, broad-based, flexible, and humble approach to understanding the global economy.

BIG SHIFTS IN THE GLOBAL ECONOMY

The global economy is constantly evolving as the participants shift the rules and incentives that govern behaviors and money flows. The complex and largely hard-to-define process involves changes in incentives, rules, power balances, politics, technologies, cultures, and innovations. Evolution happens naturally as participants find new opportunities, developing new ways to profit, position themselves, and manage risk. Evolution can also be hindered and/or driven forward by major events, such as the great recession and emerging markets and other crises.

In addition to the ongoing evolution of the global economy, other forces have the potential to more radically change its structure. These are referred to here as the "big shifts." Studied mainly outside the fields of economics and finance, they don't always get much attention. They also may not immediately appear important to participants in the global economy because they are happening over a longer term and may not be relevant to normal decision-making time horizons.

However, given the potential magnitude of change, the big shifts probably should influence longer-term decision making. That may entail where to build company capacity, what career to enter, how to invest and manage risk over the long term, and for large institutional investors such as pensions, endowments, and insurance companies, how to manage downside risk and maintain future payouts.

The five big shifts are briefly introduced here. These are broad trends that have already begun, and are likely under most conditions to continue. They are not meant to be comprehensive or all-inclusive. The exposition is highly speculative, but important enough to merit consideration. A chapter will be dedicated to each in section II of the book, along with some scenarios for how each "big shift" may affect the global economy.

Demographic Shifts

The modern global economy came into being over the last 250 years at the same time as a huge explosion of people on the planet. This is not mere coincidence; the modern economy and population growth are inextricably linked, as enablers, beneficiaries, and possibly victims of the other. Enter the field of population demographics—the study of changes in the sizes and characteristics of populations—into global economic analyses. After a long period of growth, two trends are evident in the twenty-first century. First, the total population is still growing, with more people added to the planet every year. Second, population growth is slowing with the total population thought to be leveling off later in the century.

A larger population means more demand for products, jobs, benefits, resources, and public and environmental goods. Slowing population growth means fewer workers with an increased average age. The latter leads almost invariably to a lower percentage of taxpaying workers to benefit-receiving retirees, or an increased **dependency ratio**. Most economies have obligations to their retirees regardless of how many there are. There are risks and opportunities in both subtrends, growth and slowing growth.

Ecological Change

Humans depend on a changing climate and ecology for almost all aspects of economic life—production, trade, food, health, and leisure. Though the debate about the reality and causes of climate change is thankfully coming to an end, that of what to do about it rages on. Whether the debate is cool and rational or political and hyperbolic, resulting policies can lead to changes in the global economy.

The first set of outcomes from ecological change stems from the actual physical and consequent economic impacts of a warming and less biodiverse planet. These could reach everything from coastal cities to fisheries to trade routes. Though notoriously hard to specify, the medium- to longer-term effects could coalesce into one of the greatest economic and social disruptions known to modern society.

Reactions to the *prospect* of climate change are more important to current money flows in the global economy. Government programs to combat global warming are large and growing. Tax breaks, subsidies, renewable energy quotas, and other programs have already caused major changes in global capital flows. There is more to come. People, governments, investors, and companies will continue to react to real and prospective climate change. Understanding those reactions will be key for understanding significant global economic events.

Increasing Inequality

Most of modern economic history is the story of growth and increased wealth. For the previous century or more, people have become accustomed to improvements, to feeling richer, to believing they and their children can do better. Recent data indicate that previous growth patterns are changing, with growth slowing and with most of the gains going to the wealthy. The topic is controversial. Some economists think inequality is not increasing. Some claim it is, but is not a problem. Some think inequality is the most important problem of the current century.

The data itself supports two trends that at first glance might appear contradictory. The first is that inequality between countries seems to be decreasing.[11] GDP per capita figures are converging, slowly and unevenly, as poorer countries grow more quickly than richer ones. At the same time, inequality within countries seems to be growing. The share of total income and wealth going to the top 1 percent is on the rise in the twenty-first century after many years of falling inequality. Inequality can potentially bear on a broad range of factors in the global economy, including growth trends, investment patterns, policy responses, and political stability.

Information Technology and Virtualization

Industries are being born, dying, or transforming from advances in the fields of artificial intelligence and machine learning, robotics, data analysis, and virtualization. Some of the biggest companies in the world didn't exist or barely existed twenty years ago. Others didn't adapt and are extinct. Unlike previous decades, some of technology's biggest companies are shedding the "dinosaur" stigma, taking advantage of scale and internal resources, and out-innovating previously nimble startups.

Advances are far-reaching and either are or are prepared to transform numerous elements of the global economy including labor markets, production, distribution, capital markets, consumer decisions, politics, trade, communications, social relations, and medicine. We pretty much know that. What matter here are the resulting shifts in global money flows and markets.

Because of the rapid, early, and ongoing evolution of technology and the state of global economic institutions, the effects of this big shift may be the most difficult to identify let alone quantify. Will technological advances give advanced countries an edge in manufacturing again, disrupting trade patterns? Will advances in medicine allow developed market economies to dodge the "dependency ratio" bullet? Will emerging markets economies successfully "leapfrog" into higher levels of technology without having to make the investment? Will humans find better tools to separate virtual falsehoods from reality?

Emerging Markets Influence

Emerging markets economies are increasing their share of global GDP. India and China are the big winners, which should not come as a surprise to anyone who reads the news. Other long-term gainers are some of the larger emerging markets that have grown steadily, like a number of other Asian countries, Turkey, and Egypt. Some smaller countries that started in particularly bad spots, like Rwanda and Vietnam, also gained. Other large emerging markets have done relatively well, but not well enough to keep up with India and China. Some of those, such as Brazil and Russia, have had their results beat down by crises they went through in the 1980s and again in the mid-2010s as natural resource prices dropped. There is a lot of variation over regions and times, but the overall trends are clear.

There are a few big questions here. One is why some poorer countries are growing faster and under what circumstances that might or might not continue, and for which ones and why. Also, though emerging markets overall will likely continue to grow, perhaps only pockets of those countries will carry the growth while other parts stay mired in poverty. The means, risks, and returns on investments are also unclear, as growth has often not translated into investment returns. Additionally, emerging markets economic growth interacts with demographic change, with most of the growth in big emerging markets. As those billions of people continue to strive for and achieve wealth, they most certainly will affect the planet, its resources, and investment flows.

Certainly, the big shifts introduced here are not the only or probably even the most important forces bearing on the global economy. Daily, there are shifts in prices, participants, incentives, and so on that drive the direction of the constantly evolving global economy. The shifts presented here are still postulated to be major factors bearing on global economic developments over the next five to thirty years. In our complex world, they will interact with themselves and with many other forces to evolve in a way that is largely unknowable now, but still important enough to consider and try to understand.

The next section outlines the main participants and how they interact in the global economy.

NOTES

1. What David Smick (2008) calls the "dangerous ocean of money" in *The World Is Curved.*

2. I went to a math-intensive graduate program. One of my professors, Leonid Hurwicz, who has since won the Nobel Memorial Prize in Economic Sciences, once noted that the strong sense of economic intuition that graduate students arrive with is rapidly lost as they get into the math.

3. The crisis that started in 2008 is often called "the great recession" in contrast to "the Great Depression" of 1929. There is no precise definition of a recession versus a depression, but all agree that a "depression" is worse (Federal Reserve Bank of San Francisco 2007).

4. In a 2015 study, economists from the Federal Reserve were unable to replicate the results of over half of a sample of papers taken from leading economics journals, even with the assistance of their authors (Chang 2015). As was pointed out by one reviewer, some areas in microeconomics are getting closer with the increasing use of randomized control groups to isolate the effects of policies. Replicability and counterfactuals are still problematic, but progress is being made.

5. Rodrik 2015a.

6. Some economists foresee a future where theories and models fade, supplanted by the processing of massive amounts of data by machine learning algorithms. See for example chapter 11 in Tyler Cowen's (2014) *Average Is Over.*

7. (Greenspan, pg. 292). Though central banks are known for maintaining extensive mathematical models of economies, staff are also known for their internal disagreements on the interpretation of those models.

8. This is similar to the defense used by many economists when defending theoretical models—that they need to be understood and used in context. See for example Dani Rodrik's post (Rodrik 2015b) as well as his book cited above, and the discussion by David Andolfatto from the St. Louis Fed, though Andolfatto's defense can read almost like an indictment depending on how you approach it (Andolfatto 2015).

9. A case in point of a US manufacturer taking steps to maintain market share as the USD rose in 2015 can be seen in an article by Schwartz (2015). The increase in the home currency's value can hurt exporters, but it does not mean that there is a mechanical and/or proportional export response to exchange rate changes.

10. In his two "House of Money" books, Steven Drobny's series of interviews with successful global hedge fund managers would validate the greater success of such broad-based analysis over formulaic approaches (Drobny, 2006, 2010). The methodologies put forth in the book *Superforecasting: The Art and Science of Prediction* by Tetlock and Gardner also bear more resemblance to the methods put forth here than those normally used in the field of economics (Tetlock 2015).

11. Hellebrandt and Mauro 2015.

I

THE GLOBAL ECONOMIC SYSTEM

Though the global economy is in constant flux and is perhaps more often than not beset by chaos and uncertainty, there is still a "system," or underlying framework, to speak of. This system is comprised mainly of the global economy's numerous participants, rules, incentives, and financial and physical stocks and flows. The chapters that make up section I look at these system components in more detail and explore how they work together to drive global economic events.

The *rules* are like rules anywhere else. They determine the formal legal and informal bounds within which participants operate. They are the whole set of laws, norms, traditions, and paths that guide and constrain how people move goods and money around the world. They can be informal, like social practices and norms, or formal, like official laws and regulations. The effectiveness, consistency, and permanence of rules vary, with people often trying to subvert or change them. Even if not immutable or always clear, rules matter. If people break the rules too often or by too much, they can suffer at the hands of the enforcers of the rules and/or other participants who have a stake in the rules.

The definition of a rule might seem obvious, but some examples help illustrate the diversity involved. Rules include the paperwork you need to fill out to export, the norm that you are supposed to pay for goods and services that you receive, that to trade on certain exchanges you need to follow the procedures and regulations, that money gained might need to be taxed, that Serbian border officials should not hold Macedonian fresh fruit imports to Germany at the border until they rot, that if you receive a business card in Japan you should not fold it in half and pick your teeth with it, or that if you build a power plant in France, you need to abide by environmental guidelines. Rules are numerous and appear in every part of the global economy. They can favor some groups and disadvantage others. Rules can get a bad rap as restrictions on the free market, but in truth they at least equally provide order to transactions and protect different parties to them. If rules did not exist, they would need to be invented for almost any conceivable version of a modern global economy to function.

The institutions, individuals, and societies that establish and enforce the intertwined and frequently inconsistent set of rules in the global economy are highly influential, but not omnipotent. If governments try to impose formal rules that are not consistent with existing practice, instead of increasing order they can create a foundation for uncertainty and corruption. The weaker the states, and many poorer economies have weak states, the harder it can be to create and enforce new, formal rules. Many of us observed this difficulty in Eastern Europe during the transition there from command to market economies in the 1990s and 2000s. Rather than law and order, uncertainty frequently prevailed after countries adopted EU and US laws and institutions wholesale on top of quite different, but long-standing, legal and social traditions. The more radical the departure from existing traditions and the more deep-rooted the traditions, the harder it can be to create or modify rules.[1]

Rules can be strongly influenced by those who are governed by them, and much effort is put into trying to make and shape them. As noted in chapter 4, distinguishing between "corruption" and "responsive government" can sometimes be surprisingly difficult. A myriad of examples of rule making, rule breaking, and the subsequent effects on global goods and money flows will be seen in the chapters that follow.

Incentives are what motivate people to take action, and in particular drive them to put their money out into the global economy. If returns or growth can be higher someplace outside the home economy, there is an incentive to move money abroad. If risks seem to be increasing in an economy, there is an incentive to withdraw funds. If interest rates rise in one place without an increase in risk, there is an incentive to invest there. If goods are cheaper in another country, there is an incentive to buy from there. If they are more expensive, there is an incentive to sell there. If a government introduces subsidies for green energy investments, the incentive to invest in that area increases. When a government punishes a foreign investor to protect domestic investors, it may decrease the incentive to invest there. However, if the population of that same country is large, rich, and growing, that increases the incentives to invest, all other things equal, and may counteract other disincentives.

Identifying and understanding shifting incentives are a big part of global economic analysis. It is a first step in mapping out the types of choices that people are most likely to make and understanding the waves of goods and money that move across the global economy.

The *participants* are the individuals and institutions (and the individuals within the institutions), public and private, that set and respond to the rules and incentives. Sometimes it is clear who is setting rules and who is abiding by them, and sometimes it gets very mixed up. They are divided up in chapter 2 as clearly as possible, but the divisions are still not perfect.

The introductory taxonomy above may look systematic and well defined, almost to the point where you could fit the pieces into a series of equations and solve them. To the extent possible, the chapters that follow bring in concepts and results from the field of economics that help do that. At the same time, the rudimentary taxonomy is barely a rough starting point to help organize some basic concepts and definitions. In the chapters and many examples that follow, the global economy takes a much more chaotic shape once real humans start making their imperfect decisions in a constantly changing and complex world. Rather than simplifying and trying to reduce the chaos to make it more manageable, the theme here is more one of accepting and embracing it.

The following chapter gives an overview of the historical and current state of some important stocks and flows in the global economy.

NOTE

1. Informal norms and institutions can be much longer standing and as strong as formal ones, with quite often formal rules just being the encoding of existing norms. See work from the neoinstitutional school and in particular Douglass North (1990, 2005).

1

National Economies Compared

This short exposition of the current stocks and flows of money and goods in the global economy is the starting point for the more analytical chapters that follow. Data from a variety of sources reveal where different economies stand in the global economy, some of their main characteristics, and where the money is and seems to be moving in broad terms. To be precise, money is used in the vernacular here as a synonym for income and wealth. Actually, as will be detailed in chapter 3, money is a lot more complicated than that and has different forms that are more or less "money-like." For the time being, these (important) nuances are set aside.

The main indicator used for the size of an economy is gross domestic product, or GDP. It is the sum of all goods and services produced in the borders of a country in a given year. Another common measure is gross national income or GNI, which measures the total goods and services produced by a country's citizens in a year. With some exceptions, they are usually pretty close and most of the time GDP is more widely available and commonly used. GDP works fine as a way to roughly gauge where countries stand in relation to each other. It is a good proxy for the total economic influence citizens and governments of a country have in the global economy. The identity for how GDP is normally calculated tells a lot:

GDP = Consumption + Investment+ Government Spending + (Exports – Imports)[1]

GDP defined this way is the sum total of the market value of all the goods and services that are bought in an economy over the course of a year, by people (consumption), companies adding to capital stock (investment), and the government (purchases and services from taxes and debt). Finally, if something is consumed, it is either made in the country, or imported. That's why the value of net exports is added. Countries where people buy more from other countries than they send abroad have their GDP measurement decreased by that amount. This is not highly controversial; it's just accounting.[2]

Confusingly, the identity above looks like a spending formula whereas the *P* in GDP is about product or production. It turns out it's usually easier and more accurate to calculate GDP by measuring spending than adding up actual output. It can be done that way too, and also by adding up total income.[3] The consumption method works because if something is consumed, it presumably had value to someone or it would not have been bought. The value is known—it's just the market price. Measuring output instead of consumption runs the risk of adding worthless junk to the GDP figure, since it is entirely possible to produce something that no one wants or ever buys.

Table 1.1 contains a group of countries ranked by two measures of GDP. The first is GDP in US dollar (USD) terms. In this case, the country's GDP in their own currency is just converted to USD at the exchange rate prevailing at the end of the year. The second is GDP adjusted for **purchasing power parity** (PPP).

The PPP adjustment helps capture the fact that a dollar does not purchase the same quantity of goods and services in all countries. Simply converting a foreign county's GDP to dollars ignores this fact (that is immediately evident to any tourist). Many goods and services either do not have a single world market price because they are not traded globally, or there are enough transactions costs in moving them from place to place that their world market price differs from their local price. A wide range of goods and services can cost more or less in some countries than others.

The PPP adjustment tries to account for that.[4] In vernacular terms, in "cheaper" countries the USD tends to have more purchasing power, creating a discrepancy between USD and PPP GDP. In "expensive" countries, it is the opposite. Most countries that are a lot "cheaper" are poor. In other countries, a PPP GDP may be higher than a USD GDP figure if a country tries artificially to hold down the value of its currency. By most (but not all) evidence, the Chinese government implemented such a policy to fuel demand for China's exports. As seen in the table, there is a big difference between USD and PPP GDP, even though China has become relatively wealthy.

Both indicators are useful. It might be said that GDP in USD is a better measure of wealth globally and global economic influence, whereas GDP PPP is a better indicator of how well the country is doing domestically. Many economists would feel that PPP measures are a better indicator of the real size of an economy, and these have largely become the standard.

Ignore the initials to the left of the country name for now. They will make more sense in a minute. As seen in the table, big countries tend to have big GDPs, which does not say too much. Nigeria has a larger GDP than Norway, but not many people would think of it as a richer place. Also, GDP is a flow; it is the product of the particular country during a particular year. It does not say much about how much actual wealth is in the country. Generally, it can be surmised that countries that have had a large GDP for a long time are wealthier. All those flows build up

Table 1.1. GDP in Current USD and at PPP, 2015

		GDP Current USD	*GDP PPP*
BRIC	China	10,866,443,998,394	19,524,348,171,415
DME	United States	17,946,996,000,000	17,946,996,000,000
BRIC	India	2,073,542,978,209	7,982,527,568,328
DME	Japan	4,123,257,609,615	4,738,293,560,882
DME	Germany	3,355,772,429,855	3,848,271,845,006
BRIC	Russian Federation	1,326,015,096,948	3,579,826,387,385
BRIC	Brazil	1,774,724,818,900	3,192,398,002,509
EM	Indonesia	861,933,968,740	2,842,240,508,777
DME	United Kingdom	2,848,755,449,421	2,691,808,537,207
DME	France	2,421,682,377,731	2,650,822,573,675
EM	Mexico	1,144,331,343,172	2,194,431,313,648
DME	Italy	1,814,762,858,046	2,182,579,699,550
EM	Korea, Rep.	1,377,873,107,856	1,748,776,398,234
HIO	Saudi Arabia	646,001,866,667	1,685,203,505,624
DME	Spain	1,199,057,336,143	1,602,660,452,817
DME	Canada	1,550,536,520,142	1,588,596,446,963
EM	Turkey	718,221,078,309	1,543,283,930,048
EM	Thailand	395,281,580,953	1,108,108,240,372
FM	Nigeria	481,066,152,870	1,091,697,772,067
EM	Egypt, Arab Rep.	330,778,550,717	996,638,129,040
EM	Poland	474,783,393,023	993,129,043,249
DME	Netherlands	752,547,410,447	820,725,814,742
EM	Malaysia	296,217,641,787	815,644,552,977
EM	Philippines	291,965,336,391	741,029,139,381
EM	South Africa	312,797,576,594	723,515,991,686
HIO	United Arab Emirates	370,292,716,133	643,166,288,737
DME	Switzerland	664,737,543,617	501,653,407,777
HIO	Singapore	292,739,307,536	471,630,937,869
DME	Sweden	492,618,068,569	454,867,696,457
HIO	Hong Kong SAR, China	309,928,790,732	414,375,639,981
DME	Austria	374,055,872,241	411,818,289,486
EM	Chile	240,215,707,927	400,534,442,322
EM	Peru	192,083,721,355	389,146,724,478
HIO	Qatar	166,907,692,308	321,417,765,757
DME	Norway	388,314,890,979	319,401,440,789
DME	Greece	195,212,006,432	288,778,094,737
EM	Morocco	100,359,546,358	273,358,206,500
DME	Ireland	238,020,405,900	253,634,826,262
FM	Kenya	63,398,041,540	141,950,884,423
EM	Guatemala	63,794,348,775	125,950,437,098
FM	Ghana	37,864,368,220	115,136,546,616
EM	Jordan	37,517,410,299	82,631,102,215
FM	Mongolia	11,757,940,909	36,067,684,621
FM	Botswana	14,390,863,395	35,763,294,335
FM	Chad	10,888,798,114	30,480,978,104
FM	Rwanda	8,095,980,014	20,418,305,189

over time to a big stock of wealth that contributes to quality of life and presumably continues to generate GDP.

Perhaps more importantly, GDP alone does not say much about how well people are doing in a particular country. Dividing GDP, or better yet PPP GDP, by the population gets you to per capita GDP, or national income per citizen. This is a much better indicator of how rich people are in a given country, though this should not be mistaken for the actual income that people there earn. There is a correlation, but not a direct relationship.[5]

Table 1.2 gives a ranking of GDP per capita on a PPP basis, along with growth rates over the last twenty years.

With incomes presented on a per capita basis, countries break down more clearly into broad economic categories. The letters on the far left represent the categories. An important caveat follows. These categories are not mutually exclusive, are not in any way agreed upon by everyone, nor is it all that incredibly important whether a country specifically falls into one category or another. Basically, no one really likes or agrees on these designations. However, almost everyone breaks down and uses them and they are moderately worthwhile, since countries in each grouping tend to share some basic characteristics. They are a taxonomical convenience and are used loosely enough to hopefully not become a taxonomical burden.

There are two groups of countries with rich citizens. The first are the main **developed market economies** (marked DME) that have large, diversified economies and well-developed goods and capital markets. They have all experienced high GDP over a sustained period of time, allowing them to build a large amount of wealth. They tend also, importantly, to have their own stable currencies that are widely used in trade.

The other group of wealthy countries, for lack of a better name, is called **high-income other** (HIO). These are mainly smaller countries with specific sources of wealth. Some, like the United Arab Emirates and Qatar, are energy producers. Others, like Singapore and Hong Kong, are gateway countries to much larger economies and groups of economies. Hong Kong is rich the way that Manhattan is rich; mainly it has a disproportionate share of the wealth around it.

As an example of how the categories are not mutually exclusive, Norway is a smallish country that qualifies as a DME, but that also derives much of its wealth from energy. The country of Qatar ranks at number one, but is a good example of a major difference between GDP and GNP. Some 80 percent of the residents of Qatar are foreigners. These foreigners also generate a lot of the wealth, so taking all that money and dividing it by the 20 percent of citizens there leads to a high GDP per capita. Countries like Qatar and the UAE are also notable in that they have a high GDP per capita, but have not had it over as long a period of time as the DMEs. So despite their high incomes, the economies themselves may more closely resemble the next category, the emerging markets.

The next category, also often referred to as low to high middle income countries, are the **emerging markets** (marked EM). These are countries with developing goods

Table 1.2. GDP Per Capita, PPP Basis

		2015	*Change Since 1995 (%)*	*CAGR Since 1995 (%)*
HIO	Qatar[a]	$143,788	102	3.6
HIO	Singapore	$85,209	145	4.6
HIO	United Arab Emirates	$70,238	91	3.3
DME	Norway	$61,472	90	3.3
DME	Switzerland	$60,535	186	5.4
HIO	Hong Kong SAR, China	$56,719	204	5.7
DME	United States	$55,837	666	10.7
DME	Ireland	$54,654	133	4.3
HIO	Saudi Arabia	$53,430	92	3.3
DME	Netherlands	$48,459	105	3.6
DME	Austria	$47,824	179	5.3
DME	Germany	$47,268	74	2.8
DME	Sweden	$46,420	88	3.2
DME	Canada	$44,310	140	4.5
DME	United Kingdom	$41,325	306	7.3
DME	France	$39,678	151	4.7
DME	Japan	$37,322	196	5.6
DME	Italy	$35,896	64	2.5
EM	Korea, Rep.	$34,549	63	2.5
DME	Spain	$34,527	104	3.6
EM	Malaysia	$26,891	92	3.3
DME	Greece	$26,680	158	4.9
EM	Poland	$26,135	155	4.8
BRIC	Russian Federation	$24,451	117	3.9
EM	Chile	$22,316	294	7.1
EM	Turkey	$19,618	175	5.2
EM	Mexico	$17,277	111	3.8
EM	Thailand	$16,305	200	5.6
FM	Botswana	$15,807	155	4.8
BRIC	Brazil	$15,359	176	5.2
BRIC	China	$14,239	155	4.8
EM	South Africa	$13,165	251	6.5
EM	Peru	$12,402	66	3.4
FM	Mongolia	$12,189	336	7.6
EM	Indonesia	$11,035	262	6.6
EM	Egypt, Arab Rep.	$10,891	107	3.7
EM	Jordan	$10,880	161	4.9
EM	Morocco	$7,821	86	3.1
EM	Guatemala	$7,707	110	3.8
EM	Philippines	$7,359	104	3.6
BRIC	India	$6,089	109	3.8
FM	Nigeria	$5,992	137	4.4
FM	Ghana	$4,201	263	6.7
FM	Kenya	$3,083	–9	–0.5
FM	Chad	$2,171	96	3.4
FM	Rwanda	$1,759	94	3.4

a. Data for Qatar is since 2000.

and capital markets, and that usually have their own currency that is not widely used in international trade. They usually must buy and sell other currencies to participate in global markets. Economies tend to be diversified, but often less so than the DMEs, and are often at least somewhat dependent on exports to DMEs. This is a broad category. GDP per capita may be fairly high, but like the Qatari and the UAE examples above, they have not been accumulating wealth for as long as the DMEs.

The largest of the EMs are Brazil, Russia, India, and China, also referred to as the BRICs.[6] The BRICs are the only category where membership is certain, not that the membership really means anything. The four economies have little in common other than that they happen to be big and "emerging." The EMs and BRICs tend to have had a higher average rate of growth than the DMEs in recent decades, though with a *lot* of variability. This higher average rate is one reason (and also the effect of) they have attracted considerable investment in the first decades of the second millennium. GDP per capita growth in the EMs and BRICs is extremely varied from country to country, and notoriously unstable within the countries.

Finally, the last category is the **frontier markets** (FM), which are poorer, tend to have markets that are hard to get in and out of (low liquidity), and laws that are more difficult to understand and are often inconsistently implemented. Many of them have long histories of political and economic instability. Some of these have grown quickly in recent years, attracting the interest of intrepid investors.

GDP per capita on a PPP basis is a pretty good indicator of standard of living for citizens of a country, on average. It does not say anything about whether all, most, or only a few of those citizens live well or not. Who in the country lives well and who does not (i.e., income distribution) is an increasingly important policy question that could drive global capital flows if governments try to take action on it. There will be more on that later, but it is worth taking a look at indicators of inequality within countries.

Table 1.3 presents three different measures of inequality taken from the United Nations database. They are ranked by their Gini coefficients for the most recently available year. For each of the indicators, the higher the number, the more unequal the income distribution in a country.

The Gini index is the most well-known and longest-used measure of inequality, but data is hard to come by, and methodologies for calculating it tend to vary a bit by country. For example, the figures for most of the wealthier countries (OECD data) are after taxes and transfers, or after wealthier citizens have been taxed and money has been transferred to programs intended to benefit the poor. The Gini figures tend for that reason to be a little lower than for other countries. Pretax and transfer Gini figures would be quite a bit higher. Though Gini coefficients are the most well-known indicator of inequality, two other measures are included for comparative purposes.

Regardless of shortcomings, there are some patterns in inequality data. A lot of developing and fast-growing emerging markets have relatively high inequality. In decades past, this may have been autocratic regimes' favoring their own friends and family over the general population. In more recent decades, part of the inequality is

Table 1.3. Measures of Inequality

Country	*Coefficient of Inequality*	*Atkinson Index*	*Gini 2005–2013*
South Africa	33.0	57.3	65.0
Botswana	36.5	55.5	60.5
Brazil	25.6	38.7	52.7
Guatemala	28.9	33.1	52.4
Chile	18.2	36.0	50.8
Rwanda	31.6	35.2	50.8
Mexico	21.8	34.6	48.1
Kenya	31.1	36.0	47.7
Peru	23.0	31.9	45.3
Chad	39.6	30.7	43.3
Philippines	17.8	26.8	43.0
Nigeria	37.5	28.4	43.0
Ghana	33.1	31.7	42.8
United States	15.7	35.6	41.1
Morocco	28.5	23.0	40.9
Turkey	15.7	21.8	40.0
Russian Federation	10.3	18.7	39.7
Thailand	19.9	34.0	39.4
Indonesia	18.2	17.3	38.1
United Kingdom	8.4	17.8	38.0
China	n/a	29.5	37.0
Spain	11.0	23.9	35.8
Italy	11.3	19.8	35.5
Greece	12.1	20.6	34.7
Australia	7.9	17.7	34.0
Jordan	16.4	20.5	33.7
Canada	8.6	17.4	33.7
India	27.7	16.1	33.6
Poland	9.6	17.5	32.8
Switzerland	7.3	12.3	32.4
Japan	12.2	13.5	32.1
Ireland	8.5	16.3	32.1
France	8.6	13.9	31.7
Egypt	22.8	14.2	30.8
Germany	6.7	14.1	30.6
Korea (Republic of)	15.9	18.4	30.2
Austria	7.6	15.5	30.0
Netherlands	6.5	11.6	28.9
Norway	5.3	10.2	26.8
Sweden	6.5	13.1	26.1

almost certainly related to rapid globalization as those same economies liberalized, or opened up to global markets. As certain parts of those economies have become competitive in the global economy, other parts and their workers have not, and their incomes have not grown as quickly if at all. Often, the same demographic groups who benefited under an autocratic regime had the education and connections to benefit most from the global economy as those countries opened up.

Former centrally planned countries such as China, Russia, and Poland are part of a slightly different story, since they started their latest growth phases simultaneous with a transition from centrally planned to market economies. They have seen their Gini coefficients increase in recent decades, though this time series is not shown in the data above. Under central planning no one was very rich, at least not officially, so they started from fairly low levels of income inequality.

In some of the countries where inequality has been historically high, such as in Latin America, recent economic growth has coincided with at least slightly lower inequality. The wealthy European countries tend to have lower levels of inequality, but this is on the rise according to other data. One country that does not fall into one of these patterns is the United States, which is both wealthy and for some time has had relatively high inequality. Though an interesting topic, the focus in this book is not on why countries are equal or unequal, but about how equality or inequality might affect global money and goods flows.

All this talk about indicators of national wealth assumes that they matter. Some observers have criticized the almost singular emphasis in economics on GDP and GDP growth. Critics consider these to be limited indicators that furthermore encourage policy makers to focus overly on economic growth, when what really matters are a broader range of "quality of life" indicators.[7] It might be true that economists are a little lazy and GDP is an easier indicator to work with than "well-being" and "happiness." At least people generally agree on what GDP is. Fortunately for economics, other studies have shown a solid relationship between GDP per capita and a range of quality of life indicators for both the rich and poor in a country.[8] Apparently, that ever-elusive indicator "happiness" is also pretty tightly correlated with GDP per capita.[9]

To summarize the above, some countries might produce a lot in a given year mainly because they are large, but their people are poor. Some countries may not produce so much, but they are small and their people are rich. And some countries may have money or not, but have larger or smaller numbers of rich and poor people. There is much variability, but a picture of where countries stand should be starting to emerge. Where the wealth is in the global economy is an important starting point for analysis. The purpose of these tables is to give a general idea of that.

GDP is about annual production and is a **financial flow** indicator. The indicators that follow highlight some of the main **stocks** that matter in the global economy. One place that global wealth stocks reside, at least at an official country level, is in foreign reserves. These appear in two main locations. The first is in official exchange reserves. Table 1.4 shows who has what reserves, and for reference's sake, their share

Table 1.4. Official Foreign Reserves, Million USD

	1990	*2000*	*2010*	*2015*	*% of GDP*
China	34,475	171,763	2,913,711	3,405,253	31.3
Japan	87,828	361,639	1,096,068	1,233,097	29.9
Saudi Arabia	13,437	20,846	459,313	626,989	97.1
Switzerland	61,284	53,620	270,479	602,402	90.6
United States	173,093	128,399	488,928	383,728	2.1
Russian Federation	—	27,656	479,222	368,042	27.8
Korea, Rep.	14,916	96,250	292,143	366,707	26.6
Hong Kong SAR, China	24,655	107,560	268,743	358,772	115.8
Brazil	9,199	33,015	288,574	356,464	20.1
India	5,637	41,059	300,480	353,319	17.0
Germany	104,547	87,496	215,977	173,730	5.2
Thailand	14,258	32,665	172,027	156,459	39.6
France	68,290	63,728	165,852	138,198	5.7
United Kingdom	43,145	43,075	82,364	129,600	4.6
Turkey	7,626	23,514	85,959	110,489	15.4
Indonesia	8,656	29,352	96,210	105,928	12.3
United Arab Emirates	4,890	13,631	32,785	93,929	25.4
Peru	1,890	8,675	44,214	61,594	32.1
Sweden	20,324	16,498	48,246	58,098	11.8
Norway	15,788	27,922	52,797	57,455	14.8
Netherlands	34,401	17,688	46,146	38,213	5.1
Qatar	951	1,163	31,181	36,923	22.1
Nigeria	4,128	10,099	35,884	31,334	6.5
Morocco	2,337	5,016	23,956	23,005	22.9
Austria	17,227	17,649	22,241	22,239	6.0
Jordan	1,138	3,441	13,632	16,571	44.2
Egypt, Arab Rep.	3,619	13,785	37,028	15,858	4.8
Guatemala	361	1,805	5,948	7,745	12.1
Kenya	236	897	4,320	7,548	11.9
Botswana	3,331	6,318	7,885	7,546	52.4
Greece	4,721	14,594	6,352	6,027	3.1
Ireland	5,361	5,407	2,113	2,203	0.9
Mongolia	—	202	2,287	1,322	11.3

in the country's GDP for the latest year available. Many of these are estimates, because not all countries are transparent about their reserves. Countries are ranked by their position in 2015.

Reserves are usually managed by the central bank of the country, with the funds kept in pretty traditional, short-term instruments, like government bonds, cash, or gold. Since reserves are normally in foreign currencies, holdings are in foreign currency–denominated instruments. Though reserves are usually kept on hand and not highly traded, their size means the buying and selling of reserves can affect global markets.

The bulk of reserves are normally held in just a handful of **reserve currencies**. These are mainly the currencies that dominate foreign trade and investment transactions, primarily the US dollar, euro, and yen. The British pound is still something of a reserve currency mainly because of the UK's importance as a financial center, though this may change following the "Brexit" vote of 2016. These currencies dominate partially because that is just what people end up with when they sell to or invest in other countries, and so they are "convenient" to hold. The fact that most oil and many other commodities are priced in USD helps support the reserve status of that currency.

Some reserves are held in currencies that are not important in trade but are considered "safe," like the Swiss franc. In general, and fortunately, the reserve currencies are also from countries that are considered to be more or less well managed economically. So there is some correlation between trade and investment being carried out in the currencies, and their being desirable as a store of value. The need for countries that do not have a reserve currency (most of them) to switch back and forth between their own currencies and the reserve currencies to buy and sell goods and service debt is an important theme in this book and in global economics overall.

Countries' reserve positions can be divided into some broad categories, based on why they hold them. Big economies like the United States have a lot of cash on hand because they do a lot of trading and use the money mainly to settle trades. All countries do this; it's just that bigger countries tend to have a greater volume of trade. This money does not really matter that much either for the global economy or for the country. It is not likely to either increase or decrease much as a percentage of national or global GDP and does not really go anywhere else in the global economy. As can be seen, with some exceptions the main developed market economies hold a small percentage of their GDP in reserves, almost always less than 10 percent.

A second group with high reserves consists of energy and natural resource exporters. They hold reserves, mainly in USD, because they sell a lot of oil, gas, and/or minerals, also mainly in USD. They hold the money mostly in USD or euro because the alternative would be to exchange it for their local currencies and spend it domestically. That would drive up the value of those currencies, making it more difficult for non–natural resource exporters in those countries to compete in the global economy. So they hold the money "offshore" (which is not always really offshore). This will be covered in more detail in chapter 6. Some of the larger natural resource exporters do not show large reserve positions, partly because some of their overall reserves are parked in sovereign wealth funds rather than official reserves. More on that directly below.

A third group with large reserves are big exporters that earn a lot of foreign currency because they sell a lot to other countries. They do not want to convert the foreign currency earning to their local currency for the same reason as group two. An increased currency value would either make their exports more expensive to buyers in other countries and/or decrease the profits (in local currency) that their own exporters make. The main difference between the two groups is one of perception by trade partners. The second, resource-exporting, group is seen to be prudently managing their exchange rate by **sterilizing** the domestic impact of their natural resource exports. The third group is more seen as trying to manipulate the value of their currency to make their exporters more competitive. The difference may seem subtle, but is important in the relations between nations.

The second and third groups as well as many emerging markets will also hold reserves to try to smooth out the deep cycles that can accompany being a natural resource exporter or being highly dependent on global export markets in general. If demand starts to dry up, countries can then spend down their reserves to buy their local currencies, smoothing otherwise potentially sharp exchange rate movements. Countries that allow their currencies to freely float need fewer reserves than those that anticipate trying to manage their exchange rates. Again, more on this in chapter 6.

A second place that reserves show up is in sovereign wealth funds. When countries accumulate a lot of foreign currency, at some point it becomes more than is needed to clear trades and/or manage their exchange rate. Or they may have a pretty freely floating exchange rate anyway. Sovereign wealth funds are a popular vehicle for investing excess reserves. They differ from traditional foreign reserves in that they are designed to generate a profit and/or provide a longer-term store of wealth for the citizens of the country. Since the money does not need to be available in the short term, they are able to invest in a wide range of often longer-term and higher-risk instruments, including stocks and corporate debt, property, hedge funds, entire companies, and long-term for-profit and nonprofit development projects across a wide range of countries and industries.

These funds have become important global investors in recent years with estimated wealth of around $6 trillion as of 2015.[10] In table 1.5 contains a sampling of global investments made or planned by some different countries' funds.

Significant stocks of wealth show up in another place, though it is not technically wealth, at least not yet. A number of countries have substantial value stored in the ground in the form of unextracted commodities.[11] Though not normally considered

Table 1.5.

Fund	*Investment*
State Oil Fund of Azerbaijan	Invested $1.8 billion in Chinese renminbi, both to speculate on its increasing value and as a reserve currency
Qatar Investment Authority	Holds $1 billion stake in Bank of America
Norway's Government Pension Global Fund	Will set aside $8 billion to make environmentally related investments
Abu Dhabi Investment Fund	$7.5 billion in Citigroup in 2007, helping the bank holding company make it through the great recession
China Investment Corp.	Plans to invest an increasing amount of its $700 billion+ fund in agriculture and food production

in global economics, the stocks will likely eventually influence investment flows inside and into the countries that have these resources. The most obvious cases are the oil-rich countries such as the UAE, Kuwait, and Saudi Arabia. But other resource-rich countries such as Chile, Brazil, Mongolia, and Congo are sitting on large amounts of potential wealth that have not yet entered their national accounts. This is a tricky area to get into, because once you accept it, in theory any as-of-yet unrealized wealth in any country should be counted. The value is also directly linked to highly volatile commodity prices. This topic is left aside for the time being and brought up again when relevant to specific cases.

The quick tour of money in the global economy finishes up by looking at country debt. Economists focus a lot on a country's quantity of public and private debt, and whether it is too high or not. Quantity matters, especially as the costs of servicing debt come into play and the fiscal position or debt quality starts to suffer. However, the other side of the debt coin is at least equally important for the normal workings of the global economy. Debt is not just a liability for countries and companies, but an asset for investors with real returns (interest and appreciation) that attracts money from all over the world.

As the quantity and quality of debt changes, incentives change and money moves. Debt quality is an indicator of the issuer's ability (or willingness) to pay on the debt. If it looks like a country or major borrowers within its borders may default, investors can react (or panic) and dump that debt and, importantly, the currency it is in. When a troubled debt market starts to look better, money can quickly flow back in that direction. The ebb and flow of money into and out of debt instruments in countries can be a big part of global economic activity. In the next chapter, a look at the global financial crisis of 2008 illustrates how changes in the quantity and quality of debt moved the global economy in that case.

Now for some data. Table 1.6 below shows central government debt as a percentage of GDP. This is the debt owed by the central government and does not include other important debt such as that held by companies, individuals, and other branches of government.

A couple of interesting themes emerge from the data. First, following the onset of the great recession in 2008, government debt increased quite a bit in the major developed market economies. During the great recession, as production and incomes dropped, tax revenues dropped off faster than spending, leading to deficits in those years. On top of that, many governments implemented **stimulus** programs to stabilize the economies by trying to make up for decreased consumer and business spending with increased government spending. Remember the GDP identity. If *C* and *I* are dropping, in theory the slack can be made up by *G*. Some of these programs were discretionary, but contrary to popular belief many forms of stimulus are automatic. Unemployment benefits and forms of public assistance increase sharply when economic activity falls off.

Another theme from the data is that emerging markets have tended toward pretty low and/or decreasing sovereign debt burdens over the past decade or two.

Table 1.6. Central Government Debt as a Percentage of GDP

	1990	*1995*	*2000*	*2005*	*2010*	*2014*	*2015*
Japan	67	95	144	186	216	249	248
Greece	69	93	100	98	146	178	178
Italy	92	109	105	102	115	133	133
United States	—	—	—	65	95	105	106
Spain	43	63	58	42	60	99	99
Singapore	71	67	80	92	97	98	98
France	35	55	58	67	81	96	97
Ireland	—	79	36	26	87	107	95
Jordan	220	115	100	84	67	89	92
Canada	75	100	81	71	81	86	91
United Kingdom	31	47	39	41	77	88	89
Egypt	—	—	—	98	70	86	88
Austria	56	68	66	68	82	84	86
Brazil	—	—	66	69	63	63	74
Ghana	32	76	112	48	46	69	73
Germany	—	54	59	67	81	75	71
Netherlands	77	73	51	49	59	68	68
India	—	70	74	81	67	66	67
Morocco	76	78	70	62	49	63	64
Malaysia	75	39	33	41	52	56	57
Mexico	—	—	42	39	42	50	54
Kenya	—	—	52	48	44	47	53
Poland	—	49	37	47	53	50	51
South Africa	—	—	42	33	35	47	50
Switzerland	34	53	55	58	46	46	46
Sweden	—	70	51	48	38	45	44
China	—	22	37	34	35	41	44
Thailand	—	—	58	44	40	44	43
Chad	—	—	66	26	30	37	39
Philippines	—	63	59	59	43	36	37
Australia	16	31	20	11	20	34	37
Korea	13	9	17	27	31	35	36
Qatar	11	42	53	19	42	32	36
Rwanda	—	120	103	71	23	29	35
Turkey	—	—	51	53	42	34	33
Norway	28	32	28	42	42	28	28
Indonesia	—	—	87	43	25	25	27
Guatemala	—	—	19	21	24	24	24
Peru	—	—	44	40	25	21	23
Luxembourg	—	8	6	6	20	23	22
United Arab Emirates	—	—	3	7	22	16	19
Botswana	—	—	8	7	19	18	18
Russia	—	—	56	15	11	16	18
Chile	44	17	13	7	9	15	17
Nigeria	—	—	—	—	10	11	12
Saudi Arabia	—	74	87	37	8	2	6
Hong Kong SAR	—	—	—	1	1	0	0

That is actually a big change from previous decades when many were considered debt disaster cases.

The size of the public debt and how much is too much is a topic of much discussion and controversy in economics. A couple years into the great recession, two prominent economists published an influential paper where they warned that economic growth could plummet once the debt level reached 90 percent of GDP.[12] This led to pressure to halt stimulus programs and adopt austerity measures to keep debt below the dreaded 90 percent. The paper was subsequently largely discredited when two other economists pointed out some errors in their data and analysis, starting the whole debate over again.[13] The debate of how much debt is too much remains not only unresolved, but with little consensus around it.

The International Monetary Fund (IMF), which is both influential and interested in such matters, rightly considers the speed and rationale behind debt buildup to be important, along with overall levels. In a 2015 report, they considered only Japan, Greece, Cyprus, and Italy to be in the danger zone.[14] The others in the chart above, even with debt-to-GDP ratios in excess of 100, were considered to have adequate margins of safety. They did note, however, that these margins of safety could rapidly evaporate if another recession were to begin before debt-to-GDP ratios were given a chance to decrease.

Public debt is only a portion of the total debt outstanding in an economy. It can be a little harder to define and get data on total debt, so good, consistent, cross-country comparisons are rarer.[15] For example, do credit card debt and short-term "payday" loans count, or credit extended by stores to regular customers, and if so, how are these measured? At the consumer level, different countries have many different ways that credit (debt) is created.

Private debt is important, though. It was private debt, mainly in the form of mortgage bonds, that set off the great recession. This was both a quality and a quantity problem, partially because the drive for more quantity led to lower quality.[16] As emerging markets faltered in the mid-2010s, it was again private debt at the forefront of concerns. Trillions of dollars were lent to emerging markets' banks and companies after the great recession, as investors holding reserve currencies sought higher returns than they could get in the major market economies. Investors keep watch on public and private debt serviceability and currency weakness (which are related), especially if the debt is in a different currency than their own.

This ends a quick look at where the money currently is in the global economy. As noted, some of these figures are "stocks," such as debt and reserve levels. Stocks show the current level of assets or liabilities in a certain place at a certain time. GDP on the other hand is a "flow," or actual wealth that is created in and enters an economy in a given time period, in this case a year. Whenever parts of stocks move from place to place in the global economy, they become and are recorded as flows.

Net trade in goods and services appears in the domestic GDP formula and is a large part of global flows. When people pay for goods from a seller in another country, money flows across borders in one direction, and goods in the other. In 2016,

Table 1.7.

Exports (billion USD)[a]		*Imports (billion USD)*	
China	2,304	United States	2,810
United States	2,207	China	2,040
Germany	1,612	Germany	1,366
Japan	818	United Kingdom	834
Netherlands	749	France	808

a. World Trade Organization web database

the total value of the flow of goods across borders was around 18.8 trillion US dollars.[17] Trade is covered in detail in chapter 5, but table 1.7 gives a quick look at the countries whose companies and people trade the most goods.

Another large global flow, and one of the main topics of this book, is investments made by people in one country in assets in another. Investment flows are covered mainly in chapters 6 and 7 and are a critical underpinning of almost all aspects of global economics. They can be investments in existing stocks, bonds, derivative contracts, or direct loans to borrowers on foreign markets, called **portfolio flows**. If an investor in Italy buys a US mortgage bond, that is a portfolio flow, since they are buying an investment instrument. Other examples are a Chinese investor buying a euro bond issued by Spain or shares in the US company General Electric on the New York Stock Exchange.

A characteristic of portfolio flows is that assets invested in them are relatively liquid and can be sold quickly (though not necessarily profitably) and the money can be then withdrawn from the country. These are also often referred to as **hot money** flows due to the speed at which they can move, both in and out of economies, with positive and negative consequences.

Direct lending or extension of credit lines from banks in one country to banks in another is often put into the hot money category. These interbank loans are common, either to subsidiaries of banks in foreign countries or by directly extending credit lines to unrelated foreign banks. Whether these flows are hot money or not depends on the terms of the lending contract, but even if loans cannot be canceled and called in, not being able to roll them over and refinance them can have similar consequences. During periods when hot money is fleeing, balance of payments data often shows a sharp slowing, rather than a reversal of these credit flows.

Investment flows can also be direct investments into factories, real estate projects, or other fixed assets in other countries. These are referred to as **foreign direct investment,** or FDI. FDI flows are normally fairly long-term investments and may taper back when hot money exits, but seldom go into reverse. The total value of direct investment flows in 2012 was estimated at around $4.4 trillion.[18]

Investment flows, especially portfolio flows, contribute greatly to short-to-medium-term fluctuations in currency values, with global financial volatility and crises frequently driven or at least amplified by portfolio flows. Portfolio flows might seem arbitrary at times, but in reality they react to a wide range of factors, many of which are the subject of this book: central bank decisions and interest rates across markets; domestic economic policies, including spending, regulations, and political shifts and instability; growth differentials between countries; shifts in prices and terms of trade; the search for investment yield coupled with fear; and any number of other factors, creating both investment opportunities and risks along the way. More in chapter 6 and 7.

Global pricing of everything from currencies to assets is mainly on the basis of supply and demand, and flows are the manifestation of demand. When more money is flowing in than out, currency and asset values tend to rise; when more is flowing out than in, they tend to fall. Frequently, this does not happen in a smooth, predictable, or controllable way. The sheer volume of financial flows has been growing in recent decades, with tremendous consequences for the global economy, positive and negative. This is the "dangerous ocean of money" coined by David Smick or perhaps the "global savings glut" noted by Ben Bernanke. Behind these flows, or this dangerous ocean, are millions of individual, daily decisions made by the participants described in this book. A big part of this book is about understanding the different flows and the people, incentives, and decisions that drive them.

This ends the brief introduction to where the money is. It is all just the starting point, and much of the rest of the book is about the who, how, why, and when of money moving around.

NOTES

1. Exports and imports are of goods and services.

2. Sort of. GDP is generally recognized as comparable across countries with most countries following standard methods of calculating it, but it can be controversial nonetheless. Some argue that the value of negative outputs like pollution or inefficiencies like spending on health care that does not lead to better outcomes should be subtracted. Similarly, the effect of quality improvements such as in consumer goods is rarely captured. Like any economist trying to get to a point, we will ignore those arguments here. For more on the various difficulties in defining, let along calculating, GDP see *GDP: A Brief but Affectionate History* by Diane Coyle (2014). Note also that contrary to some beliefs, imports do not subtract from GDP. When net exports are negative, it simply means that the people in the country are consuming more than what the country produces. Net exports are an adjustment to get at an accurate measurement of GDP.

3. The three methods of calculating GDP, expenditure, income, and output, are in theory equivalent, though discrepancies between them appear when applied to real data.

4. The distinction between traded and nontraded goods is important. Unless there are trade barriers in place, *traded goods and services* generally have a world market price, after accounting for the cost of getting them from place to place. They are usually not significantly cheaper in "cheap" countries unless there are barriers to moving them elsewhere. *Untraded goods and services* can vary widely in price from place to place. For a more technical exposition of PPP see Eurostat-OECD (2012).

5. GDP is a measure of total value added in an economy. Generally, people in countries with a high GDP per capita have higher take-home incomes, but the accounting route from GDP to take-home pay is a longish one.

6. This was a term coined by Jim O'Neill of Goldman Sachs in 2001 and the name stuck (O'Neill 2001). The BRIC concept is also an artificial construct, as the four economies have little in common other than their size, and is likely to fall out of use at some point.

7. For more on this debate, see again Diane Coyle (2014) *GDP: A Brief but Affectionate History*, or the much shorter review of the book by the IMF (Buchholz 2014). As an interesting note, the country of Bhutan maintains an official statistic called Gross National Happiness or, predictably, GNH.

8. The OECD Better Life project has been collecting data on a wide range of quality of life indicators in different countries. The rankings do not differ radically from the GDP per capita rankings above (OECD 2015).

9. The United Nations publishes the World Happiness Report–based surveys where people report their level of "well-being" defined by several variables. Denmark ranked as the happiest country in 2013 (United Nations 2013). The UN also publishes the Human Development Index (HDI), which ranks countries on a broader range of social indicators than just GDP.

10. Exact figures are hard to come by for many funds (Stahl 2013). See the Sovereign Wealth Fund Institute website for a ranking of the biggest funds.

11. Not everyone accepts that unextracted natural resource wealth should be part of national balance sheets. We are not concerned with national income accounting forecasts, but with how global money flows may change over time in response to the extraction of that wealth.

12. Reinhart and Rogoff 2009.

13. Herndon, Ash, and Pollin 2013.

14. Ostry et al. 2015.

15. One of the better studies is by the McKinsey Global Institute and notes that aggregate debt continues to grow post the great recession. Despite a misconception that global "deleveraging" has been widespread after the great recession, this has been limited in both the public and private sectors (Dobbs et al. 2015).

16. *The Economist* (2012b) published an estimate of total debt for a number of countries and how it breaks down.

17. World Trade Organization web database.

18. McKinsey Global Institute, *Global Flows in a Digital Age* (Manyika et al. 2014).

2

Participants and Incentives

The adage that sailing and war are characterized by long periods of relative calm punctuated by moments of sheer terror could be applied to the global economy. The main difference is that in places the terror can stretch into years, and even during periods of calm much is happening to set the stage for the next upset. In the midst of this mix of volatility, shifting incentives, often vague rules, competition, and risk are the participants who help shape and make their living from the global economy. They struggle in real time to make money, manage risk, position themselves, and maintain structure and order.

Participants in the global economy are a highly diverse group with varying characteristics, capabilities, and incentives. Escaping easy categorization, the main ones are nonetheless the subject of this chapter, along with mini–case studies illustrating their effects on global money flows. For organizational purposes, these participants are divided into those who move money and those who shape the rules of the global economic system. The edges around those categories will blur, but it is a reasonable taxonomical starting point.

At the foundation of the money-moving group are billions of individuals making billions of daily decisions that direct the flow of money around the planet. Sometimes they move money themselves, but more often their decisions aggregate up to an intermediate, institutional level. They invest money in certain investment vehicles, companies, or real estate; vote the management of public companies in or out; import and buy particular products from companies in some countries and not from others; choose to move to another country to improve their lives; travel and spend money abroad; and/or vote in ways that affect the structure and incentives of the global economy.

At the intermediate level are the managers who run the different trading and manufacturing companies, investment and pension funds, banks, and all the other institutions that move most of the money in the world. The managers who run these institutions have their own incentives, which incidentally may or may not be the same as those of the billions of people whose money they are managing and moving. The potential incentive conflicts are called **principal-agent** problems in economics and will appear throughout the book.[1]

During periods of calm the individuals, or principals, may stay in the background letting the managers, or agents, do their business (whether that is a good idea or not). During periods of uncertainty individuals can get back in the game, sidelining their agents and amplifying trends. This book concentrates mainly on participants at the intermediate level, but the incentives and potential behavior of the herds of individuals is always in the background. The decisions made by the multitude of participants at the individual and intermediate levels aggregate up to drive the events that define the global economy.

Most of the rule makers in the global economy are national and multinational public or semipublic institutions and political processes that are influenced through votes, money, lobbying, self-preservation, and power politics in states and groups of states. Sometimes these institutions move money, but primarily they set or at least influence the rules and incentives that in turn influence the money-moving participants. The term "public" is used loosely. Generally, this means not privately owned, though some of the rule-making institutions are largely private in some sense or another. Rather than try to precisely define public or private up-front, the individual descriptions below will help make this clearer.

Rule-making institutions are a varied group, established for a multiplicity of reasons to carry out a range of tasks. Consequently, they may respond to quite different incentives from each other and even be in open conflict, creating struggles for power in the global economy and adding to uncertainty. Some of them are set up to serve a narrow base of interests or to solve a particular regulatory or coordination problem. Some are set up to serve a broader base and the "public interest," at least in the country or region they are in. Adding to the chaos, what constitutes the "public interest" may be as varied as the groups purportedly defending it.

Sometimes public institutions get at least partially "captured" by private interests. **Institutional capture** is when institutions end up serving other, usually more powerful, participants than the ones they are created and mandated to serve, such as when Japanese utilities provided much of the key expertise used by nuclear regulators.[2] Some public institutions might keep the broad public interests in mind some, most, or even all of the time, but again because the public is such a diverse group, it can be challenging to identify what the "interest" is. The behavior of these institutions depends on a mix of financial and power incentives, oversight, and the political process and rhetoric. The ambiguity can make analyzing their behavior tricky, but it is better to accept, confront, and try to sort through this reality than ignore it.

How rule-making institutions end up serving different interests is all fascinating, but the ethical questions and nuances of right or wrong are not a key part of analyzing global economic events. The focus is on the institutions, their authority and capabilities, their incentives to act under different circumstances, and finally the outcomes of those actions.

As a starting point, what follows is a brief categorization and description of most of the main institutions that set the rules and move the money. Throughout the book, with analysis of different events in the global economy, these institutions and their actions will be brought out in more or less detail as needed.

RULE AND INCENTIVE MAKERS I: STATE AND QUASI-STATE INSTITUTIONS

In an open international economy, domestic institutions and their actions can drive major global economic events. Domestically based institutions are frequently more important than many purely international ones, setting the rules and incentives for the flow of global capital more than they are given credit for. Below is a short summary of the main domestically based institutions, how they can influence the global economy, and their broad incentives. The overview will be expanded and clarified as needed when analyzing events throughout the book.

The two most important of these domestic institutions, central banks and domestic law-making and regulatory bodies, have their own chapters.

Central Banks

Central banks manage the banking and monetary systems within countries. They use various tools to manage the supply of money, interest rates, and inflation, all three of which are related to each other. Some central banks have a sometimes-conflicting dual mandate to control inflation and promote economic growth. The latter is achieved mainly through maintaining monetary stability and helping sustain a flow of credit to the economy.

Most central banks are nominally "independent" of the political process, while paradoxically governors of central banks are also normally appointed by politicians. Mandates differ in different countries, but central banks usually also act as a lender to the commercial banks in the country, often of "last resort" or when the commercial markets cannot fulfill their needs. In many if not most countries, central banks also play a part in regulating commercial banks. Chapter 3 of this book is reserved for central banks, the tools they use, and their real and perceived impacts on the domestic and global economy.

Main Global Economic Influence

- Successfully increasing key interest rates, all other things equal, leads to increased demand for the home currency and an increase in the exchange rate (i.e., the number of USD you get for a euro, or yen for a Swiss franc) as money enters a country to take advantage of the higher rates.

- Interest rate increases in major market economies (i.e., United States, European Union, Japan, China) that lead to capital inflows can lead to a decreased demand for other currencies, even to the point of destabilizing the countries using those other currencies.
- Increased money supply in an economy, all other things equal, causes inflation and a decreased demand for the currency and a falling exchange rate. Since in most economies commercial banks create the majority of the money, it is often easier for a central bank to slow money supply growth than to increase it.
- Central banks may hold and actively buy and sell reserves in foreign currencies to provide funds for foreign exchange transactions, and frequently to influence the country's inflation and exchange rates.
- Bad decisions by central banks can cause harm to an economy. It is less clear if good decisions are as influential and can do much more than just keep an economy on track.

Incentives

Usually public or quasi-public, central banks are normally established to be independent from the political process, at least in theory. In practice, central banks often choose a route that is politically popular at the time, and/or serves the local banks and financial system.[3] Because they are political and *ex ante* proof of crises is hard to come by, they may err on the side of not intervening early when crises are forming. They tend to be strongly reactive and weakly proactive. Incentives are more aligned to take credit for solving a problem *ex post*, than to take the blame for making a mistake by acting too quickly to head off a problem. This may be changing, however.[4]

Mini Cases

US central bank. In May 2013 the US central bank (or Federal Reserve or Fed) signaled that it would likely start to cut back on its quantitative easing program.[5] That led investors to believe that US interest rates and the value of the US dollar might start to rise. In a rush to get out of riskier investments and prepare to invest in higher-yielding US bonds, many investors simultaneously liquidated their emerging market positions. Within a week, currencies had dropped in many markets, including 15 percent in Argentina. Whether the flight was justified solely in terms of the risk-return trade-offs is questionable. Most importantly, not wanting to be the last ones out of a falling currency, investors reacted strongly to the Fed announcement.

Swiss central bank. Because of its role as a "safe haven" or low-risk currency as well as the popularity of Swiss franc loans in Europe, the Swiss franc had been appreciating after the great recession as investors sought safety and low borrowing rates. To keep the currency from rising too much and harming Swiss exporters, the Swiss central bank tried to steady the exchange rate by selling Swiss francs for other currencies to counter demand from outside. In January 2015 the bank stopped this activity and let the market prevail. The value of the Swiss franc subsequently increased over 20 percent against the euro in a single day. The increase upset currency markets, causing the bankruptcy of a number of currency trading firms, and sharply inflated loan service costs in Central European countries where Swiss franc–based loans were popular.[6]

Legislative and Executive Branches of Domestic Governments

The legislative and executive functions of government make an economy's tax, spending, and regulatory decisions. Different systems have different degrees of overlap and separation of legislative (lawmaking) and executive (enforcement) function, though they all have some version of them. Laws are often passed as broader guidelines, with the executive side given discretion in interpretation and drafting of regulations.[7] Legislative and executive/regulatory bodies are at their best when supporting each other. If they are at odds, regulatory changes by executive mandate alone can be possible, but may have less stability or influence if not supported by the legislature. Similarly, executive branch leadership that does not agree with a law may cause confusion by stalling implementation. Conflicts can create uncertainty and instability in an economy, affecting incentives to move money in and out.

The full range of domestic spending, taxation, and regulatory decisions can change economic incentives in the global economy, leading to inflows and outflows of money. Chapter 4 is dedicated to the influence of domestic spending and regulatory policies on the global economy.

Main Global Economic Influence

- Subsidies or tax incentives to certain industries or regions can draw money into or away from countries, regions, and/or industries. Spending and regulatory decisions can shift the profitability of whole industries, nationally and internationally, by changing real prices, the cost of investments, and returns.
- Regulations can impose or relieve costs on companies and consumers, shifting the relative prices of different resources and activities, making some more/less expensive and/or risky than they would have been and others relatively lower/higher cost and less/more risky.
- Trade and investment policies can change the cost of goods and investment capital, shifting trade and investment money flows.
- Through allocations to foreign assistance programs, money can flow into developing countries.

Incentives

Governments are normally mandated to draft and implement laws to benefit voters/citizens in the country. Laws and regulations may conflict with the interests of citizens in other countries, or blocs in their own countries. Political power and job preservation are major incentives bearing on government officials, and may conflict with broader citizen interests. Both legislators and regulators are often under the influence of strong lobbying and/or elite interest groups that seek to gain or maintain power. Lawmakers and regulators may leave government to join industry groups later in their careers, so may make decisions while in office with their future employment in mind. Difficulty ascertaining the results of policy initiatives either *ex ante* or *ex post* clouds assessment of government performance, further confusing incentives.

Mini Cases

US legislature. Building on previous legislation, the United States in 2005 started phasing in a policy of subsidizing and mandating the production and use of ethanol as a fuel. This was done partly for energy security reasons, partly for environmental reasons, and largely resulting from farm industry lobbying. In the United States, ethanol is mainly made from corn. The policy led to an increase in the price of corn and subsequent increases in the prices of farmland. As corn prices rose, the price of grain-fed livestock also rose. Land that previously had been used to grow food was diverted to ethanol production, contributing to worldwide increases in food commodity prices. The recession of 2008 helped bring food prices back down, but a number of emerging markets countries were on the brink of riots from high food costs, at least partially driven by US ethanol subsidies.

Irish legislature and executive branch. For many decades in the middle of the twentieth century, Ireland was considered the hopeless basket case of Europe, with GDP growth and per capita GDP lagging EU averages. In the late 1980s, Ireland cut taxes and deregulated much of its economy. PM Garrett Fitzgerald took the reins from Charles Haughey in 1981 and built upon his predecessor's early policies promoting foreign investment. Fitzgerald further increased spending on infrastructure and education, ensuring that goods had easy access to domestic and foreign markets, and that business had a supply of skilled labor. Together these policy measures drove productivity and profits higher. As a low-tax haven with open access to the EU markets and a stable legal and regulatory regime, Ireland became a magnet for investment. Many companies, particularly US tech companies like Apple, Dell, and Intel, based their European operations there. By 2005, Ireland had one of the highest rates of per capita GDP in the European Union.

Chinese state banking system. Government credibility is strongly rooted in economic conditions, and perhaps nowhere more so than in China. In the decade leading up to 2017, signs of crisis have come and gone in the Chinese economy. Rising wages, losses of manufacturing jobs, crashes in property markets, and ever-increasing debts of all kinds have been heralded as signs of a coming Chinese crash. At the same time, government motivation coupled with huge reserves and a strong hand have kept the doomsayers at bay for far longer than would have been possible with a less focused government with fewer resources. Most imbalances cannot grow forever, but strong political will and power can perhaps push China through the transition it needs, while financing the costs of past decisions.

Departments/Ministries of Foreign Affairs/State/Defense

These institutions carry out official foreign and defense policy. They may have a role in setting that policy as well, since they frequently control the information used in decision making. They may also be involved in trade negotiations and foreign assistance decisions when matters of "national security interest" are involved.

Main Global Economic Influence

- Can wage wars directly or by proxy, harming or destroying some economies and improving others. Sometimes economies on the periphery of conflict can benefit depending on logistics, rebuilding, and refugee situations. As Brecht's Mother Courage can attest, in war there is often money to be made and lost on both sides of the battlefield and in periphery countries.
- Implement sanctions on countries, causing economic harm and altering the flows of money in the global economy. This can create both new risks and new opportunities.
- Allocate financial and military assistance to "friendly" countries.

Incentives

Difficult to determine, frequently erratic and public relations driven. Many if not most members of these organizations seek preservation or enhancement of job and status; others seek to make a name for themselves with bold moves.

Mini Case

In the spring of 2014, Russia annexed the Crimea and supported pro-Russian rebels in Eastern Ukraine. A fairly serious set of Western sanctions aimed at hurting Russian banking interests "caused" the Russian stock market to drop 40 percent in the nine months thereafter. The sanctions are also likely to have a negative effect on other, and especially German, firms that do a lot of business in Russia. In the words of a Russian investment banker encountered in Central and Eastern Europe eight months after the annexation of the Crimea: "We never expected that it would be so expensive to invade the Crimea."[8]

RULE AND INCENTIVE MAKERS II: MULTILATERAL INSTITUTIONS

Multilateral institutions help set, and monitor compliance with, rules governing interactions between other institutions, companies, and governments. They vary widely in scope and influence, with their influence often believed to be greater than it is. In reality, most major decisions that affect the global economy are still made by the domestic institutions in the first group above. The institutions in this second category all exist by virtue of some kind of voluntary, multilateral agreement between countries. Most of them are not directly influenced by special interests, but by the dominant nations among their members. As such, they are probably influenced by the special interests in those nations.

Their influence is directly tied to the power of the nations that support them. Not surprisingly, history has shown that the weaker nations run a greater risk of punishment (usually sanctions of some kind) for breaking rules set by multilateral agreements, than do more powerful countries.

These organizations are characterized by a desire to survive and reinvent themselves however necessary, even when their initial mandate has been fulfilled or rendered moot. Satisfying the wishes of the more powerful members that are normally the larger financial contributors is one way to do this. Despite some shortcomings, much of these institutions' work has with little doubt led to greater growth and stability in the global economy.

World Trade Organization, WTO

The World Trade Organization has been the main negotiator and to a lesser degree enforcer of freer trade among countries since its predecessor institution (GATT) was formed as part of the Bretton Woods agreements at the end of the Second World War. As of 2017 it had 160 members, comprising substantially all of the major economies in the world.[9]

Though begun with a mandate for tariff reduction, the WTO over the years has also concluded a series of agreements on services trade, intellectual property protection, and investment protection. As its membership has increased, its ability to gather the consensus needed to continue to negotiate and see major agreements enacted has diminished greatly. Its relative influence has also decreased in recent decades with many individual countries bypassing it to sign more limited agreements among themselves. To some degree it is a victim of its own success, with many of the "easier" tasks such as broad tariff reduction largely achieved.

Main Global Economic Influence

- With 160 members as of 2017, including all of the major economies in the world, the WTO represents the largest trading bloc in the world.
- The WTO is one of the few places where members can go with trade disputes with other countries. Though the WTO cannot force any county to comply

with its rules, it can allow member countries to increase tariffs on countries that are found at fault. However, many bi- and multilateral agreements outside the WTO have more effective conflict resolution mechanisms.
- In addition to presiding over major drops in tariffs, the WTO has been able to secure agreements on a range of other issues such as investment protections, trade-in services, antidumping, state subsidization of industries, and copyright protections.
- The WTO has become both a victim and a symbol of differences between developed and emerging economies' interests. In sum, developed nations seek better access to services in emerging markets, and emerging markets want richer countries to give up their agricultural subsidies, while leaving their own protections intact.

Incentives

The WTO has not completed a major round of negotiations since 1992. The main incentive now is to complete any deal at all, good or bad, to justify its existence. The organization's expensive, Geneva-based infrastructure is at risk.

Mini Cases

Boeing and Airbus have since 2005 been the subject of a series of complaints filed by the United States and European Union under the WTO dispute resolution mechanism. Both sides accuse the other of receiving government assistance that distorts free trade in aircraft and harms the other company. In 2012, the WTO ruled against Boeing, opening the way for punitive tariffs against US goods entering the European Union. Boeing appealed, as did Airbus in previous rulings where it was found at fault, leading to decisions in 2016 against both Boeing *and* Airbus. Many millions of dollars have been spent both on prosecution and defense. Though both companies benefit from state assistance, it is possible that it would have been greater and competition more unfair without the intervention of the WTO.[10]

Multilateral Special Purpose Entities

This is a broad category with institutions varying in scope, purpose, and influence. At times and in places, their influence may be great, and in other cases many years may go by with little evidence of their existence. Most of these were established by international agreements between nations, and are financed by signatories to that agreement.

Main Global Economic Influence

- *International Bank for Reconstruction and Development (IBRD) or World Bank.* A Bretton Woods institution like the WTO, the bank lends at often concessionary terms (low interest rates, long repayment periods, grace periods, etc.) to low-income-country governments for development purposes. World Bank loans are usually expected to be repaid, but frequently are rescheduled and forgiven. Most lending is for health, infrastructure, and education. The World Bank's research arm actively studies economic issues facing the developing world. The World Bank also collects and publishes data on member economies.

- *International Monetary Fund, IMF.* The third of the **Bretton Woods institutions** after the WTO and World Bank, the IMF was established to assist countries with short-term balance of payments problems. IMF staff often establish "conditionality," or reforms that countries must make to qualify for funds. An IMF agreement with a country has sometimes signaled that it is safe for private investors to reenter the country. The IMF has a well-regarded, fairly independent research arm that often publishes conclusions that may disagree with the institution's official policies.
- *Bank for International Settlements, BIS.* Often called the central bank for central banks, the BIS actually conducts minimal banking activity—mainly money transfers between central banks. The BIS makes influential recommendations on bank regulation, most notably the Basel Accords, and conducts well-regarded analyses of global financial risk.
- *OECD, Organization of Economic Cooperation and Development.* Established after the Second World War, the OECD consists of the main industrial countries and Mexico and Turkey. The OECD conducts studies on important events and collects data, and is a good source of both. Their reports tend to be scholarly, fairly politically neutral, and data intensive.
- *European Bank for Reconstruction and Development, EBRD, and European Investment Bank, EIB.* These were created to invest, respectively, in companies and governments for the purpose of increasing economic growth in the broader European region. Much of their activity has been in the former centrally planned states of Central and Eastern Europe.
- *United Nations, UN.* The UN is not normally considered an economic institution, but it has some influence, especially in some of the special conventions related to legal issues between countries and in setting standards that allow countries to trade more easily. It is also a good source of global economic data.
- *Organization of Petroleum Exporting Countries, OPEC.* OPEC is a cartel of countries established to collude in setting world oil prices. For decades, OPEC succeeded in restricting supply among members to keep prices high. As more oil is produced outside of OPEC member states, their power has decreased, though prices are likely still higher than they would be without their efforts. The increase in unconventional oil and gas production in the United States in the 2010s ("fracking") is undermining OPEC's historical ability to influence global oil prices.

Incentives

The main incentive that most of these organizations have is to maintain and increase their influence and funding. Whether they are relevant at any given time or not, they will seek to regain influence.

Mini Cases

International Monetary Fund. Throughout its history, the IMF has worked to assist countries with their balance of payments problems. A program with the IMF is meant to signal that a country is on a more stable path, so that private capital would return to or stop fleeing the country. In late 1999, Turkey signed an agreement with the IMF to help reduce inflation and stabilize public debt. It was believed that this would help to slow inflation, which had been running at 50 to 70 percent a year for over a decade. Investors returned, buying government bonds betting that interest rates would drop, leading to a boom in bond prices. This did happen and fortunes were made. The IMF agreement collapsed, however, around a year after inception of the program, leading to much higher interest rates and a devaluation of the currency. Fortunes were lost and Turkey entered into one of its worst recessions since its founding. The IMF was not at fault for the recession, but its actions had a significant impact on global capital flows into and out of Turkey at that time.[11]

Bank for International Settlements. The BIS hosts the Basel Committee on Banking Supervision, which makes regulatory recommendations for the banking industry known as the Basel Accords. These are not mandatory for member banks, but provisions are often widely adopted by bank supervisors (regulators) around the world. The second accord, Basel II, was widely implemented at the time of the 2008 financial crisis. The accord, which sets guidelines for determining if banks have adequate capital to maintain stability in times of crisis, has been widely criticized for leaving too much up to the discretion of the banks and allowing them to "game" the system and appear to have a lower-risk balance sheet than they actually did. The crisis revealed a number of weaknesses in banks' operations and the newer Basel III Accords were developed to address this problem.[12]

THE MONEY MOVERS: PRIVATE ENTITIES

The first two groups largely set the rules of the game. The groups in this section are the ones that move money around the globe. They work within, outside of, on the fringes of, and are constantly trying to change, the rules as they respond to varying incentives.

Large Commercial Banks

At their core, large commercial banks lend to companies and individuals and provide a range of services such as money transfers, deposit taking, check clearing, and credit card issuance. It is normal for commercial banks to make up to half of their profits on fees for services, rather than on loans. The banks included here are the ones with global reach, usually with branches abroad and that make loans across borders to other institutions.

Main Global Economic Influence

- Lenders to businesses and consumers all over the world, including providing leverage to investment funds and credit to foreign banks. The latter is an important source of funding especially in emerging markets.
- The large banks lend to their own branches and the branches of foreign banks. Others may operate only in their home countries, but still borrow on international credit markets. Lending and borrowing across currencies can cause exchange rates to shift, affecting entire economies.
- In taking deposits, clearing with other banks, lending, and borrowing, commercial banks directly and indirectly contribute to the supply and demand conditions that drive many of the main interest rates, both domestically and internationally.[13]
- They are investors of their own capital as well as depositors of funds in global assets, though this is the subject of varying regulatory limitations after many banks had to be rescued after the great recession.
- Commercial banks create much of the money in the world by making loans (more in chapter 3). They can be a force behind inflation and bubbles, as they expand credit during boom times and stymie recovery as they hesitate to lend during slow periods.
- They are the institutions that actually, physically move much of the money around the world through transfers.
- Commercial banks, through their lobbying efforts, also are influential in how the global financial system is structured and seek to protect their roles in the system.

Incentives

Commercial banks exist to profit on both loans and fees, to protect their positions, and primarily to make money for shareholders. Often the incentives of the individual managers are not the same as the shareholders or the taxpayers that guarantee deposits. Since deposits are guaranteed, managers may be incentivized to take greater than prudent risks with funds, knowing the government will ultimately reimburse depositors for any losses. This **moral hazard** problem is at the core of bank regulation policy. Following the great recession, policy makers have been addressing the question of a bank's being "too big to fail," or when its failure would threaten the health of the entire financial system. Moral hazard and the incentive to act imprudently may increase if bank managers believe they are too big to fail and can count on a bailout.

Mini Case

Latin American debt crisis. The role of commercial banks in the great recession of 2008 is debatable, since most subprime mortgages were originated by nonbank entities. Their role in the Latin American debt crisis of 1982 is clearer. From 1975 until 1982, US-based commercial banks received large amounts of deposits from oil-rich countries, as oil prices jumped. They invested much of this in Latin American sovereign debt, believing at the time that countries did not default. Lending increased 400 percent over that period, with countries largely borrowing to finance current consumption or to invest in state-owned companies. In the late 1970s, global interest rates increased to combat the inflation that followed the jump in oil prices, leading to higher borrowing costs for Latin American governments. At the same time, the global economy slumped, drying up demand for exports. In 1982, Mexico defaulted on its commercial bank debt, setting off a crisis in the region and around the world as banks stopped lending and called in loans.[14]

Investment Banking Firms

Investment banking firms' core business is creating and selling new securities. Securities are normally sold either alone or in a consortium with other investment banks or distributors with a wholesale or retail network. Sometimes the securities are the standard ones (stocks, bonds), but investment banks also develop new securities like asset-backed securities and derivatives (like CDOs) whenever they can find or create a market. Investment banks also engage in wealth management, corporate finance advisory, such as merger and acquisition advisory and financing, and trading and making markets in different securities.

Main Global Economic Influence

- Create and also trade almost all of the securities that are traded within and across borders: stocks, bonds, loans, derivatives, and so on. Derivative contracts may be between small numbers of parties, while the sale of other securities may involve many thousands of buyers. New securities can involve the movement of billions of dollars across borders, as investors in one group of countries buy investments in another. While the infamous mortgage bonds pre-2008 are one of the most notorious examples, investment banks also facilitate the investment by, for example, US-based pension funds in remittance-backed bonds issued by EU banks, or a Chinese sovereign wealth fund in bonds from a Greek shipping company.
- *Ratings agencies* assess and rate the risk of many of the securities that investment banks create, as well as sovereign and other debt. Since many investors are limited by mandate to invest in "investment grade" rated securities, getting a good rating can be imperative. Controversially, ratings agencies are paid by the investment banks, not by the end buyers of the securities. Resolving this conflict of interest between investment banks and ratings agencies continues to be a matter of policy debate.
- Through lobbying efforts, investment banks have been able to influence economic and financial policy and regulations. For example, they have been criticized for influencing and hiding from regulators the true risks of mortgage-backed securities leading up to the great recession. In an apparent, but difficult

to control, conflict of interest, regulators often end up working for investment banks after they leave their positions and vice versa.[15]

- Investment banks can be active traders, both for their own account and for money they manage for wealthy clients and institutions. For investment banks that hold official banking licenses, the amounts they can trade on their own account has been limited by post-2008 regulation.

Incentives

Investment banks seek to make money and increase their influence. Securities issuance and trading are still profitable, and investment banks work to keep it that way. The securities and investment industry regularly ranks in the top ten in spending for political influence. In a now famous bit of seriously hyperbolic, though somewhat elegant, writing *Rolling Stone* magazine's Matt Taibbi described leading investment banking firm Goldman Sachs as a "great vampire squid wrapped around the face of humanity, relentlessly jamming its blood funnel into anything that smells like money."[16]

Mini Cases

Cross-border securitization. **Securitization** is the pooling by investment banks of a group of smaller, cash-flow-generating assets into a larger and more diversified single security of a much higher face value. Almost any pool of cash-generating assets can be securitized, including mortgages, credit card payment receipts, auto loans, and remittances. Cross-border deals are common, with securitization being a popular way for local banks and companies to raise money, and with the securitized instruments in demand from large, international institutional investors. Hundreds of billions of dollars cross borders each year in securitization deals arranged by investment banks.[17]

Greek debt. In the years leading up to Greece's joining the eurozone in 2001, one of the largest and most prestigious investment banks, Goldman Sachs, helped the Greek and other Southern European governments take on more debt and structure that debt in a way that it was not readily visible to EU regulators. By structuring loans as currency trades and securitizations rather than straight loans, they were kept off national balance sheets. Greece was consequently able to enter the eurozone at a more advantageous exchange rate than would have been the case. Greek citizens and the government felt wealthier, but the de facto overvaluation may well have contributed to the longer-term competitive problems that finally came to the fore after the great recession. The adjustment after the fact may well prove to be more painful than a less-advantageous entry into the euro would have been.[18]

Investment Funds with a Global Reach

This is a broad group and includes exchange-traded funds (ETFs) and mutual, commodity trading, and hedge funds. These are quite different entities in some ways, but similar in others. They all exist to attract and manage people's money, are all vehicles for moving money around the globe, and their management and strategies all reflect the goals and psychology of their investors, manager, and mandates. Key differences between them are the types of investors they can accept, their strategies, and the kinds of investments they make.

Hedge funds. This is the most varied of the group. There is no single definition of a "hedge fund," and many do not even use hedging as part of their strategy. Investment targets and strategies are effectively unlimited, though in practice are usually defined by the fund manager and mandate. Some are fully opportunistic and broad based. Others have strategies that are more clearly defined and may invest in any number of vehicles such as listed domestic and foreign equities, private equities, government and corporate bonds, derivatives, arbitrage opportunities, commodities and futures, energy, global currencies, high-frequency trading strategies, and any number of others. Most hedge funds are leveraged, borrowing to increase returns to equity. Main investors are wealthy individuals known as "qualified investors" who have a high proven net worth, sovereign wealth funds, large institutional investors, and university and foundation endowments.

Private equity (PE) funds specialize in investment in nonlisted companies, or in listed companies that the fund intends to take private (off an exchange). Mandates vary, but are commonly to gain a controlling interest in medium-to-large-size companies and hold them for four to seven years, increasing their value during that time. Companies may use money from PE funds to expand their international operations or help finance their international growth through joint ventures. Investors are mainly institutional investors, sovereign wealth funds, and wealthy individuals. They often receive loans from commercial banks to make acquisitions and/or to leverage up their investment returns. Private equity funds were initially mainly active in the United States, but in the past decades have expanded overseas with many of the same US- and London-based companies both making investments in overseas assets and taking on international investors.

Wealth managers manage the money of the usually very wealthy. It is more accurate to see them as gatekeepers to the many other funds and investment vehicles in the world, rather than as funds themselves. Most of the money they receive ends up in another vehicle. However, their beliefs and actions determine which vehicles receive funds and when. They may engage in what is referred to as **portfolio rebalancing** for their clients, or carefully watching and reacting to changes in both investor goals and the global marketplace, responding by moving money in and out of broad instruments and locations.

Mutual funds. Mutual fund investment is open to ordinary (nonqualified) investors through their brokerage accounts or the mutual fund company. Consequently, mutual funds are highly regulated and subject to extensive reporting, transparency, and investment protection provisions. They usually have fairly strict investment mandates defined by legally binding submittals to the securities authorities. Normally fund managers buy and hold securities and cannot use shorts, derivative instruments, or leverage. There are mutual funds with mandates to invest in most global markets, developed and emerging. Before ETFs, this was how most people diversified their portfolios and got exposure to foreign securities.

Exchange-traded funds, *ETFs.* These funds are open to any investor and normally are passive, i.e., without investment managers directing the money. Money put into a passive ETF is automatically, directly, and proportionally invested in other securities according to a fixed set of rules. In most cases, ETFs invest in previously established indices. They are characterized by low fees and reasonable liquidity under "normal" circumstances. According to some they are not true funds but derivatives, since they are "derived" from their underlying securities. There are currently ETFs for almost any known market, including government and corporate bonds, domestic and foreign equities, and very specific sectors and markets. ETFs can give investors exposure to even exotic foreign emerging markets at a low cost. In addition to individual investors, ETFs are widely used by hedge funds and institutional investors. ETFs are traded on major exchanges in the same way that stocks are. At the end of 2015, about $2.9 trillion was invested in ETFs worldwide.[19]

These categories of funds are not mutually exclusive (i.e., hedge and mutual funds may invest in ETFs).

Main Global Economic Influence

- Big movers of mainly portfolio investments, or **hot money** around the world, seeking profits in global exchanges, global public and private debt markets, currencies, and in commodities of all kinds. These funds collectively move global bond, equity, and currency markets.
- ETFs and mutual funds are the vehicles that individuals most often use to invest their money. They consolidate often smallish investments from millions of people into huge, diversified investment vehicles.
- Simply because they are popular, low cost, and easy to invest in, ETFs have the potential to drive asset prices all by themselves, especially when entering otherwise illiquid or difficult-to-access markets. They have also been criticized for distorting markets, by driving up the value of the securities in the indices they track and leaving others behind.
- Hedge funds are like private investment funds for wealthy investors, often managed using particular, well-defined strategies. Their ability to borrow considerable amounts of money can make both their influence and their risk to the global economy greater than the amount of money invested in them.[20]
- Private equity funds both bring significant medium- to long-term investment capital across borders and provide investment capital that helps investee companies themselves expand across borders.

Incentives

To make money for management/ownership and then investors by receiving a percentage of assets under managements, profits, or both. Fund managers are known for benchmarking against other managers, rather than total returns. Consequently, many tend to follow the market up and down "herding" with other investors, rather than trying to buck trends. In most funds, managers do well if the fund does well but have little downside risk other than losing their job.[21] This arrangement has been criticized for contributing to excessive risk taking.

Mini Cases

Breaking the bank. Leading up to the 1990s, the Bank of England had been trying to peg the value of the British pound to the German mark. However, since the United Kingdom at the time had greater inflation than Germany, this became increasingly difficult as the real exchange rate increased. The Bank of England continued to use reserves to buy pounds, to keep the value up and help the currency markets clear at the fixed rate. Sensing weakness, hedge fund manager George Soros shorted the pound, forcing the Bank of England to spend even more. Eventually, the bank gave in, the pound dropped, and Soros walked away with $1 billion in a single trade.[22]

Breaking Argentina. After Argentina defaulted on its debt in 2001, most of it creditors negotiated terms for partial payment of around thirty cents on the dollar, rather than risk losing it all. Approximately 7 percent of the defaulted debt, however, was bought up by hedge funds seeking full repayment on it. Due to the legal language in the debt agreements and a series of court decisions, in 2014 Argentina was neither able to offer the holdouts a better deal than was negotiated with the bulk of its creditors, nor able to pay installments to main creditors unless they paid off the hedge funds. This put Argentina in the position of "selectively" defaulting on their debts for the eighth time in their history. The full case is rather complex, but illustrates how investors can both suffer and benefit from differences in financial and legal regimes across countries.[23]

Institutional Investors

These are usually large companies or institutions that invest money with clearly stated reasons, methods, and parameters. The main types of institutional investors are pension funds, insurance companies, investment arms of commercial banks, endowments, and sovereign wealth funds. Many institutional investors are not just trying to make money now, but to ensure that there is enough later to meet future obligations like pension and insurance payouts. Many are highly regulated and are investing for the so-called public trust. They are also often referred to as "real money" investors, since they invest large amounts of real, or unleveraged capital.

Main Global Economic Influence

- They are the guardians of trillions of dollars, euros, yen, and other currencies that need to be invested, often across borders. Pension assets in the 22 largest economies alone were estimated at $36.4 trillion at the end of 2016.[24]

- Because preservation of capital is central to their mandates, normally they are required to invest the vast majority of their funds in "safe" assets. They are huge consumers of highly rated sovereign and corporate debt and developed economy equities, as these are considered "safe." Within their operating and risk parameters, managers are as aggressive as possible. Their investment targets are often unrealistic and set by outside board members or political forces. Managers seek investments that can meet their tough mandates, which leading up to the great recession included AAA-rated securitized mortgages.
- They can often allocate small parts of their portfolio to investments that are considered more risky. These may include emerging markets bonds and equities, and hedge funds that in turn invest in foreign assets. Though these amounts may be small as a percentage of their total assets under management, the actual amounts can be large and sufficient to help move global markets. In 2015 it was estimated that institutional investors made up 65 percent of hedge funds' capital, with public pension funds contributing 20 percent of the total.[25]

Incentives

- Managers make money for their funds within given parameters. Because of the need to preserve and grow money to meet future obligations, forecasts are important for institutional investors. Managers are under pressure to make sometimes unrealistic assumptions about future growth in order to keep their jobs.
- To meet or beat the benchmarks. Since investment managers are normally benchmarked against peers, they cannot make less or lose more money than the other funds in their investment category. This can lead to crowd behavior and swings of risk-seeking and risk-averse behavior.
- Most institutional investors also have liquidity requirements. In addition to investment returns, they need to provide cash for the budget of the institution. This is partially for administration, but more importantly to satisfy claims such as pension withdrawals or insurance payouts.
- To perpetuate their and their investment managers' existence. Like with any bureaucracy, this reality is forgotten at one's peril. It is one reason for the herd behavior that may accentuate booms and busts.

Mini Cases

The 2008 mortgage crisis. Institutional investors seek the highest-yielding safe assets, with safe being defined by their rating from a ratings agency. In the 2000s, they found a good deal with AAA-rated CDOs such as collateralized mortgages and bought trillions of dollars' worth. The high demand from these investors, in turn, triggered a supply response to originate more mortgages. This led to a drop in quality, which was not reflected in the ratings. Eventually, many institutional investors lost billions of dollars. It is not entirely clear which institutional investors have been able to fully repair their balance sheets, or whether they may yet run into trouble and come up short on pension or insurance obligations.

Sovereign Wealth Funds

Sovereign wealth funds are pools of money controlled by governments, usually held in trust for the populace of that country. Their capital normally consists of foreign currency earnings (usually from net exports) that have accumulated outside the country. Though exact sizes are often kept secret, especially in nondemocratic states, the countries believed to have the largest sovereign wealth funds are Norway, the United Arab Emirates, Saudi Arabia, China, Kuwait, Singapore, and Qatar. Investment strategies usually include investment in countries other than the owner of the fund, though this can vary.

Main Global Economic Influence

- A large pool of capital that can move quickly into and out of investments. Though they are responsible for large amounts of global capital flows, often their identities are hidden in other vehicles. They are commonly investors in global ETFs, private equity, and hedge funds and may have considerable funds managed by global investment banks' wealth management divisions.
- May be willing to take longer-term and riskier bets than other sources of capital. They often make direct investments outside of capital markets, such as in factories, mines, and real estate.
- Often highly liquid and unleveraged, so funds can be available when other sources of capital are not (e.g., during the early years of the great recession).
- There are likely over $6 trillion in sovereign wealth fund assets under management, though many countries keep the exact amounts secret.[26]

Incentives

Main incentives are to maximize return for the citizens (or sometimes royalty) of the country, and sometimes to increase that country's influence abroad while increasing national pride at home.[27]

Mini Case

The government of Singapore fund GIC invested over $24 billion to help keep the bank UBS afloat at the beginning of the 2008 financial crisis, and was rumored to have lost around $7.4 billion of that amount as of 2011 before subsequently partially recovering.[28] Sovereign wealth funds are able to take a longer-term view than many other types of vehicles.

Manufacturing, Service, and Retail Companies

It is optimistic to consolidate so many of the companies of the world into one category. This is done more to complete a taxonomy than to provide any insight. Consider this category as a placeholder for now. In the exposition to come, as company actions are relevant to global economic events, more specifics will be brought out.

Companies form the diverse core of the global corporate sector, manufacturing and selling goods and services all over the planet. They not only sell but invest widely and employ many of the workers who then in turn make decisions that affect the global economy with their buying and investing. They compete aggressively, both responding to incentives and using their influence to change the rules of the game.

Though dynamic and responsible for significant stocks and flows of money, companies tend to move money on a more permanent basis than some other private-sector participants. Changes in company-level investment and employment can certainly drive booms and busts around the world. However, the cycles would tend to be longer than those driven by shorter-term investors.

National companies' success and governments' ability to attract investment from companies around the world (including domestically) is a factor in determining success or failure of entire economies. If companies decide China or Mexico is a better place to invest and employ than the United States or Italy, whole economies are affected. When economists talk about "structural shifts" in an economy, more often than not they are referring to the results of shifts in how companies invest and employ.

Main Global Economic Influence

- Companies are the main drivers of foreign direct investment (FDI), when an investor directly invests in a factory or company in another country. These are normally longer-term investments, as they cannot be sold on exchanges like short-term portfolio investments. Total FDI flows in 2016 were around $1.52 trillion, down 13 percent from 2015.[29] FDI inflows are considered to be more stabilizing to an economy than portfolio inflows that can be quickly liquidated.
- FDI may be in new plants and equipment, acquisitions of existing foreign rivals or partners, opening a service provider like a bank branch, opening a retail outlet, or investing in the development of natural resources like mines, depending on the sector of the company.
- Seeking investments from companies, governments will specifically change rules to attract investment and related jobs. Just as companies are incentivized by profits, governments can be incentivized by the investment and jobs that companies bring, and so change the rules and incentives to attract them.
- Companies trade in goods, buying and selling to increase their profits. Companies are a dominant force behind global trade, with both large and small companies participating at all levels and across primary (commodity), intermediate, capital, and finished goods, and often simultaneously.

- Buying investment goods from abroad. When companies buy equipment to grow, they can buy from the entire global marketplace, stimulating trade and additional investment in the companies that make the purchased equipment.
- Logistics and service companies facilitate global trade with fast and low-cost delivery, as well as through efficient handling of paperwork and customs clearance.
- They are major producers and consumers of globally traded commodities, intermediate goods, and final products for resale. In the modern global market economy, companies trade globally in commodities and intermediate goods as much as in final goods.
- Property and real estate investment companies are frequently at the leading edge of booms in markets. Though in theory they should be responding to unmet demand, in practice they can be drivers of economic activity, at least for a time. Huge costs may require capital and loans from many of the different funds listed previously, including institutional investors, private equity, and sovereign wealth funds.
- Old modes of company structure and organization are changing as companies increase global outsourcing. Frequently outsourced roles include marketing, IT, accounting, design, distribution, and manufacturing. This alters global trade patterns in goods and services, as different corporate functions may be scattered across the world.

Incentives

To make money for investors and owners, and help their management benefit and maintain their positions. Companies often make long-term strategic bets on markets, making investments that lead to short-term cash outflows with the goal of longer-term gain. Principal (management) agent (investor) conflicts are common.

Mini Cases

Auto industry. By the 1980s, it was clear that the big three US automobile manufacturers were in trouble, under threat from Japanese competitors with better vehicles at lower prices. To avoid official trade sanctions, the Japanese manufacturers imposed "voluntary" import restrictions, limiting the number of vehicles sold into the United States. At the same time, they began to invest in and build factories in the United States, mainly in the South, which had not historically been a vehicle-manufacturing hub and where unions were not active. Soon the Japanese manufacturers were turning out cars with the same quality as those made in Japan, increasingly using US management and suppliers. These investments in many ways marked a turning point, allowing the United States to preserve a critical mass of auto manufacturers, thereby maintaining the industry and its skill and supplier base.

Chemical industry. US-based Union Carbide Corporation (now part of Dow Chemical) was a major global supplier of pesticides. They built a large plant in

Bhopal, India, to supply the then-booming Indian agriculture sector, which was realizing the benefits of adopting hybrid seeds and the increasing use of fertilizers and pesticides. In 1984, an accident at the plant exposed five hundred thousand people to toxic chemicals, killing and injuring thousands. The Bhopal disaster has since been held up as an example of the potential negative impacts of powerful foreign companies investing in developing countries that lack adequate regulatory systems. The case arguably acted both as a shorter-term barrier to additional foreign investment in developing countries, and as a longer-term catalyst to improve regulation.[30]

Changing rules. Company investment into a country or region can bring growth, employment, and tax revenues. As such, both national and regional governments compete with each other to attract companies. At times this may take the form of entire country–level reforms, improving the business environment. Other times, governments may offer tax incentives, giving companies long tax holidays in exchange for investment. One such case by Costa Rica in 1997 attracted semiconductor manufacturer Intel and is credited by some for changing the orientation of that country's economy. Intel accounted for over 10 percent of foreign investment and 20 percent of exports until the plant closed in 2014.[31] Critics look at this and other cases, and claim that the competition for investment creates a "race to the bottom" of corporate giveaways and few sustainable benefits. Others note the significant job and export gains and often domestic "satellite" companies that emerge around large investments such as Intel's.

Commodity Producers and Own Account Commodity Traders

Commodities are the basic building blocks of the global economy and include the foods, energy sources, and metals and minerals that go into global supply chains. A subgroup of often large companies produces and does primary processing of these products. They sell to traders, speculators, and final end users.

Main Global Economic Influence

- Significant investors, especially in emerging and frontier markets where many remaining, untapped reserves are located. Many African countries and Mongolia saw massive commodity-related investment booms in the 2000s (that were followed by equally precipitous busts). Despite volatile prices, commodities remain the almost exclusive source of wealth (and power) for a group of oil-rich Middle Eastern states and a major source for a wide range of countries from Chile (metals); Australia (metals, coal); Indonesia (petroleum products, mining, and palm oil); Norway and Canada (fuels); and New Zealand (agriculture).
- Commodities are critical inputs for a wide range of industries. Price swings influence the profitability of companies, the budgets of countries, and national price levels and/or inflation rates. They can drive global capital flows both directly and indirectly as the overall economies and capital markets of commodity-dependent countries rise and fall with prices.

- Many governments control the extraction, use, and export of commodities within and from their borders, trying to maximize domestic royalties and benefits by encouraging processing and downstream industries, rather than just the export of raw materials. Policies can lead to greater levels of development, but also price distortions and inefficiency that make otherwise unprofitable industries appear profitable.
- When prices are high and shortages feared, state and quasi-state commodities companies may "ring fence," or maintain for exclusive national use, even commodities produced in other countries. For some time, wealthy Gulf State governments have been buying farmland in foreign countries, with unlimited rights to export home.[32] Similarly, Chinese commodity companies have extracted abroad and stockpiled in China. The behavior can increase price volatility on global markets, as traded markets are thinned out and supply and demand become less transparent.

Incentives

- To make money for their shareholders by managing and reacting to supply and demand conditions through investments, trading, and stockpiling.
- For state-run or -influenced suppliers, to ensure that national companies have an adequate supply of key commodities.
- For state-run or -influenced suppliers, often to provide, especially energy, commodities to the companies and citizens of a country at below world market prices.
- To profit by providing contracts to customers that help them hedge against large price swings.

Mini Case

African growth. Chinese investment in Africa represents one of the biggest FDI booms in the 2000s. Most investment has gone into natural resource extraction, mainly metals, minerals, and fuels. The subsequent exports from Africa fed China's economic boom and were processed by Chinese companies to sell into other countries. China became the largest trade partner for the African continent. Total investment is hard to estimate accurately but is likely near $28 billion as of 2015, a significant sum in an economically depressed continent. Some observers believe the investment was a major contributor to record growth rates in many African countries in the first decade of the 2000s. Investments in infrastructure and human resources may continue to fuel growth, even as direct investment slows.[33]

Individuals

Behind every institution, company, bank, or government are people. They buy, invest, manage, push for greater returns as shareholders, shop for life insurance, vote for change and for things to stay the same, and so on. Like the proles in Orwell's *1984*, if roused to act together, they can change the world. Fortunately or unfortunately, that rarely happens.[34] However, individuals, like any group of decision makers, can be prone to herd mentalities, fueling trends, bubbles, and busts. They also may not be fully tuned to the nuances of policy and may push for changes that are not necessarily in their economic interests, as the 2016 vote for the United Kingdom to leave the European Union and perhaps the Trump presidency in the United States can attest.

Main Global Economic Influence

- As consumers, individuals may buy lower-cost and/or higher-quality (or just preferred) goods from other countries, driving trade deficits in one country and surpluses in another.
- As consumers, you can feel their wrath when they get behind a cause. Informal or formal boycotts of products from other nations have caused changes in global money flows and policies. These may be for causes like labor or the environment, or because of dislike of a country's politics.
- Behind most companies, banks, investment banks, and institutional investors in the global marketplace are many, many people making individual decisions that in the aggregate are significant. They put their money in and can take it out.
- As voters, individuals influence trade treaties, subsidies, and taxes and support wars, economic sanctions, and any number of other factors that may change the incentives and flows in the global economy.
- Individuals, as both consumers and managers, can be prone to cognitive biases in the way that they react to events and may act as much on the basis of emotion as raw analysis.[35]

Incentives

Highly dependent on circumstances, making summary difficult, but some combination of money, personal pride, status, and national pride.[36]

Mini Cases

US homeowners. A driving force behind the global financial crisis of 2008 that got less attention than the banks and mortgage brokers were the millions of individuals that got into the frenzy and bought houses, some of which they could afford, then increasingly ones they could not. Individuals took out home equity lines of credit, decreasing their equity and increasing their debt, and added to global economic risk. Even in places with stricter mortgage standards than the United States, Spaniards, Irish, and Italians all made decisions that increased risk in the global market. Then, when the property bubble burst and their houses were worth less than the debt on them, many people walked away, again increasing risk and real losses.

Japanese "housewives." The Japanese have traditionally had an unusually high savings rate, leading over time to massive pools of savings that were historically invested in Japanese government bonds. When Japanese interest rates plummeted in the 1990s, primarily women head-of-households opened individual trading accounts and sought higher returns in foreign markets. The movement of this huge pool of savings abroad frequently made up 20 percent of all global foreign exchange activity at the times when the Tokyo market was open. Often household savings were invested unleveraged, but some of the trading accounts gave households the ability to borrow additional funds, increasing both returns and risk. Given the fragmented nature of this investment pool, it is hard to predict its behavior, even as it moves global markets.[37]

That ends the short summary of the main participants in the global economy, keeping in mind caveats about mutual exclusivity of categories, exhaustiveness, and fairness and accuracy of characteristics. It is merely a taxonomical starting point.

There are a lot of categories even in this summary, but sometimes it takes a wide variety of participants to make global economic events happen. To see how many of them worked together to wreak havoc, let's have a closer look at the global financial crisis of 2008.

CRISIS IN 2008! AND THE ROLES THEY PLAYED

A short exposition of the great recession of 2008 illustrates how multiple participants and their incentives combined to create a major global economic event. Figure 2.1

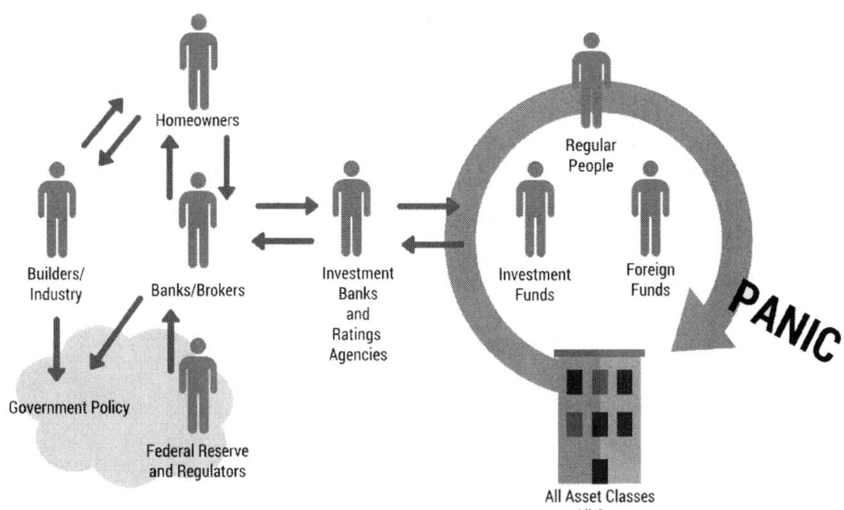

Figure 2.1. Linkages in the 2008 Crisis

summarizes the main players and the links between them. A major theme is that nearly everyone did pretty much what they were supposed to do. By "supposed to do," they did their jobs and followed their incentives. Economists say there was an "incentive-aligned" set of conditions leading to the crisis. That most failed to notice the system was heading for breakdown is perhaps less of a problem than that they were not incentivized to notice. For those whose job it was to notice, the incentives were still mixed whether to ignore the signals or not.

The buildup to the crisis started in the early 2000s. Some would say it followed directly from the bursting of the .com Internet bubble in 2001. The US Fed at the time followed its incentives and kept interest rates low to help the economy recover from the crash. Interest rates on home loans were also low, so people were incentivized to buy homes, which they did. As more homes were bought, prices started to go up, so builders stepped in and did what they were incentivized to do. They built more homes. Since home prices were going up, investors were happy to support the whole effort and finance the purchase of more homes by buying up securities backed by mortgages. Mortgages were considered safe and paid better than the main alternative safe asset, government bonds.

The US government helped out and followed its incentives to support homeownership by guaranteeing many of the mortgages, essentially taking the risk out of them. The usual "experts" on TV needed airtime, and they grabbed on to the fact that things seemed to be going pretty well and repeated that point again and again. They claimed that home prices never go down and the global economy was in the middle of a "great moderation" that had tamed the boom-and-bust business cycle. With the smart people saying there was no risk, mortgage-backed securities became even more enticing to investors, who wanted more. Returns were good and risks were low.

The investment banks did what they were supposed to do and came up with some creative new ways to package the mortgages into marketable securities, so they could sell them to investors. They also helped expand the market by selling these securities to investors abroad, especially in Europe, where returns on other "safe" assets were lower. They also sold mortgage-backed securities to the Chinese and other emerging markets investors, who had accumulated large amounts of USD reserves from all of their exports. Many of the investors whom the investment banks were selling to could only buy highly rated securities, so the investment banks went to the ratings agencies to get a AAA rating for them. At first, this was easy to do, because the mortgages were taken out by people who could afford the homes, and in any case, they were perceived to be government backed.

So far, so good. But people kept doing what they were incentivized to do, and the market grew. People wanted more, bigger, and second and third houses, and to refinance and take money out of homes they had for new homes. Home prices kept going up with high demand fueling more building. At the same time, investment banks had created a voracious global appetite for their products, with institutional investors everywhere wanting more of these AAA-rated, low-risk, high-return securities. Investment managers were under a lot of pressure to generate returns for their clients, and these were a perfect fit. Builders were making a lot of money building new houses, and politicians were happy with all the employment and homeownership created by the boom.

There was demand for houses and for the mortgage-backed securities that went to finance the houses. So to generate more loans, the mortgage brokers and investment banks started to accept looser standards on the mortgages. Brokers stopped asking for money down and verifying income. They "innovated" and offered low "starter" rates for a limited time, and mortgages worth more than 100 percent of the house value. People still wanted houses, and now you could get one with no money down and no job, and even get cash in your pocket. Lots of people thought that was a good deal and took advantage of it. Since the experts said house prices never go down, mortgages were still risk free. There was no reason for consumers not to keep buying houses, and investment banks to keep packaging the mortgages into securities and selling them.

When the government-backed guarantee companies refused to guarantee the loans based on looser standards, some private players stepped in. AIG, a large American insurance company, started to guarantee the securities with instruments called credit default swaps, which paid off if mortgage bonds didn't. In one year 40 percent of AIG's profits came from premiums on these guarantees, all from a division of fewer than two hundred people in a company with tens of thousands of employees. No reason to stop that; they were making good money with no risk. If investors were worried, they need not be, because the securities were still rated AAA because AIG had a AAA rating.

The investment banks paid for the ratings, and if they didn't like the one they got, they would shop the security around to another rating agency more amenable to issuing a higher rating. Eventually the ratings agencies did what any good service provider does and let the customer know they are always right. If the customer thought the security should be AAA rated, then it probably should be. Even better than that, ironclad laws of finance theory proved that diversification would reduce risk, and nothing could be more diversified than a security backed by thousands of different mortgages. AAA it was. Investors trusted the ratings agencies, and in any case these were some of the highest-yielding investments around. Not to buy them would mean your fund might have lower returns than the competition and you could lose your job.

Everyone was still doing exactly what they were supposed to do. The problem is, the situation had reached the point of no return. It was broken. Too many houses were built. Too many people had bought too many houses that were too expensive, with too little income, and too many investors had helped that happen. But it happened with everyone doing what they were incentivized to do.

The whole thing started to unravel when inevitably people without jobs or without good enough jobs could not make payments on their mortgages. The people who bought the AAA-rated securities stopped getting *their* payments, and the value of the securities started to drop. As people could not make payments, they had to sell their houses (or the banks did it for them), so home values started to drop. As people saw the value of their houses drop below the balance on their mortgage, more of them started to walk away from their houses and their mortgages. The downward spiral became as self-reinforcing as the previous upward spiral.

In the meantime, the people who had bought the securities ran into trouble. They tried to sell them to get them off their books, but the buyers disappeared. As values fell, the asset values of investors' portfolios fell. They were often leveraged, borrowing money to buy the assets, and needed to pay their creditors. So they sold other assets, which led to the drop in value of other assets that were not related to the problem securities. They also began to look more critically at other assets they had. Maybe those Greek and Italian government bonds were not as safe as they thought. Or maybe the notes on all those developments in Ireland and Spain were risky, or maybe all those credit lines extended to fuel consumption through Eastern Europe warranted more scrutiny. As everyone started to peek more closely at the assets, they saw risk everywhere. It was not just American mortgage bonds, after all; they were just the first to stop performing. The same web of incentives had replicated the risk around the world. At the height of the crisis, no one knew who did or did not have any money, so pretty much everyone stopped lending.

It is not 100 percent fair to say that everyone did their job. A few people probably did not do their job very well.[38] The first are the ratings agencies. They followed their incentives, but they did not do their jobs. Their incentives were to make money for their private, profit-driven companies. Their jobs were to accurately rate securities. If they had done their jobs, it is possible that the crisis would not have happened, since a lot of the investors who bought the securities were required by mandate to invest only in AAA-rated investments.

The second are the bank and securities regulatory agencies. People did try to do their jobs, and some of those lost them. Others simply went along for the ride or didn't want to stop a boom that seemed to be going well, or just didn't understand it. The reasons for regulatory failure are complex, but it is fair to say that regulators fell under some influence from the huge amounts of money being made during the boom times. Regulators frequently go to work for investment banks as a next career step, so no reason to upset anyone. There is no excuse, but that is the reality. Perhaps they followed their incentives, but they did not do their jobs very well.

Most of the rest of the people were just doing their jobs. You cannot expect more from a prospective home buyer who can get a house for no money down, a mortgage broker who gets a commission on each sale, an investment banker who gets a bonus based on creating new securities and selling them, a central bank that might get blamed for wrecking the economy for increasing interest rates, or an investor staring at a high-yielding security that a reputable agency had just rated the highest investment grade.

That is why incentives are so important in economics and why analysis of global economic events and trends requires analysis of a broad range of participants and incentives. The incentives were aligned to make the crisis happen, and are aligned in some way to make almost all events happen. That is the magic of bubbles and busts, and why they are so hard to control.[39]

This completes the overview of the main participants. In the sections that follow, this foundation is built on to go more deeply into how some of them work, and how they and the incentives they feel drive global economic events.

NOTES

1. The CFA (Certified Financial Analyst) Institute Research Foundation published an excellent summary of the principal-agent problem (Shah 2014).
2. Numerous articles and allegations abound. See, for example, Nakamura and Harlan.
3. That said, there are well-documented cases of high tensions between central banks and main branches of government, one case in point being the Bank of Japan and the Japanese ministry of finance.
4. During a September 2015 speech, the head of the US Federal Reserve Bank, Janet Yellen, implied that managing financial stability influenced Fed decision making. This represents a more proactive, and risky, approach than many central banks had been previously been comfortable, or mandated, to undertake (Federal Reserve Bank of the United States 2015). See Cooper (2008) for arguments supporting intervention.
5. Quantitative easing is explained in detail in chapter 3, but suffice it to say for now that cutting back led people to believe that US-based interest rates would rise.
6. *The Economist* 2015e.
7. As a general rule, common-law countries such as the United States and United Kingdom tend to leave more regulation making to executive branches, whereas much of Europe has a civil law system in which the legislatures are traditionally much more specific about how the laws are to be implemented.
8. As told to William Infante, a US businessman based in Mongolia.
9. WTO website.
10. The dispute is quite complex, though good public documentation is available. See the WTO website for a start, particularly the section *DS316: European Communities—Measures Affecting Trade in Large Civil Aircraft.*
11. As noted by one reader of this manuscript, the IMF has been instrumental in getting a number of countries on track toward stability and sustained growth. For example, effectively forcing Bulgaria in 1997 into a currency board that stripped the government of its ability to print money has been credited with allowing that country to join the European Union ten years later. Paul Blustein's (2001) book is a bit critical of the institution, but also highlights the extreme difficulty of making policy at times of crisis and gives a good overview of the string of financial crises of the late 1990s.
12. See this OECD working paper (Slovik 2012).
13. They may also manipulate those rates to their benefit, as with the so-called LIBOR scandal. The Council on Foreign Relations (2015) published a good, brief explanation of the LIBOR scandal.
14. The FDIC (1997) published an excellent summary of the crisis.
15. There are many examples, but for one example see Lewis (2014) and Kolhatkar (2017). Specific cases of the revolving door in the United States between investment banking and

government include Hank Paulson (thirty-two years at Goldman Sachs, became secretary of the treasury); Robert Rubin (twenty-six years at Goldman Sachs, became secretary of the treasury); John Corzine (twenty-two years at Goldman Sachs, became governor of New Jersey); Robert Hormats (twenty-seven years at Goldman Sachs, became undersecretary of state); Michael Froman (Citigroup 2001–2009, became the US trade representative).

16. Taibbi 2010.

17. Though many deals are privately placed and hard to track, some estimates for the US and EU market are available in Basurto et al. 2015.

18. The story has many different angles; see Cohan (2015), Dunbar and Martinuzzi (2012), and a more dissenting view at Story et al. (2010).

19. Investment Company Institute 2016.

20. Stevenson and Corkery 2014.

21. For many years, the standard compensation structure was based on 2 percent of assets under management and 20 percent of profits.

22. The story is well told by Sebastian Mallaby 2010.

23. The issue was finally resolved in 2016. For the story and outcome see *The Economist* 2014d and Caliari 2015.

24. Willis, Towers, Watson, 2017. The OECD estimated total global pension assets at $34 million in 2013. *OECD Institutional Investors Statistics* (database) and OECD 2014.

25. Managed Funds Association 2015.

26. Sovereign Wealth Fund Institute 2016.

27. The Abu Dhabi's fund Mubadala's investment in Ferrari is a case in point.

28. Ismail 2011, Bloomberg.

29. UNCTAD, Global Investment Trends Monitor, February 2017.

30. For an overview and retrospective, see Taylor 2014.

31. *The Economist* 2014e outlines the controversy.

32. *The Economist* 2009a.

33. Stevis 2014 and *The Economist* 2013c.

34. It is happening perhaps less and less according to some observers. See Tyler Cowen, *The Complacent Class.*

35. Much research has been conducted over the past decades on the types of biases that enter into human decision making. Two of the most important books on the topic are *Judgment under Uncertainty: Heuristics and Biases* and *Thinking, Fast and Slow*, both by Daniel Kahneman and Amos Tversky (1982, 2011). For a more practical application of the principles, see *Behavioral Finance and Wealth Management* by Michael Pompian (2012).

36. See Jonathan Haidt's *The Righteous Mind* for a psychologist's glimpse at the diverse factors that drive voter behavior.

37. The traders are colloquially referred to as "Mrs. Watanabes." See Smick (2008), chapter 5, or for a short summary, Fackler 2007.

38. Alan Blinder (2013) in *After the Music Stopped* identified seven "villains" in the 2008 crisis, including regulatory shortfalls and the ratings agencies. I would agree on all of his villains, but most of them were doing their jobs.

39. For a similar perspective on the incentive problem in the crisis, see Raghuram Rajan (2010). See also Eichengreen (2011) for a concise and balanced summary of the 2008 crisis.

3

Central Banks, Interest Rates, and Money

Not long ago a book on the global economy would not have had a chapter on central banking and money. However, as Mohamed El-Erian noted in his suitably titled book, since the great recession, central banks are *The Only Game in Town*. Not only are they essential participants in domestic economic policy, but in the process of conducting that policy, they have a profound effect on global money flows. This chapter covers money, central bank operations and incentives, and actual and potential effects on domestic and global economies.

MONEY, PRESENT AND FUTURE

If global economics is about money moving around the planet, it probably makes sense to start by defining it. There are numerous resources on the history, definitions, management, and problems caused by money, so only the basics are repeated here. Money performs three functions in a modern economy:

1. Unit of exchange. You can use it to get the goods and services you need, and receive it for whatever goods and services you produce. It basically makes trade easier than if you had to trade whatever you make or do for each item on a grocery list. It is easy to see why money had to be invented when humans got out of their hunter-gatherer stage and barter was no longer a viable option.
2. Unit of account. Money can be used to measure and record the value of things and services.
3. Store of value. You can use money to store value and save it for later.

For a long time in the history of money, it was either made from something like gold or silver, or it was backed up by one or a combination of these two metals. Money that is backed up by metals at a fixed ratio is usually referred to as a **gold standard**. Under a gold standard, new money cannot be brought into circulation in the economy unless more gold is obtained to back it up. This limits the amount of money in circulation, and so naturally limits monetary policy. Basically, there is no monetary policy outside of getting more gold. This constraint is considered either a strength or a weakness of the gold standard depending on your politics.[1] Historically, such a system has usually lasted until the central authority runs low on gold and decides to go ahead and issue more currency anyway.

The United States established and maintained a loose form of global gold standard after the Second World War to help stabilize the currencies and economies of the major combatants in the war. For several decades up until 1971, every dollar issued in the United States was backed up by a quantity of gold at the rate of one ounce for every $35. At the same time, by agreement the major European currencies were all pegged to the USD at fixed rates, so in theory their currencies were also backed by gold. They just needed to exchange their currencies for dollars, and then they could go exchange those dollars for gold. It was in reality more nuanced than that; see the footnote for references.[2] As of 2017, no country any longer uses a gold standard, although the debate occasionally returns.

National currencies are normally now "fiat" currencies; that is, currencies that exist because the laws and regulations of a country establish it as "legal tender." A fiat currency is not backed by any precious metals and can be created (and destroyed) more or less at will, or by "fiat." Its value is determined solely by supply and demand. Supply is mainly determined by commercial banks (more on that later), central bank policies, and the bank regulatory system. Demand is driven by the underlying strength of and activity in the economy and, weird as it may seem, the amount of "faith" that people have in the currency and its management. Yes, currency values when currencies are not backed by specific amounts of precious metals or anything tangible are "faith-based," which to date has worked well, as long as faith is maintained.

When faith in a currency is lost, however, values can plummet, as seen in cases throughout history and regions. In Bulgaria in 1997, people lost faith in their monetary authorities and abandoned their currency mainly for German marks. At one point, few in the country would accept the Bulgarian lev. This has not happened with a major currency for some time, though the Russian ruble perhaps had a brush with abandonment in early 2015. In more minor currencies, the Zimbabwean dollar fell precipitously through the 2000s and the Venezuelan bolivar may be heading for equal infamy in 2017. A common consequence of lost faith is hyperinflation in the local currency, as demand for the currency dries up and it loses its purchasing power.[3]

True fiat money–based national currencies have really only been the norm since the United States moved away from the quasi-gold standard in the 1970s. That is a relatively short time period in the over two-thousand-year history of money. The system seems to be working fine for the time being as a medium of exchange, and certainly fine enough for people to want to move and chase fiat money all over the planet.

The future may see additional evolution in the forms that currencies take. Increasing interest and use of virtual fiat currencies such as Bitcoin are made possible by large amounts of distributed computing power and wide connectivity. Their popularity may herald at least a partial displacement of national currencies at some point in the future. Not issued by any central monetary authority, they are in some ways the ultimate fiat currency, moving even further away from any sort of precious metal standard. Virtual currencies have become popular in recent years largely because of tax avoidance and anonymity, where illicit products can be bought and sold without alerting authorities.[4] Just like cash, except you don't have to be there to hand it over or pick it up.

Virtual currencies will probably continue to gain in popularity, especially as security issues get resolved. Bitcoin has run into a number of problems with theft, which have probably kept it from being more widely popular even as its value increases. The economist Hyman Minsky once said that anyone can create a currency; it is getting people to accept it that is hard. So far virtual currencies have not been widely adopted and are still in their infancy, with numerous contenders besides Bitcoin. It is possible that the next virtual currency will emerge serendipitously from one of the numerous online payment clearance systems. It would be a (long) series of small steps from denomination in one currency or another to some more neutral medium of exchange, which could then take on increasingly currency-like characteristics.[5]

In chapter 1, the term "money" was used loosely and largely incorrectly as a proxy for wealth, as noted there. I promised a correction was coming. Economists define money in diverse ways, which can vary from the concept of wealth used in chapter 1. Money supply in an economy is normally measured using *M* terms. M1 is the most restrictive, and is the total supply of currency and checking deposits; that is, the money that is easiest to get hold of and spend. M2 is a broader definition and includes M1 plus savings and smaller time deposits less than $100k in the United States and similar amounts in other countries. M3 is more expansive and includes M2, plus larger time deposits and is one way of defining what is called "broad money."[6] The wealth discussed in chapter 1 is a combination of all these, plus longer-term investments.

CENTRAL BANKING, PRINCIPLES AND REALITIES

Central banks are favorites of critics from across the political spectrum as shadowy instruments of the government (from the right) or evil instruments of greedy capitalists (from the left) set out to devalue and destroy national currencies (libertarian viewpoint). The financial press attributes divine qualities to central banks as the single entities capable of saving a floundering economy. It is hard to figure out if central banks are the big, scary smoking machine in *The Wizard of Oz* or the harmless little man pulling the levers and doing little. In truth, they are a bit of both. Here is what they do, what they probably don't do, and why they matter for the global economy. Be patient on the last point. It will take a little while to get there.

In most countries, central banks are hybrid government entities. Some may be fully part of the government, like the Bank of England, which was at one time private and then nationalized. Others like the US Federal Reserve (US Fed) and the Bank of Japan may have components that are actually owned by private commercial banks and investors.

A key tenet of central banking in modern economies is central bank "independence," or lack of influence from government. Another key tenet is a lot of tension around this supposed independence. In theory, central banks should influence monetary policy from a long-term perspective free from meddling politicians and their short-term electoral goals. In practice, rarely does a central bank take a position that completely conflicts with the political winds of the time, partially because doing so can ironically lead to a loss of that "independence."[7]

In the case of the US Fed, though nominally independent and with parts of the system owned by private commercial banks, the head is appointed for a four-year term by the president and confirmed by Congress. It is also the banker to the US government and coordinates closely with the treasury. It is telling that the website is a .gov and not a .com or even a .org. The Fed is actually pretty succinct about this, stating that it is "independent within the government" rather than "independent of the government."[8] Almost all of the profits from Fed operations go to the treasury. Losses, should there be any, would quickly become a public policy issue.

Most central banks have two main, not always compatible mandates: to control inflation and minimize unemployment.[9] Some, like the European Central Bank (ECB) are influenced heavily by countries like Germany that had scary historical experiences with hyperinflation and have traditionally been more anti-inflation oriented.[10] Some, like the US Fed, have a more balanced role and tend to be willing to accept some inflation if trying to cut inflation would also hurt employment.

The mandates are significant, but central banks seem to have powerful tools to achieve them. Let's take a look first at the so-called conventional tools used in "normal" times, and then the "unconventional" ones used in times of crisis. The unconventional tools have been used to unprecedented levels since the great recession.

Conventional tool #1. Central banks can influence interest rates in the economy by adjusting reserve requirements, or the amount of reserves that banks must hold at the central bank. In principle, the more reserves banks hold at the central bank, the lower the rate at which they lend those reserves to each other in the active interbank market. The interbank rate has different names in different economies, but in the United States is the federal funds rate, in the United Kingdom the LIBOR, and in the eurozone the Euribor. It's a matter of supply and demand that a greater supply of reserves for a given level of demand leads to a lower price, or interest rate, on lending them. The anticipation is that lower interbank rates will then lead to lower lending rates to businesses and consumers in the economy, which will in turn stimulate the economy. All other things equal, of course.

Central banks can adjust reserves by setting a reserve requirement for banks. More commonly, reserves are altered by central banks' buying or selling of bonds, normally short-dated government bonds, through commercial banks that they use as intermediaries in the bond market. This is called **open-market operations**. When central banks buy bonds from intermediary banks they pay for them by increasing that bank's reserves, so overall reserves in the system increase. The intermediary bank in turn credits the account of the seller of the bond, increasing liquidity in the economy or "loosening" monetary policy. When central banks sell bonds through intermediate banks, reserves and liquidity decrease, "tightening" monetary policy. The owners of the bonds need to want to buy or sell them, so the transactions happen at or just on the favorable side of market clearing rates.[11]

As noted, central banks create reserves by electronically crediting the banks' reserve accounts at the central bank when they buy bonds from them. These increased reserves are an asset for the member bank. Simultaneously, a bank deposit, which is a liability for the member bank, is created in the name of the seller of the bond. The central bank also picks up an asset, the bond, and a liability, the reserves. Both the member bank's and the central bank's balance sheets increase in size, but net worth does not change for either of them, or in the system as a whole.

The popular press often reports that the central bank is creating or "printing" money by creating these reserves and buying bonds in open-market operations. That is not technically true. From an accounting perspective, the process is one of asset swaps, not asset (or money) creation. Between the member banks and the central bank, short-term bonds are swapped for reserves. Between the member bank and the seller of the bond, one liquid asset (bond) is swapped for another (cash). Asset composition, but not net worth, changes in the economy.

Reserves, despite popular opinion, are not lent out, or at their post–great recession levels even required for lending. They stay in the central bank, outside the broader economy, and are mainly used to clear interbank transactions. Except at far lower levels than have existed for many years, commercial banks do not need more reserves to make loans, and they can always borrow that money from the Fed anyway through the discount window (see tool #2). In sum, conventional open-market operations are designed to affect interest rates in short-term lending markets. As central banks buy assets, interest rates can drop both from the increased reserves and the higher bond prices coming from the bank's entry into the market (rates drop as bond prices rise). The reverse is true when central banks sell.

Conventional tool #2. Central banks can in theory create as much money as they want and lend it to member banks through what is referred to as their "discount window." When it lends, the central bank electronically credits member banks' accounts at the central bank. They also set the interest rate at which they lend that money. This short-term interest rate, then, in theory should ripple out to affect other interest rates in the economy. In practice, it definitely affects the interbank lending rate, but the influence on other rates can be less clear.[12]

Commercial banks usually only borrow from the central bank when they need extra money to clear the interbank transactions that are required when customers move money from place to place. Even then, the bulk of lending happens in times of panic when interbank lending markets dry up.[13] Under normal conditions, commercial banks don't borrow much from central banks. Borrowing is especially unnecessary in economies carrying out quantitative easing where banks have plenty of reserves to clear transactions (much more on this later). Not borrowing from central banks severs the direct channel by which a discount rate translates to lower rates in the economy, mitigating the effect of this policy lever. That said, financial institutions do watch this benchmark rate as an indication of where the central bank is trying to steer things. Setting expectations is a surprisingly important part of central banking, even when direct effects may be elusive.

Despite popular conception, modern, developed-economy central banks don't create much money at all. They mainly create reserves, and banks don't lend reserves. Almost all of the money in the economy is created by commercial banks. When banks create loans, they create deposits, and in doing so create money.[14] Banks don't need a central bank to create money for them. They have a banking mandate, which allows them to create money in the process of making loans. A central bank's ability to create money (at least under conventional monetary policy) is less impressive when looked at in this broader context. People, especially ranters and ravers on TV, talk a lot about central banks' "printing money." In a modern monetary system even in desperate times, this is rare. And in any case no one "prints" much money anymore.

Despite the aforementioned limitations, central bank rate policy does matter. Betting against a central bank is risky, so interest rates do tend to align around the rate targeted by the central bank. Also, if the central bank is lending at a low rate, banks in need of liquidity would be foolish to borrow at a higher rate from somewhere else. By keeping rates low, central banks encourage people to borrow, and so encourage the banking system to create money by making loans to fulfill demand for money. In contrast, higher rates would discourage people from borrowing, and lead to fewer loans and less money creation. That is how it works at least in theory. Practice and reality, as will be seen, can be more complicated.

Unconventional tools are those used outside of "normal" conditions, or when conventional tools are not having the desired effect. That was the case during and in the aftermath of the great recession. The Bank of Japan had been using such tools for some time, following its economic crash in the 1990s. The US Fed and the Bank of England began in 2008, with the ECB starting a bit later, mainly because of differences in mandate and conservative German dominance of the ECB. German memory of hyperinflation in the 1930s continues to color their attitudes toward aggressive monetary policies.

Unconventional tool #1. During the great recession the Fed and Bank of England realized that buying their usual quantities of their usual government bonds was not having much effect on the economy. So they started doing what the Bank of Japan had previously, buying a lot more government bonds of different, longer maturities and also buying commercial bonds, mainly mortgage bonds, from both banks and other investors who held them. This was a controversial move and had a cryptic name—**quantitative easing** or QE—to preserve the mystery of the central banking system among the public (not really).

Where conventional policy stops and where QE begins is a somewhat nebulous point and, of course, the subject of the kinds of hair-splitting debate that economists are notorious for. For the most part, QE begins when the central bank purchases anything other than its normal mix of short-dated government bonds, and/or when the quantity of reserves created get larger than what banks actually need to settle accounts between themselves. Most QE programs stick with interest-bearing instruments. However, considered unorthodox even by the standards of central bank unorthodoxy, the Bank of Japan's more aggressive program has purchased large quantities of ETFs, making it a major owner of shares in Japanese companies.[15]

Since banks have little reason to hold reserves in excess of what they need, central banks may pay interest on reserves to entice banks to play their game. The Fed started doing this in 2008. As a nontrivial departure from conventional policy, doing so in the United States required congressional authorization. The ECB has actually gotten away with paying negative interest on accumulated excess reserves, simply requiring banks to hold them as part of the ECB QE program.

QE has various goals, depending on how it is carried out. Buying longer-dated government bonds, mainly at three- to ten-year terms and beyond, puts upward pressure on price and lowers yields (or the real rates) on those bonds.[16] Whereas conventional monetary policy mainly affects short-term rates in the interbank market, QE can help decrease interest rates on the huge stock of longer-term debt in the economy. Also, by buying mortgage-backed securities when the market for them was illiquid, the Fed became a sort of buyer of last resort, providing liquidity to a market that was beset by panic. Investors were able to get volatile assets off their books, stabilizing their balance sheets and freeing up cash for investment in other areas. As they reinvested in other assets, prices rose and yields dropped on those as well. One knock-on effect was lower corporate bond interest rates, thereby increasing cash flows to the larger corporations in the bond market. Finally, paying interest on the reserves that were created helped recapitalize banks hit by the recession.

When central banks buy assets from banks during QE, just like with regular open-market operations, there is no net "money" or assets created in the traditional sense. One type of asset in the system is being traded for another. Central banks obtain the bonds (assets) and create reserves (liability); commercial banks get reserves (assets) and create bank deposits (liability); sellers gain cash and lose their bond asset. Again, the net worth of the system does not change, at least according to the accounting relationships.

That last caveat about the accounting relationships appears because of considerable heated debate about whether money is actually created during QE. From an accounting perspective, it is an asset swap where net assets in the system do not change. However, the debate continues along a couple of lines. The first is whether it matters when assets change shape and get more liquid (i.e., get turned to cash). If the sellers take the cash and go buy goods and services, new money enters the broader economy with potentially both stimulating and inflationary results. That does not happen in practice with QE. There is no clear transmission mechanism between asset purchases under QE and money entering the consumer economy. Sellers normally use the transaction as a chance to rebalance their portfolios into new assets with different risks, returns, and/or terms. The sellers are investors in asset markets, not consumers, and any price effects would happen in asset markets.

Whatever one's stance, some money was almost certainly created if the assets were bought in imperfectly liquid markets. Any time a large new buyer enters a market, prices shift upward. That is supply and demand. Net money creation then would be the difference in pricing that occurred with the entry of the central banks into these markets. In some areas of the markets like medium-term treasuries, the price difference may not have been much. In the market for mortgage-backed securities, especially early on, it was likely greater. This is supposed to happen; asset inflation is the mechanism by which QE works.[17]

An important question is where investors reinvested the proceeds they received through QE purchases. Anecdotal and some empirical evidence suggests it was reinvested in government bonds, other assets domestically and abroad (especially bonds and the extension of lines of credit to foreign banks), back into property through corporate channels (seen as lower risk than individuals), in the so-called shadow banking system that then lent to a variety of end consumers, and back to large businesses that are less risky than smaller businesses and consumers.[18]

Figure 3.1 shows the increase in Fed, European Central Bank, and Bank of Japan assets since 2006. It represents the total value of bonds and other assets that the central banks have bought since 2008, with corresponding amounts being deposited in commercial banks' reserve accounts. For the Fed, the total is around $3.3 trillion of additional reserves between 2008 and 2015 when QE was ended.[19] The Fed basically quadrupled the size of the balance sheet it held in "normal" times. The situation is similar for the other central banks.

How to conduct monetary policy in a post-QE environment is one of those questions that keep some central bankers up at night. In uncharted territory, economists don't agree on how and with what effect the asset positions will be unwound. In any case, large reserve positions may well undermine use of the discount rate as a future policy lever to combat inflation. Some sources do not see any problems, while others, including the BIS, see possible complications ahead.[20] Perhaps one of the biggest questions is to what extent central banks' basic mandates were fulfilled with QE, maintaining a stable economy and an inflation target. Lacking clear counterfactual

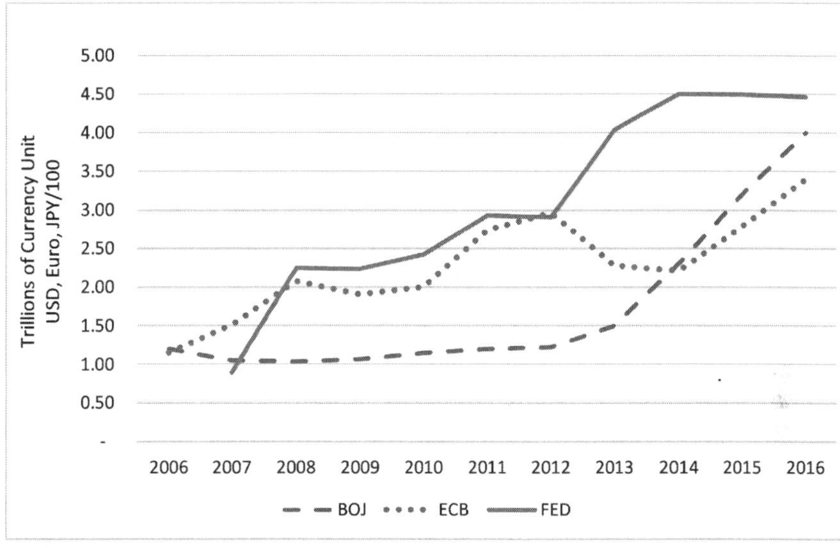

Figure 3.1. Central Bank Asset Growth
Source: US Federal Reserve Bank, Bank of Japan, European Central Bank.

cases, the costs and benefits of QE during this period will be analyzed and debated for decades to come.

Unconventional tool #2 and beyond. Central banks are normally mandated to be what is referred to as the "lender of last resort." That is, if liquidity dries up in the banking system and banks will not lend to each other to settle transactions, the central bank can step in and lend. This is something of an extension of conventional tool #2, but for different reasons under different circumstances. It was common in the early days of the great recession. Following panic and illiquidity in the overseas dollar market, the Fed even extended extensive credit lines to foreign central banks as an international lender of last resort. Given the increased size of dollar markets since 2008, there is some question whether the US Fed could do that as effectively again.

In theory, this money-creating tool could be extended even further and central banks could actually create real, net money and inject it into the nonbank economy. Economists refer to this as **helicopter money**, after Milton Friedman coined the term in 1969. Central banks could directly purchase government bonds at auction, rather than only in the secondary market. They could also directly finance companies or credit consumer accounts. Helicopter money is generally considered to be a poor policy choice that could radically undermine the "faith" in a fiat currency and lead to currency flight and hyperinflation.[21]

At this time, no major economy engages in helicopter financing. However, it is worth questioning when large-scale, long-term purchases of government bonds in the secondary markets start to resemble direct financing of government spending. As of mid-2017, the aggressive Japanese QE program has led to the BOJ's holding over one-third of Japan's public outstanding debt stock.[22] Certainly, the BOJ's willingness to sop up bonds in the secondary markets affects investors' willingness to buy the bonds in the first place, helping ensure ongoing demand for debt to finance deficit spending. The gap between BOJ policy and helicopter money gets more tenuous as time goes on. As economies battle with low growth in a deflationary environment, direct money creation will become more tempting. For the first time in many decades, helicopter money is getting serious airtime in policy circles.[23]

That covers the main so-called conventional and unconventional tools. Most central banks also regulate banks and influence their lending practices. Bank regulation is not as frequently considered an economic policy tool, but given the role of lending in money creation, perhaps it should be. Central banks usually set commercial banks' reserve and capital requirements. The reserve requirement is the amount of reserves a bank needs at the central bank, usually a percentage of the total amount it is authorized to lend. The reserves ensure that banks can meet their clearing needs with other banks when people move money between banks.

The capital requirement is similar, but is the percentage of the total amount a bank can lend that must be held as capital, usually equity, in the bank. Capital is a buffer against changes in the value of the bank's balance sheet. Higher levels are considered safer, but also restrictive of lending. Banks tend not to be reserve constrained, both because of current huge excess reserves after QE and because they can just borrow from the central bank to cover. However, they are often capital constrained, so increasing the capital requirement can reduce the amount of money that commercial banks create through loans.

To control risk in the system, central banks and other authorities set rules on the conditions under which loans are made. The low interest rates and the stabilization of bank balance sheets through QE were meant to return normalcy and lending to the financial system. At the same time, to reduce risk after the last debt-fueled crash central banks implemented regulations that have decreased lending in certain areas. In particular, banks' lending to economically important consumers and small to medium-size businesses decreased post-recession at least partially because of these regulations. Interest rates may be low, but loans are harder to get. More on this later, but hold open the idea that bank regulation may influence economic activity as much as the discount rate and open-market tools.

Keep in mind that since this is being written in 2017, the focus has been on lowering interest rates and getting people to borrow and banks to lend and create money. If the economy were booming along and there was inflation, central banks would throw these levers into reverse to try to increase interest rates, decrease people's interest in borrowing, and slow the rate of money creation.

It would seem the ability to create money at will and control interest rates are awesome qualities to justify any wonder that a mortal might feel toward central banks. As seen, in reality central banks actually create very little net money. Also, part of the reason for such awe is the lingering assumption that interest rates are the tiller by which an economy is steered in the modern globalized economy. The assumption is based on two main assumptions about central bank policy and interest rates.

The first assumption is that central bank interest rate policies determine the rate at which money is lent into the broader economy.

As economic activity slows, central banks use their policy levers to lower interest rates, hoping to get cheap loans out in the economy to stimulate more borrowing, investing, and related economic activity. This is the textbook mechanism. After central bank responses to the great recession, rates on government bonds dropped and rates on corporate borrowing followed suit. Whether lower policy rates extend to a broader range of borrowers is less clear. Let's look at some data from the United States in table 3.1.

Lending rates did go down, but not evenly. The policy discount rate dropped the most, and others followed to a more or lesser degree. They dropped the least on the two rates that are perhaps most poised to stimulate the economy, consumer and small business lending. They dropped the most on large commercial loans, at a time when US companies had large cash stores (on average). After a financial crisis, lenders have usually been burned and don't want to make cheap loans to their riskiest customers, such as consumers and small businesses. New, tighter bank regulations make it harder to do that anyway. Consequently, interest rate policy hits limitations just when it needs to work the most. While some rates drop, they are perhaps not the ones most likely to jump-start economic activity.

The second key consumer rate, on mortgages, came down significantly. Whether that helped stimulate the economy or not leads to the second assumption about central bank interest rate policy effectiveness. This is the "easy money" assumption. For policy to work, *more* money needs be lent to (or borrowed by) spending consumers and investing companies. During the housing boom, a consumer who gets a house for free in a rising market doesn't care about small changes in the interest rate. The Fed gets blamed for inflating the housing bubble with low interest rates, but rates are probably not the main culprit. The availability of *easy* money trumps cheap money. And money was easy.[24]

Table 3.1. Selected Rates

	2007	*2008*	*2009*	*2010*	*2011*	*2012*	*2013*	*2014*
Discount rate	5.9	2.4	0.5	0.7	0.8	0.8	0.8	0.8
Prime rate	8.3	5.0	3.3	3.3	3.3	3.3	3.3	3.3
Mortgage rates	6.3	6.0	5.0	4.7	4.5	3.7	4.0	4.3
Consumer lending, credit cards	12.8	12.0	13.6	13.4	12.4	11.9	11.9	11.8
Commercial loans	6.3	3.3	2.6	2.7	2.6	2.2	2.3	2.3
Small business loans	6.2	6.1	5.7	5.6	5.7	4.8	4.2	5.5

Sources: Federal Reserve, Freddie Mac, SBA. Small business loan rates are for SBA loan program rates at January of each year.

Table 3.2. Lending Volumes (in $ billions)

	2007	2008	2009	2010	2011	2012	2013	2014
Mortgages originated	1,260	740	550	490	480	570	790	820
Small business credit outstanding	650	680	650	620	600	580	550	530

Sources: Federal Reserve, FDIC databases, Freddie Mac

By 2012, money was cheap but not easy. It was cheap to the banks, but they were lending to the government and large companies rather than the broader economy. That's anecdotal, so some data appears in table 3.2 above.

Though rates were low, post-recession banks lent less to housing, consumers, and small businesses. Interest rate policy was strangled by risk aversion, a lack of consumer desire to borrow, and bank regulatory policy, just when it needed to stimulate the economy. Unless broader lending (and spending) is stimulated, monetary policy can stay limited to banking and investment markets. This is beside the point that stimulating lending may be a bad idea following a debt-fueled boom and bust. But stimulating the economy through interest rate policy is central banks' main tool.

With QE it is important to underscore the difference between additional liquidity and inflation in asset markets, and stimulation of consumption, investment, and potentially consumer price inflation. QE involves purchases in assets markets and is almost certainly inflationary there; it was designed to be. Transmission mechanisms to the broader economy where economic activity and inflation can be generated are harder to find. The sellers of bonds to the Fed during QE spent the proceeds on assets, not goods and services.

There is evidence, however, of money creation post–great recession. Table 3.3 shows broad money growth in several countries, consisting mainly of bank deposits.

In the United States, money supply increased during the housing bubble, which makes sense. It might seem less than expected, but that is not how mortgage markets worked. Banks might initially create money for a loan, but their balance sheet would contract again as loans were packaged into mortgage-backed securities. Much of the money invested into those securities had already been created. During the period examined after 2008, with the exception of the United Kingdom, Fed and other major market central bank policies led to modestly increased money creation. What channels that money took through the economies is less clear, but perhaps more rather than less went through investment rather than consumption channels.

The real effects of central bank policy on the domestic economy are complicated. Central banks' record on slowing down economic activity and combating inflation is pretty well documented. However, when stimulation is required, whether even unconventional policy levers can do much is less clear. As renowned financial economist Mohamed El-Erian notes, despite the enormous burdens and expectations put on central banks, "the fundamental problem confronting central banks is their ability to effect systemic and lasting change."[25]

Table 3.3. Broad Money Growth for Select Countries

Country Name	*2005*	*2006*	*2007*	*2008*	*2009*	*2010*	*2011*	*2012*	*2013*	*2014*	*2015*
Australia	8.5%	15.1%	18.2%	17.0%	3.2%	10.1%	8.0%	7.3%	6.7%	7.0%	6.2%
Switzerland	6.9%	4.6%	3.3%	4.0%	7.6%	5.5%	11.2%	13.0%	4.1%	4.6%	0.1%
China	16.7%	22.1%	16.7%	17.8%	28.4%	18.9%	17.3%	14.4%	13.6%	11.0%	13.3%
United Kingdom	13.8%	14.1%	15.8%	17.8%	–0.1%	4.0%	–4.4%	0.8%	2.1%	–2.5%	1.9%
Japan	0.5%	–0.7%	0.6%	0.7%	2.1%	1.7%	2.9%	2.2%	3.5%	3.0%	3.1%
United States	8.1%	9.0%	11.7%	8.2%	5.5%	–2.7%	6.7%	4.9%	4.4%	5.1%	3.4%

Strangely enough, central bank actions can have a more well-defined effect on the global economy. This is the case both in the countries with the main reserve currencies and emerging markets. The next sections finally get us out of the domestic and into the global economy.

GLOBAL EFFECT #1: EXCHANGE RATES

Though central banks may not influence all interest rates in an economy, they do affect some of the main ones global investors care about, such as government and corporate bond yields and the cost of lines of credit extended to foreign banks.

Investment managers scan the globe for the highest returns, in what is called the global **search for yield**. All other things equal (and that is important), when interest rates go up in a country, investors follow. The higher the interest rate difference, the more investors will leave the economy with the lower rate for the one with the higher rate. When investors do that, they sell the currency they were in and buy the one they are investing in. Since currency prices are subject to the forces of supply and demand, this buoys the value of the currency of the economy with the higher rate, while putting downward pressure on the exchange rate of the currency with the lower rate.

The next point is important and is probably a bigger driver of both exchange rates and investment returns than the actual interest rate. If you are an early investor, you not only get the higher interest rate, but you also benefit from currency appreciation as other investors follow you. The opposite holds on the exit, and investors who get out late can suffer losses from currency depreciation that rapidly overshadow interest rate gains. The rush to get in and out is a big reason that currencies, especially in emerging markets, bounce around so much.

Interest rate increases can be such a good way to increase currency values that they may be implemented just for that purpose. The Turkish central bank increased rates in January 2014 after the Turkish lira dropped nearly 20 percent against the euro and USD. The action helped stabilize the lira as demand increased when investors took advantage of the higher rates. The Russian central bank did the same thing in December of the same year, hiking interest rates 6½ percent in the middle of the night. In that case, things were going badly enough in the broader economy that it did not make much of a difference and the Russian ruble continued to fall. However, once the panic subsided, the higher interest rates almost certainly did help the subsequent ruble recovery.

Longer-term differences in broad central bank rate policy can also affect exchange rates. As mentioned, the ECB has traditionally been more aggressive about controlling inflation than the Fed, so under similar circumstances would tend to keep rates higher. As the United States was pulling out of the recession in 2012 the Fed kept rates low. The ECB kept rates fairly high and was more conservative about quantitative easing than the Fed. Consequently, even though the US economy was growing faster, the USD did not climb much against the euro.[26] People were still chasing higher bond rates in the eurozone. This all changed later, as the ECB implemented its own QE program and the USD rose as it tapered back on its program.

As with most rules in economics, interest rate changes affect exchange rates "all other things equal." Often all other things are not equal. Interest rate increases when something is seriously wrong with the economy won't have the same effect. That was the Russian case, mentioned above, as well as the cases of the Asian and Latin American crises of the 1990s. Similarly, when Greek government bond rates went up in 2010, money did not immediately follow those higher interest rates even though they were denominated in euro. People were worried about default, an exit from the euro, or both. To reliably move exchange rates, the risks should be more or less similar before and after a rate increase, though much higher interest rates can at least partially compensate. When there are problems in an economy, investors will require a **risk premium** on rates, and sometimes even high rates will not be enough to compensate for risk.

Frequently, when investors buy into bonds in a different currency from their own, they hedge with futures contracts or derivatives that allow them to minimize exchange rate risk. The real increase in interest rates that they get after paying the costs of the hedge is called the **covered interest spread**. Hedges can be expensive, though, and quickly eat into the real spread.

Some data can illustrate both how central bank interest rate policy effects exchange rates, and the important role of market psychology in the global economy. In May of 2013, the Fed signaled that it might, maybe, at some point decide to cut back on (or "taper") QE and reverse its policy of buying assets to put downward pressure on medium-term interest rates. Emerging markets currencies and stock markets slid as investors fled back to the USD, interpreting the Fed's signal as suggesting, all other things equal, that interest rates would rise on medium- to long-term US dollar denominated securities. In January of 2014, the Fed subsequently announced a fairly modest reduction in bond buying under its quantitative easing program, and there was some recovery. Figure 3.2 shows these drops and the slight though temporary recovery among the emerging markets currencies.

Why would an announcement by the Fed that it would slowly reduce the bond buying under QE cause these emerging markets currencies to drop? First some background. After 2008, with post-recession interest rates low in the developed market economies, investors had been seeking out higher rates of return in emerging markets. Evidence indicates that some of the proceeds from selling bonds during QE also ended up in emerging markets. In all, with the reduction of developed market interest rates to near zero in 2008 and 2009, several trillion USD made its way to emerging markets, helping drive up asset values, economic growth, and the value of the currencies.[27]

Now to 2013. A planned reduction in QE meant that at some point longer-term US rates might start to go up, so investors moved money back into USD and out of those currencies.[28] In fact, medium- to long-term USD bond rates had not increased

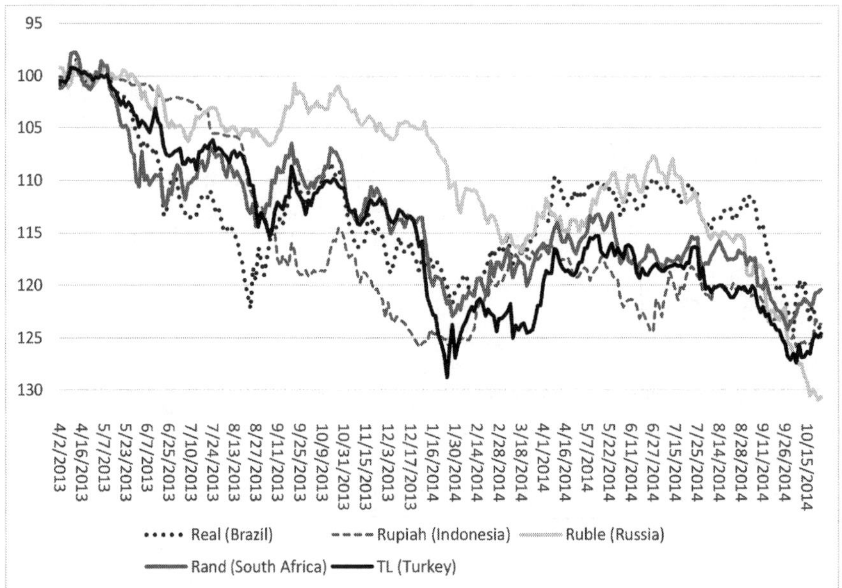

Figure 3.2. Selected Emerging Markets Currencies against the USD
Source: Murat Ucer, Turkey Data Monitor.

and actually continued to fall for some time after the announcement was made. This is where psychology comes in. Investors know what happens when interest rates change, and figured that they better get out before USD rates went up and the emerging markets currencies dropped. The drop became a self-fulfilling prophecy. Anyone who did not panic and bail out would get left behind and be stuck reconverting to USD at a lower rate. Adding to the tinderbox, some weaknesses had already begun to appear in these economies before May 2013, with capital inflows well below previous peaks.[29] Investors were getting nervous before the announcement, compounding the effect when it finally happened.

The global economy is complex, with events playing out in different ways in different markets. One of the world's largest bond investors bet on rising interest rates anticipating the end of QE. However, instead of being praised as a visionary for getting out of a market before it dropped, he lost billions. Bill Gross, the founder and CEO of PIMCO, the world's largest bond trader and bond fund manager, felt that the end of QE would see increases in interest rates as all the extra liquidity left the market. As such, he announced PIMCO's exit from government bonds early on in 2011. Unfortunately, rates continued to drop and bond prices rose for years afterward, costing his company and investors billions of dollars, and him ultimately his job.[30]

Economics blends the potentially mechanical with the actual psychological. Emerging markets investors with itchy fingers on sell buttons did not want to get stuck if rates went up. So they created a self-fulfilling prophecy that led to a drop in emerging markets currencies well before any real change in policy. At the same time, Gross did not want to be the last one stuck in a global sell-off of US treasuries, so got out sooner rather than later. However, there simply continued to be enough demand for treasuries even after the "tapering" of QE that bond prices kept going up and interest rates down.

It turns out that QE was perhaps not as asset inflationary or interest rate depressing as some people had thought, at least as far as government bonds were concerned. In one case, the thought it might be was enough to wreak havoc on a bundle of emerging markets' currencies. In another case, the reality that it was not led to the demise of the career of a man referred to as "the king of bonds."

Even if central banks have challenges spurring lending to real humans in their own economies, rate changes or rumors of them can affect exchange rates in intended and unintended ways. These cycles of interest rate adjustments, yield chasing, and risk fleeing have repeated themselves over and over in the world, driving booms and busts. The cycles have been and are likely to continue to be a reliable part of global economics, though the timing less so.[31]

GLOBAL EFFECT #2: ASSET BUBBLES (AND BUSTS)

When credit increases, it goes somewhere. The low-interest money created by banks since the recession may not have gone to consumers and small businesses. But it did get invested. Similarly, the liquidity created by QE went into other assets once the bonds were sold to the central banks.

When central banks promote liquidity and keep rates low and commercial banks are creating money, the investors (note, not consumers) who end up with the money will seek out the best returns they can for their risk profiles. This creates demand for other assets, driving prices up. If investors are after higher returns, the assets they buy will be riskier than short-term, developed-economy government bonds (which are the safest out there). As more investment enters other asset markets, prices will go higher than they otherwise would have in a non-QE equilibrium. Higher prices for assets whose underlying risk has not changed can ultimately lead to increased volatility as investors' fingers get twitchy on the sell button, not wanting to be the last one out if markets fall.

In the monetary expansion of 2008–2014, a number of asset classes globally began to increase in value. Though capital flows data is not definitive, price increases provide some indication of where the liquidity went. These include US domestic stocks, US high-yielding debt (aka junk bonds), foreign stocks, foreign bonds, real estate, and automobile loans.[32] If interest rates on safer assets go up, money could flow out of these riskier assets, just like it did out of emerging markets securities. Of course, the inflection point where investors start to react and sell is hard to identify. It depends on many factors, only one of which is the set of core interest rates influenced by central banks.

INFLATION AND GLOBAL INTEREST RATES

Inflation is defined as an increase in the consumer price index (CPI). The CPI is calculated by pricing thousands of goods and services around a country on a regular basis. Those prices are then weighted according to what surveys determine to be a representative "basket" of goods and services consumed by the average person in the country (though rural consumers are often excluded). Changes in those weighted prices then turn into the CPI and any increase (decrease) in that from month to month becomes the inflation (**deflation**) rate.[33]

Inflation can have multiple causal factors, most of which come down to supply and demand for goods, services, and currencies. One driver of inflation is "excess demand" in an economy, when consumers and governments want more goods and/or services than the economy can supply at current prices. Prices go up because demand exceeds supply. A rapid increase in money supply can create excess demand: more cash in people's hands, same old productive capacity. That's the concern with helicopter money.

Inflation can also be driven by supply shocks: products get more expensive because they cannot be produced at the same price and same levels as before. This happens when, for example, droughts occur in multiple grain-producing countries at the same time as they did during a high-inflation period in the mid-1970s; a country that is a major producer of something enacts export restrictions, like China did for rare earth elements in 2011; when prices are set administratively as they were in many centrally planned economies before the 1990s; and/or when a cartel is able to control and inflate the price of a key commodity, like OPEC did for energy products in the early 1970s or De Beers has done with diamonds for over a century.

In wealthy countries, single commodities are usually a small part of the overall consumption basket. These sorts of limited, sectoral price increases rarely affect the overall inflation rate by much. The last time was probably in the 1970s when both food and energy prices increased at the same time, which along with looser monetary policy drove overall price levels and economy-wide inflation. These two items were a larger part of the consumption basket than they are now. In poorer countries, single commodity price increases can drive inflation a lot more, since food staples and energy are a bigger percentage of overall consumption.

Increased labor cost is an often-cited inflation driver. Central bankers keep a close eye on unemployment, hypothesizing that decreasing unemployment (scarce workers) can drive the price of labor up, which then drives up the cost of goods and services. This is, in theory, a simple supply and demand relationship. However, it's not clear how low unemployment needs to get for wages to increase and inflation to kick in. Economists have a fancy word for the threshold, the nonaccelerating inflation rate of unemployment (NAIRU). It is a great term, but no one knows what the rate is. They thought they did. Then conditions changed, and in the 2000s and mid-2010s unemployment dropped below the dreaded NAIRU and nothing happened.[34]

Central bankers also don't know whether, how soon, and by how much they should raise rates in response to employment conditions. It's a hard job. The relationship between unemployment and inflation can be affected by productivity, the possibility of import substitution, the shifting importance of the labor component in production and service provision, the structure and flexibility of companies and the workforce, how competitive the market is, as well as other factors. On top of all that, central bankers need to keep in mind that increased wages might actually be a *good* thing for the economy overall, especially in light of increased inequality and the importance of consumption in GDP growth.

A final reason for inflation, which has historically been more evident in emerging and frontier market economies, is currency depreciation driven by a loss of faith in the currency. When people bail out of a currency, the value drops relative to world market prices and those goods become more expensive in local currency terms. This is a fascinating event that happens fairly frequently to different degrees. Global hedge fund managers watch these events carefully, both as opportunities to lose and make money. Some examples include emerging markets currencies during the so-called taper tantrums in 2013; the Russian ruble in 2014 and 2015; the Mongolian tugrik between 2012 and 2015 as commodity prices slumped along with faith in the economy; and the Bulgarian lev in 1997. Though depreciation for any number of reasons can set off inflation, it can be particularly sharp when there is a loss of faith involved.

An explicit part of all central bank mandates, inflation is one of the main indicators central bankers keep an eye on. Without going into too much depth, generally inflation around 1 percent to 3 percent is considered "good." Lower than that and people start to worry about **deflation**, which is dropping prices. The effects of deflation are, again, debated, but generally considered to be "bad," mainly because real interest rates can become very high. A real interest rate is the interest rate minus (more or less), the inflation rate. If interest rates cannot go to less than zero, and if there is, for example, a –5 percent rate of inflation (i.e., deflation), then the real interest rate is 5 percent.

A real interest rate of 5 percent is considered fairly high, at least for slower-growth, developed market economies, making money expensive in a recovering economy. To break this lower bound on nominal interest rates, central banks in Europe and Japan have experimented with negative interest rates on certain funds held with them by commercial banks. So far, there has not been much pass-through effect to rates charged to companies and individuals, but time will tell. The main outcome of negative interest rates may end up being decreased bank profitability, as spreads tighten.[35]

Higher inflation than the 1 to 3 range is also considered "bad." It is hard to say exactly what that is, but anything over 4 or 5 percent will definitely get the attention of a central bank and probably prompt an increase in interest rates to try to slow the economy down.[36]

Since central banks make much of their policy based on inflation rates, global investors keep a close eye on them and their underlying drivers. A change in inflation in a particular market can presage the kinds of capital flows that move currencies and markets, and drive both investment gains and risks.

SOME (REASONABLY EDUCATED) GUESSES ABOUT POLICY AND OUTCOMES

This section moves further into the unknown, briefly introducing some final topics on central bank policy, growth, inflation, and interest rates. To start, central banks' tool kits rest on some postulated causal relationships that are the mainstay of textbook economics. Like many staples in economics, economists often disagree on them, they definitely do not always hold, and they sometimes seem to break down just when they matter the most. A discussion of some of them is included here as policies around them will drive ongoing interest rate changes and money flows between economies.

Assumption One: Low Interest Rates Lead to Increased Economic Activity

This may be true, but it need not be the case. Economic activity requires some combination of demand for consumer consumption and business investment, a willingness of banks to lend, and a desire for companies and consumers to take on debt to invest and consume more. In the most recession-affected countries, for most of the post-2008 recovery this failed to happen. During the run-up to the great recession (and as a major causal factor), consumers and businesses took on debt and ran into trouble when the economy fell apart. So they "deleveraged," decreasing their debt, investment, and consumption, either by choice or because of job or profit loss or more stringent regulations. In such an environment, the channels by which low interest rates stimulate an economy are unclear.

While low interest rates cannot single-handedly create an economic recovery out of thin air, most economists would agree that higher interest rates will slow an economy and stymie recovery from a recession. So again, central banks may not help much by following the best policy, but can hurt by following a bad one.

It is worth digging a little more deeply into how low interest rates can influence economic activity. Table 3.4 outlines some channels that low interest rates (all other things equal, of course) can take through an economy, and some of the reasons they may or may not have the desired outcome.

It's not a simple relationship. Nor is it simple to determine when and to what degree different channels are likely to be reliable transmitters of interest rate effects. A lack of counterfactuals complicates historical analysis of a low interest rate policy. Regardless, awareness of the channels and their potential and limitations is a starting point for a better understanding and clearer analysis of particular situations. A similar table could be constructed for the effects of higher interest rates, with many of same channels active, but in reverse. Despite current sentiment to the contrary, it is entirely possible that higher interest rates will be the main concern during the period that this book is in print.

Table 3.4.

Channel	*Channels and Comments*
Increase GDP through the *C* or consumption component of GDP	If consumers are willing to borrow more to consume and banks are willing to lend, lower interest rates can help increase consumption and GDP. After a credit crisis, like in 2008, banks may not be able or willing to lend and consumers may be shedding debt, so effects are muted.
Increase GDP through the *C* or consumption component of GDP	Lower interest rates increase prices of bonds and can have a secondary inflationary impact on other assets as investors go elsewhere for yields. This can have a **wealth effect** where people feel richer and spend more. This would affect those with large investment portfolios more than the middle class and below.
Increase GDP through the *C* or consumption component of GDP	If rates are low, all other things equal, consumers may decide to consume in the present period rather than save at low rates.
Decrease GDP through the *C* or consumption side of GDP	Lower interest rates can decrease income from and accumulation of fixed assets and anticipated retirement income, causing people to consume less both in retirement and while saving for it.
Increased GDP through the *I* or investment component of GDP	Lower interest rates lower investment costs, increasing investment, if investments still yield good returns, which is less likely during a weak economy when low interest rates prevail; companies adjust their WACC to the new rates, which they may not;[a] businesses need access to capital to invest, while a lot of small businesses operate and invest on retained earnings.
Increased profits for companies with debt, increasing *I* and *C* depending on what is done with profits	Companies that have borrowed a lot may find their cost of borrowing decreasing in a low interest rate environment, increasing profit. Investing this profit or distributing it to shareholders can increase GDP. Many companies post-2008 are retaining profits or buying back their shares to boost stock prices. The latter can have a wealth effect if stock prices rise.
Can lead to capital flight from economy, seeking higher returns elsewhere	This can positively affect investors, but potentially lead to exchange rate instability at home and abroad especially if capital returns, bidding up exchange rates and harming exports just as the economy is recovering.

a. Bryant and Jones 2015

Assumption Two: A Faster-Growing Economy Leads to Inflation

This relationship can but does not always hold, especially in the developed market economies where even high growth is not very high by global or historical standards. Some periods of high growth have seen low inflation, and vice versa. It depends on a range of factors. The converse is also not always true. The 1970s in the United States had a period of low growth and high inflation, or **stagflation**. Inflation and its various drivers matter because central banks try to combat it preemptively by reacting to leading indicators, rather than waiting until it appears. Tracking inflation and knowing which central banks are particularly sensitive to which indicators of inflationary pressure can help in understanding where rates are likely to rise first.

Assumption Three: Higher Interest Rates Will Slow Inflation

Higher interest rates raise the cost of investing and borrowing to buy goods, so at the margin, people slow investing and buying. It is also more beneficial to save since returns are higher, so again, at the margin, people should save more instead of spending. Historically, in most countries higher interest rates have slowed inflation. If there are serious problems in the underlying economy, or if inflation is chronic, raising rates may not matter so much. For almost two decades, Turkey had an inflation rate that hovered between 40 and 80 percent with interest rates almost always higher than that.

Interest rate increases designed to counter underlying currency weakness and prop up exchange rates may also not slow inflation. This is particularly the case when consumers and especially retailers believe that inflation will be high. Retailers can rapidly lose working capital and their businesses from underestimating inflation, which is one reason that so called **expectation-driven inflation** is so hard to beat. Its roots are often in millions of individuals fighting for survival.

Assumption Four: The Fed and Other Central Banks Will Be Able to Increase Economy-Wide Interest Rates

Economists disagree on whether central banks' increased balance sheets will affect their ability to influence interest rates (and so control inflation) if inflation starts to rise. After QE, the discount rate matters less because banks no longer need to borrow to supplement their reserves. Central banks will target the interbank rate and so probably increase the rates they are paying on their huge reserve liabilities. Fortunately, increased rates are likely to coincide with either increased stability in or drops in central banks' bond portfolios, possibly helping by sopping up liquidity and limiting interest payouts. The economic and political implications of significantly higher payments to banks are not entirely clear.

Perhaps more importantly, interest rates like any price are primarily driven by supply and demand. The end of QE did not result in higher rates because there was enough additional demand in the market to make up for the loss of QE liquidity. If inflation starts to accelerate, will central banks be able to counter that demand with their traditional levers given the enormous amount of liquidity in the global economy?

These four and other similar assumptions may be broadly correct. However, questioning them and others like them and understanding the conditions of their validity is an exercise that will help refine an understanding of how monetary policy reacts to and affects a continually evolving global economy. Across various markets, we are likely in the coming decades to see multiple instances of high and low interest rates, attempts to control both inflation and deflation, and ongoing, often rapid movements in and out of different currencies. These events will take place in an at least slightly (and sometimes radically) different context than they previously occurred. Questioning assumptions and understanding when this time things really are different helps keep our understanding updated and reactions to them nimble. The second section of this book outlines some, occasionally a bit outrageous, scenarios that also challenge assumptions in looking toward the future.

Much of this book has by default focused on a state of low interest rates. This chapter ends with a few notes on what might be expected in an increasing interest rate environment.

Effect One: Bond Prices Will Fall

There is a clear, mathematical relationship between interest rates and bond prices. When interest rates go up, bond prices drop.[37] The longer the maturity of the bond, the larger the drop. Governments, central banks, pension funds, commercial and investment banks, insurance companies, and so on are holding large quantities of bonds. When interest rates are low, even small, nominal increases translate to large percentage increases. A half percentage point increase from 6 to 6½ percent is only 8 percent, but a half percentage point increase from ¾ to 1¼ percent is a 66 percent increase. Could a rout in the bond markets weaken the balance sheets of financial companies and funds that previously just suffered through a period of low returns?

Effect Two: Exchange Rates Will Shift

Interest rates affect exchange rates, and not all central banks will seek to increase rates at a similar speed. For example, for cultural reasons, the Fed may increase rates more slowly than the ECB. If so, similar inflation rates could lead to a rise in the euro versus the USD. As of 2016, the Fed was quicker to influence rates upward than the ECB, though more for reasons of getting back to a "normal" monetary policy than to quell inflation.[38] Central banks may hesitate to raise rates just to keep their economy's exchange rate down.

Effect Three: Asset Allocations Will Shift around the World

Inflation and interest rate differentials could set off significant portfolio reallocations across assets and economies. An overall increase in rates can send investors into more interest-bearing and fewer equity instruments. They will also move money to the places with the highest interest rates (allowing for risk differences). As rates rise on low-risk, interest-bearing instruments, investors may also keep shifting out of riskier instruments and locations, causing values to drop and risk premiums to increase. In countries with under-controlled inflation where central banks hesitate to raise rates, investors tend to escape low or negative returns on cash and bonds, by going into property and equities, or simply fleeing the currency. Mere anticipation of this scenario can cause it to happen.

Effect Four: Short-Term Borrowers Will Suffer More Than Longer-Term Borrowers

Interest rate increases drive down the values of longer-term interest-bearing assets. Those who borrowed in the short term to buy longer-term assets may find their cost of capital higher than their returns. That is a squeeze called a **maturity mismatch**. Short-term borrowing at 1/2 percent to buy a 10-year bond yielding 3 percent works, until the borrowing cost goes to 4 percent and the value of the bond drops 20 percent. Institutions with these mismatches can profit in the short term, but be decimated after rate increases. A maturity mismatch can be compounded by a currency mismatch.

These are possible effects based on past experiences and the way the system developed post 2008. After the great recession people got used to behaving as if interest rates never go up, or if they do, they will go up only a little. It is worth looking at the longer term, and what interest rates have actually done. Figure 3.3 shows long-term interest rates from 1790 to 2016. Clearly, there are other periods in history in which people thought that rates were stable and were going to stay that way. This time may be different, but history says it probably won't be.

Figure 3.3. Long-Term Interest Rates, 1790 to 2016
Source: Data is from Bianco Research LLC, 2016.

NOTES

1. This is not as clear cut as many traditional "left" or "right" issues, though those on the right and libertarians tend not to believe that money supply should be actively managed and see strength in the rigidity of the gold standard.

2. Despite popular belief, individuals in the United States were not able to go to the Fed and get an ounce of gold for $35. However, other countries that held USD could. It was the aggressive selling of USD to the US Treasury for gold by France in the late 1960s (and the age-old nemesis of gold standards, a need to finance the Vietnam War) that led the United States to abandon gold as a basis for the dollar. See Eichengreen (2011) for a good summary of the program and the nuances involved, which are too extensive to get into here.

3. Hyperinflation is commonly defined as inflation of greater than 50 percent per month. Commonly, a loss of faith is presaged by monetary authorities' rapidly increasing the money supply, but that need not be the case. Once enough people start to abandon a currency, its value can keep plummeting under its own steam.

4. Silk Road, one of the largest exchanges of illicit goods and services including drugs and contract killings, was closed by the FBI in late 2014. For the story of the capture of its alleged founder "Dread Pirate Roberts" and the subsequent trial see Greenberg 2015.

5. For an overview of virtual currencies, how they differ from national fiat currencies, and regulatory issues see the IMF report, He et al. 2016.

6. For a summary, see these notes from the US Federal Reserve 2015 and the Federal Reserve Bank of New York 2008. Though these measures of money have historically been important in economics, they are decreasingly so in open economies with free movement of capital, "shadow" banking, and credit systems.

7. A notable exception was US Fed Chairman Paul Volcker's very politically unpopular decision to raise interest rates toward the 20 percent range in 1982 to put a stop to inflation. History now remembers this as one of the boldest and most correct moves in central banking. Cases also abound of revocation of independence when central banks don't follow political tides, such as the Peruvian case under Alan Garcia in the 1990s.

8. The ownership structure of the Fed is a bit confusing, with the twelve banks in the Federal Reserve System in theory owned by the member commercial banks, Federal Reserve Bank, 2016.

9. These can vary a bit as they are stated. The Fed is mandated to achieve "maximum employment, stable prices, and moderate long-term interest rates," Federal Reserve Bank 2016.

10. History is being made as this book is written, with the ECB implementing loose monetary policies that not long ago would have been unthinkable.

11. The actual owners of the bonds were mainly large institutional investors, hedge funds, sovereign wealth funds, mutual funds, and other large global money managers. They sold because at the offered price, they believed it would be more advantageous to change their portfolio composition than to continue to hold the bonds.

12. The rationale behind the applications in the modern, post–great recession world, of these and the unconventional levers to follow has been written about extensively elsewhere. See, for example, the narratives in *Big Picture Economics*, by Naroff and Scherer (2014) and any number of quality books about the great recession such as *This Time Is Different* by Reinhart and Rogoff (2009) and *Crisis Economics* by Nouriel Roubini (2010).

13. Such as in 2008 and 1907.

14. This is contrary to the way money creation is normally described in textbooks, but it is correct. See Standard and Poor's research paper, "Repeat after Me: Banks Cannot and Do Not 'Lend Out' Reserves" by Paul Sheard (2014) and the exposition by Roche (2011).

15. Nakamura et al. 2016.

16. Remember the inverse relationship between bond price and interest rate.

17. Former Fed Chairman Ben Bernanke is renowned for saying that QE works in practice, but not in theory.

18. Solid evidence is lacking in many areas. See, for example, the case for emerging market asset price inflation by Lavigne et al. 2014. Some researchers suspect QE has led to wider asset price inflation simply because of supply and demand relationships, but given time lags and noise in data, results are not conclusive. See Joyce et al. 2011.

19. Federal Reserve Bank 2016. The site gives a constantly updated picture of the Fed's balance sheet.

20. See the BIS annual report, BIS 2014.

21. Some do advocate such interventions. The Modern Monetary Theory school and some mainstream economists such as Paul Krugman have questioned whether direct injections would be problematic when inflation is persistently low.

22. This could reach nearly half by 2017 according to Buckland and Nozawa (2015).

23. For a summary of issues, see S&P chief economist Paul Sheard's (2016) article, "Helicopter Money and the Monetary Garden of Eden."

24. The concept of cheap versus easy money comes out in this study by Painter and Redfearn (2002) of the effect of interest rates on housing. Low rates affect housing starts in the short run, but not homeownership. Developers react to low rates to expand the supply, but low rates alone do not get individuals to buy homes.

25. El-Erian (2016), pg. 144.

26. Eventually, the USD did increase sharply in value as the discrepancy between deflationary Europe and a growing United States became increasingly evident.

27. This led to claims of a much-publicized "currency war" in Brazil as authorities there worked in 2010 to counteract the accretive effects of financial inflows on their exchange rate. After the "tapering," Brazil's currency dropped and the ministry of finance struggled with ensuing inflation and the higher cost of dollar-denominated sovereign debt.

28. Like most events in the global economy, there were likely multiple causal factors. For some of the countries in the chart, weakening growth and softening global commodity prices were likely a parallel driver of the drops. Short sellers, anticipating drops, can also then put downward pressure on a currency.

29. See chapter 2, "Understanding the Slowdown in Capital Flows to Emerging Markets," in the 2016 IMF World Economic Outlook.

30. The event was widely reported in the financial press. See for example *The Economist* 2014.

31. I have been warned by a respected reader of this manuscript about predicting crises and will not claim to do that. However, the sorts of more moderate, but still considerable, ebbs and flows of EM currency values are likely to continue due to the dynamics discussed here and throughout the book.

32. It has been difficult to precisely ascertain how QE affected prices in different asset markets. On longer-term highly rated bonds it was probably significant, as that was the purpose of QE. On domestic stocks, it is harder to say since increases in stock values also coincided with increase corporate profitability. In emerging markets, again there is some evidence, but not

definitive. The reports cited offer various viewpoints. See Fratzscher et al. 2013, Barroso et al. 2016, the IMF report by Roache and Rousset, and the McKinsey report by Dobbs et al. 2013.

33. Though inflation is a key economic statistic used in policy decision making, it also serves as a case of the ambiguity inherent in economic data. The basket used in the United States is reconfigured every seven or so years, so it probably does not reflect almost anyone's actual consumption patterns. More importantly, inflation is not really an economy-wide number, but affects regions and people quite individually. Yet even minute changes in the reported rate are regularly watched, commented on, and acted on.

34. Even though unemployment dropped, for a number of reasons wages did not increase as much as they had historically. It's an example of why hard-and-fast rules, even related to supply and demand, need to be looked at carefully in each case rather than blindly followed.

35. For a summary of the mechanics of affecting real interest rates, see the BIS report by Bech and Malkhozov 2016. For a country like Greece with price levels that are probably too high for the country to be competitive on global markets, deflation, though painful, is the main short-term mechanism for regaining competitiveness.

36. Central banks tend to treat even moderate inflation as more of a problem than it might actually be. Economist Robert Barro (2013) noted a negative relationship between inflation and growth, but results were only statistically significant when cases of greater than 20 percent per year inflation were included.

37. There is sometimes confusion here. If you hold a bond to maturity, you get the full return you signed up for. But if you try to sell it in the secondary market after rates go up, its value will be lower than before. Interest rates went up.

38. "Other things" include weaknesses in the eurozone periphery, changes in attitude/orientation at the ECB, demographic shifts from aging, and low productivity growth.

4

Domestic Policies and Global Repercussions

Events don't happen by themselves out in an isolated world called the "global economy." In truth, a great many of the incentives and rules that impel and constrain participants in the global economy are rooted in domestic policy. The linkages going both directions, however, tend to be underemphasized. To quote the former Singaporean ambassador to the United Nations:

> Most prominent economists believe that the nation state is the most important unit of economic analysis . . . The perspectives of economists differ dramatically from those of [in business] . . . if policymakers do not understand that we now live and function within a single global economy, they could make hugely flawed decisions or could take actions that could damage the world.[1]

Though unfortunately most people probably care more about avoiding hugely flawed financial decisions than damaging the world, understanding the interplay between domestic and global economies can help in avoiding both.

The emphasis here will be on two main areas, fiscal policy and regulations. **Fiscal policy** is the framework of taxing, spending, and borrowing within an economy. Regulations are the rules established to govern economic behavior. Among other effects, both can create incentives that draw people, goods, and investment in from around the world; create disincentives that drive money out of the domestic economy that otherwise would have stayed there; either reward or punish people for playing by or breaking rules; and/or change relative prices, so that purchases or investments become more or less profitable than before.

Taxing, spending, and borrowing are the components of fiscal policy. Taxes have redistributive and diversionary effects. They redistribute money out of taxpayers' hands and redirect it to others' through government spending. Taxes are diversionary because governments spend on different things than people and companies do.

Less money goes to certain investments and purchases, and more money to others. Countries may end up with fewer investments and employment in mega yacht manufacturers, and more in the production of staple food products, schools, and roads. Or there may be more in mega yacht manufacturers depending on spending decisions. But economy-wide spending won't be the same as if there were no taxes.

For practical purposes, taxes are charged in each individual economy, so despite a web of legislation to prevent it tax avoidance is a big money mover in the global economy. Tax rates and breaks are watched carefully by global companies and investors. Countries and special tax zones attract money by lowering tax burdens, either with a lower rate and/or helping hide money from authorities in other countries. Table 4.1 lists a few of those locations and what they have offered taxpayers at different times.[2]

Tax havens allow people to hide money, and low-tax areas allow them to be taxed at a lower rate. The first are increasingly rare, at least for those trying to get away from tax authorities. In the last decade, the US Internal Revenue Service (IRS) especially has made it more difficult for US-based investors and companies to hide their

Table 4.1.

Tax Haven	*Their Deal*	*Comments*
Switzerland	Ability to open numbered accounts, making it hard for authorities in other countries to see who holds the account.	Recently discontinued for US citizens under pressure from the US government, but Switzerland was the center of anonymous accounts for many years.
Cayman Islands	Income tax rate is zero, and ability to set up companies where ownership is hard to determine.	Over 60 percent of Fortune 500 companies had a subsidiary there in 2014, booking profits that probably were not earned there.
British Virgin Islands	Zero income and capital gains taxes, and a sophisticated and low-cost financial sector.	One of the biggest and still growing havens, a favorite of Chinese businesses and wealthy citizens. Profits are booked here.
Ireland	15 percent tax rate on corporate profits, compared to 42 percent average in the US and 23.5 percent as an EU average.[a]	Fully legal, as are the practices of shifting profits to Ireland to avoid taxes in higher-tax countries.
Montenegro	Numbered and untraceable accounts, one of the last truly anonymous banking centers.	This practice has been discontinued under pressure from the US government.
Panama	A favorite location to nearly anonymously register companies that can be used to hide money.	A large Panamanian law firm was subject to a data leak in 2016 that exposed many government leaders trying to hide ill-gotten funds.

a. Dalton 2012. To be fair, most larger US corporation take advantage of various tax loopholes and pay less than the 42 percent rate.

earnings. That is not to say they don't try. With a sophisticated enough network of shell companies registered in places that the IRS will probably not think to look (Delaware apparently being one of them), people are still managing to hide money.[3] It is getting harder, though. The United States has successfully used the specter of terrorism and the money that funds it to pry open most of the traditional tax havens. Whether terrorists could just use cash rather than the international banking and payments system was seemingly beside the point.[4]

People from other countries have it a bit easier. For one, most countries rely more on value-added taxes for revenue, rather than high corporate tax rates. Incentives to evade are also lower. Also, unlike the United States, a lot of countries do not tax global income (i.e., any income earned outside the home country). So for most legally obtained earnings, authorities don't care so much. Their tax authorities have also not been able to beat the international banks into submission the way the IRS has. Ironically, it is currently quite a bit easier for a corrupt or tax-evading foreign national to invest their ill-gotten gains in the United States than it is for a US citizen to do so in a foreign country. In particular, when investing in US real estate, if the money comes from overseas, requirements are loose in verifying whether its origins are legal or not.[5]

The use of the second type of international tax shelter, low-tax areas, is widespread and for the most part perfectly legal. At least use is widespread if you have the money, global reach, and accounting department to take advantage of these opportunities. They are used extensively and creatively by multinational companies and their accounting departments. The main tool is called **transfer pricing**, which is the use of accounting entries to change where profits end up. You direct profits toward low-tax areas, and losses toward high-tax areas.

Here is an example. A US-based company is subject to an approximately 42 percent tax rate on profit in the United States (federal plus state tax). Profit in Ireland is subject to a 15 percent tax, and lower for some companies. A common tactic is to manufacture a small part of a product or perform some service in a low-tax area like Ireland. The company then sells that Irish-made product or service to the US-based division of the same company at a higher than fair market price. The division doing the buying is based in a high-tax area, but because of the high price makes very little profit or even loses money after overpaying for the purchase from the low-tax location. The profits are made in low-tax Ireland, and the US operations are less profitable or may even lose money. Transfer pricing can lead to high costs and inefficiencies at the company level. But the benefits of lowering the tax burden can quickly make it worthwhile.

Transfer pricing and related money flows are an important element of global economics, and most international companies use transfer pricing in one way or another.[6] For Ireland, provision of these kinds of services is a big part of the Irish economic "miracle," whereby Ireland went from being one of the poorest to one of the richest countries in the European Union in a few decades.

Though numerous global companies have used these tactics for some time, they came into view of the US public in 2013 and 2014 during a series of congressional hearings on Apple Inc. Officials from the company took the stand and were very forthright about how they legally use low-tax areas and transfer pricing to lower their US tax burden (or evade US taxes, depending on how you feel about it). The core of their approach was to set up offshore entities in low-tax areas, and/or areas that had favorable rules about what was taxed. Some of these entities apparently did not even have employees, but controlled billions of dollars in revenue.

The key was not just to locate in a low-tax area, but more importantly to locate in areas that did not tax nondomestic sources of income for entities that are based there. So an Apple subsidiary in Ireland (where Apple had also negotiated a special 2 percent corporate tax rate) did not have to pay taxes on profits it made in other countries while operating from its Irish base. By playing this shell game at multiple levels, Apple was able to, perfectly legally, make much of its profits "stateless" to use the term from the hearings.[7]

In another example, PepsiCo manufactures the syrups for its soft drinks in Ireland. It marks them up and then sells them to subsidiaries in other countries with higher tax rates at a very high price that locks in the profit in Ireland, and ensures that the subsidiaries do not have as much profit.[8] Ireland is certainly not the most efficient place to make syrups and ship them around the world. But lower taxes make it better than basing these operations in the United States or in mainland Europe.

It remains to be seen whether these kinds of activities will continue into the future or whether companies such as Apple are exploiting loopholes that violate the spirit of tax laws. In the summer of 2016, EU authorities ruled against Apple's use of an Irish base to avoid mainland taxes and presented the company with a $14.5 billion tax bill.[9] Whether or not they succeed in this levy will be widely watched.

Tax inversions are cross-border acquisitions in which a company in a high-tax area purchases a similar company or rival in a low-tax area. It then relocates the headquarters from the high-tax to the low-tax area and reports more profits there. As a high corporate tax economy, the United States has seen the most inversions with many of them occurring in the 2010s. Tax inversions are politically sensitive, for obvious reasons, in the higher-tax countries. The future of inversions is unclear as governments have begun to crack down on this obvious source of tax evasion. In 2015, the US government reacted by making adjustments to the tax code that kept pharmaceutical giant Pfizer from purchasing a smaller rival in Ireland and moving its headquarters there.[10]

Tax breaks and **tax credits** are specific reductions in taxes designed to incentivize people to behave differently than they otherwise would. Tax breaks can, for example, encourage companies to invest more in certain sectors or locations, to cover employees' health insurance, replace certain types of equipment, conduct research and development activities, or to buy homes. Large companies are frequently given tax breaks to make an investment in a certain country or region, as seen in the previous example of Intel in Costa Rica.

A tax break has essentially the same effect on global money flows as a direct payment. The main difference between a tax break and a subsidy or direct payment is that you need profits to benefit from tax breaks. If your company is losing money, you care less about tax breaks, unless the tax breaks are what pushed you into a loss position.

Local and national governments commonly offer a range of tax breaks to entice companies to locate in their area, often competing with one another to offer the best deal. The practice is both widespread and controversial, with critics claiming that governments are competing to get the least amount of benefit from investment as possible while subsidizing rich companies. Proponents claim that such incentives are essential for attracting investment. In any case, they are common enough to redirect significant capital around the global economy from where it otherwise would have gone.[11]

In addition to taxes, government spending is a big driver of incentives throughout the global economy. Whenever a government is willing to spend money, you will find people willing to sell, build, consult, kill, lie, cheat, and steal for that money. People chase government money all over the planet. The area around Washington, DC, is not one of the wealthiest in the United States because it is a seat of manufacturing and technology prowess. There is big money to be made from securing government procurement and subsidies.[12]

Figure 4.1 shows total government procurement (i.e., what the government spends on buying outside services) for a group of OECD countries. To give an idea of the amount of money here, the total central government budget of the United States was around $3.7 trillion in 2012. So procurement was over $1 trillion for the United States. Money is spent on many areas but can include military hardware, computers, bridges and all their components, lots of consulting services, pencils, energy projects,

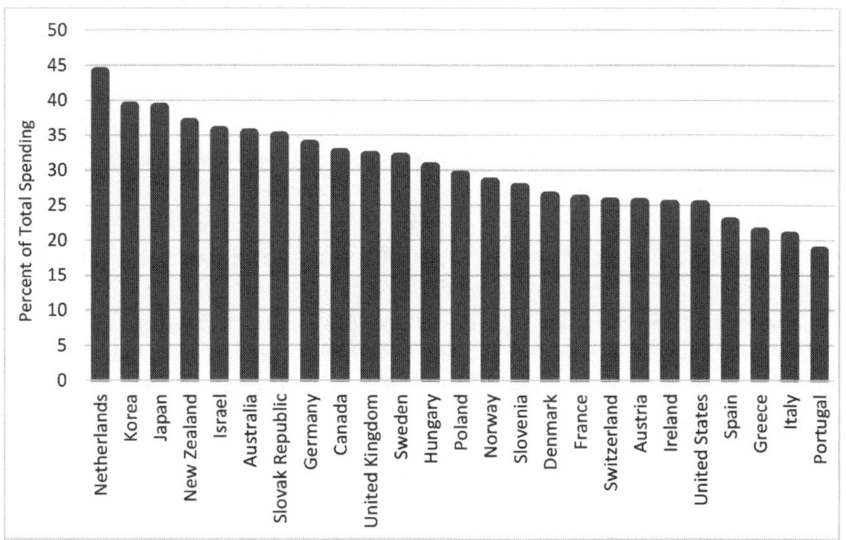

Figure 4.1. Procurement as a Percentage of Total Government Spending

Source: Government at a Glance 2015, OECD Publishing. Data is from 2013.

you name it. Procurement can draw in money from other countries, directly or indirectly. For example, EU alternative energy subsidies have drawn in foreign energy operators, raw materials, and much foreign-made equipment. Direct payments and tax breaks for these programs amounted to over $100 billion in 2012.[13]

Governments often try, legally and illegally, to steer public-sector procurement away from foreign companies and toward local ones. Legally, because most countries allow discrimination in at least some areas. For example, defense and other national security–related contractors are frequently required to be national companies. BAE Systems is a UK-based defense (or defence) company that moved its headquarters to the United States to take advantage of the much larger US market and not have to worry about being barred from procurements.

Governments discriminate illegally because many of the same governments (like the United States and many EU governments) that effectively bar foreign companies from non-national-security-related procurements are signatories to a WTO protocol that says they will not do that. Examples will follow, but suffice to say that high government spending can change global trade and investment patterns as investors move to take advantage of that spending.

Government spending can also drive money out of a country, especially if investors are concerned that it is reaching unsustainable levels that cannot be financed by future revenues. How much debt is "sustainable" is a matter of a heated debate in economics. High deficit spending drives concerns that taxes will increase in the future to service the debt, that the money supply will be increased to monetize the debt, driving inflation, or that there may be a default. Investors watch fiscal deficit and debt levels fairly carefully, not wanting to be the last ones out if things go badly. Concerns about high debts and default risk have led to investors fleeing a wide range of countries over the years, including Greece, Argentina, Russia, Brazil, and Mexico, among others.

Government spending is a significant money mover, but when governments want private money to do something, as often as not they use regulations. Regulations are rules that provide much of the structure to an economy. Though often vilified, without regulation many parts of economies and societies simply would cease to function in any recognizable way.

Most regulations are carried out by the executive functions of a government, with the laws that enable them created by the legislative side. Enabling legislation is commonly vague, with the executive side firming up the rules before implementation.[14] This latter point is important, as it gives the executive branch **bureaucratic discretion**, or flexibility, to interpret the law and carry out its regulations in a way that may be different from what some lawmakers might have had in mind. Laws can also be intentionally vague to avoid offending potential supporters and ensure the coalition needed to pass them.

Flexibility in regulatory implementation can make it harder to foresee the shape of final regulations after a law is passed. It also means that bureaucracies can change regulations when deemed necessary, as long as they can convince the courts that the change is consistent with the original legislative intent. Rule changes may come about because someone is trying to find a way around the regulation and thinks there is a loophole that still meets legislative intent.

Bureaucratic discretion then is tricky. Flexibility to adapt is important, but it also opens bureaucracies up to institutionalized (lobbying) and criminal (payoff) versions of outside manipulation. The process of making regulations is further complicated by the complexity of economies and the lack of economic knowledge and real economy experience of many lawmakers. They say there are two things you never want to see made: laws (regulations included) and sausage. I have seen more laws than sausage made, and lawmaking gives sausage a bad name.

The sheer quantity of types of regulations and potential effects on the global economy mean that there is no way to begin to cover them all. Also, regulations frequently combine subsidies, penalties, and tax breaks, so sometimes there isn't a clear distinction between regulations and fiscal policy. The goal in this chapter is to define a basic framework, and then use that to look at specific cases. Below is a sampling of areas of domestic regulation and how each can influence global money flows:

- *Environmental/energy:* Change the relative prices of pollution by taxing or regulating it, which can change the relative price of producing in one country versus another; make certain sources of energy relatively lower cost than they would have been otherwise, changing investment flows from one to another; change the relative prices of alternative energy by subsidizing it (both of these first two can change global energy production, investment, and trade patterns); forbid certain technologies/methods from being used (e.g., charcoal fires); require the use of certain technologies, boosting the industries that supply them (e.g., catalytic converters and platinum); set strict limits on the amount of certain emissions, forcing industries to close, leave to other countries, or invest in different technologies; fuel efficiency standards change the relative desirability of different vehicles from different countries and using components from different countries, such as clean diesel engines from Europe and batteries from the United States and Japan.[15]
- *Labor:* Set and enforce minimum wages and benefit levels, changing the cost of labor versus capital and changing the cost of labor in a whole market versus other markets; make it more or less difficult to hire and fire, changing the relative all-in cost and risk of labor across markets; set child labor laws and minimum workweeks, changing the relative cost of labor, but possibly increasing education and longer-term competitiveness in some markets; set domestic labor quotas for foreign investments, changing the cost, risk, and return profiles of the investment; prohibiting foreign labor in certain areas can change direct or compliance costs (e.g., Mexico and cross-border trucking).[16]
- *Bankruptcy law and efficiency of administration:* Changes the risk of investing by changing the costs and probability of recovering assets after business failure.
- *Pensions and savings:* Tax-shielding private pension laws can drive the accumulation of massive pools of money that are then invested all over the world

through individual and group accounts; lower taxes on dividends can make equities more attractive for savings and investment, shifting money out of other instruments and markets; pay-as-you-go pension schemes versus defined contribution can affect fiscal balances and the sustainability of government debt in certain countries, eventually potentially disrupting interest rates, inflation, debt sustainability, and growth; changes in pension fund investment regulations can open and close global markets for large sums of money.

- *Financial regulation:* Bank capital requirements decrease risk in the bank and the system, and affect returns to investing in commercial banks; sound bank regulation lowers overall system risk and cost of capital; large variations in national financial regulation regimes can change relative prices and risks of investing in one area versus another, leading to movements of capital, and can lead to overall greater risk in the system.
- *Capital controls:* After several financial crises in emerging markets, some countries make it more or less difficult or more expensive for "hot money" to exit the economy quickly if there is a crisis; some countries limit access to foreign investors and/or require domestic partners in many or all industries, especially with regard to foreign direct investment. There will be more on these in chapter 7.
- *Food policy:* Food safety laws make it more difficult for countries to trade food across borders—some are warranted and some are another version of protection from foreign competition; food subsidies can make some countries' food much cheaper on foreign markets, increasing demand and leading to negative outcomes for farmers in countries with more limited subsidies; different domestic testing and labeling requirements increase costs of the food trade, changing relative prices.
- *Medical:* Health systems in some countries are able to enter into pools to negotiate with drug and device makers for better deals, and in some countries it is not legal (like the US public system); public medical research spending can drive investment in certain markets over others; differences in cost/quality trade-offs between different medical systems can move money across borders as customers seek lower costs (to emerging markets) or specialized treatments (to developed markets).
- *Contract law:* Enforceability of contracts and speed and cost of enforcement can change risk-return calculations in different markets.

The above is a nonexhaustive list of types of regulations that can drive global capital and trade flows. Actual effects can be difficult both to predict before regulations are implemented, and to measure accurately once they are in place. Each case needs to be analyzed separately, looking at the particular incentives that are created or altered by changes in relative price and risk levels.

The appendix to this chapter provides some more detailed case studies on the effects of domestic policies on the global economy.

AMBIGUITY, INFLUENCE, AND THE MAKING OF POLICY

In theory, monetary, fiscal, and regulatory policies are made by governments for the benefit of the citizens of the country.[17] In reality, academic studies and the glaring news that hits the press every day make the case that special interests and those who lobby for them greatly influence domestic policy. [18] A 2014 working paper by two professors from Princeton and Northwestern Universities concluded that in the United States, organized interest groups representing economic and business elites had substantial influence on policy, and that ordinary voters had little to none.[19] The study surprised few people, but was still particularly stark in its evidence.[20]

While citizens of European countries can get smug and think that their systems are different, there is little to indicate that is the case. Latin Americans and Africans generally know better than to assume otherwise, and ample evidence of elite influence emerged from the Asian financial crisis under the so-called Asian growth model. Countries under single-party rule are almost without exception no better, and may even be more transparent since interest groups tend to be more concentrated around the ruling elite.[21] Singapore may be the exception that proves the rule.[22] The term *corruption* is often used to describe undue elite interference on and benefit from policy. As will be seen, though corruption certainly occurs the natural ambiguity of policy effects can make it difficult to apply such a catch-all term.

The first theme of this subsection is the role of political power in economic governance, and in particular regulatory policy. Political process is inseparable from economic policy formation, with the exact lines where technocratic competence ends and political influence begins often hard to unravel. Global economic history is rife with stories of political influence over economic rules.

Though most of the time it hums along without incident, economic and financial regulation can fail, becoming a proximate if not leading cause of economic instability and the rapid exit of global money flows. Sometimes it is a sin of omission, when regulatory capacities are simply not authorized or up to the task of monitoring and maintaining order in the financial system. Weak institutions, particularly in banking, monetary, and securities regulation, are a characteristic of many emerging and frontier markets economies. The pace of financial innovation, in recent decades further accelerated by rapid advances in technology, is relentless and well funded. Regulatory agencies are almost without exception less so.

At other times close coalitions between the regulators and regulated lead to loose oversight, or the sort of **regulatory capture** noted in chapter 2. The 1997 Asian financial crisis was enabled by both weak regulatory bodies unprepared to cope with newly open capital markets, as well as the particulars of the Asian model at the time with close links between state regulators, politicians, and powerful businesses. Regulators, including the famed technocratic "Berkeley Mafia," were encouraged to look the other way as risk piled up in the system.[23] Similarly, regulatory failure leading up to the 2008 great recession has been at least partially blamed on the "revolving door" of employment between powerful investments banks and regulatory agencies in the United States. Links can be made between weak, captured, or dirigisme regulation, and the severity of many financial booms and busts throughout the past decades.

Less than independent regulatory bodies may not be all negative, especially in the short to medium run. Leading up to the crises starting in 1997, the leading Asian economies saw decades of unprecedented growth. Though like most hot topics in economics the conclusions are controversial, evidence suggests that the close business and government linkages helped support that growth, at least for a time. Similarly, Chinese influence over state banks and monetary authorities has certainly changed the path of that economy multiple times, including possibly saving it from crisis at least in the short term and perhaps buying the economy the time it needs to outgrow debt and make needed transitions.

We can take as a given then that elite, government, or special interests often lurk behind regulatory action and inaction. What is called corruption often appears evident after the fact, but is often less so when viewed in real time, especially when it is embedded into the institutional structure of a particular economy and society. At what point did the so-called Asian model go from being an envied driver of impressive rates of growth, to a corrupt "crony capitalist" regime? Evidence points to this being more a matter of when performance began to wane, rather than any objective assessment of interlinkages and mutual backscratching. Even the impressively corrupt Suharto regime in Indonesia was seen as a bit of an economic miracle worker in its heyday, and Vladimir Putin's Russia experienced some of the best growth in the post-Soviet era.

Some of the controversy in economic regulatory regimes stems from the problem of **moral hazard**, or when governments explicitly or implicitly generate guarantees that transfer risk from private to public parties. A strict theory of the free market holds that people manage risk better when they personally suffer from the result of their bad decisions. Management of a modern economy, however, often entails putting in safeguards to keep that from happening.

There are usually good reasons for the safeguards. Deposit guarantees keep bank runs and major liquidity crises at bay, but mean that banks that lose depositor money can count on the government to cover any losses. That may encourage greater risk taking by banks and appears to do just that. If an institution is considered **too big to fail**, it means that failure would lead to systemic risk in the financial system and so it should be protected from failure. However, management of such a protected institution now need not worry about failure, so may take more risk than would be prudent. The fixed exchange rates that prevailed leading up to the Asian financial crisis helped protect investors and exporters from fluctuating exchange rates and were a major part of policy at that time. However, they encouraged borrowing in foreign currencies without hedging. When the fixed exchange rates broke free, borrowers were exposed to massive losses. A similar argument is made about IMF lending. If investors know the IMF will come and bail them out, they may take greater than prudent risks.[24]

Clearly, there are both up and down sides to offering the guarantees that can generate moral hazard, but it is almost impossible to imagine a modern economy without such guarantees. Regulators usually work to manage the risks of moral hazard with additional regulations. For example, banks that accept government deposit guarantees are then subject to rules about what they can invest in. Banks that want to grow to "too big to fail" get regulated even more. Finding the correct balance of guarantees versus regulation is hard and subject to imperfect knowledge, potential regulatory capture, and the major discrepancy in money and capability between highly motivated financial sector players and career regulators. It is hard to stay a step ahead of market forces. The extreme self-interest and motivation of market players is self-evident, as is apparently their ability to work the system.

Mancur Olson was one of the great economists who died before he could get a Nobel Memorial Prize. His basic premise was that the advantage of collective action (i.e., the ability to organize for self-interest) goes to smaller groups with a focused agenda. Large, disparate groups, like voters who just want a decent life, get left behind in democracies. They find it nearly impossible to come together and rally for basic, common causes. Also, once policy changes are made and interest groups grow up around them, they become difficult to reverse. Consequently, rather than old programs closing down when policy goals shift, new programs can end up being implemented alongside them. Policy survivability explains such paradoxes as the US government's subsidizing tobacco growing at the same time as trying to discourage its use.[25]

This brings us to the second theme of this subsection, the role of ambiguity in policy making. The same challenges identified earlier in reaching definitive conclusions from economic analysis play heavily into policy making. This ambiguity helps make the assessment and evidence of elite influence on policy both less stark and more nuanced. Special interests can press for changes that are both detrimental and beneficial for a larger part of the population. Problematically, we often just don't know which they are. Both *ex ante* and *ex post* policy analysis is difficult, with the actual effects of economic policies notoriously hard to accurately evaluate. In many (though certainly not all) cases, it can be hard to say for certain whether what a special interest succeeds in achieving is good or bad for the economy as a whole, or even the majority of the population. Also, what is good in the short run may be bad in the long run, or vice versa. What is good for a large group may be bad for a smaller one, or vice versa.

Sometimes hard-to-evaluate factors such as being in the "national interest" get thrown into the mix. Ongoing sugar and cotton subsidies in the United States, film subsidies in France, and EU GMO restrictions are just a few examples of policies that many economists would find questionable, but are considered to be in the national interest in the respective countries. Interest groups take advantage of the natural ambiguity around policy outcomes to press for what they want, downplaying the potential negative effects and loudly emphasizing the positive.

Special interest groups get tarred with a broad brush of being corporate stooges, and many may very well be. At the same time, there are plenty of special interests that appear to be pushing for the "common good," like tighter environmental policies, improved social welfare programs, or improved childhood education and health care. However, and importantly, they are inevitably going to be doing so in ways that not everyone is going to agree on or where the broader, economy-wide impacts are unclear. Most people may want cleaner air or to take care of senior citizens and children. However, there may be serious disagreement on the costs and benefits of different types of programs to achieve those goals, in addition to whether any program at all can or should be implemented.

Defining the "common good" is slippery and changes depending on what part of the "common" people you are talking about. A particular program for cleaner air (common good), might lead to less employment (another common good), lower pension assets (potentially a common good) when the stock of polluting companies is held by pension funds, or tax revenues (needed to implement a range of beneficial programs).

With shifting demographics in most countries leading to an aging population, critical and difficult policy decisions will need to balance the needs of younger members of the population with older ones. The debates around these choices will be full of confusion about who will gain, relative costs and benefits, and when they will occur. Everyone might agree in principle that keeping the old from suffering and educating and ensuring opportunity for the young are "common goods." However, there might be little agreement on the amount of money to be allocated in each direction, the types of programs to be implemented, and their relative costs and benefits.

If developed market economies really do enter a prolonged period of low growth, or secular stagnation, they will be faced with increasingly difficult questions of redistribution of existing income, rather than being able to rely on economic growth to fuel new programs. This makes the debates all the more contentious and raises the stakes, probably without any better tools than economists have now for analyzing policy impact. Domestic policies shaped by these realities and ambiguities will attract and repel global money flows in complex ways. Some of those will be explored in section II of this book.

A common conclusion of simulations that ask regular citizens to make fiscal policy decisions is that most want to both lower taxes and increase spending. The deficit spending common to most countries may reflect actual voter preferences, regardless of whether it is good for the long-term health of the economy. Quite simply, like economists, individuals have a hard time with policy feasibility, trade-offs, and impact assessment. The left-wing Syriza party was elected in Greece in 2015 because people wanted to maintain low retirement ages, high public expenditure outlays, and to stay with the euro. That is what the people want, but that does not make it possible. Eventually, trade-offs were made under conditions of extreme uncertainty. Policy making is ambiguous and hard even when everyone is actually trying to do the right thing, despite the black-and-white dichotomies drawn by the media's talking heads.

Even if the common good is agreed on as maximizing growth, no school of economics or side of the political spectrum can claim a monopoly or even a majority of policy directions that universally achieve that goal. Latin America and Africa in the 1970s and 1980s (and to a lesser extent to the present day) are a graveyard of well-meaning leftist policies that bankrupted governments, led to unrealistic expectations, and are widely agreed to have held back growth. Mexican land reform, though effectively distributing land to the landless, also inadvertently held back agricultural production and tied people to unprofitable patches of land that they could not consolidate, sell, or borrow against even as agriculture scaled up elsewhere and farm-gate prices dropped.

On the right, there have been any number of experiments with excess domestic austerity after economic crises decimated public finances. In retrospect, these may have locked countries into low growth paths, rather than allowing them to rebound. *Ex-post* analyses on the austere domestic policies the IMF enforced on a range of countries after the Asian financial crisis of 1997 indicate that these policies may have made the crisis worse.[26] An ongoing, almost doctrinaire belief in supply-side economics led to an experiment slashing income taxes and waiting for a supply response in the US state of Kansas. To date, the result is deficits and cuts to education and infrastructure programs that probably do help growth.[27]

Programs of all types often come with "feel-good" press around them. However, that does not necessarily make the program good for the overall health of the nation, however that is defined. Sometimes they are, sometimes they are not. More often than not, no one actually knows because no real, rigorous, independent analysis has been done. And if it has been done, it is likely inconclusive, bores people, and makes for tedious news. There is enough ambiguity in policy analyses that with the right spin, even fairly clearly bad policies can be made popular and good ones derided.

As a case in point, one effective way to control costs in public health programs is independent panels to look at rigorous research on what specific treatments for specific conditions have proven effective versus ineffective. Effective treatments are then paid for by insurers or the state, and ineffective treatments (and treatments lacking sufficient evidence) are not paid for. This is normal in most countries, and most economists would agree that it is a good idea. In 2008 in the United States, there was an attempt to give these panels more influence, and so determine how patients would be treated. A major PR campaign was launched to discredit the proposal, saying it got in the way of the doctor-patient relationship and would result in "death panels" of bureaucrats deciding who lives and dies. It is unlikely that defeat of this proposal resulted in better health outcomes and it certainly led to higher costs, but the public generally felt good about the defeat.[28]

Analytical ambiguity, confusion on outcomes, news-cycle attention span, the outsize influence of special interest groups, and political infighting and instincts all make for a highly complex environment within which domestic, and by extension, global economic policy is made. That said, the purpose of this section is not to pass judgment on the system or to just say nothing matters since nothing can be definitively known.[29] The goal is to introduce the political realities within which economic policy is made, and to underscore the importance of standing back and rationally analyzing the balance of power with humility and with one's eyes open.

Understanding who the special interests are, what they want, how powerful they are, and how much credibility they can capture can help a lot in understanding the direction and persistence of domestic economic policy, and in turn its influence on the global economy. As anywhere in economics, incentives matter in fiscal policy. In his book *Predictioneer's Game*, Bruce Bueno de Mesquita (2009) tells how he has made a nice living out of following brazen self-interest and using that to predict outcomes. You should do the same.

UNINTENDED CONSEQUENCES OF POLICIES

Making economic policy is hard. Successfully changing the incentive structure of even a small part of an economy depends on predicting the behavior of the sometimes millions of people who will react to the proposed policy or policy change. It does not help that laws usually end up as a patchwork of compromises made to get enough legislators to vote for them. It also does not help that market participants are creative and will try to find an easier way to make money than the policy intended. The result can be unintentionally bad and/or ineffective policy. Even when policy goals are achieved, there can be other effects that were not anticipated. This is the so-called law of **unintended consequences**: that no matter how well conceived a policy is, something is going to go wrong. In practice, that something can end up being profitable for a particular group(s), so they will fight hard to keep the policy from being corrected.

Sometimes unintended consequences are domestic. Sometimes, though, even if the policy is successful by some measures in the domestic economy, there are unintended consequences that are felt internationally. Chapter 3 included an example of how a change in the US quantitative easing program wreaked havoc on a group of emerging markets currencies. Probably the best way forward is to look at a few more examples.

Ethanol Production in the United States

Seeking environmental benefits and greater energy independence, the US government began a series of regulatory, tax, and subsidy programs to increase the production of the grain alcohol ethanol for use as a fuel. By 2014, approximately 10 percent of motor vehicle fuel sold in the United States was ethanol. The United States became the largest ethanol producer in the world, with most of it coming from corn. Corn, unfortunately, is not a very efficient way to make ethanol.

- Domestic unintended consequences: Increased incentive to grow corn led to other previously higher-value crops being pushed out of production, leading to increased imports of those crops; ethanol incentives led to marginal farmland being put into production, potentially degrading the land; the net environmental impact of ethanol production appears to be negative, especially when coal is the main fuel used to provide power to processing plants in the ethanol-producing areas.[30]

- International unintended consequences: Increased global food prices, as corn is diverted from food use to ethanol production and land that was used for food crops is diverted to ethanol production. Emerging markets were especially hard hit, with high prices leading to civil unrest in 2007 before the commodity slump that followed the great recession.[31]

EU Renewable Energy Subsidies and Quotas

The European Union has set aggressive targets for renewable energy consumption, with some countries setting even higher national targets. There has been considerable investment to meet the goals. At the same time, Germany has voted to shut down its nuclear plants.

- Domestic unintended consequences: Prices for energy have gone up, as the higher cost of renewables has been subsidized by the end user—this was largely anticipated; the use of coal as an energy source increased after the laws came into effect because of its low cost (much lower than cleaner gas) and the desire by power producers to offset the increased prices from renewables.
- International unintended consequences: Coal imports from the United States have increased, just as coal use has been declining in the United States; electricity imports by the most aggressive "green" countries have increased, stemming from the need for base-load power when renewables such as wind and solar are not producing reliably, with much of these imports from dirty coal-burning sources.[32]

Proposed California Industrial Emissions Standards

The State of California was proposing emissions standards on cement production plants that would have forced them out of the state. California cement plants already met the highest standards in the country.

- Domestic unintended consequences: Cement with a high weight-to-value ratio is expensive to transport, so cost would have increased considerably in California, though this was largely understood; pollution from transport would have increased.
- International unintended consequences: Given that California is a coastal state, it would be lower cost to bring cement into many markets from abroad, mainly from China, than from other states. Since Californian cement plants are some of the cleanest in the world, the attempt by the state to improve emissions would have the opposite effect on the global environment as cement was imported from dirtier plants in China.

Drug Prohibition Policies

For decades, countries and especially the United States have prohibited many recreational drugs. With constricted supply, the price of drugs increased considerably along with the incentives to provide them. Since drug provision is illegal, those who do provide them naturally operate outside of the law.

- Domestic unintended consequences: The increased cost of drugs beyond what normal production and distribution costs would be has arguably led to well-financed and violent criminal gangs controlling the trade, leading to increased instability and policing and prison costs.
- International unintended consequences: Since many drugs are best produced in climates different than in the main markets and are also labor intensive to produce, production is mainly in low-income countries with particular climatic conditions. The criminalization of the drugs in these and the transit markets has led to violent conflicts between drug traffickers, local law enforcement, and local populations.[33] Production has also helped to fuel political movements that the main Western democracies find threatening.

Egyptian Energy Subsidies

Egypt used to heavily subsidize the energy consumed by local industry, leading to a boom in investment in energy-intensive industries (e.g., fertilizer, cement). The companies were able to buy the power below its market and production cost. The goal was to increase local output and employment.

- Domestic unintended consequences: The capital-intensive nature of most of the businesses that opened meant that little employment was actually created, especially given the cost of subsidizing. At some level of subsidy, the subsidy was believed to have been "exported," leading to a net negative value-add for the economy.
- International unintended consequences: A number of the investors in these industries were from other countries, so local firms benefited less, though the populace bore the cost of the subsidies.

APPENDIX: CASES IN DOMESTIC POLICY AND THE GLOBAL ECONOMY

Some case studies can help illustrate the interplay between domestic policy choices and the global economy. Obviously, any short case studies are going to contain oversimplifications with numerous missing counterpoints especially with regard to overall effect. Sources for additional readings are given for those interested in more detail.

Policy	EU renewable energy targets (regulatory policy, enhanced with fiscal incentives)
Description	The European Union has set a series of targets for member countries for the percentage of energy that must come from renewable sources by 2020. Percentages vary from 10 percent (Malta) to 49 percent (Sweden), with a total overall target of 20 percent. Some countries have gone beyond the EU mandate.
Global impact	• High spending on renewables has attracted considerable global investment to the European Union. In 2011, total foreign direct investment in the EU renewables sector rose to \$77 billion from \$55 billion in 2010.[a] • Trade in targeted areas has increased. For example, by 2012 Chinese companies had an estimated 80 percent of the photovoltaic cell market in the European Union. The fate of EU producers has not been so positive, as their market share dropped proportionally.[b] • Some EU companies have emerged as global players. For example, Siemens is a global leader in and major exporter of wind turbine production, likely helped by the start it got on EU projects. • The cost of power has gone up, driven by the higher cost of renewables, perhaps leading to a loss of EU competitiveness, especially among small and medium-size companies.[c] • Since renewables are costlier than traditional fossil fuels, many EU-based power producers used the cheapest fossil fuels for that part of the output that can still be produced in that way. Consequently, the use of coal in the European Union increased, though this is the dirtiest way to produce electricity. The increased use of coal also gave US-based coal producers a new market, as the US market increasingly turns to natural gas of which there is now an abundance due to hydraulic fracturing technologies.
Comments	There are pros and cons to any environmental policy, with the pros often more difficult to measure quantitatively than the cons since they tend to happen over a longer period of time. Most voters continue to support the programs despite the costs. The longer the programs are in place, the more those who benefit from them will defend them and the more difficult they will be to change, regardless of whether change is needed.

Policy	Chinese exchange rate management (monetary policy)
Description	The Chinese government pursued a policy of a weak yuan throughout much of the 2000s. To maintain this, the Chinese government kept large amounts of foreign currency earnings from entering the domestic economy where they would be exchanged for yuan, driving up inflation and raising the real exchange rate.
Global impact	• The earnings needed to be invested somewhere outside China, and as it was largely in USD, much of it ended up in the United States. • The inflow helped to keep money cheap (low interest rates) and plentiful in the United States in the 2000s, which helped to fuel the housing bubble and to keep government borrowing costs low, before and after the crisis. • The inflow has allowed the United States to continue to finance a large trade deficit, much of it with China.
Comments	It is fairly common for countries with large export earnings to keep foreign currencies parked outside of their economies to help control inflation and to manage their exchange rates. Others with similar policies include the United Arab Emirates, Saudi Arabia, and Norway.

Policy	Support for hydraulic fracking in the United States. There is not a single policy, but support comes from a combination of clear individual mineral property rights, a looser regulatory environment than in the European Union in certain areas, tax breaks for exploration, and a strong investment climate that led to rapid adoption of fracking in the United States.
Description	Hydraulic fracking is the extraction of oil and gas from previously inaccessible shale formations by injecting sand and chemicals into a well at high pressure. This has already and may continue to radically change the balance of energy power in the world, and the flows of money between countries.
Global impact	• Fracking made the United States the largest oil and gas producer in the world in 2016, overtaking Saudi Arabia in oil and Russia in gas.[d] Oil price volatility will shape the data in coming years, but the trend appears to be set. • A large segment of the tanker shipping industry was dedicated to bringing crude to the United States. With the United States becoming increasingly self-sufficient, the industry will either need to orient itself elsewhere, or suffer, along with the Korean and Chinese shipyards that supply the global market for ships. Since current capacity was created assuming both US and Asian imports, it may be hard to reorient capacity elsewhere. • Geopolitically, the wealth of the Middle East may decrease at a time of increasing instability, inhibiting governments' ability to buy peace among their populations. Since most shale oil is only recoverable at $50 to $60/barrel or greater, low-cost Middle Eastern producers can still make some profits, even as they struggle to balance budgets. However, natural gas is cheaper to extract from fracking and can become a

	substitute for oil. As of 2016, the United States had some of the lowest natural gas costs in the world and could become a major exporter • Russia is the largest natural gas producer for the European Union. If the European Union either adopts fracking or imports from the United States (costlier than Russia), it could shift the balance of power in the region and damage the Russian economy. • Increased supply from US fracking was likely the main driver behind a precipitous drop in oil prices in 2014 and 2015. There are likely also strategic reasons, with Saudi Arabia maintaining supply to try to drive fracking companies out of business. Interestingly, few speculators in the futures markets were able to see this coming despite developing long-term changes in supply conditions.
Comments	The global effects of fracking will depend on which countries adopt it. The influence on the environment is mixed. Fracking can be harmful to the environment. However, the gas obtained is far cleaner than coal, a bit cleaner than oil, but less clean than wind and solar. Other than existing nuclear plants, gas is the source of base-load power with the lowest greenhouse gas emissions.

Policy	EU banana import restrictions and preferences
Description	The European Union has traditionally favored banana imports from its former colonies in the Caribbean and Africa, rather than from the Central and South American countries. The latter are able to produce bananas more cheaply than the former colonies.
Global impact	• EU buying power and money has been going to former colonial countries, at the expense of producers in Central American countries. • EU consumers pay higher prices for lower-quality bananas. Importing from Central America would benefit consumers and would shift considerable money from banana-producing regions in the Caribbean and Africa to Central America. • A trade dispute was put before the WTO and won in 1997 by US-based banana companies in Central America, imposing penalties on a range of EU imports from Scottish cashmere to French cheese. The total value of exports affected was over $500 million. • The United States brought this case before the WTO because most Central American bananas are produced by large, US-based companies. When the largest one, Chiquita Brands, made a $500,000 contribution to the Republican Party in the United States, the Democratic president at the time, Bill Clinton, went into action and had his administration bring the case to the WTO almost immediately afterward.[e] It may have been a coincidence.
Comments	This is a case of diversion of trade for political reasons. Importers and producers from African countries had been able to maintain their position through lobbying, rather than from being the best and/or lowest-cost producer. Similarly, US companies lobbied the US government to act on their behalf.

Policy	Russian debt default
Description	In 1998, following a series of problems and poor policy choices relating to its domestic economy, Russia defaulted on its sovereign debt and devalued the ruble. Russian domestic debts (called GKOs) were previously very popular investment instruments for international investors due to their high yields and relatively high trading volumes.
Global impact	• Foreign investors lost billions of dollars, in what was at that time the largest sovereign debt default in the world. • Emerging markets indices dropped around the world, with falling exchange rates, increasing bond spreads (and financing costs), and dropping stock markets. Though they subsequently recovered, billions of dollars were lost at the time.[f] • The increased spreads on emerging markets debt led to the failure and subsequent $3.6 billion bailout of the hedge fund Long-Term Capital Management in the United States, which had made bets on narrowing spreads that were highly leveraged with short-term bank loans.
Comments	The Russian crisis of 1998 is an example of financial "contagion" (i.e., when linkages and similar investor sentiments between interrelated economies cause a crisis to spread from one country to others).

Policy	US DARPA and DOD funding of a decentralized communications network and a satellite positioning system
Description	The Internet was originally developed by the US Department of Defense as a decentralized "packet switching" communications network that could withstand a nuclear attack by diverting traffic across multiple, decentralized nodes rather than point to point. GPS was to help guide ships and other military conveyances.
Global impact	• The Internet exists, with consequences too numerous to mention. It is possible to speculate on whether and in what form the Internet would have taken without US government research support, but it would probably not be the same. • GPS exists, with consequences also too numerous to mention. Unlike the decentralized Internet, GPS takes a massive up-front investment to put into effect. It is beyond what most companies would be capable of undertaking, and is in some sense a true "public good" in that a for-profit version would be hard to exclude nonpaying users from.
Comments	It is interesting to speculate on how and if these technologies would have been developed by the private sector alone. Scope, performance, and probably access and effect would have likely been quite different.

Policy	US and EU agricultural subsidies
Description	The United States and the European Union maintain huge farm subsidy programs, with 57 billion euro spent by the European Union and around $20 billion by the United States in 2014.[g]

Global impact	• Subsidies in countries that are major agricultural producers anyway can lead to overproduction and exports of surpluses at low prices. This can keep food prices, and production, in other countries low, having a positive effect on consumer prices and an adverse one on farmer incomes and farm employment. • Overproduction in the United States and the European Union that leads to underproduction elsewhere may have negative implications for food security if disease or poor weather conditions cause drops in US or EU production. • To compete with subsidies in the developed market economies, many poorer countries also try to protect and subsidize their markets, even if they cannot afford it. This leads to wasted resources. • With major markets protected by subsidies to local producers, companies in other countries cannot realize competitive advantages to freer trade. The sugar lobby in the United States is notorious for protecting only a handful of producers, keeping prices high and sharply restricting imports from poorer countries that could and should be major producers for the US market. • Subsidies have led to poor-quality land being brought into production, which can require more fertilizer, pesticides, and mechanization, which negatively affect the environment.
Comments	In the United States, though farm subsidies are widely believed by economists to be inefficient and distortionary, beneficiaries spent $52 million on the 2012 election and were able to secure ongoing support.[h]

a. OCO 2012.
b. EU Prosun news 2013.
c. Karnitschnig 2014.
d. US Energy Information Administration 2016.
e. See Barkham 1999.
f. See Fry et al. 2002.
g. *The Economist* 2015
h. For up-to-date information, see the Environmental Working Group's (EWG) database on farm subsidies.

NOTES

1. Mahbubani 2014, pp. 86–88.
2. For a comprehensive investigation into tax havens and their use, see the compendium by the International Association of Investigative Journalists. Their website, icij.org, has a section dedicated to financial secrecy.
3. There are two takes on the seeming lack of US clients discovered in 2016 when account information was leaked from a Panamanian bank, the so-called Panama Papers. The first is that US authorities have succeeded in preventing US entities from using tax havens. The second is that most of them don't bother because they can easily hide money in the United States in states like Delaware and Nevada.
4. One source estimates that between 21 and 32 trillion USD was hidden in offshore accounts as of 2010, compared to a global GDP of around 80 trillion USD. See Henry 2012.
5. See, for example, Story and Saul (2015) for an investigative article, part of a series on the wealthy from emerging markets hiding their assets in the United States.

6. As a UN (2013) report notes, estimates on the value of transfer pricing are hard to obtain, but estimates are that 30 percent of global trade is intracompany and potentially prone to such activities.

7. For a summary of some of the issues, see Schwartz and Duhigg 2013 and *The Economist* 2013d.

8. For the story, see Leonhardt 2013.

9. Doyle and Bodoni 2016.

10. See this Bloomberg article by Mider and Drucker (2016) for a description of inversions, and some of the largest ones to date. The OECD BEPS project is focused on shedding light on and reducing tax avoidance behavior. See OECD 2015 for an overview.

11. Much has been written about the topic. For an overview and analysis, see the 2012 IMF working paper by Abbas and Klemm 2012.

12. The DC metro area ranks third, only behind an area in Connecticut where many hedge funds are located, and Silicon Valley. See table 2 of the US Census Bureau report by Bee (2013).

13. See the report *Subsidies and Cost of EU Energy* 2014 by the European Commission.

14. This varies depending on the type of legal tradition. Common-law societies like the United States and United Kingdom tend on average to have shorter laws that allow more interpretation later, and civil-law societies like Germany and much of Northern and Eastern Europe tend to be much more precise about regulations in the actual enabling legislation.

15. The 2015 case of German company Volkswagen's cheating on emission tests for its clean diesel technology shows the extent to which rules can promote both good (billions spent on the development of technology) and bad (cheating on tests when the technology fell short) behavior and lead to billions of dollars diverted from where they otherwise would have gone. For a summary see the BBC article by Hotten 2015.

16. The since-rescinded ban on Mexican trucking companies crossing into the United States was estimated to cost consumers $400 million annually. See Alexander and Soukup 2010.

17. Dictatorships might be thought to be different. However, with the exception of a few fully totalitarian states (e.g., North Korea), most rulers in nondemocratic countries are sensitive to public sentiment. Legitimacy that they do not get through elections can come from other sources such as subsidies to the populace (Venezuela, Cuba, Iran, Egypt), increased international standing (Russia, Qatar), or economic performance with broad-based benefits (China, Singapore, Chile previously).

18. There is no shortage of cases of special interests influencing laws and regulations. One case of influence on regulatory agencies is outlined in a broadcast of secretly taped meetings between investment bank Goldman Sachs and the agency tasked with regulating them. See "The Secret Recordings of Carmen Segarra," 2014. Another case has the sugary drinks industry lobbying to continue to allow government food stamps in the United States to be used for their products. See Pear 2011.

19. The study is by Gilens and Page (2014). See also Lee Drutman's (2015) book on lobbying.

20. A 2016 Gallup poll found that 86 and 84 percent of the survey group respectively believed that their elected representatives were too beholden to financial backers and special interests. Gallup News Service, June Wave 1. June 1–6, 2016.

21. See Bueno de Mesquita and Smith (2012) for a good summary of how interest coalitions are formed in both democratic and single-party states. They conclude not surprisingly

that the public interest is much better served in democracies, though the coalitions required for rule can be startlingly limited.

22. *The Economist* (2016c) published a summary of the system and its legacy.

23. See, for example, Stephan Haggard (2000) and Sharma (2003).

24. The same can perhaps be said about countries, though as one former IMF economist reviewing this manuscript noted, the stigma of an IMF bailout was negative enough to keep many middle- to upper-middle-income countries from playing that game.

25. Olson's (1965) main book on the topic is *The Logic of Collective Action: Public Goods and the Theory of Groups*. *The Economist* (1998) has a summary of Olson's work in their obituary of him.

26. The Asian financial crisis of 1997 is probably understudied today. For readings on the role of the IMF see Blustein (2001), the relevant chapters in the two books by Joseph Stiglitz (2002, 2006) as well as the IMF (2003) retrospective. For a summary of the issues and more of a defense of the IMF, see John Head 2010. The IMF is also considering that it may have made similar errors in recommending austerity after the 2008 crisis. See Blanchard and Leigh 2013.

27. To be fair, effects from the Kansas tax cuts have not yet had a chance to play out fully at time of publication, though lawmakers are starting to revolt.

28. Attempts have been made to subject policy decisions to rigorous analysis. Former US president Ronald Reagan decreed that the Environmental Protection Agency under William Ruckelshaus undertake cost-benefit analysis to determine net regulatory benefit. The reference cited here gives an in-depth review of how the relative merits of a regulatory activity were assessed, as well as the considerable ambiguity involved (Call 1985).

29. The normative part of this argument, that is, what *should* be done, is a different topic and outside this book's scope. A lack of absolute clarity of outcomes is not an excuse to not take action.

30. See Searchinger 2008.

31. Actionaid International USA 2012 is one of many analyses available of the outcomes.

32. *The Economist* 2013e.

33. See, for example, Reuter 2009.

5

Global Trade and Trends

Trade in goods and services is the most visible part of the global economy. Nearly everyone every day buys or sells a good or service that originated in or is heading to another country. Goods and services move one direction, and money comes back the other way. Trade and trade theory are core topics in most international economics courses. Though this book touches on the core principles of modern trade theory later, most of the focus here is more pragmatic: who is trading, what is traded, the agreements and rules that govern international trade and how they are evolving, and whether/under what circumstances more trade is a "good" thing.

Economic theory has countries trading to exercise comparative advantages, or because one is intensive in some factor, or had a "factor resource windfall." The premise here that countries don't trade, but the people and companies *in* countries do, is more than pointless semantics. That people trade is the basis for understanding increases or decreases in trade, as well as when and why groups advocate for or against more trade, and the likelihood they have of fulfilling their agenda. Following the money, as usual, helps in understanding current and future likely trends.

Table 5.1 summarizes what was traded (at least legally) in 2014.[1]

The table is clearer about some things than others. The importance of commodities and fuels in trade is evident. People often think of trade in terms of shirts, electronics, and other tangible consumer goods. That's only the most visible part of the story. A lot of what is traded, and produced, in the world are primary products, like oil, coal, minerals, and metals. As is an important theme in the book, commodities are usually priced and traded in the main global reserve currencies, particularly the US dollar.

Harder to see in the table is the prevalence of intermediate goods, or the goods used to make final products. It is tricky to break these out accurately from trade data, since one person's final product and another's intermediate good can be categorized in the same way. For example, most trade data does not indicate if a solid-state

Table 5.1. Total Trade 2014

Export Category	*Billions of USD*	*% of Total*
Total merchandise	18,816	
Commodities/fuels	8,912	47
Food products	1,456	8
Automobiles	1,347	7
Other, manuf.	7,101	38
Total services	4,644	
Travel	1,183	25
Financial services	334	7
Other services	3,127	67
Total Trade	23,460	
% of World GDP	29	

Source: World Trade Organization, statistical database

drive that crossed a border was going to go into a computer (intermediate good) or whether it was a drive for personal use (final product). There are 5,300 categories in trade data reported under standard UN protocols. That may seem like a lot, but in most cases there are no usage distinctions.[2] An in-depth 2009 study by the OECD found that trade in intermediate inputs made up 56 percent of trade in goods and 73 percent of trade in services between developed market economies. Since if anything supply chains have continued to decentralize since that time, the percentages are unlikely any less now. Intermediate goods are traded both between and within companies, depending on the structure of their supply chains.[3]

Table 5.1 is also static, showing trade volumes for only one year. Though trade volumes and values dropped in the early years of the great recession, according to WTO data by 2016 they had recovered to well above 2008 peaks. Growth trends since 2008 have been slower than before that time, but still positive. Some of that slowness reflects generally weak recoveries after the recession, and some simply a drop in fuel and other commodity prices.[4]

WHO TRADES WITH WHOM

Trade flow data by product and country is readily available. The two main sources are the ITC Trade Map and UN Comtrade. Both offer limited access to their data sets for free and both get their data from the same source, transactions reported by countries' customs departments. Almost all countries report into these databases. You can see how much of pretty much any product a country imports and exports (legally). Because the data is disaggregated into 5,300 categories, both identifying the right category and then summarizing the data can take some time. Table 5.2 shows the largest merchandise importers and exporters in the world in 2015.[5]

Table 5.2.

Rank	*Exporters*	*Value*	*Share*	*% Change YOY*	*Rank*	*Importers*	*Value*	*Share*	*% Change YOY*
1	China	2,275	13.8	–3	1	United States	2,308	13.8	–4
2	United States	1,505	9.1	–7	2	China	1,682	10.1	–14
3	Germany	1,329	8.1	–11	3	Germany	1,050	6.3	–13
4	Japan	625	3.8	–9	4	Japan	648	3.9	–20
5	Netherlands	567	3.4	–16	5	United Kingdom	626	3.7	–9
6	Korea, Republic of	527	3.2	–8	6	France	573	3.4	–15
7	Hong Kong, China	511	3.1	–3	7	Hong Kong, China	559	3.3	–7
	—domestic exports	13	0.1	–16		—retained imports	134	0.8	–11
	—re-exports	498	3.0	–2					
8	France	506	3.1	–13	8	Netherlands	506	3.0	–14
9	United Kingdom	460	2.8	–9	9	Korea, Republic of	436	2.6	–17
10	Italy	459	2.8	–13	10	Canada	436	2.6	–9
11	Canada	408	2.5	–14	11	Italy	409	2.4	–14
12	Belgium	398	2.4	–16	12	Mexico	405	2.4	–2
13	Mexico	381	2.3	–4	13	India	392	2.3	–15
14	Singapore	351	2.1	–14	14	Belgium	375	2.2	–17
	—domestic exports	174	1.1	–20	15	Spain	309	1.8	–14
	—re-exports	177	1.1	–9					
15	Russian Federation	340	2.1	–32					

As with a lot of economic data, raw trade data can be hard to interpret correctly. To take a popular example, Apple iPhones worth around $2 billion were imported into the United States in 2009, according to official trade data. However, over 90 percent of the value of that $2 billion is made up of components imported from Japan, Korea, Germany, and, actually, the United States. But since the final assembly takes place in China, the full value of the iPhone is recorded as an import from China.[6]

To address these sorts of data ambiguities, trade agreements between countries often mandate that traders in participating countries keep a careful accounting of all intermediate good values that comprise a final product. Known as **rules of origin**, these requirements ensure that a specified percentage of the final product's value originates in the countries that subscribe to the particular trade agreement. Verification and enforcement can be administratively burdensome, contributing on some level to increased costs of trade.

Note also in the chart above that Hong Kong and Singapore rank in the top fifteen exporters. However, most of their exports are **re-exports**, or products that were manufactured elsewhere and are destined elsewhere, but passed through and landed at the Hong Kong or Singapore ports. They were exported in essentially the same condition in which they were imported.

The degree to which people trade across borders depends on numerous factors that ultimately come down to the money to be made versus the cost of "doing business"—in this case trading. Various costs are associated with importing and exporting. The main ones are:

- *Transport costs.* Proximity, good transport infrastructure (roads, rail, ports), and low port fees all can hold these costs down. It is no surprise that countries close to each other or with good infrastructure links tend to trade more among themselves.
- *Paperwork and standards.* Moving goods between countries can require a lot of paperwork, such as permits, correct goods classifications, proof of origin documents, and health and safety certificates. These can sometimes add significantly to the cost, especially when expensive laboratory tests, labeling, and/or other compliance costs apply.
- *Information costs.* Potential buyers in one country may not know what is available and at what cost in other countries, and sellers may not understand what the demand is. Quality and exact standards may also be hard to verify and compare. The Internet has helped lower the cost of obtaining information, but misinformation can be as common as information.
- *Wholesale and related costs.* Having a product that costs less than a competing one in another country does not mean it will be worth selling it there. Wholesalers and retailers take a big part of the final sales price, and even if you sell direct, costs related to warehousing, returns, warranties, repairs, and product liability insurance will likely still apply.

Table 5.3.

Item	*United States*	*European Union*
Milk and cream mixture, 1% fat or less	$.34 liter	13.8 E/100 kg
Plastic tubes, pipe, and hoses	6.5%	6.5%
Fresh bananas	Free	132 E/1,000 kg
Plain steel wood screws	12.5%	3.7%
Electrical motors	4.4%	4.7%
Golf clubs	4.7%	2.7%

Sources: Tariff information is available from a number of sources. This data came from the US International Trade Commission for the United States, and the European Union database for the EU. Tariff data is reported according to a universally recognized coding system called the Harmonized System of Tariffs (HTS).

- *Customs duties (tariffs) and quantitative restrictions or quotas.* **Tariffs** are taxes that countries charge on imports. Most countries have them and charge them on many if not most imports. Table 5.3 shows the US and the EU tariffs on a small list of products that they charge to each other and other countries with which they do not have a free trade agreement. Tariffs can be either per item or per unit of value, and can also be temporary and/or seasonal. **Quantitative restrictions** or **quotas** are rules that limit the import of certain products to a preestablished quantity.
- *Sanctions and restrictions.* These are outright bans on either the countries that certain products can be shipped to or from, or the types of products. These can increase the cost of trade considerably, but do not by any means put a stop to it. In fact, they can make trade even more profitable by making it harder.

Given costs, obstacles, and the complexity of trade-related rules, it may be surprising that trade happens at all, but apparently people are sufficiently determined.

Recall the net exports part of the GDP definition. If a country's companies increase their exports, all other things being equal (as always), the country's GDP goes up. Consequently, export growth is a central tenet of many countries' economic strategies and related policies. Subsidies have been a popular, though hardly low-cost, way for governments to encourage exports. As a direct or indirect (i.e., tax break) payment to exporting companies, subsidies make trading more advantageous for companies. Usually subsidies target specific sectors, applying to more than one company. They are widespread, and also illegal under many trade agreements because they are considered unfair competition.

Before moving on to those agreements, a few comments about near-term trends in international trade are worth making. Complex, competing forces push both for and against increasing global trade in the future. Though not assured and with a number of fits, starts, and some reversals, most indications are that global trade in both goods and services will continue to increase. On the side of increased trade, logistics and the administrative work required to trade between nations are increasingly efficient and low cost. Most likely, the world has not seen the full extent of virtualization's ability to connect buyers and sellers and transact business anytime and anyplace, nor of consumers' appetites for global goods and services. As emerging markets' economies continue to grow, so should demand for a wide range of globally produced goods and services.

A desire to source the cheapest intermediate inputs and production equipment is likely to keep those major components of international trade booming. Also, the types of supply chains that were built up to support, for example, the production of electronics goods in Asia or automobiles in North America, are hard to move. Simple inertia will likely keep certain areas of global production centered in certain countries for years to come.

Should new trade agreements continue to tackle barriers to trade in services, it is likely that services trade growth will outpace that in goods. Many financial, insurance, real estate, retail, and other services continue to be very nationally oriented, though there is little inherent, nonregulatory, economic reason for that.

Contrary to these trends, other factors are pushing against increased global trade, and toward more local and regional production. As the cost of labor equalizes across countries, it makes less sense to locate production solely or mainly on the basis of cheap labor. The gains from doing so are just not as high (in relative terms) as they once were, for example to sourcing from China in the 1990s. Similarly, with decreasing low-skilled labor value-added in more sophisticated products, labor becomes a less important input. Along these lines, "smart" machines and improvements in robotics and automation are increasingly substituting for low-skilled human labor, making labor cost less important in deciding where to set up production.

At the same time, rapid and continuous adaptation to changing consumer preferences is increasingly important in the modern marketplace. Producing smaller batches of highly customized products may make more sense in more and more cases than ordering up large batches of even cheaper homogeneous products. If so, production closer to the point of consumption becomes more appealing. The so-called fast-fashion industry pioneered in Spain by Inditex is a case in point.[7] Consumer movements in wealthy countries may also help reinforce a move toward local rather than far-reaching global production. The "locavore" movements that have sprouted up mainly in the liberal and upper-middle classes strive to buy locally produced products.

Another global recession, spikes in fuel prices, radical technological advances in distributed energy, or nationalist populist movements and policies could all slow down or reverse trends toward more trade. Some individual markets will also slow, such as slowing of the petroleum trade as fracking continues apace in the United States. Populist policies are a wild card, with potential effects ranging from a handful of small "feel-good" policies blocking foreign goods to all-out trade wars. Though there are numerous forces competing in both directions, on balance global trade is probably more likely to continue to increase in the coming decade than decrease. There are too many people with too many incentives to make it happen.

TRADE AGREEMENTS

The global rules on trade are enshrined in a multitude of trade agreements between countries. The agreements and rules are the result of a long trend toward freer trade after the Second World War as a reaction to the prewar, Great Depression–era mercantilist movement. Proponents of **mercantilism** seek to restrict imports and protect domestic producers under the assumption that trade is a zero-sum game: exports are good (they make money) and imports are bad (they lose money). Many economists and policy makers believe that mercantilism helped prolong the Great Depression and increase tensions that led up to the war.

Of all the legally imposed **trade barriers**, tariffs and subsidies get the most attention when trading partners sit down to negotiate deals.[8] That's probably because they are the most obvious, transparent, and in some ways easy to address of the different trade barriers. The tariff a company pays to sell into another country depends on the agreement(s) that exists between the two countries. Table 5.4 shows the main types of agreements in place and how they contribute to trade liberalization.

Table 5.4.

No agreement	Exporter pays whatever tariff the importing country has posted on its schedule. This may be high or low depending on the product and the importing country. Most global trade occurs between nations with some sort of trade agreement in place.	Increasingly freer trade this direction ⟶
World Trade Organization (WTO) member	As of the middle of 2017, 160 countries were members of the WTO. Upon becoming a member, a country agrees to consistently apply a usually lowered schedule of tariffs to other members. These schedules are negotiated upon entry of the country to the WTO, or when all members conclude an additional agreement among themselves (known as "conclusion of a round").	
Bilateral or multilateral free trade agreements	These agreements are between two or more countries negotiated outside the WTO. The tariffs between members of these agreements are almost by definition lower than under WTO rules. Often these agreements include services and provisions for protecting investments, intellectual property, the environment, and/or labor and can include a customs union as a special case. Though often referred to as "free trade" agreements, they frequently achieve less than free trade.	
Economic union	In an economic union, trade is fully integrated and other steps are taken to integrate economies. There is no easily definable distinction between countries that are party to comprehensive bilateral or group FTAs and those that are part of an economic union, although a "common external tariff" is often implemented on countries that are outside of a union.	

The WTO has been the largest and the most important of all the trade-related institutions for the latter half of the twentieth century. It is the successor institution to the General Agreement on Tariffs and Trade (GATT) founded after the Second World War to reopen global economies to each other after the conflict. From its founding in 1948 until present, the average tariff charged to a member state by another member state dropped from over 20 percent to less than 4 percent. Tariffs have been reduced in a series of "rounds" named after the country or city that was the primary sponsor. Notably, the last successful round of WTO negotiations was the Uruguay Round concluded in 1994. Since then, not much has happened. The Doha Round, which started in 2001, has made almost no progress. Even when members abandoned more contentious goals for further tariff reduction in favor of smaller reductions in administrative barriers, as of mid-2017 they have failed to reach a full agreement.

Before moving on, it is worth making a few general statements about the WTO. First, one of the main barriers to further lowering tariffs is that tariffs have already been significantly reduced on the wide range of products that aren't controversial. In that sense, the WTO is partially a victim of its own success.

Second, agriculture is among the main areas of controversy, and it is a sensitive area for many governments both because of food security concerns and because of powerful agricultural sector lobbies. Any agreement would need to address both tariffs and subsidies. The agricultural subsidy policies of the United States and the European Union linger as the main barriers to lower tariffs (and reduced subsidies) on agricultural products. A number of emerging market countries like India that have suffered famines in the past and are sensitive about food security have also blocked efforts to remove barriers and liberalize agricultural markets.

WTO member countries are also finding it difficult to reach agreement on services, especially financial services such as banking and insurance. In this case, it is the developed market economies that are pushing for lower barriers to entry (not technically tariffs), while the emerging markets are more interested in protecting their domestic service industries from the big global players. Concerned about maintaining control of their financial systems, emerging markets' regulatory authorities sometimes also weigh in against the entry of large foreign financial firms.

The WTO's current troubles also arise from its success bringing in so many members that the whole group cannot seem to agree on anything at all. For a new round to be concluded, all 160 members have to agree, at least to a degree. Then, two-thirds of the countries' lawmaking bodies must accept or adopt the agreement as law. That takes a very long time and is fraught with risk of failure all along the way. Only when all countries have agreed, and the requisite parliaments ratified the agreement as law, can a new WTO agreement be enforced on all members, at least in theory. This brings us to the next broad comment on the WTO.

Though it is the main body facilitating lower trade barriers, the WTO has a hard time enforcing its rules on its unruly members. The WTO's enforcement mechanisms are stronger in theory than in practice. If a country violates the rules in a way that hurts another country, the WTO can allow the aggrieved country to levy higher tariffs on the violating country's goods. But the enforcement and appeals process is seemingly endless. The United States and the European Union have been going at each other over subsidies to the commercial aircraft manufacturers Boeing and Airbus for decades, with little to show for it except for a few headlines, headaches, and massive legal expenses.

The other problem with enforcement is that even if a country wins, it might not really "win." In 1997, the United States won a judgment against the European Union on banana imports. The European Union was found guilty of illegally blocking the import of bananas from Central America (where US-based companies control the trade), in favor of bananas from its former colonies in Africa (where EU-based companies control the trade). As punishment, the United States got to greatly increase tariffs on French wine and cheese, which served only to hike the price of these imports to the United States and enrage US consumers. The WTO has no ability to stop a country from doing something; it can only allow indirect punishments that may carry unintended consequences.

So that is the WTO. Following its recent failings, whether due to its previous success or not, the institution does not seem poised to drive further trade liberalization. As a consequence, governments that believe freer trade between their countries would be beneficial have been actively striking their own **free trade agreements** (FTAs). Sometimes these are between two countries (bilateral agreements) and sometimes multiple countries (multilateral agreements). These non-WTO agreements became increasingly prevalent and popular, especially since the flagging of the WTO Doha round. The European Union has signed over a dozen bilateral FTAs plus several customs union agreements, and it was negotiating over a dozen more as of 2017.[9] The United States has FTAs with twenty countries, and it has pushed forward on significant regional trade agreements, such as the Trans-Pacific Partnership (TPP)—though these efforts seem to have come to a halt with the election of the populist Trump administration in 2016. Table 5.5 gives a list of some of the main free trade agreements currently in force.

Unlike the WTO, the signing of these bi- and multilateral agreements proceeded at full speed in the twenty-first century, though political infighting and impasses in the US Congress and other countries' political systems slowed momentum toward the middle of the 2010s. As noted, populist anti–free trade backlashes following Brexit and the election of Donald Trump in the United States are also taking a toll. However, despite some setbacks, these free trade agreements are still likely to be the main way that trade policy is conducted for the medium term and likely beyond. Having made some broad, sweeping statements about the WTO, it is only fair to mention a few generalizations about these other bilateral and multilateral free trade agreements.

First, they are technically illegal under the WTO. WTO membership requires that members treat all other members equally. This is called the "most favored nation" principle. Since the WTO is with a weak enforcer, members just ignore this technicality, though it does weaken the credibility of the institution.

Table 5.5.

Agreement	*Participants*
NAFTA, North American Free Trade Agreement	United States, Mexico, Canada
EFTA, European Free Trade Agreement	Norway, Switzerland, Iceland, Liechtenstein
CEFTA, Central European Free Trade Area	Macedonia, Albania, Bosnia and Herzegovina, Serbia, Moldova, Montenegro
Mercosur	Argentina, Brazil, Paraguay, Uruguay, Venezuela
AFTA, Association of South East Asian Nations (ASEAN) free trade area, and China	Indonesia, Malaysia, Brunei, Philippines, Singapore, Myanmar, Thailand, Cambodia, Laos, Vietnam—agreements signed with China
CAFTA-DR	United States, Costa Rica, El Salvador, Honduras, Guatemala, Nicaragua, Dominican Republic
EU-Chile, EU-South Korea, EU-Mexico US-Chile, US-Oman, US-Korean, US-Morocco	This should be kind of clear.

Second, bi- and multilateral agreements create a massively complex network of often contradictory trade rules that can take a lot of effort to unravel. A big issue has to do with rules of origin. For example, the United States has a free trade agreement with Chile, and Chile has a free trade agreement with China, but the United States does not have an agreement with China (as of 2017). The last thing the United States wants is for goods to come into Chile from China without any tariffs, and then be re-exported to the United States without any tariffs under the bilateral free trade agreement. Doing so is generally illegal under free trade agreements and is called **transshipment**.[10] So goods coming into the United States under the US-Chile agreement have to show that they are some percentage Chilean, which varies depending on what the product is. Rules of origin are complicated in a global marketplace, since many products have components from all over the planet. Remember the iPhone example. Proving rules of origin can generate a lot of paperwork, and a lot of potential for fraud. Consequently, the lack of a global or even moderately unified trade regime ends up supporting a lot of lawyers and customs brokers who really do not need to have a job at all. That ends up being a transaction cost that increases the cost of trade and cuts into gains from freer trade.

Third, FTAs may lead more to **trade diversion** than the absolute increase in global trade that would be expected under a full WTO-type agreement. Trade diversion is when trade shifts from one country to another, without any increase in overall volume or value. Evidence is largely circumstantial and historically based, since it is impossible to know what would have happened otherwise once an agreement is signed. However, trade diversion is a common criticism leveled at FTAs.

An advantage of these bilateral and multilateral FTAs is that with only a few signatories, they can readily deal with a lot more than just trade in goods. They can, and often do, address trade in services (which the WTO has been weak on), protection of investments, food and product safety, environmental issues, labor rights, and anything else that country negotiators (or their lobbyists and/or constituents) think is important.[11]

As free trade agreements and areas evolve and encompass more aspects of economic integration beyond tariffs, at some point they become more than a free trade area. One stage that a free trade area may reach over time is a **customs union**. Technically, a customs union is a trade area where all of the participants apply the same tariffs to imports from outside the union. The European Union is a customs union (and more than that also), so for example, France cannot decide to increase its tariffs on goods from the United States without getting an agreement to do so from all of the other members. Because of this **common external tariff**, countries are able to integrate trade among themselves more closely. There is no way for importers in one country to "cheat" and bring in goods from an outside country cheaply, and sell them to their neighbors. Consequently, there is less need for border checks between members. The European Union also maintains customs unions with non-EU countries, such as Turkey. Mercosur, noted in the table above, is a free trade area and is also a customs union.

In cases where integration between economies continues to increase, other stages can be reached. The European Union started as a free trade area only covering certain goods in the 1950s, and has evolved to a much fuller economic integration, including a single currency and central bank. The Gulf Cooperation Council (GCC, Bahrain, Kuwait, United Arab Emirates, Oman, Qatar, and Saudi Arabia) has also moved beyond a free trade area, with a common patent office and no restrictions on investments or services trade, though efforts to form a monetary union are delayed. The United States began as a much less integrated group of states that grew closer over time, largely through court-level interpretations of the Constitution. There are no absolutely clear definitions of what these more integrated areas are or are not and when they pass from one stage to another, though it is possible to split hairs arguing for one definition or another.

BENEFITS AND PITFALLS OF FREER TRADE

Trade policy formulation is a high-stakes business. Negotiators are committing their countries to long-term agreements with considerable money at stake and, truthfully, often hard-to-quantify benefits and costs. Different industries, companies, and individuals benefit and lose in different ways from freer and more restricted trade. Groups take sides, hire lobbyists, and try to advance their side's position. These positions may not all be well grounded in economic theory or evidence, though the complexity and ambiguity of evidence means there is usually at least something for each side to anchor its position on. Understanding the main arguments and evidence presented and who is on each side can help in seeing where incentives might lead politicians in the future as one side or the other prevails. The two camps, pro and against free trade, both have their arguments. Let's take a look at a summary of the debate and the evidence.

Comparative advantage is the theory most often cited as to why free trade is universally beneficial, even if it does not actually support this precise conclusion. The theory was originally put forth by David Ricardo in 1817. The basic tenet is that a country can benefit from trade even if all of its producers have an absolute cost disadvantage in all of their products. They do so by having their companies focus on producing the products which they are least bad at, and export those, and import other things. The theory is clever, makes a lot of intuitive sense once you understand it, and has a simple and elegant mathematical exposition.[12] Though two hundred years old, comparative advantage remains the primary intellectual basis for a large percentage of pro-trade arguments. It is a powerful argument that a country can gain from freer trade even with producers that cannot do anything at all better than producers in other countries.[13]

Critics of free trade tend to focus on the details behind comparative advantage that are left out of the "pro" arguments. The positive results of comparative advantage and its voluminous extensions over the years rest on important simplifying assumptions. Among those are a low enough cost of transitioning both human and physical resources into industries where a country has a comparative advantage once the country is open to trade. Anyone who has ever had a job, in the private sector anyway, knows how hard it is to turn a wine cask into a loom, a baker into a candlestick maker, or a bumper installer into a software engineer. The theory also assumes that the terms of trade will not change. That is, if all the bumper installers turn into software engineers in one country, and all the software engineers turn to car makers in another, the relative prices of the two products cannot shift. If they do, the producers in one country lose out. That is a big "if" for any business owner closing one factory to open another (if it were so simple).

Consequently, many narratives supporting more restrictive trade focus on local workers who get displaced by lower-cost and/or higher-quality imports. In a theoretical world, they just start doing another job that reflects the real advantages that exist in the country they live in. In the real world, they may not have the skills, or there may not be any jobs like that because there are too few investors or too little demand in other countries, or maybe the transaction costs of transitioning to new industries are too high. There are lots of reasons why people lose their jobs to imports and don't get new ones. Or at least they don't get new ones that are as good as their old ones.

Supporters of free trade argue that the total gains from freer trade are high enough to compensate those who lost their jobs or income and still have the economy come out ahead. It appears, from theoretical models anyway, that this should be true and the gains are in fact high enough. But for all sorts of reasons compensation of those who lost their jobs can be hard to execute in a meaningful way. It is hard to figure out what to do. Do countries or companies just pay people for the rest of their lives for losing their jobs or for taking a lower-paying job? Where does the money come from to do that, how do we know if someone lost their job from trade, and how are the "winners" correctly identified and taxed? Though direct transfers are easy to envision, they are not politically very popular or very feasible to implement.

In one form of compensation, many countries have job-training programs for workers displaced by trade.[14] As has been discovered, it can be challenging to effectively retrain skilled workers in one area in another skilled area. This is especially the case when jobs lost are in manufacturing, and jobs gained are in services. And if the jobs lost are fairly well paid and/or high skilled, it can be hard to match incomes after transition to a new industry. Some studies show that workers often just end up in lower-paid jobs in the same industry they worked in before, and that those who do switch industries end up with even lower compensation.[15] Another study found that while higher-wage workers subject to import competition were able to maintain their incomes as they moved to new jobs, lower-wage workers were not, and in addition were subject to more job instability.[16] A 2013 study indicated that 44 percent of job losses in the US Midwest between 1990 and 2007 resulted from imports, with each $1,000 in imports leading to a $500 reduction in overall income. Government compensation programs made up only $58 of that.[17] Other studies find that most job losses have been from automation, not trade, so additional questions arise about figuring out who lost their job because of what and who is due compensation.[18]

In summary, there is substantial agreement among economists and even politicians on the gains from trade and the need to compensate the losers. However, there is not much agreement on how to compensate losers, or many really good, large-scale successes to point to. Up until the 2016 double shocks of the so-called Brexit in the United Kingdom and the election of Donald Trump to the presidency of the United States, the problem of compensating globalization's losers was largely relegated to academic debates. These events didn't make the compensation problem easier to solve, but they do bring it square into the middle of policy debates. Whether this leads to any real policy innovations remains to be seen. To date, the focus is more on restricting free trade than better allocating its gains.

That is what the two sides say, in brief. Table 5.6 contains what some of the economic studies say. It's important to reiterate the challenges of definitively proving complex effects with economic data and analysis, and trade analysis is no exception. Given the time lags between when an agreement is signed and when the effects take place and data become available, it is nearly impossible to clearly establish causation of positive or negative effects from numerical data alone. Too many other events could have happened during that period that could have also contributed to the same outcomes. A lot of trade impact analysis is done with models that imperfectly and rigidly simulate outcomes, rather than with real data. Even minor changes in model assumptions can lead to quite different results.[19]

Table 5.6.

Study	*Summary/Conclusions*
"Trade Liberalization and Growth: New Evidence," *World Bank Economic Review*, 2008	Of twenty-four emerging markets countries studies, thirteen showed a positive experience with trade liberalization, five negative, and with six the data was inconclusive.
"The Economic Impact of the Free Trade Agreement (FTA) between the European Union and Korea," *Report for the European Commission*, May 2010	After the FTA, trade increased considerably (fact). Estimates of net gains *from simulations*, estimate .08 percent of GDP for the European Union and "up to" .084 percent for Korea.
"Trade Liberalization, Exports, and Technology Upgrading: Evidence on the Impact of MERCOSUR on Argentinian Firms," *The American Economic Review*, 2011	The Mercosur free trade area does appear to have increased Brazilian firms' purchases of advanced technology. This may lead to increased efficiencies and exports even outside the Mercosur.
"NAFTA Revisited: Achievements and Challenges," *Foreign Affairs*, 2006	Claim a net positive gain, again on the basis of simulations. Also noted increases in trade and investment and upgrading of technology.
Council on Foreign Relations, Backgrounder, 2014	Meta-analysis, or summary of a range of studies, mainly indicating that impacts of NAFTA were small, but generally positive.
"Do FTAs Matter for Trade?" *Asia Pacific Economic Cooperation*, May 2015	Study of outcomes of 144 Asian FTAs indicates that trade did increase after FTAs, but it is less clear if new exports were created or trade was just diverted to FTA members. Impact on GDP was not possible to estimate.

Overall, in the above and in others, studies tend to conclude that freer trade does, on average and under "normal" circumstances, bring net economic benefits to a country. How large those benefits are depends on how much trade patterns actually change and what happens if people do lose their incomes from freer trade.

To summarize the literature on the subject, the claimed and often empirically supported benefits of free trade are as follows:

- Greater economic growth. Theoretically, and as seen above to a lesser extent empirically, this is believed to be correct under a fairly wide range of conditions.
- Access to lower-cost and/or higher-quality goods for consumers. This can be quantified, is generally agreed to be true, and leads to higher real consumer incomes and potentially lower inflation.
- Access to lower-cost, high-quality production equipment and intermediate inputs for companies. This can be quantified and is generally agreed to be true,

and can lead to higher productivity and employment growth for firms that are able to take advantage of it.

- Larger markets for all producers of goods and services (if included in the agreement). This is true by definition and can lead to greater economies of scale and job growth, if the industry is scalable.
- Increased efficiency and competitiveness through increased competition. The "dynamic" gains from trade are difficult to quantify empirically, but are considered by some to be among the most important, driving both better consumer goods and services and firm-level productivity. For certain, competition increases with freer trade. Actual results are driven by the responses to that competition; companies may get stronger or may go out of business.[20]

The claimed and also often empirically supported costs of freer trade are as follows:

- Jobs (good ones) can be lost when imports are cheaper and/or higher quality than the products produced at home. It is hard to know the net effects, since jobs can be gained in other areas, but job and/or income loss has been validated in certain sectors and cases.[21]
- Production can be shifted to emerging markets where environmental laws are less strict, increasing detrimental side effects such as global carbon emissions or deforestation. This effect can be substantiated, though mainly in case studies and theoretical models due to time lags and a lack of counterfactual data.[22]
- When jobs go overseas, labor rights including child labor may not be respected. A case in point has been the conditions at the Chinese Foxconn plants that make iPhones, and these are certainly not the worst of the conditions.[23]
- Opening up an economy "too soon" can lead to a decline of the productive base. Conclusions can be drawn either way, which lies at the heart of the so-called infant-industries argument covered in chapter 8.

There is plenty of ammunition out there both for and against freer trade to keep the sides arguing with each other for a long time. As of the beginning of 2016, the planet seemed to be on a pretty sustained and continuing seven-decade path toward freer trade rooted in the anti-mercantilism and globalist sentiment of the post–Second World War era. There were some movements toward mercantilism during the great recession, but they came to little and the overall movement toward greater globalization continued. Should anti-globalization backlashes continue to gain momentum, the world could see more of the anti–free trade rhetoric that characterized the 2016 US election cycle and some parallel events in Europe, such as Brexit. As of the middle of 2017, the world is either experiencing a minor hiccup in its decades-long march toward freer trade and greater globalization, or is on the cusp of a serious reversal.

Tables 5.7 and 5.8 contain a summary of the main groups that lobby for and against free trade in the developed market economies. In the emerging markets, some

Table 5.7. Pro Freer Trade

Businesses that are globally competitive and/or export oriented	This is a wide range of businesses; some seek greater access to foreign markets, and some may want to import to their home market from existing or planned plants abroad. For companies whose overall operations are not under direct threat from imports, freer trade affords more options and flexibility. Retail companies support free trade.
US and European chambers of commerce	The US and European chambers largely support free trade, but also seek to negotiate provisions in agreements that are favorable to their national companies. Chambers of commerce in Europe have a closer relationship with unions and may be more concerned with workers' interests. In Europe, support for free trade varies by country, with emerging Eastern and Northern Europe more supportive than the industrial giants of France, Germany, and Italy.[a]
Economics and business academia	Since many arguments for free trade rest on free market economics, academics in economics and business departments have more influence here than in many other areas of policy making. Legislators seem to be fairly responsive to technocratic, expert witness in this area.
Libertarian think tanks	Libertarian policy institutes or "think tanks" are often supported by pro-trade businesses and write many of the policy papers that lobbyists use to influence debates.

a. See the Pew Research Center report by Stokes (2015).

of these are similar, but some are the exact opposite, since what may hurt workers in developed market economies can help them in emerging markets. There is a mix both on the right and the left of the political spectrum, for and against freer trade. As electoral cycles come and go, keeping an eye on who has influence can help in understanding how trade rules are likely to evolve. For example, conservatives in developed market economies have historically supported freer trade. However, populist strains emerging in the right wing of conservative parties in the 2010s are eroding this position over time.

The pro–free trade side is largely populated by businesses and economics-related academia. In truth, putting all of them into a single "pro" category is a vast oversimplification. Business groups mainly lobby for trade policies that are beneficial to them, whether or not that leads to freer trade.[24] On balance, those policies tend toward freer trade. Businesses can be more interested in the service market access and investment and intellectual property protections that come with many of the bilateral and multilateral FTAs signed outside the auspices of the WTO. Tariffs on goods (excluding agricultural products) are usually already fairly low even without an FTA.

Table 5.8. Against Freer Trade

Labor unions	Some of the most vocal opponents in the developed market economies are labor unions, since they frequently represent exactly the types of skilled production workers most threatened by global competition. The votes can be split, however. Rather than outright opposition, labor groups will often lobby for provisions that protect US workers from lower-cost foreign labor, while opening foreign markets in the sectors that union members work in. In emerging markets, labor unions are split. In protected industries, they logically tend to side against freer trade.
Populist political movements	Though until recently the purview of left-wing populist movements, more recent years have seen a coupling of right-leaning populist politicians with traditional manufacturing workers to form a general antiglobalization movement. This is particularly evident in the United States with the Trump administration and the Brexit vote in the United Kingdom.
Businesses with large investments in local production	Certain industries with high sunk costs are difficult to make more productive or to move overseas. Traditionally, businesses opposed to freer trade in developed market economies have been in steel, automobiles, and textiles, though this varies depending on how well positioned the companies are and how flexibly they can relocate overseas. A number of large US manufacturers came out in support of the Trump administration's "border adjustment tax."
Farm lobby	Farmers in the United States and European Union benefit from subsidies that would not be permitted under freer trade regimes, since they give an unfair advantage to national producers. Agriculture has been excluded from many agreements, and continues to be one of the main sticking points in all free trade agreements. Emerging markets producers are split. Some like India are opposed to freer trade in agriculture because of historical food security concerns. Others like Brazil, New Zealand, and Argentina have highly competitive producers and favor freer trade.
Non-economics and nonbusiness academia, think tanks, some consumer groups	Outside of economics and business schools, it is fair to say that much of academia globally opposes freer trade. Arguments are related to loss of union jobs, labor rights, and environmental effects of poor regulatory regimes in lower-income markets.[a] A variety of left-leaning and farm lobby think tanks and consumer groups oppose freer trade. Consumer groups are split, as consumers can be beneficiaries of freer trade.

a. For a good example, see the lengthy book by Mander and Goldsmith (2006).

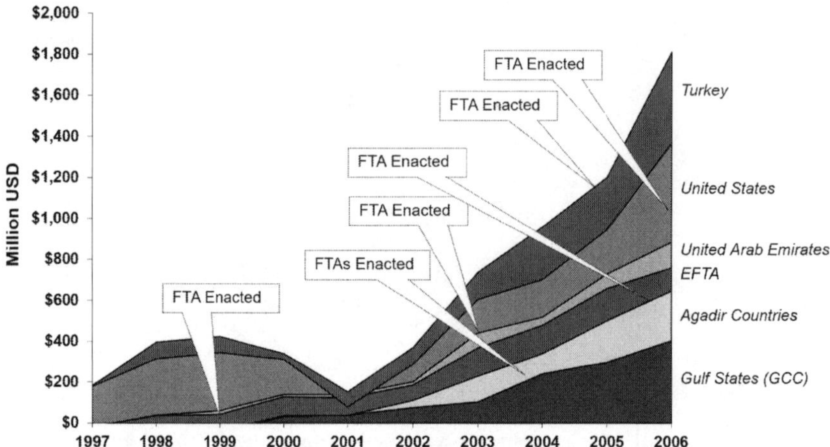

Figure 5.1. Trade Gaps with Signatory Countries, Morocco
Source: UN Comtrade, Booz Allen Hamilton, Andrew Vonnegut.

Historically, trade has increased between FTA members after ratification. It is less clear if FTAs lead to higher levels of overall trade or whether this is the aforementioned trade diversion occurring. Also uncertain, and important for the "benefits of free trade" debate, is that even as trade volume increases, benefits may accrue unequally between countries. Figure 5.1 indicates changes in net imports to and from Morocco and selected trading partners before and after signing free trade agreements. The usual caveats about correlation and causation apply. Although causation cannot be established, overall trends seem clear.

The chart shows the gap between imports and exports, or the trade deficit, between Morocco and each country or trading bloc. In each case, companies in the other signatory countries sold more into Morocco after the agreements were signed (and often before), than Moroccan companies were able to sell into their countries. Trade did increase and Moroccan consumers increased their consumption of goods that they clearly preferred over domestic goods. Also, companies in the countries that sold the goods to Morocco benefited, as presumably did their employees. However, exports and most likely production (and jobs) in Moroccan firms lagged. On an overall basis, did the economy, companies, and workers benefit? That is hard to know, but if the increased net exports coincided with lower Moroccan production, the answer can be negative especially if increases in consumer benefit and net income were not offsetting.

The chart was taken from a report that identified some of the reasons Moroccan companies were not able to increase exports to new markets as effectively as companies in those markets increased their exports to Morocco. For one, lower tariffs into the Moroccan market were new for all the other signatories to the FTA. However, the new markets that Moroccan companies got access to were already fairly open. Their markets were already full of low-cost goods that were similar to what Moroccan companies could export, making it more challenging for Moroccan companies to increase their exports.

Morocco's human capital was also inferior in most respects to the human capital found in the trading partner countries. The agreements covered mainly sophisticated manufactured goods, and half of the Moroccan population at the time was illiterate. The workforce very well may not have been capable of efficiently increasing or shifting production and competing against better prepared workforces in new international markets. Trade negotiations, especially between economically unequal economies, frequently benefit from considering these kinds of factors and working various forms of relief into agreements.

A QUICK LOOK AT TRADE THEORY

Starting with Ricardo, economists have a long history of developing theories of international trade. The above section contained a quick look at Ricardo's theory of comparative advantage, and some reasons the results may or may not hold. Much work has been done extending that body of theory, mainly in allowing for an unlimited number of goods,[25] economies of scale, brand preferences, imperfect competition,[26] and shifts in advantage stemming from stages of the product cycle.[27] The papers cited are considered the seminal ones, but there are hundreds of others that continue down similar lines. Most, but not all, conclude that under a range of assumptions there are net positive returns to trade even after the "losers" are compensated.

As comparative advantage models were developed, they naturally spawned a wide range of theories as to why trade happens the way it does: that is, if trade can be advantageous, what sorts of patterns is it likely to take? A leading trade model is the Heckscher-Ohlin (HO) model. The model notes that if a country has an abundance of some factor, people will use that to make and export goods. Probably thousands of papers and dissertations have been written exploring this point. Not to be overly blunt, but if a country has considerable oil and few forests, it seems unlikely that the citizens of that country would decide to produce and export paper, rather than petroleum derivatives and energy-intensive products.

The real issue with the HO model is not that it might be a bit simplistic on the surface, but rather its lack of predictive power. Whenever there are nuances involved (all the time in the real world), it can break down. Wassily Leontief showed it to be wrong in the case of the United States as far back as 1954 in what became known as the "Leontief paradox." He questioned why the United States should be exporting labor-intensive goods if it was a capital-intensive country, though that is what the data showed. That was followed by a long line of papers noting the theory's poor predictive power.[28]

The Rybczynski theorem is another popular theory that seeks to predict how economic growth will affect trade. There is a bit of math involved to get there, but it concludes that when a country increases the amount it has of something, it will make more from that, and less from other inputs. It would predict that when US companies discovered shale oil and gas, they would not let it sit there unused and move on to the next discovery. Or that when oil was discovered in Saudi Arabia, the companies there would not let it leak into the sea and focus all their efforts on getting the world to buy more of their dates and figs. Or that Chinese companies would forget about all the low-cost labor they had in the 1990s and the lack of arable land and decide to export food instead of manufactured goods.

Despite the shortcomings of these two models, they continue to be staples of undergraduate and graduate-level trade courses. Every textbook I have reviewed includes long sections on these two theories. The critique here may admittedly not be very fair. However, it is probably fair to say that few decision makers in industry or government use these models either directly or are in intellectual debt to them indirectly.

As trade theory has evolved by extending and relaxing assumptions of the core models, a number of other offshoots have appeared. The first is new trade theory, or NTT, which followed the line first established by Paul Krugman and Elhanan Helpman in the papers previously cited, integrating economies of scale and imperfect competition into the debate. NTT notes that scale effects help certain world-dominating industries build up in certain areas and retain dominance even in the face of global competition. The implication is that when companies are newly exposed to free trade, they may not encounter what is referred to as a "level playing field." Empirical validation of NTT has been mixed, but its core tenets do hold under certain circumstances.[29]

Less influential in policy circles, the area of New Economic Geography was also largely an offshoot of work by Krugman. It has grown into a more interdisciplinary field and examines such diverse factors as technology dissemination, transportation and transaction costs, and the emergence of highly competitive industry "clusters" in certain areas. Some practitioners of New Economic Geography dispense with the more rigid neoclassical models that have dominated trade for a century, allowing them to better focus on regional effects and the development of activist policies to counter negative effects of trade.

Much of the more recent work on trade theory has continued to extend the concepts briefly described above. In truth, academic work has often failed to keep pace with the dynamics on the ground, either theoretically or empirically. On the theoretical side, shortcomings are related to a failure to keep pace with the rise in interfirm trade, the role of and linkages to investment and growth, consumer tastes and decisions, trade in services, the fragmentation of trade across final products and services, information and technology dissemination, and other factors related to the relentless pace of globalization. A desire, and a mathematical need, for simplicity and to stay above the chaotic fray that constitutes global trade on the ground, has stunted the growth of more relevant and useful theoretical models that adequately capture global trade patterns and trends.

Empirically, challenges of both measuring impacts from trade and showing consistency with theoretical models are stymied by the usual difficulties of extracting conclusions from large, noisy data sets over long time frames. The apparent lack of consistency between current theories of trade and empirical realities might stem from data difficulties. Or it might be due to the need for new theories. Unfortunately, this has been difficult to definitively ascertain.

On a policy level and in terms of understanding where trade models may lead us in the future, the dominance of neoclassical models has coincided with the aforementioned seven-decade march toward freer trade. The basic models and their extensions have by and large supported this transition. At the same time, the increasing sophistication of these models has laid bare some of the rather serious assumptions and complications behind the arguments for freer trade. If public and political winds do continue to shift against freer trade, there will be ample academic and theoretical support for such a shift.

The main theories of international trade offer some, but limited, insight into the dynamics on the ground. Understanding and decision making are probably better served by returning to the world of human behavior and incentives to trade, rules of production and trade, and costs of all kinds, including the costs of trade.

NOTES

1. Data is hard to come by, but the world sees considerable illegal trade, mainly in drugs, arms, people, money, stolen goods and art, and endangered species. See *Illicit* by Moisés Naím (2005) for an overview.

2. See the UN Comtrade and ITC Trade Map databases and related documentation for more data on information on how it breaks down.

3. See the OECD working paper by Miroudot et al. 2009.

4. WTO, statistical database.

5. WTO, World Trade Statistical Review, 2016.

6. See the report and other related research by Xing (2013) of the Asian Development Bank Institute.

7. For a short history and overview of the industry see Caro and Martínez-de-Albéniz 2015.

8. The Trump administration in the United States in mid-2017 had been discussing implementing a "border adjustment tax." The tax would be recognized by trading partners as a trade distortion similar to a tariff, but in reality is more of a form of corporate tax relief for exporters.

9. European Commission.

10. For a news story on alleged attempts by a Chinese aluminum smelter trying to transship Chinese aluminum to the United States through Mexico, see Patterson 2016.

11. See the IMF article by Ruta and Saito (2013) on the legal framework behind global supply chains, and implying that these agreements are *mainly* about topics other than tariffs.

12. The exposition will not be repeated here, but a Google search will turn up one of the perhaps thousands of places it is detailed.

13. Yes, I referred to a "country" as a trader. Though this is not technically correct, it is described this way in classical trade theory.

14. See, for example, the Trade Adjustment Assistance (TAA) program for US workers hurt by NAFTA. The European Union has a wide range of programs.

15. See the OECD (2005) for an overview of the arguments, data on job displacement from trade, and programs and results.

16. Autor et al. 2014.

17. Autor et al. 2013. See also Acemoglu et al. 2016 for an estimate of around two million jobs lost in the United States from Chinese imports. Note that these are not net losses, nor does the study consider consumer income gains from the imports.

18. See Hicks and Devaraj (2015).

19. See *The Economist* (2015g) for a summary of results from models estimating outcomes from the Trans-Pacific Partnership.

20. Several studies support this premise. Bloom et al. (2015) showed increased innovation and productivity among European firms most exposed to competition from Chinese imports. See also Anderson and Yotov (2016).

21. There are hypothesized, though not empirically determined, conditions under which there is only a net job *loss*, at least for some time and in the tradable sectors. Even if jobs are lost, it may be that the increased consumer incomes that come from lower-cost imports will create new job opportunities. See the OECD (2005) study cited previously.

22. The paper by Revell et al. (2014) on the proposed FTA between the Mercosur countries and the European Union highlights both positive and negative potential outcomes. These are hypothetical and theoretical, model-driven results, though backed with sound logic and analysis.

23. Reports are plentiful, but see for example Barboza and Duhigg 2012. The unregulated international maritime industry was covered in a series of reports by Ian Urbina (2015) of the *New York Times*.

24. A case in point is the support for the 20 percent so-called border adjustment tax by some prominent US exporters in 2017.

25. Dornbusch, Fischer, and Samuelson 1977.

26. Krugman 1979. See also Helpman 1981.

27. Vernon 1979.

28. Leontief 1953, Deardorff 1982. See also Schmidt and Kulkarni 2014.

29. For an early example, see Deraniyagala and Fine 2001.

6

International Payments and Exchange

The international payments system is the court recorder of global economic activity. Nearly everything (legal) that happens in the global economy passes through countries' national payments systems, and lucky for us, gets recorded into standardized accounts along the way. That the topic only gets one chapter is less a testament to its importance, than that most of the components that become part of the balance of payments accounts are covered in detail in other chapters. This chapter summarizes the main terminology and topics, then addresses implications of imbalances that can occur in the accounts.

International payments methodology defines and classifies accounting entries between nations. It's easy to get bogged down in technical details and forget that behind those sterile entries are millions of real people making billions of decisions that define the global economy at any moment in time. These individual transactions are the foundation of international payments, not the entries themselves, which just show the aggregate end results. Understand the people, incentives, and behaviors behind the flows, and accounting entries in and out of countries start to take on more meaning.

BALANCE OF PAYMENTS LEDGERS

The **balance of payments** (BOP) is an accounting of all the money that comes in and out of a country during a period of time, sort of like an income statement for countries. Like most concepts in economics, at its roots it is driven by the financial and spending decisions of companies and people around the world. When people buy a product, or a stock or a bond, sell a machine, send money back to their home country, or spend money as a tourist in another country, it shows up in the balance of payments of both countries. The balance of payments accounts represent the sum total of these cross-border trade and investment transactions. In fairness, the balance of *payments* might be a slight misnomer since it is more a register of transactions.

Though people talk of a country having this or that balance of payments position, "the country" is only along for the ride. It just happens that the people undertaking a given transaction are in two different countries. It usually does not even matter what country they are from, just what country they happen to be in when a transaction takes place. For those who have taken accounting, a country's balance of payments works under the concept of double-entry bookkeeping. For those who have not, just know first that any action shows up as both a debit and a credit in each country's account, and second that the balance of payments is just that, a balance, and it always balances and sums to zero.[1]

Table 6.1 summarizes the structure and main categories in the balance of payments.

The numbers to the left of each category are there for reference and correspond to the standard IMF classification of the accounts. Anyone with the desire can find lots more information on each account on the IMF website. Knowing exactly what goes into each category and how different nuances and discrepancies are accounted for is interesting, but mainly if you are an accountant.[2]

The balance of payments ledger is divided into two sides, the current account and the capital and financial account (historically referred to just as the capital account). On the left-hand side of the table, the current account is dominated by the balance of trade, imports minus exports, of both goods and services. If there are more im-

Table 6.1.

Current Account		*Capital and Financial Account*	
1.A.a Merchandise trade	Imports (–) and exports (+)	2.A Capital account	Transfer of ownership of fixed assets, debt forgiveness, transfers of intangible assets
1.A.b Services trade	Travel/tourism, financial services, etc.		
1.B Investment income	From investments abroad, i.e., dividends, interest payments	2.B Financial account	Net foreign investments: direct, portfolio/securities, credits/loans, in reserve assets
1.C Current transfers	Workers' remittances, government grants to other countries		
Adjustment for statistical discrepancy			
Overall balance			=0

ports than exports, then the country is running a **trade deficit**. The opposite, and it is running a **trade surplus**. Both goods and services are included in the current account. If a Moroccan call center helps customers of a French bank, there is an inflow to the Moroccan current account, and an outflow from the French current account. If only goods and not services are included in a summary of the balance of payments, that is the **merchandise trade balance**.

The current account also records income received from investments in other countries, and income paid to people in other countries who have an investment in the home country. For example, if I live in the United States and own a mutual fund with Japanese stocks in it and those stocks pay a dividend, that creates an inflow to the US current account and an outflow from the Japanese current account. There is also a category in the current account called unilateral net transfers where mainly foreign assistance and donations are logged. Workers' remittances, or funds sent home by workers abroad, also are recorded in the current account; oddly enough, though, only if they are sent home to support consumption rather than to make investments. More on that later.

These other categories in the current account tend to be smaller than trade and have less bearing on overall payments balances. There are exceptions, however, that can be important in certain cases. Some countries such as India, Mexico, and the Philippines are highly dependent on workers' remittances, so changes in those levels can greatly affect these countries' balance of payments. Some poorer countries are dependent on foreign assistance, another category in the current account. Many companies establish subsidiaries in Ireland to take advantage of low tax rates. The Irish balance of payments has an outsize primary income component in its current account where profits that flow through those subsidiaries are recorded.

On the right-hand side of the table, the capital and financial account includes the flow of funds for investments back and forth between countries. If someone in your country buys an asset in another country, that is an outflow from your country's capital account (and an inflow to the other country). If someone in another country buys an asset in your country, that is an inflow on your country's capital account (and an outflow on theirs). All the buying and selling of stocks, corporate and government bonds, factories, and so on, ends up recorded here, in the capital and financial account. Remember that the returns, like dividend or interest payments, on those investments show up in the current account.

Also included in the financial account are increases and decreases in the reserves that countries hold in the currency of another country. For example, when Russia increases its euro reserves, the transaction shows up here in its balance of payments. As noted, some economies' currencies are used as a reserve currency, mainly the United States, the European Union, the United Kingdom, and a few others. When a country increases its reserves, monetary authorities normally purchase assets issued by the reserve currency economy, creating an inflow on the reserve currency economy's financial account. These inflows are a major benefit of being one of the few issuers of reserve currencies.

The US dollar's popularity as a reserve currency has led to massive inflows on the United States' financial account over many decades as foreign countries bolster their reserves and buy up US dollar assets. The inflows have allowed the United States to maintain a persistent trade deficit (which shows up on the current account) and consume more than it otherwise would be able to. In short, other countries' accumulation of USD reserves and their subsequent purchases of US assets like treasury bonds offset or "fund" the chronic trade deficit. Remember that the two sides balance, with an outflow on one side (trade deficit on the current account in this case) balanced with an inflow on the other (asset purchases on the financial account).[3]

The content of chapters 1, 2, 3, and 4 on the participants, central banks, and domestic policies all ties heavily into what happens in the financial account, and chapter 7 to come is largely about trading through the financial account. The participants in the global economy of chapter 2 both make the rules for trading in international financial assets and trade in them. Central bank policies of chapter 3 affect the returns that can be earned in a country, which in turn influence inbound money flows to take advantage of those returns, or outbound flows in pursuit of higher returns elsewhere. The domestic policies of chapter 4 help determine how attractive a country's assets are for investment by outsiders, affecting the types and quantities of flows on the financial account.

All these factors and players affect the flows of FDI, portfolio investments, lines of credit to banks, and other investment components that make up the capital and financial account side of the balance of payments. The story of investors and entire economies riding and sometimes crashing on waves of capital account financing is a big part of what came before and what follows in this book. The importance and stability of activity in these accounts varies across different countries and time periods. Stability is key, since the underlying behavior that drives wide swings in the accounts can also drive swings in countries' exchange rates, inflation levels, GDP, employment rates, and other indicators.

It is worth making some broad generalizations about the different accounts, how they function and fluctuate, and why that might or might not matter. Remember, these are broad generalizations and each individual case and context should be understood when analyzing balance of payments accounts and activities.

Emerging markets economies tend to experience more volatility in their balance of payments than developed market economies, especially those with reserve currencies. Since the two sides of the balance of payments need to balance, the frequently observed volatility on emerging markets' capital account leads inevitably to volatility on the current account. Imports will plummet along with capital account outflows, in particular as outflows put pressure on the currency value.

Instability can also originate on the current account side if for any number of reasons a trade balance takes a wide swing. Volatility can emerge when even short-term shocks to the current account, such as a drop in exports leading to widening trade deficit, cannot be financed through inflows on the capital account. Even anticipated current account imbalances can lead to a drying up of capital account inflows if creditors expect problems and turn off the taps.

Current account fluctuations driven by trade shocks are common in economies heavily reliant on commodities trade, since commodity prices are notoriously unstable. When the price of oil drops, for example, energy-producing countries that have not sufficiently diversified into non-energy-related exports see wide swings in their trade accounts. They may then use the reserve positions built up during boom times to help at least temporarily finance imports during times of low commodity prices. This "burning" of reserves leads to inflows on the capital account, filling the export earnings gap and thereby propping up the current account and allowing consumption of imports to continue, at least for some time.[4]

Countries whose exporters are highly dependent on certain markets can see their current accounts swing into deficit when demand shifts in those markets. There is an old adage that when the United States sneezes, Mexico gets the flu. Similarly, many of the same emerging markets affected by the "taper tantrum" of 2014 had already seen their exports to the Chinese market start to drop off after a slowdown in industrial production there. Merchandise trade between developed market economies tends to be more stable, with one year's trade balance usually pretty well correlated with the previous years'.

Historically, certain countries such as Germany, Japan, and China (though the latter is changing) have maintained long-term trade surpluses. Many if not most other nations including the United States have maintained long-term deficits. As noted, the United States has maintained a trade deficit for decades, financed over that period by capital account inflows. Current account deficits, in particular trade deficits, are not necessarily a problem if there are adequate balancing inflows on the capital and financial account side. In fact, trying to address a trade imbalance through trade policy while ignoring what is happening on the capital account is likely to be futile. This is an essential reality that is more often than not ignored in political rhetoric around trade deficits and policy.

Account 2.B, the financial account, is where a lot of the short-term action in the global economy appears. Through the financial account, wide swings of money flood into countries to pursue short-term investments, and equally wide swings retreat at the first signs of trouble. It would not be much of an exaggeration to say that many booms and busts are channeled through the financial account. The shortest-term and most volatile flows are the portfolio flows. However, bank and private credit flows can also change direction quickly, depending on the terms under which money was lent.

Money moving in and out of the financial accounts has other knock-on effects. The buying and selling of the country's currency that accompanies the in- and outflows can drive exchange rate volatility. Fluctuating exchange rates can then move any number of other variables, such as costs of imported company inputs, values of products on export markets, financing costs, and ultimately investment and employment. Managing and especially moderating financial flows are a major goal of policy makers, especially when the flows are directed toward the exit. Watching and acting on these flows are a major focus of global investors. This is where fortunes are made and lost in global markets. The investors who trade in the areas that make up the financial account thrive on, suffer through, and can end up driving much of the currency and asset volatility in global markets.

A tricky thing about the balance of payments and global economics is that certain balances can seem to be really "out of balance" for a long time with apparently few consequences. As noted, the United States has run a persistent merchandise trade deficit for decades. This has been the subject of a lot of worrying. The United States can run a trade deficit because (so far) it has compensated for it in other ways. First, there is a positive balance (surplus) in services: the United States exports more services than it imports. Second, people in the United States receive more money from their foreign investments than what others get from their investments in the United States, for now. Finally, and most importantly, lots of money comes into the United States to buy assets of all types (stocks, bonds, real estate)—in part because of the reserve status of the USD.

Quite simply, for decades the trade deficit in the US current account has been made up for by adequate inflows on the capital account. As long as this keeps up, there is no crisis in the US balance of payments. Pundits have been predicting the collapse of this balance for a long time, but *so far* gambling against it has been a sucker's bet. As noted, trying to address a fully financed trade deficit through trade policy alone is likely to be futile, unless of course that trade policy so inflames trade partners that they abandon the US dollar as a reserve currency. The consequent drying up of capital account inflows would resolve the trade deficit, but would also almost certainly lead to lower levels of US consumption and a much lower US dollar.

The United States is not alone. Lots of countries have run trade deficits for many years without much clarity on how and how long it will be sustained. Sometimes there is a severe readjustment (crash), sometimes accounts slowly and calmly draw back into balance, and sometimes the trade deficits just seem to continue indefinitely. Much of how things turn out is driven by how the deficit is financed through the capital and financial account and why.

Two examples help illustrate the point. Greece maintained a persistent trade deficit through much of the 2000s, mainly driven by the importation of consumer goods purchased by its population. The trade deficit was financed largely by borrowing from abroad when low-cost credit lines and bond markets opened up after Greece adopted the euro. An advantageous conversion rate to the euro from its previous currency, the drachma, helped make imports even more affordable and desirable. Once the credit lines were cut off after 2008, so was financing for imports (among other things), and the Greek economy went into a severe tailspin. A lack of credit and an inability to increase exports meant Greece could no longer finance the same level of imports. This quick summary is clearly an oversimplification of a complex scenario, but it is largely correct.

Poland also maintained a trade deficit during the late 1990s and 2000s, partially driven by consumer goods imports, but also because investors were pouring money in and companies there were importing equipment to increase productive capacity. A large amount of the deficit was financed by permanent, direct investment in the economy by companies from abroad, and not short-term capital flows like in Greece. In fact, Poland's FDI as a percentage of GDP from 1996 to 2006 was three to four times that of Greece.[5] Direct investment is generally considered to be more stable than portfolio financing, as it does not simply leave and/or demand repayment when things go badly. More importantly, it contributes directly to the productive capacity of the economy, churning out the goods and exports that are needed to keep the accounts in balance. Through the great recession, both countries struggled, but Poland emerged in far better shape.

All the beating into the ground of the links between the current and capital and financial accounts might seem redundant and tiresome. Part of the emphasis is reactionary. The relationship too frequently gets glossed over in the off-the-cuff analyses that appear in the popular financial media. Everyone wants to talk about the trade deficit, but it really is impossible to do that without understanding and analyzing what is happening in the capital and financial accounts.

Insightful analysis of global economic events requires drawing links between the behaviors that drive flows on one set of accounts and the behaviors and consequences on other accounts. Especially when analyzing bubbles and crises, there are endless and often productive debates among economists about whether the problem originated in the current or capital account. It is important to understand how they fit together, even if perfect analysis is illusory for the usual reasons related to data quality, causality, and imperfect tools.

Investors and lenders should probably take more account of the composition and trends in target countries' balance of payments in their risk assessments. One of the problems in acting on observed imbalances, as noted, is that countries can maintain even apparently unhealthy deficits for a very long time. Often, the ultimate collapse is triggered as much by a seemingly unrelated event outside the borders of the country. Hindsight is great, but it can be simply hard to know when to act. Difficulties aside, investment flows and the levels and composition of trade are not secret and can readily be integrated into analyses and risk management assessments.[6] The art of managing risks in crises and benefiting from recoveries rests as much as anything on a good understanding of payments accounting and the related stocks and flows. Boring old accounting coupled with understanding the incentives behind the fingers on the buy and sell buttons can be a good start to keeping an eye on potential volatility.[7]

At first blush, there appear to be few definitive parameters governing this kind of analysis. The frustration becomes a little more bearable if two more things are considered. First, people have made (and lost, or just managed to preserve) considerable wealth moving money in and out of global assets as long as they have an exit planned and/or are hedged (or are either very skilled or very lucky). An understanding of these accounts is essential to basic global investment risk management.

Second, once imbalances blow up, they often do so in a spectacular manner, with the rebound off the bottom often equally sharp. Every major global financial crisis has (so far) been followed within a few years by a rebound where money was made. Of course, the past is not always an accurate indicator of the future. If something radical has changed, it might not be. You have to think it through. Understanding the implications of payments balances requires being comfortable with nuances and ambiguities, and carefully balancing current flows and conditions against historical outcomes.

The gateways of international financial flows are the exchange rates. The next section covers what they are, how they change, and why they matter so much.

EXCHANGE RATES AND BALANCES

The exchange rate is the ratio at which one currency is traded for another, or more accurately the price of one currency relative to another. When people buy goods, services, and assets abroad, they normally need to exchange money to do it. Changes in the rate at which they can make that exchange can affect their pricing and investment returns. When a currency's value relative to another one increases, it is said to be **appreciating**. When its value drops against another currency, it is **depreciating**.

Changes in exchange rates come about in two ways. The most obvious is when the market price of one currency changes versus another on world markets. If the value of the Chinese yuan against the euro goes from 6 to the euro to 5 to the euro, the euro has depreciated and the yuan has appreciated. You can get fewer yuan for a euro. That is a change in the **nominal rate** of exchange.

A change in what is called the **real exchange rate** happens independent of changes in the market rate and is driven by differences in inflation between two economies. If inflation is running at 10 percent in China and zero in the European Union, even without a change in the nominal exchange rate, the real exchange rate (yuan/euro) will have appreciated 10 percent over the year. The price of goods and services in China cost 10 percent more in euro terms, and therefore now a euro buys 10 percent less in China than it did before. The change in Europeans' ability to purchase Chinese goods and services is the same as if the nominal rate had changed without any difference in inflation.

To keep the real exchange rate constant between two countries, the currencies need to revalue at the same rate as the inflation difference between their economies. In the example above, to keep the real exchange rate and euro purchasing power constant, the euro would have to appreciate 10 percent against the yuan. Changes in both the nominal and the real exchange rates need to be considered when looking at price changes between currencies. China is in fact a good case study of real exchange rate adjustment. During the 2010s, inflation was higher than that of its main trading partners as the economy boomed and wages rose. Though its nominal exchange rate remained controlled, China's real exchange rate appreciated with the

Table 6.2.

Currency Value Appreciating	*Currency Value Depreciating*
Imports are cheaper. More can be purchased abroad with each unit of currency.	Imports are more expensive. Less can be purchased abroad with each unit of currency.
Exports cost more to trading partners, making it harder to export.	Exports are cheaper to trading partners, making it easier to export.
Potentially less inflationary pressure, since imported goods can be bought cheaply, keeping price levels down.	Potentially inflationary, as the higher price of imports can affect overall price levels in an economy.
Investments can be made abroad more cheaply.	It is more expensive to invest in other countries.
Investments in other currencies return less in local currency terms.	Investments in other currencies yield more in local currency.
Debt held in other currencies becomes less expensive and easier to pay off.	Debt held in other currencies becomes more expensive and more difficult to pay off.

inflation and was reflected in a declining trade surplus as its exports became costlier for others to import.

Table 6.2 summarizes the main ways that changes in a currency's value can affect an economy and therefore, its traders and investors.

Import and export prices change in direct proportion to exchange rate changes. This clearly matters for trade. All other things equal, exports should increase and imports decrease as currencies become cheaper, and they often do.[8] In other cases, all other things are not equal. Empirical evidence of exchange rate changes on non-commodity trade volume is often less clear than might be expected, especially over the shorter term. In fact, trade patterns can be fairly well established and price inelastic over a wide shift in exchange rates.[9]

Trade volume may or may not be affected by exchange rates for numerous reasons, many of which are behavioral and/or are related to strongly held preferences or longer-term business decisions. Drivers in the United Kingdom won't just stop buying BMWs and start buying Acuras because the value of the euro went up 5 percent against the yen, and revelers won't forgo that bottle of Jack Daniel's in Argentina because the real lost a few percent against the US dollar. The more specialized and less substitutable the item, the less especially small changes in exchange rates matter. Final price is important, but is usually only one consideration.

Institutional factors also contribute to trade stability. Most non-commodity trade is in intermediate goods, not in the final goods that consumers see and buy. Global supply chains for such goods are fairly well established and can be rigid in the face of exchange fluctuations, especially in the short term. Suppliers may be connected to the buyers legally or financially, or may have long-term relationships that help them manage diverse types of risk, of which price is only one. In other cases, supply chains may span several markets with different currencies that even out exchange effects, and/or suppliers may be willing to take a lower profit for some time before giving up market share.[10]

Structural factors may also overshadow effects of exchange rate changes. Fracking in the United States was a much larger contributor to decreased energy imports between 2015 and 2016 than any decrease in the value of the USD. The correlation between a weaker dollar and reduced energy imports is indisputable, but the cause was unlikely a change in exchange rates. There were other things going on.

Though often fairly stable in the shorter term, changes in nominal and/or real exchange rates can drive changes in trade patterns more significantly over the longer term. The stabilizing factors noted above can start to shift. When this happens, it is said that a country is experiencing an increase or decline in trade competitiveness or its **terms of trade**. If trade competitiveness decreases without offsetting capital account inflows, the effects on the balance of payments can be negative and severe. A number of Latin American currencies appreciated throughout much of the early 2010s. For a time, exchange rate appreciation was both offset and driven by demand for regional exports and by money flowing in through the capital accounts looking for higher investment returns. When the capital inflows and export demand slowed, many of these countries (like Brazil and Argentina) found themselves with overvalued exchange rates. Quick and painful exchange rate adjustment was required to mainly decrease imports and to a lesser extent increase exports to get their trade accounts back into line with reduced capital account flows.

Greece's lack of trade competitiveness contributed to its inability to resolve the financial account crisis it ran into post 2008 when credit lines dried up. A devaluation that makes exports more competitive on world markets and home goods more competitive against imports would be a normal way to compensate for a reduction in financial account inflows. Technically, Greece could not devalue its nominal exchange rate since it is part of the eurozone. Instead, the Greek economy had to rely on the much more painful process of wage reduction and deflation to adjust its real exchange rate. An even bigger concern was its (related) lack of domestic policies to make the country attractive for investment to get financial flows moving again.[11] Greece was not able to attract the capital and financial account inflows needed to offset either the reduced credit lines or its trade deficit.

While appreciation and depreciation indicate a currency's direction relative to others, people also worry about whether a currency is over- or undervalued at any particular level. The assumption is that if it is one or the other, a correction could be on the way, and corrections can be painful. Whether a currency is over, under, or fairly valued can be surprisingly difficult to figure out. In economics, a theoretical "equilibrium" exchange rate would be the rate that would put certain payments in balance, for example where imports equal exports. In the real world, it is difficult to establish whether a currency is over- or undervalued, partially because it can be hard to distinguish between short-term volatility on accounts flows and long-term trends until the trend is pretty far along.

The Economist magazine, in recognizing this difficulty and making light of it, has since 1986 published a currency value scale that it calls the "Big Mac" index. It simply compares the price of a standard product, the McDonald's Big Mac, across countries and notes where the cost is above (overvalued exchange rate) or below (undervalued exchange rate) the norm. Reacting to criticism that it does not adequately account for "cheapness" in lower-income countries, *The Economist* developed an adjusted index that accounts for differences in PPP per capita income.[12]

Exchange rates fluctuate for numerous reasons, and like other price changes are normally driven by shifts in the supply and demand for a currency. Under normal circumstances money supply is not rapidly changing, so demand shifts mainly move exchange rates around.[13] If people want to buy more goods and assets that are priced in a particular currency, all other things equal, the price of the currency goes up relative to others. If people are selling more assets and not choosing to buy goods that are priced in the currency and so are either selling the currency or buying less of it, the price goes down. The demand shifts are manifest as increases or decreases in funds flowing through the balance of payments accounts.

Table 6.3 notes some of the main factors behind changes in exchange rates, and some (not always true) generalizations as to the degree and time frame of the changes. All but the last example are from changes on the demand rather than the supply side.

Though market-driven supply and demand factors underlie most levels and changes in exchange rates, countries do try to manage both supply and demand to smooth the rates and extents to which their currencies bounce around. The way a country manages its exchange rate is called the **exchange regime**. Though there is a lot of variation within them, there are basically three main exchange regimes.[14]

1. **Fixed or pegged rate**. The exchange rate is fixed to another currency or weighted basket of currencies, usually the main trading and investment partners. Only about 10 percent of countries maintained a fixed peg as of 2017. A fixed rate can be difficult and expensive to maintain. Countries that maintain a fixed rate need to carefully manage demand, often against market forces. They normally use their foreign currency reserves to do this. If global demand for their currency is not sufficient to maintain the fixed rate, they can end up spending a lot of their reserves buying their home currencies to create artificial "demand" to keep the price at the fixed rate. Sometimes they run out and then are left both with no reserves and a lower currency value. Many of the emerging markets currency crises in Asia and Latin America in the 1990s involved a fall from an unsustainable peg that was probably defended too long. Since those crises, fixed rates have become much less widespread. Switzerland pegged the franc to the euro in 2011, but was forced to abandon the peg and increase the value of the franc in early 2015. The Swiss central bank had been managing demand by creating new francs and using them to buy euros, but ultimately found the cycle hard to maintain in the face of undiminishing demand for francs.

Table 6.3.

Factor Influencing an Exchange Rate	*Comments on Outcome*
Changes in balance of payments, such as in trade, investment, and/or remittance flows	Can be strong effects, as permanent as the change in the payment flow. May be rapid.
Shifts in interest rate differentials between economies	Often severe revaluations in small economies, and can trigger other outcomes. Duration varies.
Perceived longer-term changes in competitiveness, a general improvement or deterioration in the country's position over time	Significant changes over time, though there can be a herd mentality at times, which may result in sharper adjustments
Speculators betting on currency movements, often triggered by other factors	Short term, sometimes severe shocks, but often just "normal" volatility, unless the volatility triggers other problems
Security, risk reduction, and a lack of better alternatives (i.e., best currency option of all the bad ones)	Happens particularly during times of crisis, like the flight to the US dollar during the great recession
Shift in composition of currency reserves. A reserve economy may see demand shift for its currency, and an emerging market may see the overall value of its reserves shift.	For the reserve economy, long-term trending with minor volatility; for emerging markets, exchange rates effects should be minor
Perceived policy, "talking the currency up/down"	Usually minor and short term, but depends on credibility of monetary authorities and other tools at their disposal
Differences in inflation rates, even with a fixed nominal rate, a country with higher inflation will see decreases in their real exchange rate	Slow and steady, over the medium to longer term
Official policy, type of exchange regime (see discussion) and credibility of that regime	Varies, but a voluntary or involuntary shift from one regime to another can precipitate a shock
Rapid increase in money supply not supported by economic fundamentals	Sell-off of a currency after a loss of credibility, can be from an actual increase in money supply or flight to other currencies

2. An extreme, and usually effective, way to peg a currency is with a **currency board**. Under this regime, the country picks a foreign currency to peg to. It then maintains one unit of foreign currency for each unit of its own currency, so anyone who wants to exchange at the pegged rate can do so without question. The country then cannot issue new domestic currency without having more foreign currency in reserve. There is little risk of speculators' attacking the currency, since the monetary authorities will always have enough currency

to defend the current exchange rate.[15] A number of economies have tried currency boards, with Hong Kong among the foremost examples. Other recent examples include Argentina (linked to the USD, but dropped it as USD appreciation made their economy uncompetitive), Estonia, and Bulgaria. Both of the latter countries adopted currency boards to gain the monetary and fiscal stability needed to join the European Union in 2004 and 2007 respectively. Estonia adopted the euro in 2011, while as of 2017 Bulgaria continued to use the lev, which remains pegged to the euro (previously the USD). A currency board is clearly as much a monetary as an exchange regime.

3. **Managed peg or managed float.** Monetary authorities seek to maintain the currency value within a certain range, but let it float freely in that range. These are common regimes, with a wide range of variability in how they are carried out. Most emerging markets use this type of hybrid regime. The volatility of a full free float can be painful, but a fixed peg lacks flexibility and can be hard to maintain. So a managed float provides a middle ground. Countries maintain different ranges for different reasons. Turkey, for example, manages its currency partially to facilitate trade and investment with its most important trading partner, the European Union, since importers, exporters, and many investors don't like rates that bounce around unpredictably. Turkey's managed float also helps control inflation and keep interest rates steady. The country is prone to expectations-driven inflation, and the exchange rate is one of the main data points that merchants look at when setting prices.
4. **Free float.** A currency is free to move without bounds. The large, nonemerging markets economies have more freely floating currencies. The United States, the European Union, and Japan's exchange rate regimes fall into this category.

In reality, almost all countries, even those with freely floating currencies, will try to manage the value of their currencies in some way. This is especially the case in times of rapid appreciation or depreciation.

Maintaining exchange rate stability is particularly important for countries that export natural resources or whose exports are otherwise heavily concentrated in particular sectors. These countries seek to avoid **Dutch disease**, named after a phenomenon the Dutch encountered in the mid-twentieth century. When the Dutch discovered natural gas off their country's shores in the North Sea in the 1960s, they were initially pleased with all the money that gas exports were bringing in. At that time, the Netherlands had its own currency, the guilder. The more they sold, the more foreign currency they converted into guilders to spend at home.

The reliable laws of supply and demand drove up the value of the guilder, and it became cheap for the Dutch to travel overseas and buy things from abroad. It was great for a while. Then the Dutch realized that the increase in the value of the guilder that was fueled by all the gas exports was making their manufactured goods uncompetitive on global markets. It did this in two ways. The first was by making guilder-denominated goods more expensive on foreign markets, simply from currency appreciation. The second was that the flood of money into the Netherlands was causing inflation, which was driving wages up and making it more expensive to make things, thereby driving up the real exchange rate. The term Dutch disease was since coined to describe this substantial real and/or nominal exchange rate appreciation driven by a surge in natural resource exports.

After the Dutch example, natural resource exporting economies have figured out how to **sterilize** their foreign currency earnings, mainly by keeping them in foreign currency and outside the local economy. A number of natural resource exporters do this. It's one of the reasons (besides to smooth out the effects of commodity price swings) countries such as Saudi Arabia, Norway, Qatar, and the United Arab Emirates have such large reserves, some of which are contained in sovereign wealth funds. By keeping and investing the foreign earnings outside the country, they avoid appreciating currencies and price inflation.

Other countries also sterilize their foreign currency earnings, but not to guard against natural resource–driven currency and price inflation. They do it just to keep the value of their currency lower than it otherwise would be so that their exports stay competitive in foreign markets. This is often frowned upon by trading partners that may be rightly concerned about **currency manipulation**. It can be hard to prove definitively that a country is manipulating its currency, though an expansion of foreign reserves is telling. China has been accused of holding down the value of its currency for much of the 2000s. The country accumulated over $3 trillion in foreign reserves, as the nominal (but not always real) value of its currency remained relatively constant against that of its main export market, the United States.

Some investors make their living speculating on movements of foreign currencies. If they believe a currency will go up, they buy it or assets denominated in it, either directly or through futures or derivative contracts. If investors believe a currency will go down, they short sell it. All of this speculative buying and selling can increase market liquidity, but can also cause a currency to fluctuate for no other reason than that. It tends to irritate governments, which is one reason governments keep reserves on hand to absorb speculators' "hot money" at least a bit. Sometimes speculators can blow a pegged or managed currency out of the range where the government wanted to keep it. As seen before, George Soros and his fund were able to do that to the British pound, making a lot of money in the process.[16]

It should be getting clearer that fluctuating exchange rates can pose considerable risks to companies, investors, and governments. Exchange rate volatility by itself has been shown to be correlated with lower levels of investment in the affected country.[17] However, the greater risks to players in the global economy come from foreign exchange exposure, which is coming up in the next section.

FOREIGN EXCHANGE EXPOSURE

Transacting across currencies frequently generates some kind of foreign **exchange exposure**, or the risk that a change in the exchange rate can increase or decrease a cross-border transaction's expected return. Foreign exchange exposure affects transactions in goods, services, and financial instruments alike.

The risks are evident in financial transactions across currencies. Take for example the common practice of cross-currency lending, usually either in the form of a bank credit or bond. The lending may be across borders, or simply in a different currency from an institution within the borrowers' borders. Frequently, the loan is granted in one of the major reserve currencies, like the USD or the euro. If the borrower has a different domestic currency or earns money in a different currency than what the loan is in, changes in the exchange rate will change the repayment terms for the borrower. If their home currency drops, the borrower will need to pay more in their own currency to service the loan and interest. If they are luckier, and their currency appreciates, payback will be relatively cheaper for them. The sharper the exchange rate swings, the more seriously affected is borrowers' ability to repay their obligations.

Cross-border lending is one of the most common international financial flows. According to the Bank for International Settlements, as of September 2014 total USD credits (loans and bonds) extended to nonbank emerging markets companies amounted to $9.2 trillion, up over 50 percent from the end of 2009.[18] Similarly, in the 2000s Eastern European households and businesses commonly heaped on debt, taking out loans denominated in euros, Swiss francs, and to a lesser extent British pounds. When cross-currency lending builds, so does the risk of exchange exposure, and subsequent financial crises.[19] During the great recession and in its aftermath, currency market volatility often greatly altered the repayment terms of a large swath of foreign currency loans. Initially, terms improved as many non-European emerging markets avoided the negative effects of the crisis and their currencies appreciated, but then turned sharply worse as local currencies depreciated with a rise in the US dollar.

People may borrow in currencies other than their own with minimal exchange risk if their revenues or income are in, or are tied to, the currency that they are borrowing in. More often, they borrow because interest rates in the foreign currency are just lower than in the local currency. Lenders like these loans because they can get higher returns than in US-based assets, and in theory, don't have to worry about exchange risk because the loan is in their own currency.[20] As long as the currencies remain stable relative to each other, or if borrowers' home currency is appreciating, such loans seem cheap to borrowers and advantageous to lenders.

The risk of pain and default starts to loom larger when there are sharp drops in exchange rates and borrowers find it hard to service their loans. If a local currency depreciates, for example, 10 percent against the currency that the loan is in, a household or company borrower may struggle a bit but still make their payments. As the depreciation increases in magnitude, debt gets increasingly hard to service. Lenders start getting nervous about repayment, especially if the drop in currency value is (as is often the case) related to other underlying structural weaknesses in the economy reflecting broader declines in output, employment, and collateral values.

Once exchange rates start to fall, having liabilities denominated in other currencies can have mutually reinforcing repercussions throughout the entire economy:

household and company debt service costs go up, leading to decreases in wealth and profits, leading to lower hiring, layoffs, and wage cuts, leading to drops in consumption, which depresses GDP and profits, and so on. In such a downward spiral, if loans go into arrears, willingness to lend evaporates, further depressing the exchange rate and the economy.

Though exchange exposure continues to be a common risk, policies to minimize the risk of major exchange-related crises have improved over the decades. The percentage of debt that emerging markets borrowers have taken on in their own rather than foreign currencies has increased considerably since the major crises of the 1980s and 1990s. Overall lower debt and greater levels of reserves have allowed countries to use reserves to buffer volatility in capital flows, often arresting a dropping currency before too much damage is done. Over the long run burning through reserves is usually a sucker's bet, but judicious use can help stabilize short-term currency movements. These factors and better and more transparent economic and monetary governance practices have allowed many emerging markets to increase resilience and better prevent full-blown economic meltdowns. Though the 2014 emerging markets adjustments were painful, they were nothing like previous crises.[21]

Investors and borrowers working in currencies other than their national currency can protect themselves from exchange risk by hedging. Hedging was introduced in chapter 3 with covered interest spreads. If investors and borrowers do not hedge for exchange risk, they make what are called uncovered or **naked trades**. The Japanese household traders introduced in chapter 1 are renowned for making these kinds of uncovered trades, trading their own currencies for foreign ones and buying securities bearing higher interest rates. The yen went through a long period of depreciation, allowing traders to frequently make exchange gains in addition to the returns from their foreign investments. When the yen started to appreciate again in the mid-2000s, many households did lose money as the value of their foreign currency holdings dropped in yen terms.[22]

Those lending in their own currency normally do not hedge, since they are not, technically speaking, taking on exchange risk. This is a common institutional practice, with major reserve currency lines of credit frequently made to banks and companies whose main currency is not the one they are borrowing in. Lenders presume that the borrower is either going to hedge or take on the full risk of a devaluation. There are many examples. Banks that were lending euros into Central and Eastern Europe before the great recession (which were then lent to businesses and households) were usually not hedged. Similarly, both domestic and foreign lenders that lent to Latin American emerging markets after the great recession usually put all of the exchange rate risk on the borrower. The borrower may assume all the risk, but that does not mean the transaction is risk-free.

If there is a devaluation, and the borrower cannot pay and subsequently defaults, the lenders can be forced into what the financial industry refers to as a **haircut**, or some combination of a change in payment duration, interest rates, or a markdown in the value of their loan and/or interest payments. Lenders hate haircuts and usually write strong language into lending contracts to avoid them. But sometimes the borrower fails to pay and there is inadequate collateral to fully secure the loan. Lenders ignore at their peril the kinds of macroeconomic imbalances that can cause a devaluation and subsequent default. In fact, often little macroeconomic risk management is built into extended credits, especially during times when economies appear stable and borrowers' home currencies are appreciating. The fact is, hedging is expensive and cuts into returns.

Exchange risk is not only a problem (or opportunity if it goes your way) with financial transactions. Traders of goods also run into it. Take an example of a trader in the United States who wants to buy twenty cars from Germany for resale in the United States for €1 million. Let's say the German company is willing to ship the cars for a 20 percent down payment with the balance due upon delivery. Assume the USD/euro exchange rate is 1:1 at the time the down payment is made, so the buyer pays $200,000. Now, let's say that two months later when the cars arrive, the USD has fallen and the rate is 1:.9. The buyer was hoping to pay $800,000 (€800,000), but now they have to pay $880,000 (still €800,000). If their planned profit was $80,000 on the transaction, they just lost it. Of course, the exchange rate could have moved in the opposite direction, thereby yielding an exchange rate gain, increasing profits.

Trade-related situations like the one described above happen all the time. Depending on short- and long-term purchasing contracts and payment terms, supply chain importance, demand elasticity, and the relative market position of the buyer versus the seller, if exchange rates turn the wrong way someone in the transaction stands to lose money and/or market share. Trade volume may or may not decrease at all, though value might. Outcomes vary considerably, and as noted previously, contrary to a strict reading of economic theory, especially in the short term there can be swings in rates with little bearing on overall trade volume.

The example of the car purchase from Germany is a simple one. In reality, supply contracts are very much situation-dependent, and may be written differently, putting the foreign exchange risk on someone other than the buyer, or sharing the risk between the buyer and seller. Traders of goods often use hedges. The buyer can, for instance, buy a call option on the euro to protect against an increase in the exchange rate. There will be more on this in the next chapter. German car maker Porsche became something of a legend in this regard in the mid-2000s after buying a series of puts that allowed it to fully ride out subsequent drops in the value of the USD.[23]

Foreign exchange exposure, or the threat of it, is one of the main reasons it would be difficult for Greece or Italy, for example, to abandon the euro and go back to the drachma or the lira. In a unified euro zone, there is no foreign exchange risk. Greek debt held by German and French banks is denominated in euro, and Greek borrowers pay both the principal and interest in euros. That does not mean there is no default risk, but at least there is no exchange risk.

If Greece left the euro and went back to the drachma, one thing is certain: the value of the new drachma would be lower than the euro, maybe by as much as

30 to 40 percent even after the dust settles. Some choices, all with serious consequences, would need to be made. One option would be to keep all of the Greek euro debt in euro. In that case, Greece and Greek companies would need to pay those debts in euro, while presumably generating most of their revenue in newly devalued drachma. To say the least, this would be challenging given the difficulty Greece has already experienced generating euro revenues. Greek borrowers would need to pay 30 to 40 percent more to service their euro debt.[24] Significant pain and defaults would be likely.

The second option would be to exchange all the euro debt for drachma debt, preferably at a pre-devaluation rate. That would make it easier to pay, but it would also be in violation of the debt contract, is basically illegal, and would constitute a default. Foreign and domestic debt holders would have big holes blown in their balance sheets as they revalued their assets in devalued drachma.

Either option would ensure that the Greek government and companies would have a hard time getting new credit, at least for a while.[25] In an economy that is so integrated into and reliant on international credit markets, it seems this would be a problem. At the same time, perhaps the Argentinian "Great Depression" of 1998–2002 is illustrative of both the conditions in Greece in the 2010s, and the possible outcome of a withdrawal from the euro. The Argentinian crisis culminated with a collapse of its currency board in 2002 that had kept the peso at parity with the USD for a decade. Though there was much turmoil at the time, perhaps auspiciously, credit lines returned and the Argentinian economy recovered relatively quickly afterward.[26]

Large economies with reserve currencies and emerging markets do not have equal control over their currencies and monetary policies. In what is referred to as the **impossible trinity**, emerging markets economies can manage two of the following three variables under normal circumstances: their exchange rates, their monetary policy, and/or their capital inflows and outflows. Most emerging markets have chosen to try to manage the first two, leaving capital flows up to the market. Problems arise, however, when capital outflows during a crisis obliterate a country's ability to control its exchange rate. Then they lose control over the other two parts of the "trinity." Traders know this and fear getting stuck in a currency that looks like it might collapse. Their quick departure then exacerbates the volatility.

It should be clear by now that there are benefits to having your currency be one of the main reserve currencies. People in reserve currency economies borrow and trade globally, in whole or in large part, in the same currency that they generate at home. Currency mismatches (i.e., having your liabilities denominated in a foreign currency with most of your cash flows and assets in local currency) are rarer. Since governments and companies in other countries desire to hold your reserve currency, there is an intrinsic, natural level of demand for the currency, which tends to reduce volatility and can provide something of a floor under its value. The demand, as seen in the last chapter, can finance trade deficits and allow a country's citizens to consume more than they otherwise would be able to. Markets where you can buy hedges are more liquid, and cheaper. You can also borrow and invest in your own currency. Basically, most aspects of exchange exposure become easier to deal with when your home currency is a global reserve currency.

That said, even reserve currency economies cannot control their monetary policy as much as they would like, or perhaps need to in order to manage future financial crises. Having so much of your currency in foreign markets and subject to the whims of a global cadre of unpredictable traders can be a blessing when the global economy is stable, but also a responsibility and potentially a curse if you need to re-exert control.[27] The story behind the fits and starts by which the Chinese renminbi has moved toward reserve currency status since 2010 is a case study of both the risks and potential gains.[28]

COMMON SHOCKS AND CONTAGION IN A GLOBAL ECONOMY

In a globalized economy with free capital and trade flows, economic events in one location can trigger reactions in other economies. This is referred to as **financial contagion**. Similarly, a **common shock** is when a global event affects multiple countries in similar ways. Economists debate whether and when these are the same or different phenomena, and even if contagion occurs at all.[29] The precise definitions are best left for academic debate, with effort here put into understanding the events, transmission methods, and effects.

A few points can be stated initially without too much controversy. It is certainly accurate that events in one country can affect other countries. Also, the transmission mechanism behind contagion and common shocks is the activity that appears in the trade, capital, and financial accounts in the balance of payments. Finally, contagion at least initially happens mainly with hot money, or portfolio investments and lines of credit that investors can pull quickly out of at least semiliquid markets. When investors get wind of emerging risks, they can pull money out of stock, bond, overnight lending, credit, and currency markets, essentially heading for the exits as fast as they can. More complex are the myriad external drivers and internal facilitators of these events. The discussion and cases that follow will seek to shed some light here.

We saw an example of what most would agree was a common shock in chapter 3. When the US Federal Reserve signaled a potential decrease or tapering in QE, investors fled emerging markets. The chart showing declines in exchange rates against the USD is reproduced here as figure 6.1.

These countries all shared similar characteristics before the drop, including recent increases in exchange rates; recent increases in asset markets where bubbles were feared; a recent history of international portfolio investors entering for higher returns when the developed market economies slashed interest rates after the great recession; and investor fear that they could be harmed if exchange rates or asset prices in those countries were to drop. Pre-existing nervousness about a devaluation became

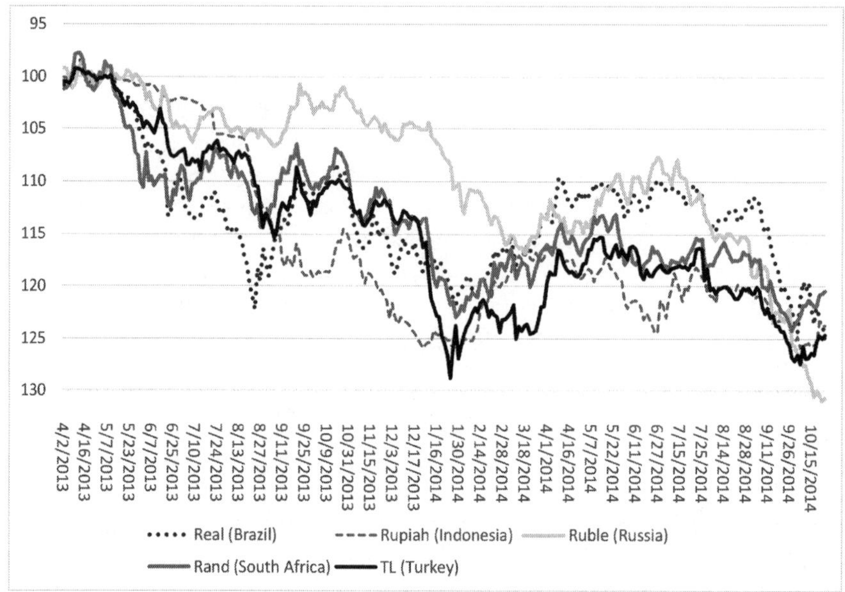

Figure 6.1. Selected Emerging Markets Currencies against the USD
Source: Murat Ucer, Turkey Data Monitor.

self-fulfilling, helping drive the capital flight and the subsequent shock. Speculative opportunism also likely played a part, with short sellers putting further downward pressure on the currencies. Another example of a common shock was the flight of capital from peripheral euro countries after the onset of the 2008 crisis. Portugal, Ireland, Italy, Greece, and Spain (the so-called PIIGS) were all affected by similar perceptions of high risk.

One of the most often cited examples of contagion is the Brazilian currency crisis of early 1999. This occurred several months after a late summer 1998 Russian debt default and the collapse of Long-Term Capital Management (LTCM), a US-based hedge fund that had made large bets on emerging markets interest spreads.[30] Research indicates that the Brazilian crisis was largely triggered by increased emerging markets lending rates following the Russian crisis. The crash of LTCM was predicated by a failure of bond spreads to revert to a longer term mean, and led investors to question and get increasingly nervous about the Brazilian bond and currency markets.[31] A combination of spooked investors and speculators betting against the country drove the currency down.[32] Some more minor version of crisis may have happened eventually anyway, but the Russian and LTCM crises provided the tipping point and added fuel to break the Brazilian real.

In a global economy, there is nothing very profound about the concepts of contagion and common shocks. They are a natural result of globalized financial and trade markets coupled with human market behavior and risk aversion. Investors in countries that share certain characteristics would be expected to react to outside events in a similar way. As they react, economic variables then change in similar ways. As can be seen from figure 6.1, however, they do not all react the same and some are affected more than others. Similarly, during the 1999 Brazil crisis, many other global and regional bond markets and currencies became more volatile as a result of the same set of events. It was Brazil's economy that went into full crisis mode.

Whether events set off a crisis or not depends on a complicated mix of factors, including real and perceived risk. The riskier a country is in "objective" terms, the greater the chance of a crisis. Objective measures of risk include leverage, degree of foreign exchange exposure, level of reserves, recent increases in exchange rates, central bank mandates and credibility, dependence on particular export markets, and government policy actions and intents, among others.

Beyond objective risks, perceived risk can also increase the chance of a crisis, even in a country without major red flags. Such a country can still be hurt by an outside shock, especially if investors believe it is vulnerable. Just the act of investors selling off assets and currencies can set off a series of events that can edge a previously seemingly stable country toward crisis. This is the tricky and interesting part. In the examples above, did Brazil, Eastern Europe, and all those emerging markets actually get riskier following some discrete event, or did investor sentiment and subsequent actions change in a way that ensured that they became riskier?[33]

It is hard to radically change the fundamentals of an economy overnight. Changing the way those fundamentals are perceived, however, seems to happen readily. The investor reactions that drive common shocks and contagion are perhaps not as much driven by events as they are by a longer-term probable mispricing of risk in the affected economies in the first place. The precipitating event perhaps merely revealed risk that was already in plain view, causing investors to reprice it quickly. A global event or crisis in one country should not suddenly reveal risks in other markets to investors. But that is what seems to happen as frequently as cases of slow, systematic repricing of risk. In sum, investors seem willing to tolerate risk as long as everyone else is. Once the herd shows signs of losing tolerance, risk multiplies as it heads for the exit.

Whether and how countries react to shocks varies considerably. Money is made and/or investment risk controlled by those who correctly assess which countries really do have the (objective perhaps) problems that investors fear, and which ones are likely to rebound quickly once the shock and panic are over.

Common shocks and contagion can be set off by multiple events. How they actually unfold depends on what the precipitating event is, what actually happens when there is a crisis in a country, the state of the economy in the country, where the crisis originates, and what sorts of connections exist between countries. Financial markets are global. Nearly anything that causes investors and creditors to rapidly change direction can result in a common shock or contagion effect.

Here is a simple framework for thinking about contagion and common shocks that illustrates the most common ways that they work.

Country 1, the country of Stabilia: investor in and trade partner to country 2.

Country 2, the country of Crisisia: this country is less stable and falls into an economic crisis, leading to some combination of bond/payment defaults, decreased stock market value, and/or drop in exchange rate.

Country 3, the country of Reservia: a country that maintains one of the global reserve currencies. Companies and banks in both Stabilia and Crisisia have loans in this currency.

Below are some ways shocks and contagion can happen between different countries.

- Investment connection 1. Stabilia's companies and banks have made substantial investments in Crisisia. Outside investors in Stabilia have become concerned about the effect of Crisisia's economic crisis on Stabilia's banks and companies. As investors pull their lines of credit and portfolio investments from Stabilia, markets and currencies drop, contributing to a crisis there. The Asian financial crisis of 1997 was as much driven by a withdrawal of credit lines by foreign banks as from any tradable instruments.
- Investment connection 2. Stabilia and Crisisia share many of the same investors, who are suddenly starting to notice certain unsettling similarities between the two countries. Crisisia just defaulted on its debt, but the debt-to-GDP ratio in Stabilia is looking very similar. Crisisia's exports have dropped, but Stabilia has a similar export mix. Maybe risk conditions are similar and investors are now looking more closely, or maybe they are just perceived as similar. Both can have the same result. The real and perceived existence of bad debt was an important factor in the Asian financial crisis when credit lines dried up and defaults and currency devaluations swept across the region.[34] The withdrawals of lines of credit and from bond markets across four countries in Southern Europe and Ireland after the 2008 great recession may be attributable to the same kind of investor herd behavior—fleeing any markets that might seem to carry similar risks.
- Investment connection 3, portfolio rebalancing. If investors in Crisisia start to take a loss, the overall real or perceived risk of their portfolio increases. To decrease that risk, the portfolio manager may withdraw from all emerging market countries that fit the same broad risk profile. Stabilia may be one of those countries. This can be both a common shock and contagion effect. After the Russian default of 1998 and the "taper tantrum" of 2013, investors pulled back from a wide range of emerging markets.[35] Similarly, sovereign spreads increased simultaneously across the main Asian markets in the 1990s once trouble began, indicating that investors were concerned about higher risk in a broad swath of similar countries.[36]
- Investment connection 4, liquidity. As similar countries, some funds and companies invested in both Crisisia and Stabilia. Facing severe losses in Crisisia, highly leveraged investors were forced to sell their Stabilia shares to meet cash requirements in Crisisia. Unfortunately, markets in Stabilia suffered as a result, leading to more sales and losses. During the 2008 crisis, diverse asset markets plummeted across the globe as investors sold assets to raise cash. Similarly, Asian investors sold Russian securities in 1998 to raise capital to meet obligations in

their own crisis-ridden countries, leading to drops and ultimately a crisis in Russian markets later that year.[37]

- Trade connection 1. Companies in Stabilia that depend on selling products to Crisisia suffer a sharp decline in exports when crisis hits Crisisia. Stabilia's balance of payments becomes destabilized. To make matters worse, investors in Stabilia may suddenly get concerned about their balance of payments and, anticipating a devaluation, pull investments from Stabilia.[38]
- Trade connection 2. Price decreases in Stabilia's key exports, whether following a crisis elsewhere or not, can destabilize any economies that also depend on a similar export mix. The drop in commodity and especially energy market prices from 2014 to 2016 led to balance of payments crises in major exporting countries such as Brazil, Russia, and Saudi Arabia. Similarly, the devaluation of the Taiwanese dollar in 1997 led to a drop in export earnings and contributed to a crisis in Korea, whose companies exported many of the same products as those exported by Taiwan.[39]
- Banking connection. Banks in Reservia have lines of credit extended to banks in both Stabilia and Crisisia. When the lines to Crisisia start to underperform and payments are missed, the Reservia banks withdraw credit from Stabilia as well, both to increase liquidity and lower exposure to emerging markets. This is particularly problematic when lines of credit are short term and need to be renewed mid-crisis.[40]
- Interest rate movements. Investors are constantly adjusting portfolios to gain returns and avoid risk on interest-bearing investments. If Reservia increases its interest rates, investors may seek returns in a lower-risk reserve currency economy. Drops in emerging market assets and currency markets may follow, as occurred during the so-called taper tantrum of 2013–2014.
- Financial market connections. Financial markets can be interlinked simply by investor behavior. As many emerging markets are fairly illiquid even relatively small flows can affect a country's currency value. An IMF researcher has speculated that short positions taken out on emerging market currencies as a hedge against their Russian positions in 1998 may have led to downward pressure on those other currencies.[41]

It should be evident from the discussion that contagion and/or common shocks have psychological as much as technical roots. Note use of the words "perceived" and "concerned" in the examples above. We don't really have better terms than those. Complex mathematical models may show clear cause and effect in contagion. In reality, the problem is often as much perceptual and behavioral. When people believe that contagion or shocks are likely, they become more likely. If the situation really is dire, so much the better and all the more reason for an investor to react. If it is not, perception can suffice send investors running for the door.

Global hot money investors are nervous people. When they think things might go bad, they might just pull their money out. Those actions ensure that things actually do go bad, which means that next time they may get out even faster and in greater numbers. The real contagion problem may not be from one country to another, as is often assumed, but from the psychological effect that carries over from one bubble and crisis cycle to another. This hypothesis might be a starting point for some useful research.

With contagion, it is hard to tell when an actual problem will develop. Sometimes it happens, and sometimes it doesn't.[42] And sometimes it happens a little. This is one of those instances where it is important to analyze the particular conditions, stocks, flows, and vulnerabilities in each potential case. It may not happen if a shock hits a country that is truly unique to that country. That the Russian slowdown after sanctions were imposed in 2014 did not spread further indicates that there are in fact real transmission mechanisms beyond emerging markets jitteriness. Policy reactions also matter. For example, if a country like Stabilia has strong foreign reserves and a stable macro economy without a lot of debt, the government may be in a position to step in, stem the panic, keep the currency stable, and minimize outflows.

The section on payments and exchange rates concludes by emphasizing again the current global financial system's volatility and complexity. A massive quantity of money is out there chasing returns all over the world, driving booms and busts along the way. Since the middle of the 2000s, economists have been concerned about a **global savings glut**, and that the global economy may have reached a stage when there is an excess of money chasing too few investments.[43] What is "excess" and "too few" is the subject of much debate and nearly impossible to address definitively. However, refer again to David Smick's "dangerous ocean of money" that is free to move from one country to another, buoying markets in one and decimating the other, then moving on to reverse that process when the time comes. Everyone loves the money on the way in and hates it on the way out, and it almost always seems to head out at some point. Long periods of low interest rates leave investors even more desperate for returns, and even more nervous about losing money since it takes that much longer to make it back. Whatever the case, the large, shifting pools of money are here to stay. The task at hand is to understand and learn to better manage the pools and the risks and rewards they bring.

NOTES

1. This explanation should be taken as a stylized and practical summary for how the balance of payments is recorded. In reality, there are nuances that can alter some of the conclusions made here. For those interested in the nuances, see the official manual from the IMF (2013).
2. The previously cited IMF Balance of Payments Manual is the standard reference for those interested in the details of balance of payments compilation.
3. The ability of reserve currency economies, and especially the United States, to offset trade deficits with other countries' purchases of assets has been called the "exorbitant privilege" of having a reserve currency. See Barry Eichengreen's (2011) book of the same name, or this McKinsey report by Dobbs et al. (2009) for a discussion of the pros and also the cons of being a reserve currency country.
4. This strategy assumes a certain cyclicality and reversion to a mean price level in the commodity in question. Structural changes to commodities industries, such as the emergence of fracking in the petroleum industry, can throw off strategies to use reserves to finance imports in the short term and force a longer-term change in import consumption levels.

5. Data from OECD, IMF, and the World Bank.

6. The IMF maintains the most detailed data available to the public, with the OECD and World Bank providing more accessible summaries. The Institute for International Finance, a trade group for financial institutions, maintains a separate database using mainly IMF data that is accessible only to its members.

7. See, for example, Moritz and Taylor (2009), who indicate that crises are presaged by the accumulation of credit.

8. The Marshall-Lerner condition sets forth the elasticity conditions under which a change in exchange rate will lead to a change in value of trade, rather than just volume.

9. Commodity trade tends to be priced in reserve currencies, mainly the US dollar, so has its own dynamic. Overall demand can be quite elastic or inelastic, depending on the commodity and available substitutes. The author wrote a paper (Vonnegut 2000) concluding that investors do not rapidly make decisions based on the expected net present value of their decision, but take switching and other option costs into account. As a result, decisions are "sticky."

10. See the World Bank study by Swarnali et al. (2015), which credits supply chains for the decreasing responsiveness of exports to exchange rates. See also Ruta and Saito (2013) in an IMF article outlining the movement to supply chain–based trade.

11. According to the World Economic Forum, Greece came in at number 81 in its 2016 global competitiveness rankings, right between Tajikistan and Armenia.

12. Despite its non-serious origins, the Big Mac index is well cited and has been the subject of a number of dissertations and journal articles.

13. There are exceptions. Big shifts in money supply usually stem from unorthodox monetary policy (e.g., "printing" money and injecting it into the economy).

14. See this report by Collyns and Mohammed (2014) of the Institute of International Finance for an analysis of trends in exchange rate regimes.

15. During the Asian financial crisis, speculators did unsuccessfully attack Hong Kong's currency board.

16. It is not worth repeating the story here, since it is told much better by Mallaby (2010).

17. See Oskooee and Hajilee 2013.

18. Bank for International Settlements 2015.

19. See for example an article by Ghosh et al. showing the link between foreign debt accumulation, financial vulnerabilities, and crisis.

20. The exposition here is extremely general and is simplified for the purposes of describing the problem of exchange risk. In the real world, cross-currency lending is a varied, complex, and not always well-understood phenomenon. See the Bank for International Settlements (2015) for an overview of some of the issues and complexities involved in more accurately categorizing cross currency lending. As much, for example USD, lending does not originate in the United States, tracking flows can be rather difficult.

21. See the IMF World Economic Outlook, April 2016, chapter 2. Though as the report notes, some other risks may have increased. As capital markets become more integrated, there is evidence that domestic investors are accentuating net outflows by exiting their home markets alongside international capital flows.

22. For more on this topic, see the literature around what is referred to as the "carry trade" in currencies.

23. Milne 2005.

24. As with most statements in economics, there are caveats. Greek companies with euro revenues and drachma expenses could benefit greatly.

25. Gelos et al. (2011) show that a history of default is not a major barrier to tapping credit markets again, at least in the near future. However, their research shows that perception of the quality of domestic institutions does matter, an area that Greece is fairly weak on.

26. See the World Bank working paper "The Anatomy of a Multiple Crisis" by Perry and Servén (2003).

27. See the special report on the world economy in *The Economist* (2015h), which outlined a number of potential perils and that the size of the US economy has shrunk relative to the size of the overall global USD market. See also Smick (2008) where he discusses the increasing size of global capital flows and the difficulties controlling them.

28. For an excellent summary, see Wildau and Mitchell.

29. For varying viewpoints see, for example, Moser (2003), an IMF working paper by Ozkan and Unsal (2012). For a skeptic's view, see also "Does International Financial Contagion Really Exist?" by Karolyi (2003).

30. The crash of LTCM is one of the great global case studies of hubris followed by a train wreck. The fund was established by some of the most successful traders at the time and two economic Nobel laureates. It is well documented in a number of places, including *When Genius Failed* by Roger Lowenstein (2000).

31. See Fry et al. 2002 for an analysis linking the fall of LTCM with the subsequent Brazilian crisis.

32. Baig and Goldfajn 2000.

33. Financial contagion has been the subject of much research in the academic economics literature, with models showing a wide range of conditions under which contagion can occur. See for example Kodres and Pritsker 2002.

34. Theoretical research by Italy Goldstein and Ady Pauzner (2004) shows that even when countries have fundamentals that are not related to each other, if they have the same groups of investors, contagion can occur. The fear of exit by the investors is enough to drive a self-fulfilling crisis. An IMF staff paper by Tressel (2010) notes that a crisis in one country may set off deleveraging across a wider range of economies.

35. For example, see Dungey et al. (2007).

36. Baig and Goldfajn 1998.

37. Sharma 2003.

38. As an example, decreased oil exports from Russia to Asia in 1998 following the Asian financial crises caused the Russian current account to swing from a large surplus into deficit, further helping destabilize the Russian economy and lead to the default of 1998.

39. See Blustein (2001) for a narrative account of the effects of contagion spreading across three continents in 1997 and 1998. See also Sharma (2003).

40. According to an OECD (2012) Policy Note, such a credit retraction occurred across Eastern Europe after the onset of the great recession. It was also prevalent during the Asian financial crisis. See Van Rijckeghem and Weder (2001) for an analysis of lending-driven contagion. For a case related to the Italian interbank market, see Mistrulli (2011).

41. Moser 2003.

42. For example, the Argentinian crisis of 2001 did not lead to increased volatility in related markets. See Eichengreen (2002).

43. Former Fed Chairman Ben Bernanke (2005) did not invent the term, but is attributed with bringing it into the mainstream in a 2005 speech.

7

Investor Decisions, Moving Economies

Spread across the surface of the planet are millions of people making investment decisions every day, some investing their own money and many others the money of the institutions they work for. They include investment officers at pension funds, CFOs at manufacturing companies, middle-class Europeans buying vacation homes in Costa Rica, future retirees buying shares through their individual retirement accounts, hedge fund managers speculating on bond prices in Malaysia, commercial banks' lending money to branches in other countries, and many others. They gather information from the market, respond to signals, follow their incentives, and send billions of dollars around the world.

Most individual investor decisions are not significant enough to matter much on their own. Markets are usually too large and liquid for single institutions to move them, unless people are deliberately trying to corner or manipulate them.[1] At the same time, though focused on their own portfolios, investors across multiple companies and markets are reading many of the same signals. As those signals change or are perceived to be changing, investors can respond in the same way especially as actions of other investors are reported on. The resulting "herd" activity can multiply into the sorts of booms and busts regularly experienced across countries, regions, and markets.

The money sent around the world by all these individuals and institutions forms the second major core of the global economy, after trade in goods and services discussed in chapter 5. In terms of international payments and accounting, their activity appears mainly in the right-hand side of table 6.1, and more specifically account 2B. This chapter expands on the investment categories that make up the capital and financial accounts, and some of the ways and reasons those investments are made.

The first main subcategory of flow that appears in account 2B is foreign direct investment (FDI). An investment flow is classified as FDI when an investor actually owns (i.e., has direct title to) and controls their investment in a country that is not their own. An FDI is normally held over the medium or long term, partially by intent and partially because most of these kinds of investments are not easy to quickly sell.[2]

Common examples of FDI are when a company in one country opens a manufacturing plant or a branch of their service network, like a bank, in another country. Outright purchase of all or a controlling interest in a company, whether by a company in the same or a related industry or an investor looking for a financial return, is also counted as FDI. Even when a minority, noncontrolling interest is taken in a private transaction (i.e., not on a public exchange), the purchase would be classified as FDI. On an individual level, buying a home or property in another country is classified as FDI in national accounts.

FDI normally involves a fairly long-term investor commitment. The investment may not be expected to start to pay off any time soon, and may be part of the investor's longer-term global strategy. The FDI investor is usually planning to stick it out in the country for the longer term, making money back over a period of years. As the OECD notes, "FDI provides a means for creating direct, stable and long-lasting links between economies."[3] If things go badly, investors usually stay and try to work things out. Like hot money investors, they may be concerned about changes in policy in a country, or in exchange and interest rates. But those concerns do not usually cause them to try to take their money and leave. For one, usually they can't, because their investments are not liquid. Selling factories, real estate, and service networks takes time. Trying to do so quickly can lead to losses.

Governments generally like FDI. It is money that comes in to stay, creates jobs, has been shown to bring additional know-how and technology to a country,[4] and is easier to control by host-country governments than many other forms of investment. FDI can be harder to attract to a country than more liquid portfolio investments, because it usually comes in in large chunks and investors need to trust that they will be treated fairly.

As figure 7.1 indicates, emerging markets have been receiving an increasing share of global FDI. These inflows can help stabilize currencies when shorter-term investment flows are more volatile, as long as FDI investors don't get spooked at the same time. Though longer-term trends show steady increases, 2015 saw some slowing in emerging markets at the same time as portfolio flows were on the way out.

Figure 7.2 shows which countries are getting the bulk of FDI. The United States leads, though this does not take into account that much FDI enters China through Hong Kong and Singapore and so should be counted as Chinese. On the other hand, it also does not take into account that investment into the United States also enters through the British Virgin Islands, a tax haven.

Like FDI, portfolio investment also falls into balance of payments cell 2B in table 6.1. Unlike FDI, portfolio investment targets traded securities in another country, like stocks, public and private bonds of all types, currencies, derivative instruments, and/or futures linked to a country. Short-term credit lines extended across borders between companies and banks also fall into this category, even if such credits are not

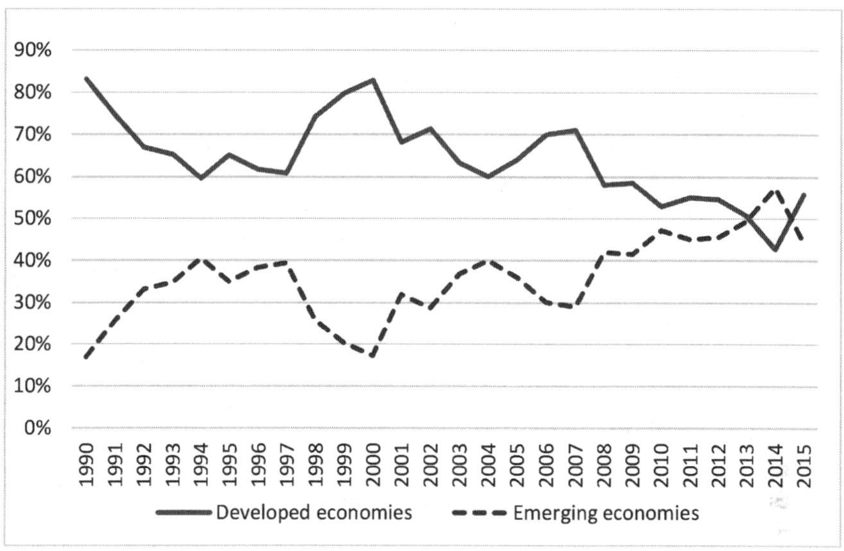

Figure 7.1. FDI Inflows, Percentage of Total

Source: UNCTAD. The UN sometimes uses the term "developing countries," though in this case the data is dominated by the main emerging markets.

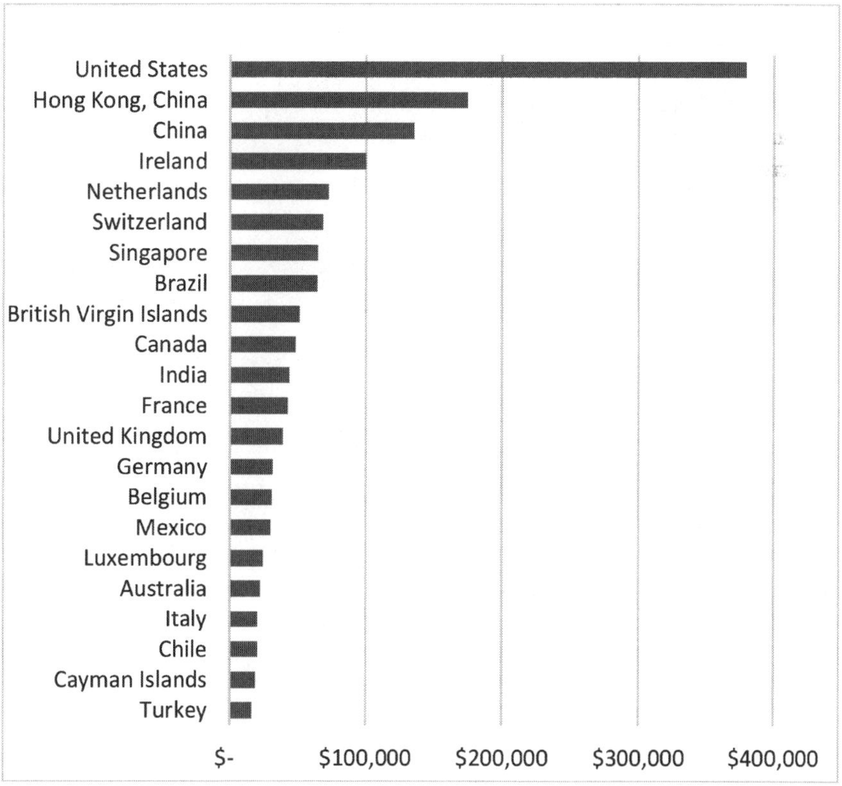

Figure 7.2. FDI by Destination, Millions of USD

Source: UNCTAD. The UN sometimes uses the term "developing countries," though in this case the data is dominated by the main emerging markets.

technically traded. Portfolio investments are characterized by some level of liquidity and being able to be bought and sold relatively easily under normal market conditions. Frequently, there is some sort of public exchange that enables the trades. The portfolio investment that appears in account 2B is not only capital that originates outside the country. Much of this can be domestic capital that is globally mobile and mixes freely with the international capital on its way in and out of a country. Increases in emerging markets wealth make capital of domestic origin increasingly important in global capital flows.

As noted, these short-term investments are also referred to as **hot money**, since the investment capital can rapidly come into and then flee a country. Much of the money that left emerging markets and led to a drop in exchange rates after the Fed announced it would "taper" quantitative easing in 2013 and 2014 was portfolio investment, or hot money.[5] When portfolio investments are made, the investors' home-country currency is normally exchanged for the currency where the investment is located. This creates the potential for foreign exchange risk if the investee country's currency drops. Avoiding that risk is one of the reasons hot money is so hot. No investor wants to be the last one out when things go bad. The 3 percent premium they were getting on the emerging markets bond goes away pretty quickly when the currency drops 10 percent as coinvestors flee the country before they do.

There is a lot of debate about hot money. Countries love it on the way in and hate it on the way out. On the way in, government deficits get financed, interest rates can drop, currencies can strengthen, and investment floods into fancy new housing developments and commercial buildings. Stock markets rise, making people feel rich, and exchange rates go up, which can moderate inflation, make imports look cheap, and allow people to travel easily abroad.

When hot money is coming in, people start to forget it's hot. They start to believe that the money is there to stay and "this time is different." These beliefs help these cycles repeat themselves. Stories circulate about how the money is coming in because the economy is in great shape and on a "sustainable" (a favorite word) growth path, government policies are sound, and a country "deserves it," so no need to worry about risk. Investors love our country. On the way out, all that sentiment goes into reverse, and often the very same governments that took credit for the boom get blamed for the bust.[6]

The post-2008 crisis cycle is a case in point. Between 2009 and 2013, hot money invested in emerging markets doubled to over US $9 trillion as investors fled low interest rates in the developed market (reserve currency) economies. The financial press reported how well the emerging markets were doing and how they had dodged the recession bullet. They were touted as an essential part of any investor's portfolio. Then it all went into reverse starting in 2013, as investors became concerned that the inflows had inflated asset values and currencies, and the main reserve currency, the USD, started to look comparatively more attractive. Tipped by the Fed's "tapering" announcement, capital of both international and domestic origin went "hot" and fled the countries in which it was invested.[7]

If common shocks and contagion had a best friend, it would be portfolio investment, handled by nervous investors who love risk when things are going well and hate risk when they are not. There are no friends or favors in portfolio investment, just nerves, bonuses for making money, and job losses for underperforming your peers (i.e., failing to get into rising markets early enough, or getting out of falling markets too late). Hot money managers are investing to make money and manage risk in the short term. Everyone knows that in theory, but policy makers can forget it in practice, believing that they are somehow immune to the vagaries of the hot money mentality. Hot money movement has been at the center of nearly every financial crisis in recent decades: Mexico in 1994, multiple Asian countries starting in 1997, Russia in 1999, Turkey in 2001, the great recession of 2008, emerging markets generally in 2013–2015, and so on. That said, hot money was also what fueled much of the economic booms that presaged those crises. That point gets less attention, but is essential to understanding why it can be attractive.

Some countries have tried to limit the negative effects of fleeing hot money by imposing **capital controls**. These are restrictions on short-term money flows, usually affecting money on the way out of a country. Policy makers in the wealthy developed market economies and the main international financial institutions such as the World Bank and IMF have historically opposed controls on global capital movement. Since the 1970s, these institutions have largely successfully convinced emerging market countries (and others) to loosen or eliminate restrictions on the free movement of capital in and out of their countries. Many bilateral and multilateral free trade agreements also contain provisions for opening up, especially, emerging markets to freer movements of capital.

Critics claim that pressure to open capital markets has come from free market ideologues and developed countries' financial industry lobbyists seeking new speculative markets. There may be some truth to this, but economists from across the political spectrum would make other points in favor of freer capital markets. Emerging markets are often short of funds and need lines of credit and investment to fuel growth. The old saying is: if it can't get out, it won't come in. The fear is that emerging markets will not attract the capital they need if investors are not able to get it out when they so desire.

Overall, it is fair to say that the proponents of freer capital controls have had their way for most of the past few decades with a steady opening of global markets to all types of flows. At the same time, the detrimental effects of hot money shocks are increasingly on display and under critique as of the mid-2010s. More economists have looked at the steep booms and busts of the previous decades and concluded that unfettered capital markets can cause undue harm, and that hot money should be subject to greater control. The IMF has revised some of its current positions and released a set of guidelines on capital controls' benefits and guidelines for use.[8]

As always, even those who may agree on the benefits of capital controls in principle are divided on how to go about actually imposing them. Capital controls can take different forms with different outcomes. Common forms are differential tax rates on money that is taken out of investments held for only a short time, caps on how much local currency can be transferred into hard "reserve" currencies, limits on the sums that can be taken out of a particular country at one time, various types of waiting periods for withdrawal, or limits on foreign ownership of assets. Each type of capital control has its own possible benefits and risks under each circumstance in which it is applied. One risk is that portfolio investment flows can be hard to separate from all the other types of flows in and out that are needed to keep a country's economy humming along. More notoriously, they can be disguised as other types of flows by motivated money managers, limiting their impact.

Experience with controls is varied, with much more experience and data needed. As an early case, during the 1998 Asian financial crisis, the Malaysian government limited outflows of foreign capital for a short period, becoming the subject of fierce criticism. However, the limits most likely helped to avert some of the worst of the shocks suffered by neighboring countries.[9] More recently, following the 2008 financial crisis Cyprus and Iceland both implemented stringent capital controls to keep money from fleeing their banks and decimating their currencies. As of mid-2017 Iceland had finally removed the last of its controls and some in Cyprus remained in place. Critics would have grounds to claim that the controls deterred investment into these economies, though as is often the case in economics, the counterfactuals are not clear. What would have happened otherwise remains unknown. Controls seem to work best when, as *The Economist* summarized it, "as a means to buy time for broad reforms . . . not [as] an enduring solution on their own."[10] The debate is far from over, but is moving away from extreme openness and toward acceptance of additional controls on international capital flows.

The last main driver of capital flows on the capital and financial account is remittances, which is the money that workers living abroad send back to their home countries. Often this goes back to support family members or to make investments that will support the worker in the future. Some countries are major net exporters of remittance payments while others are importers. For some nations like Mexico and India, remittances represent critical cash inflows that help to "balance" the balance of payments. Remittances allow imports and investment to be higher than they otherwise would be, and their disappearance would leave a hole in the balance of payments.[11]

Though remittances appear in the balance of payments accounts, they can be hard to accurately categorize. For example, wages sent home appear in the current account as trade in services, but investments sent home appear in the capital account. If you don't want to go down a statistical rat hole, just leave it that both inflows can help balance outflows elsewhere. As wealth shifts and opportunities for work appear and disappear, labor deficits and surpluses across countries come and go. Consequently, remittance payments and where they come from can vary, with rapid short-term changes bearing on the payments balances of the sending and receiving economies.[12]

Total global remittances in 2012 were an estimated $529 billion. Table 7.1 shows the main sources and recipients of remittances.[13]

Table 7.1.

Sources of Remittances		*Recipients of Remittances*	
United States	123,273	India	69,350
Saudi Arabia	27,645	China	60,246
Canada	23,909	Philippines	24,453
United Kingdom	23,601	Mexico	23,219
Germany	21,031	Nigeria	20,568
United Arab Emirates	20,347	Egypt, Arab Rep.	20,515
France	19,283	France	19,451
Spain	18,595	Bangladesh	14,060

The four categories of global money movement (FDI, portfolio investment, trade, and remittances) are approximate, and may not be mutually exclusive or accurately reported in balance of payments accounts. They are a decent starting point, though, for looking at sources and stability of flows in different markets.

SECURITIES AND TRADING METHODS

All other things being equal (which they often are not), direct equity investments, trade transactions, and remittances are normally conducted directly through the movement of money between bank accounts. When someone wants to buy something in another country, they deposit money in the account of the seller. It works the same regardless of what is being purchased (i.e., real estate, a factory, a good or service, or labor in the case of remittances). It's pretty much like a transaction at home, except the money flows across borders. A purchase price is negotiated between a buyer and a seller, and money changes hands.

Portfolio or hot money investment typically works a bit differently. Most of the time investors are buying and selling securities instruments or currencies on an open market or some sort of exchange with lots of buyers and seller. Most of the rest of the time, they are extending lines of credit. Exchanges work differently than direct buyer-to-seller transactions, though money does ultimately flow back and forth between bank accounts. On exchanges, investors expect to be able to see historical prices and a "revealed" price (particular price for a particular security that is known at a particular time).

Portfolio investors also expect **liquidity**, which is another way of saying they want the ability to get in and out of a particular investment at will without experiencing a big deviation from the current market price. Under "normal" or noncrisis conditions when the number of buyers and sellers is roughly matched, in a liquid market even large quantities of securities can be traded at or near the market price. A large number of well-balanced buyers and sellers in a market is what creates the liquidity. When the balance of buyers to sellers goes off and/or the number of participants drops, it is said that liquidity is "thin" or has "dried up." Liquidity can characterize an entire market, like the stock exchange of Thailand, or a single or group of securities, like shares in the Turkish cement producer Aslan on the Borsa Istanbul.

Markets will turn illiquid when everyone is quickly trying to either get in or out, usually out. Illiquidity risk is a major reason portfolio investors try to get in or out before the proverbial stampede begins. If they wait, they will need to trade in a low-liquidity situation and pricing will suffer and/or the trades will not happen. Liquidity is relative. Even frequently traded securities on large exchanges can become illiquid in the face of big enough purchases or sales. In mid-2014, following large money flows in and out of the same markets at the same time, liquidity became a problem even in major developed market economies.[14] Even the notoriously liquid interbank markets became illiquid at the height of the 2008 financial crisis. Some assert that markets may be becoming less liquid overall as investment banks are required to pull back from their trading and market-making activities by post-2008 financial regulations.[15]

Unlike portfolio investors, foreign direct investors do not expect liquidity. There may only be a select few eligible buyers or sellers, so anyone who wants to quickly exit a foreign direct investment may have trouble finding a buyer and be headed for a big "haircut" (i.e., a loss). That is why FDI investors generally operate with a longer-term investment time horizon.

Emerging market exchanges are notorious for having liquidity that dries up just when it is needed most. Sometimes in thin markets that are in the midst of a bubble, valuations can reach extreme highs, but anyone trying to sell any quantity of stock will end up just crashing the market instead of cashing out. In the Montenegrin stock market in the mid-to-late 2000s, investors enjoyed returns of hundreds of a percent over short periods of time, but faced liquidity barriers to exiting the market. Selling even moderately sized positions could cause the stock price to drop precipitously.[16]

In a securities (or any) market, you have some people wanting to sell and some wanting to buy. The sellers are offering what is called the "ask" price and the buyers are offering the "bid" price. The ask price is obviously higher than the bid price, or the trade would have happened already. The difference between the bid and the ask prices is the "spread." In illiquid markets without many buyers and sellers, the spread can be sizable, as in multiple percentage points of the value of the asset. You can lose money just on a spread, even if the value of the asset increases nominally. Sometimes if you want to sell, you can only sell a little at the bid price, and then need to sell the rest at a lower price.

Spreads can move fast and almost always move in a direction that costs the trader money. The lower the liquidity in the market, usually the worse the spread. Buyers will try to force the price down, and sellers will try to force it up. Traders have strategies to try to keep the spread from moving against them, like distributing their orders over time or sending mixed signals into the market like staged buy and sell offers (illegal in many markets, by the way). Usually, liquidity dries up and spreads increase just when an investor needs to get in or out. That is the nature of the game, and it is why hot money investors have the odd combination of a herd mentality *and* no friends.

Hot money managers and traders can make side investments (or bets) to decrease their risk. These are called **hedges**. In the discussion on covered interest spreads, the hedge was the side investment that protected the investor against drops in the exchange rate. If bond values went down, the value of the hedge was expected to go up, providing some protection. Since hedges require the purchase of other securities, they are not free. They need to be well designed to provide protection without eating too much into returns on the main investment.

While it is almost always possible to find some sort of hedge, it is not always possible to find a cost-effective one. As an aside, the concept of a hedge is not really related to what are called hedge funds. The common vernacular is simply historical, and owes to the particular strategy of the first fund in that group that was later to be dubbed "hedge funds."

Table 7.2 contains a short overview of the main securities traded globally.

Table 7.2.

Security/Instrument	*Description*
Stocks	Share of ownership in a company, may be traded on a public exchange or privately held (the latter then becomes a direct investment, not a portfolio investment). Different classes of shares have different characteristics. Most traded shares are called "common" shares, though "preferred" shares that are more like a stock-bond hybrid are also traded.
Government bonds/bills	Bonds issued by national or regional governments, usually to cover spending deficits. Normally, these have some sort of at least implied guarantee of payment by the country, or sovereign, as they are known. Sovereign bonds are frequently traded on secondary markets once they are issued, though liquidity in more obscure national or regional bond issues may be low and only traded through specialized traders usually at investment banks and who "make a market" in the security.
Corporate bonds	Bonds issued by companies to finance expansion or ongoing operations. May vary a lot in quality/risk/return. These may or may not be traded on secondary markets, and may or may not be liquid.
Lines of credit	Money is widely lent across borders on both a short- and long-term basis, often by banks or institutional "real money" investors to banks. When lent on a shorter-term basis, these loans take on the characteristics of hot money.
Commodities	A basic item used in production, such as metals (e.g., gold, copper aluminum), main food staples (e.g., wheat, corn, beef), or energy sources (gas, oil, coal). These are usually traded locally and internationally on both spot (buy the product now) or futures (buy the obligation to buy or sell the product later) markets.
Currency	Currencies issued by national governments are usually traded locally and often internationally.

Most of these instruments can be invested in through multiple methods, as outlined below.

Method 1: Going Long and Short

You can go "long" and "short" on all types of different securities, but the most typical ones are common stocks and bonds. Making a **long trade** is simple. You buy something and hold it, hoping the value will go up. If it does, you make money upon selling (as long as you can sell). That second part is important because as noted, markets with high reported returns may not be liquid. When there is panic, liquidity can dry up fast and it can be "haircut" time!

Short trades are more complicated. When you go *long*, you are waiting for the value of the asset to go up. When you go *short*, you are betting that the price of the investment will go down. Instead of buying the asset, you are *selling* it. Only in finance and con schemes can you sell something you don't actually own. With short selling, you sell the asset, and then if/when the price goes down, you buy it back to *cover* your position and get to keep the difference in price. That puts you back to a zero-ownership position, just like when you buy (go long) and then sell the security. With shorting, if the asset goes up in value, you lose. To go short, normally you need to find someone to lend you the asset. Exchanges that allow shorts (not all do), will help arrange that for you, or you enter into private-party contract (which would then be a type of derivative; more on that later).

A nice thing about shorting is it doubles the amount of gambling you can do: you can make bets on both rising and falling prices. Sometimes it can be easier to identify losers than winners, so there is a bigger pool of investments to choose from than just going long all the time.

The bad thing about shorts is that loss is potentially unlimited. If the stock goes to zero on the long bet, the maximum loss is the investment amount. On a short where the stock keeps climbing, the investor will need to cover it no matter how high it goes. Most exchanges have rules about how much trouble an investor (gambler) can get into with shorts and will force a buyback of the security before things get too out of control.

Another disadvantage of short positions is you cannot hold them indefinitely. When this author started shorting housing stocks in 2005, he had to close out his positions even if eventually he would have been right and made money. To make money on short positions, the investor(s) needs to accurately predict the price direction, and equally important, at least the rough timing of the drop in value. As a final note about shorts, since markets have generally trended up over time, making investments in short positions runs against the countervailing trend. Most investors in shorts are not looking for long-term holds, in any case.

Method 2: Options

Options are just what they sound like. When you buy an option you are buying the option to buy (this is called a call) or sell (this is called a put) a security at some point in the future. The point in the future is any time before the expiration date of the option. The option becomes worthless when it expires. Options for a wide range of mainly stocks, bonds, and indices are traded on major exchanges.

Each option has several characteristics. First is the premium. That is what you pay for the option, or the right to buy or sell the security in the future. For stocks, the premium is usually for an option on one hundred shares of a stock. The premium differs across different options, and often the bid-ask spread is significant, since options markets are usually not very liquid. Generally, you pay more for a premium that is: for an expiration date that is further out; for a stock that many people think is going the same direction you do; and for a stock that has a price that is close to the strike price of the option. The strike price is the price that the stock needs to reach for you to profitably "exercise" your option. Exercising your option is when you actually use the option to buy or sell something. You need to exercise or sell your option before the expiration date, or it becomes worthless. If you don't hit your strike price, you lose some or all of your premium, depending on whether you were able to unload it onto a greater fool (more later; big concept in investment) before the expiration date or not. But thanks for playing.

That is a lot to fit in one paragraph, so an example may help clarify the concept. Table 7.3 gives an example of a put on Apple stock when the stock itself was at $150 per share. Remember, with a put you are betting that the price of the stock will drop. When you buy the "put," you are buying the option to sell the stock at a specified price (sell it short) in the hope that the stock price will fall lower.

The options in this case expire seven months from the time of this quote. The strike price is on the left. That is what the stock needs to drop to for the option to be "in the money" and therefore possible/advantageous to exercise. So if you buy at a 110 strike price, you have bought the right to *sell* 100 shares of AAPL at 110 any time in the next 7 months. If it goes to $100/share, you make $10 a share. But not really. Because it costs you $1.88 a share or $188 to buy the option, really you make $8.12 a share, minus the trading fees. The other numbers show the change, the bid-ask spreads, and the "open interest" or options out there.[17] See that the bid-ask spread on your option is .11. That is quite a lot even though Apple is a widely traded stock. You need to keep the spread in mind when estimating profits from your trade.

People buy options mainly because they allow investors to gain greater control over a lot of shares of stock for not much money. In the example above, for $188, you get the right to sell short $15,000 in AAPL stock (100 shares times $150 at the

Table 7.3.

Strike	*Option*	*Bid*	*Ask*	*Last*	*Change*	*Open*	*Volume*
105	105.5 Put	1.30	1.37	1.34	0.00	15	2,814
110	110.0 Put	1.88	1.99	1.99	0.00	1	8,008
115	115.0 Put	2.69	2.75	2.74	0.00	16	2,746
120	120.0 Put	3.75	3.85	3.8	0.00	92	7,761
125	125.0 Put	5.15	5.30	5.3	0.00	19	4,767

Source: Section of AAPL Options Chain. Data from TD Ameritrade.

time of purchase). That is a lot of stock for not a lot of money. Options give you leverage if you want to speculate on the direction of a stock.

People also frequently buy options to lower the risk of other investments. As noted, this is called "hedging" and is common in the global economy. Here is an example. Say that a USD-based investor has a big position in a foreign government bond market, say Argentina, and they are (rightly, history would say) concerned about default risk. They may expect the stock market in Argentina to drop should there be a government default. This is probably correct, as certain events like those tend to be correlated, or they are trends that move together. Consequently, the investor may purchase a put option, or "hedge," on the Argentinian index. The premium they pay gives them a little bit of insurance (or a hedge) against being fully exposed to the Argentinian bond market. If the bond market tanks, they will make up some or all of the losses in gains from the put (minus the premium they paid to buy the put).

This is the main way covered interest spreads work. You may buy a put option on the currency or market to cover the exchange risk you have on a bond position. It might cost 10 percent (for example) of the value of your bond position, but it protects you from risk. Covered interest spreads work because of hedging, and options are one way to create that hedge.

Method 3: Futures

Futures are the right, and obligation in fact, to buy or sell actual commodities at a specified price at some point in the future. Those commodities are commonly currencies, agricultural products, or energy products, but can be any number of things. A lot of people mix futures up with options. If you enter a futures contract and hold the contract to maturity, you will own (and need to pay for) the actual items specified in the contract. If an option reaches its expiration date, it expires harmlessly (or relatively harmlessly since you may have lost money), as it was just an option.

For example, if you have a futures contract to buy one thousand feeder cattle and you hold that future to the expiration date, you will own one thousand physical cattle and need to figure out what to do with them, how to pay for them, house or transport them, and keep feeding them. It is possible to buy options on many futures contracts. In those cases, you are not required to execute the transaction because it is just an option. To trade futures, you need to open a specialized futures account and show that you have the financial capacity to perform on your contracts. In reality, it is not as hard as it probably should be to start trading futures. Transactions are usually highly leveraged, so trouble can come quickly.

A lot of futures contracts are held by commodity producers and end users, to help them stabilize their prices. A candy factory may buy sugar futures to lock in pricing and reduce risk. A sugar producer may do the same to lock in their sale price. Though futures markets were started to help producers and consumers of commodities stabilize prices, in the modern world many more contracts are held by speculators who are simply betting on prices going up or down. Speculators are said to benefit the futures markets by providing liquidity. However, there are also well-documented cases where their activities have caused increases in prices and volatility for end consumers.[18]

Method 4: Derivatives

Derivatives are the subject of much talk and controversy. Investor Warren Buffett has called them "financial instruments of mass destruction." They are powerful, mysterious, even creepy. The problem with generalizing about them is that there is more variation in this category than any other. Derivatives are by definition nothing more than a security that is "derived" from another security, or that is based on it. That is where the name comes from. Mystery solved, sort of. Derivatives are everywhere and cover nearly every type of investment imaginable. Some derivatives, like options, are traded on exchanges, but most just come into existence when two parties decide to make a contract. These are called over-the-counter, or OTC, derivatives.

Some of the most common types of derivatives and some reasons why people might purchase them are detailed below.

- Option: This was already described. An option is a type of derivative, since it is derived from some underlying stock, futures contract, currency, or bond. Long-term options that mature up to three years after issuing are called long-term equity anticipation securities, or LEAPS. Cute name; they leap forward. Finance does not have much that is cute.
- Forward: This is any contract where two parties agree to buy and sell a specific item at a specific price on a specified future date. When these are customized to the buyer and seller, they are forward contracts. When they are standardized and are traded on exchanges, they are just futures. Some people buy forwards to speculate on price movements, and some do it to lock in prices of commodities that they will need to buy or sell in the future.
- Swap: Swaps are the most confusing, probably because they have so many different potential permutations; if you don't know what else to call it, call it a swap. At their root they are nothing more than an agreement by two parties to trade cash flows in the future at some point and under a set of defined conditions. Here are two examples. A common type of swap is an interest rate swap where one party that holds a bond with a fixed rate of interest agrees to swap the interest stream with another party that holds a bond with a variable rate of interest. They may do this to speculate on interest rate changes, to hedge against them, or just because different types of investors prefer different types of cash flows under different conditions. Another type of swap encountered before is the famous credit default swap (CDS) of 2008 crash fame. In this case, if the underlying security defaults, the two parties "swap," with one party getting cash and the other getting the defaulted security.

- Warrant: A warrant is like an option, but it is not standardized and the warrant itself and the underlying securities are usually issued by a company. Like an option, it gives the holder the option to buy a particular security at a specific price and time. Unlike a standardized option, a warrant can have as many conditions written into the contract as the parties want. That is the great thing in general about OTC derivatives. For example, it may be written into a warrant that it can only be exercised if a share price hits a certain level, there is a certain amount of rainfall, or if there is a recall on Skittles. Spurious examples, but the point is that unlike standard options, anything goes. There can be both call and put warrants. They are commonly used to facilitate transactions, as so-called poison pills to make a takeover costly for a buyer, or to incentivize top management by linking pay to company performance.
- Structured notes: A common type of structured note is when a loan is taken out, and the interest rate is determined by something other than the prime or interbank rate at the time. For example, a company that makes bubble gum may want to take out a loan where the interest rate is tied to the price of sugar or dental visits. Anything is possible in the derivatives market. You just need people to agree on the contract.
- Exchange-traded funds, ETFs: A lot of people would argue about whether ETFs are derivatives or not. It does not matter; they need to be covered someplace, and they are "derived" from underlying securities. More on these below.

Two things about derivatives make regulators worry (everything makes financial columnists and politicos worry). The first is the amount that are outstanding. No one knows the total quantity for certain, since a lot of derivatives are based on private contracts that are not disclosed (i.e., OTC). Here are some data points. According to the Bank for International Settlements, as of December 2013 the total nominal value of OTC derivatives contracts outstanding was $710 trillion. That is about ten times global GDP. Total market value was $18 trillion, down from $27 trillion two years before.[19]

Nominal value includes the full face value of the underlying securities, regardless of whether it is even in play as part of the derivatives contact. Market value is a better indicator of what is actually at risk. Consider an interest rate swap on $100 million in government bonds. The nominal value includes the $100 million face value of the bonds. The market value would reflect the perhaps $3 million in interest payments that are the subject of the swap. There may be billions of dollars of securities underlying a swap contract nominally, but the actual amount that can be gained or lost over time is just a small fraction of that.

Both of these sum up to a lot of money. The problem is, it is hard to know if it matters whether outstanding derivatives contracts are one or one hundred times global GDP.

That gets to the second thing that concerns people about derivatives. No one understands the linkages between different derivatives contracts, and between them and financial institutions, including ones that are insured by the public, and the linkages between them and institutions that the public relies on, like pension funds. As mentioned, many if not most derivatives contracts are between private parties. On the one hand, it is only their business. For example, you and your teacher may agree that if your grade is less than a 90 on the midterm, you will buy them a case of beer to improve your grade. That can qualify as a derivatives contract, a swap in fact. It should not concern regulators (but may concern school officials). On the other hand, if the derivatives affect banks and pension funds, and ultimately the stability of the global financial system, they might be more of a threat to people's business, and therefore of greater concern.

It is worth looking at a couple of examples of when private derivatives contracts between companies did matter, and in fact posed "systemic" risk to the financial system. At the height of the housing bubble leading up to the 2008 crash, a private insurance company called American International Group (AIG) was writing derivatives contracts related to mortgage-backed securities (collateralized debt obligation or CDO). The contracts, which they offered to both hedgers and speculators, were called credit default swaps, or CDSs. The value of a CDS was directly related to the performance on a particular CDO. You can see why it was a derivative; it was derived from the underlying security, the CDO. When the CDO defaulted, the CDS paid off. It was a way that investors could theoretically remove the risk from a CDO. Poorly rated CDOs just needed to get a CDS issued by AIG, which had a AAA rating, and then suddenly investors had an investment-grade security.

A lot of people mistakenly called the CDSs "insurance" on CDOs, though unlike insurance you did not actually have to own any CDOs to buy a CDS. If you thought that the mortgage market was going to tank, you bought these. A lot of people did and made money that way. However, and importantly, they did so mainly because the US government bailed out AIG and made good on their contracts. If the government had not, AIG would have gone under and not been able to service the contracts. They wrote far too many CDSs to be able to pay out on.

This is related to another difference between these CDSs and insurance. Insurance is a highly regulated business, with insurance companies required to hold substantial investments, reserves, and usually reinsurance to ensure that they can pay off claims if things go bad. AIG was not subject to these requirements. AIG had, emphasis on had, a AAA rating on its balance sheet. Unlike with its insurance products, it did not hold loss reserves on its derivatives. It just issued them, and because it was considered to be a highly credible company, people bought them without a second thought. AIG made a lot of money doing this, for a while.

When the mortgage market fell apart, AIG simply did not have the money to pay on its contracts. That mattered because a lot of the buyers of the CDSs were pension funds, other insurance companies from all over the world, basically institutions that really could not afford a default. That is one reason they bought the CDS in the first place. The chain reaction if AIG had actually been allowed to default would have been politically and financially problematic. Real companies that held money in the public trust, and needed the risk protection of the CDS and thought they had it, would have seen big holes blown in their balance sheets.

Instead, the US government stepped in, took over AIG, and made good on its contracts. This was an unusual move, since AIG was not a bank and was not really regulated, at least not as part of the financial system. But it had made bets that regulators and others feared would jeopardize the global financial system when they went bad. It also threatened pension systems that in reality the United States and other governments probably would have had to rescue if AIG had not paid off on the CDSs. The US government actually paid those claims in full and has been probably rightly criticized for doing so. Speculators who bought CDSs and should have been aware of and taken account of the risks that AIG was taking, also got paid off in full. That is how it goes, though.

This is a case (or would be if AIG had been allowed to fail) of what is called **counterparty risk**, or the risk that the other party to a contract cannot fulfill their part of it. Despite making tons of money writing these contracts, it was not enough to actually cover them when things went bad. The point, anyway, is that though AIG was a private company entering into private derivatives contracts with other private companies, its behavior put the entire global financial system at risk.

A second case illustrates when the risk appears out of nowhere, which is unrelated to the previous example of misjudging risk in a major financial crisis. In 1998 a hedge fund called, not super appropriately, Long-Term Capital Management (LTCM) "blew up," as is said when funds lose a lot of money. LTCM was founded by a group of top quantitative analysts, including two who won a Nobel Memorial Prize in economics. They were clever people, but probably overreached in extending their academic work to real-world trading. Unfortunately, a condition in the markets that their models told them was nearly impossible happened, after they had borrowed billions of dollars to fund their positions. The standard probability distribution underpinning their models is well behaved and helps theoretical models solve, but often does not reflect the unfolding of events in the financial world. Too many of their derivative positions started to go bad at the same time, and they were about to default on billions of dollars of loans from banks when the Fed stepped in and arranged a bailout in order to avoid that.[20]

The broader problem is that with trillions of dollars of derivatives of thousands of different types outstanding, it is really quite impossible to figure out if there are any more cases of potential systemic risk out there. Sometimes they just appear.

On a limited scale, the discussion of whether derivatives themselves are "safe" is somewhat irrelevant. At their roots, they are just contracts between private parties. What matters is less the instrument than the leverage. Leverage is the amount of a total investment that is borrowed or that can be controlled without putting down all the money. When a company borrows money to expand or pay its bills, it is leveraging. It now has access to more money than just what it had in the bank, and the more it borrows, the more leveraged it gets. When you buy an option, you are leveraging your investment, since you can control more stock than you are paying for. Common home mortgages are simply leveraged buyouts of real estate.

When LTCM made its big bets, it was highly leveraged, or it had borrowed to make those bets and did not have ready money to pay off when they went bad. When AIG wrote all those CDSs, it created insane amounts of leverage, worth many multiples of what its equity alone would have supported.

Leverage is a key part of the global economy. Companies with a lot of cash on hand make money providing it. Investors increase their returns on scarce equity by using it. A lot of money is made on leverage. With the partial exception of the large, real-money institutional investors described in chapter 2, almost everyone uses leverage. It is not going away. But leverage does increase risk in the system. More often than not, good risk analysis should focus on the risk that comes from leverage, not from a particular class of instruments, like derivatives. The main problem with leverage, as you may guess, is when it is used to make risky investments, like AIG did, like mortgage lenders did, like LTCM did, and like will probably happen again and again. Follow the leverage and the risk, and you can find the next crisis.

Another category of derivative, exchange-traded funds or ETFs, have become a big enough phenomenon in recent decades to deserve some additional time. They allow investors an easy way to achieve diversification, access to hard-to-reach markets, and a certain amount of liquidity. Over time they have grown from a relatively obscure investment vehicle to one worth \$3.9 trillion in 2017 up from \$2 trillion in 2014, or about one half of the US fund market.[21]

The instruments described above, with the exception of many types of derivatives due to their being private contracts, can be accessed directly by individual investors through brokerage accounts. Individual investors can go long and short, and can buy options and futures. At the same time, it can be hard for individuals to invest enough in individual instruments to get good "diversification." Diversification is investing in different types of assets that tend not to go up or down at the same time. When assets move up and down together at the same time and with the same market conditions, they are said to be correlated. When they go up and down at different times, they are said to be uncorrelated. Modern Portfolio Theory says it is better to own a group of diversified, or uncorrelated, assets. This retains returns, while smoothing out volatility.

If individual investors or even good-size institutional investors try to diversify across a large number of assets, the trading fees will start to eat into returns. Also, when investing in foreign securities, the cost of opening a brokerage account in each country and wiring money there is expensive. Probably the best way for individuals and many institutions to invest in a wide range of instruments around the globe has been through exchange-traded funds, or ETFs. These are used widely by both individual and professional/institutional investors.

The concept behind ETFs is that rather than buying into individual securities, an investor can buy a defined chunk of securities in one or multiple countries by buying a single ETF. Usually, it is clearly defined up front exactly what an ETF will invest in, and how. Consequently, the management fees of ETFs are much lower than traditional mutual funds. For the most part, there is no real management to speak of, just administrative buying and selling of the particular securities that the ETF is mandated to invest in. No one tries to pick the best stocks or bonds in the group. They just buy the whole group. In that sense, management is defined as "passive," rather than the "active" analysis of individual securities that make up a traditional fund.

In the early days of ETFs, they were easier to define because they just tracked indices. For example, if you wanted to invest $1,000 in the S&P 500, rather than trying to buy shares in 500 different companies with your $1,000 investment, you could just buy SPY, which is the ticker symbol for an ETF for that index. As with any instrument, ETFs have evolved, making them harder to define. Some ETFs no longer just have a passive investment strategy. Table 7.4 gives some examples of the wide range of ETFs available.

Before ETFs became very popular around the turn of the twenty-first century, mutual funds were the main mechanism investors used to diversify and/or access otherwise difficult-to-get-to markets. Mutual funds are funds that are managed by "professional" investors who actively trade their portfolios of assets to try to maximize returns. The reality is that because of lower management fees, ETFs have tended to outperform traditional mutual funds in almost all cases.

While having these professional mutual fund managers watching your money may seem like a good idea, very rarely do they manage to attain or beat the returns of similar passive vehicles. Mutual fund advertising on every media on the planet gives a pretty good indication of where at least some of your money is going. A 2014 report from Standard and Poor's shows that only 3.78 percent of 687 mutual funds remained in the top 25 percent of performers over two years. The 2016 follow-up report indicated that over a five-year period, approximately 90 percent of professional money managers underperformed their respective indices once their fees were

Table 7.4.

Symbol of ETF	*Investment the EFT Gives Access to*
SPY	S&P 500
DBB	Invests in an index of futures contracts on important industrial metals, outside of gold
PGX	Tracks an index of investment-grade preferred shares
SJNK	Invests in an index of short-term, high-yield debt held by US corporations
ERUS	Tracks an index of large Russian shares on the Moscow exchange, the MSCI Russian 25/50 index
FXI	Tracks large-capitalization Chinese shares on the China FTSE 50 index
SDS	Tracks the S&P 500 index, and gives a 200 percent return to *decreases* in the value of the index. Known as a "leveraged ETF," the value of these shares decreases just by holding them due to the derivatives they must invest in to give a 200 percent return.

accounted for.[22] Some other studies show even lower performance.[23] In case anyone was wondering if the wealthy got a better deal on managed funds, hedge funds, which are generally only available to the very wealthy or professional money managers, have similar performance records, though with more variability.[24]

As more investors make use of ETFs, a number of questions arise. Since they are defined usually by an index, investors pouring money into ETFs are increasing demand only for what is in that index. A security or even a whole market segment left out of indices will be at a disadvantage no matter how good the company or segment is. One that is included may get undeserved premium pricing. Supply and demand trump fundamentals every time. On the flip side, the existence of an ETF for a market can drive previously nonexistent demand. Emerging or previously hard-to-access markets can get a bump in value after an ETF is formed to access them. Access and convenience seem able to drive demand, especially when transaction costs were previously high.

Some have voiced concerns that as ETFs become more widely traded than the individual underlying securities, that movements in and out of ETFs can drive liquidity problems in those underlying markets. A side effect could be precisely the sort of illiquidity and price volatility that ETF investors were seeking to avoid.[25] A final concern about ETFs stems from the passive investment strategies that drive their low fees. Modern corporate governance structures function at least partly because activist shareholders can remove ineffective management. With so many passive investors, a major part of corporate checks and balances disappears.[26]

ANALYZING GLOBAL INVESTMENTS

Many good books have been written on the process of analyzing and valuing investments in US and global securities.[27] Generally, doing that for global investments is not radically different. Below is a short review of the basic tools, and some things to look out for when investments transcend national borders.

Financial statements, namely the income statement, balance sheet, and cash-flow statement, are still the main tools for firm-level investment analysis, almost no matter where or what country you are talking about. Financial statements across borders usually follow similar global standards. The only time I ran into anything radically different was when looking at statements from the old communist days in Eastern Europe, which were more physical goods oriented, and less financial. A good knowledge of accounting and financial statements is an absolutely necessary precondition for investment analysis. It is not sufficient, since financial statements may not be accurate, but it is necessary.

There are some pitfalls to be on the lookout for when looking at financial statements in countries other than your own. Different countries' accounting systems allow revenue to be booked in different ways. Sometimes companies can book it as soon as an order is received, and there is little relationship to whether any money actually ever showed up or not. It may be difficult to discern the source and composition of revenues, and whether sales are coming from core products, or services to related companies (who sometimes never pay). The latter is one of many tricks that emerging markets companies (and others) have used to inflate revenue. With balance sheets, a major thing to look out for is just lying. People lie about the value of inventory and equipment, about what they are likely to collect, and about the amount of debt they have or may just forget to list vendor debt, or shareholder debt. That happens at home of course too, but auditors may have more trouble catching it abroad.

Unfortunately, a major difference between accounting systems is that the most important of the three types of statements, the cash-flow statement, is optional in a lot of places. It is odd, but a lot of people don't actually understand that a company can be "profitable" (i.e., showing a profit on its income statement) but still be going bankrupt. It is easy. There are sometimes critical outflows that are not considered current expenses (for the income statement). These might include debt repayments, capital investment requirements, or increases in working capital resulting from anything from growth to changes in vendor terms.

It might seem strange to bring up financial statements in a global economics book, but global economic flows are at their roots financial flows, and a lot of these flows are going back and forth between companies' balance sheets. Anyway, every functional human being should be able to do basic financial statement analysis. Fortunately, there are a lot of solid resources available for free on the Internet to help out. What takes more time, and can be important depending on what your goals are, is actually understanding the truths and not so true things behind financial statements. Some hints of those were given above, but there are many more.

Broader analysis of whole foreign and international markets in government bonds, currencies, stock markets, and so on is obviously more difficult with numerous factors coming into play. At the same time, good financial statement analysis skills provide a foundation for broader market analysis. Just like companies, market prices move because of changes in stocks, flows, other prices, perceptions, and other factors that drive changes in supply and demand. Just like the starting point of company-level analysis is an understanding of the starting position and related stocks and flows, the same holds for broader markets. Much of this book is dedicated to trying to understand the underlying forces driving these flows.

The main purpose of analysis is to get to a fair and accurate valuation. Again, there are lots of good resources out there that go into a lot of depth. The three main valuation methods are quickly defined here.

Discounted Cash Flow (DCF)

The DCF method is the most theoretically and technically correct method of business valuation.[28] It starts with a forecast out over time of the amount of cash an investment will generate for the owner after all expenses have been paid and ongoing investments made. That cash flow is then discounted through time, because a dollar today is worth more than a dollar tomorrow. Those discounted cash flows are then added up along with the amount that is needed to be paid for the investment. That gives the total value. There are obvious flaws to this methodology. For one, no one can accurately forecast the future. So the future cash flows are just a guess. An educated one, but a guess. The better the DCF is done, the more the future cash flows are caveated and the more different scenarios can be run for different conditions.

Another flaw in the DCF is the choice of the discount rate. There is no good, both practically and theoretically sound methodology for picking it. Worse, small changes in the discount rate can lead to big changes in valuations. So DCF is the theoretically and possibly practically the best method, though still very imperfect. It also takes a lot of time and requires a lot of information. A good DCF does force you to really get to know the investment and all of its sources of revenue and risk.

Though DCF methodologies are not perfect, expected cash flow remains the most valid way to value a company or other investment. In the mid-1990s, I spent several years combing through the rusting assets of former state companies in Eastern Europe, analyzing investments for a consortium of US-based investors. It is uncountable the number of times I would enter a hollowed-out, rusted factory and hear all about how it was incredibly valuable because it was "the diamond in the rough," or "the only factory like it in the country," or "the biggest," or "had more employees than any other one," or any number of other totally irrelevant proxies for value. Investments are valuable for one reason alone: they generate income.[29]

I was reminded of this minor point several years later during the .com boom leading up to the 2000 bust when everyone was busy betting on companies that were losing millions of dollars a year. At the time, serious analysts at major investment banks were talking about how profits did not matter anymore and using all sorts of unorthodox metrics to value companies. I laughed, did not invest, and did not lose money when it all crashed. And it did crash; it had to. There was no cash being generated by the companies, nor any real prospect of it (the most important point).

Something else happened, though, which was distressing. I did not lose, but because I did not invest I also did not make any money, and a lot of other people did.

So that gets to the next point. As they say, cash is king. It is the only thing that really matters, except when it doesn't. There are two other common valuation methods that are probably more widely, and some would say more effectively, used than the DCF method.

Market Equivalence and Previous Transaction

With this method, different metrics on traded markets (market equivalence) or nontraded markets (previous transaction) are compared with each other to shed light on relative under- or overvaluation. Single investments are not only valued in this way, but whole markets can be.

The most common of these methods is probably comparing the price per share to the earnings per share (PE) ratios of the company you are trying to value to the broader market.[30] If its PE ratio is lower than that of similar companies on the market, it might be cheap. If it is higher, it might be expensive, or overvalued. During the .com boom, the favorite metrics were not earnings, but were page views or registered subscribers, regardless of whether that led to anything else, like any sort of cash flow or revenue. The market equivalence method does not pretend to give any sort of objective value. It just tells you where one asset or market is relative to the rest of the market or to another market. You will often hear analysts talk about, for example, the average PE of the Indian index being lower than the average PE of the Chinese one, implying greater value for money in India, greater investment opportunity, or something similar.

There are many flaws to these methods. To compare based on the PE or another metric, there cannot be any other big differences between the investment being valued and the companies it is being compared to (or the two markets being compared). Usually, there are. Companies and sectors may have different strategies, levels of debt, growth histories and prospects, management, markets and submarkets, and so on. Markets will additionally have very different future prospects, regulatory regimes, and risk profiles.

Extensive additional analysis and judgment should be used when applying this method. It may make more sense to compare two similar chemical companies to each other than to compare two technology companies, one that makes memory chips and one that makes cute phones and tablets that everyone loves and people are selling their kidneys for. You have to think it through and try to make adjustments. The problem with adjustments is it can be hard to know what to adjust and by how much. Adjustments can become arbitrary and lead to hand-waving and ranting that is not grounded in any reality. But then again, reality may not lead you to make the best decisions in the crazy world of financial markets either.

The other problem with this method is that it assumes your benchmark company or market is not grossly under- or overvalued. If you think the Indian market is a great deal at a PE of 6 because the Mexican market has a PE of 25, it may just be that the other market is way overvalued and ready for a big fall. That is what happened in the .com boom. Some profitless Internet companies were bid up in price because other profitless Internet companies had a higher price and the same number of useless page views. It turns out that one was not in fact undervalued, but that they were both equally worthless. Finally, the method only works when you have a comparison value. In liquid, traded markets, you often do. In other types of transactions on private markets, there may not be many or any known comparable transactions.

But herein is observation number one of valuation: it is largely subjective, and even if such a thing as an objective valuation exists, figuring that out may not make you any money. Even if you are right, it may take a very long time before values return to where your model says they should be (if they ever do). Bad valuation and good nerves may make you more money than good valuation and staying power. Lots of money is made (before it is lost) during crazy valuation bubbles no matter how little sense they seem to make either at the time or in retrospect.

•

During asset bubbles, trying to buy and hold on the way up is sometimes referred to less than affectionately as "greater fool" investing. It basically says that if prices are going up, objective valuation does not matter as long as you can sell to a "greater fool" at a higher price than what you paid. Money can be made doing this way outside of the parameters given by any rational valuation model. It is made easier by the fact that the talking heads on TV are talking up the prices at the same time. You just cannot be the last one out when things fall apart. Big money is made, and it has nothing to do with any rational, consistent, or theoretically sound valuation methodology. Here is where the greater fool method worked (for a while) in recent memory:

- Asian stocks, 1990s
- Japanese stocks and real estate, 1980s
- US real estate, 2000s
- US .com stocks, late 1990s
- Peripheral Europe real estate, 2000s
- Eastern European stock markets, 2000s
- Chinese equities in general, and particularly penny stocks, early 2000s until 2014
- Brazilian stock and currency markets, late 2000s early 2010s

These are largely viewed as crises, and fortunes and economies were crushed by them. But considerable money was made leading up to them. Bubbles are fun and profitable. Use a rational cash-flow model to value investment opportunities and you may miss out on the fun and profit.

Observation number two of valuation: even though there is no perfectly objective method, cash does seem to matter. Cash methods can help in relative valuations or to get an idea of which assets are under- and overvalued relative to each other. Cash-flow analysis, whether on a company or market level, takes time, but can pay off. Perhaps more importantly, cash flows can give an idea of when values are getting bubble-like and markets may be at risk of a crash. They cannot unfortunately help pinpoint when a bubble will burst, but they can help identify trends. In each of the crises above, values were out of line from where a reasonable cash-based valuation model would indicate they should be. Cash can help let us know when things are out of balance, in a traditional range of markets like stocks, bonds, futures, derivatives, and even real estate.

Here is an example related to housing. Beginning around 2005, people in the United States talked about a housing bubble. But prices kept going up and the skeptics were getting proven wrong. Why did some people think there was a bubble? Below are two charts related to housing prices. Figure 7.3 shows the overall trend in housing prices between 1980 and 2016. If you put your hand over the part after the decline, it does look like prices are getting out of line. However, the trend lines do not look that out-of-line, especially if you follow the trend line from the late 1980s and just figure the boom was a recovery from an early 1990s slump.

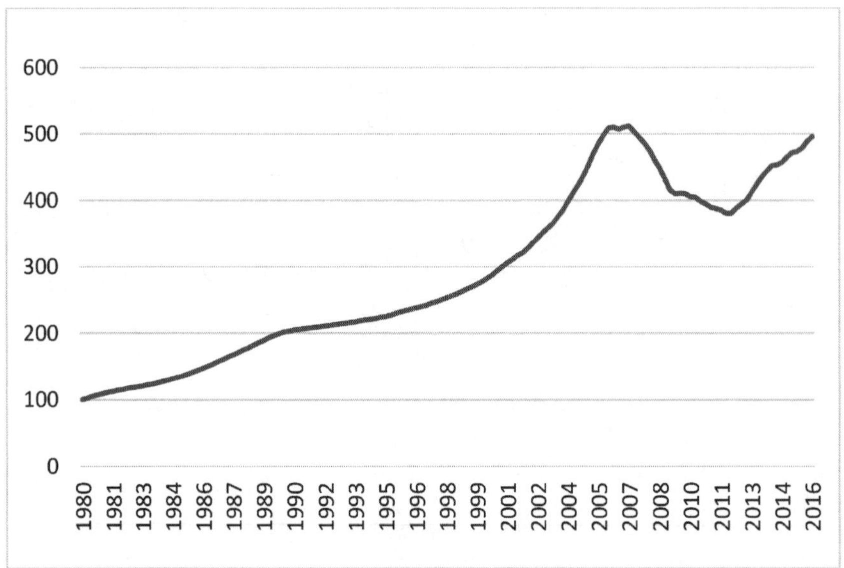

Figure 7.3. House Price Index
Source: Case-Shiller data as archived with the Federal Reserve Bank of St. Louis.

More importantly, just because prices are going up does not mean housing is getting unaffordable or that people might stop paying on their mortgages. Instead, the chart may be interpreted to mean that household wealth is increasing, making the economy even more stable. Low interest rates at the time also make payments cheaper, meaning prices can go up without having an adverse effect on family finances. Unless people start to default on their mortgages, there is no crisis.

Figure 7.4 is more related to a cash flow–type valuation. It compares house prices to rents. This matters because rents better reflect what people are able to pay for housing. First, at the margin, it is renters who get converted to owners. Also, in the rental markets rents represent a cash return on investment to owners and a cash expense to renters. As houses increase in price, owners' need for rent to cover the investment costs will at some point exceed renters' ability to pay. If cash returns matter, and they ultimately do, what renters can pay must at some point be linked to sales values. As the two drift apart, either the houses will sit empty because rents are too high, or rents will be inadequate to cover the investors' expenses. Both should have the same ultimate effect of bringing prices back down. The two should not become overly disjointed. And they were quite disjointed in 2006 and 2007.

Comparing rents to house prices is not the same as a DCF valuation. The two methods do, however, rest on the same principle: that cash flow matters for value.

The main conclusions on valuation are as follows. First, there are no truly objective, foolproof methods of valuing global stocks, bonds, property, or anything else to either get at an objective "fair market" value or to determine if one asset is over- or undervalued relative to another. There are proxies, all of which have pros and cons,

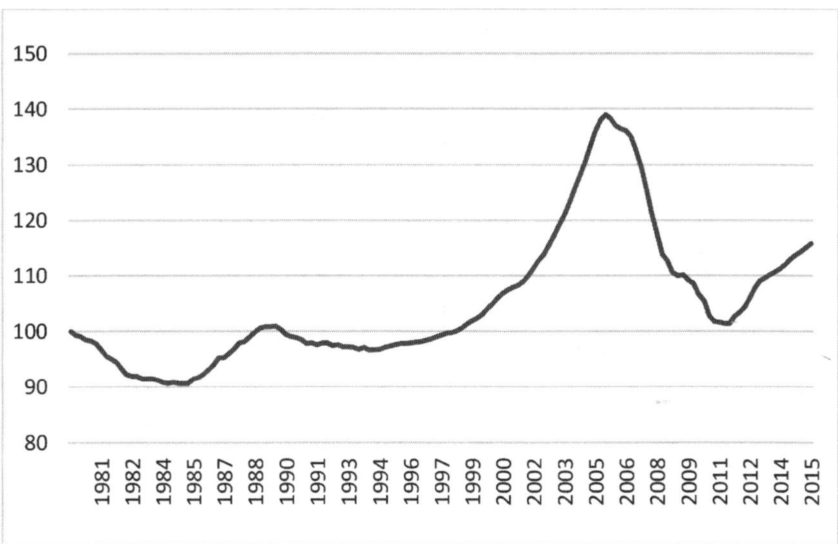

Figure 7.4. Rent-to-Price Index

Source: Case-Shiller and Federal Housing Finance Agency data, archived on the Lincoln Institute for Land Policy site, originally from Davis et al.

and different levels of usefulness in different circumstances. The only value that matters ultimately is the value that the buyer and seller agree on. Valuation is subjective, and like the rest of economics can be highly dependent, often for long periods of time, on perceptions and behaviors rather than what would seem to be economic and financial realities.

Second, market equivalence methods can help in (all other things equal, of course) trying to figure out if something is relatively under or overvalued, though that does not mean that the whole benchmark market is not under- or overvalued. You have to take extenuating factors into consideration.

Finally, cash flow–based methods may be utterly useless in making short-term decisions in bubble conditions, but can potentially be a useful tool for figuring out when certain markets are getting out of line or when certain markets may be undervalued. They are not perfect, but can be a starting point for useful analysis.

Analytic valuation methodologies are useful mainly because the alternative, the unaided human brain, is even worse at making decisions.[31] This is probably as good a place as any to bring in some of the concepts in the field of behavioral economics and finance. Threads of this have been woven throughout the book, specifically when looking at bubbles, crashes, and the quick and panicky movements of money in and out of markets.

The roots of behavioral economics and finance are found in the work of Daniel Kahneman, Amos Tversky, and Paul Slovic.[32] These individuals showed through a long series of well-designed experiments that humans are remarkably poor at accurately assessing quantitative and statistical data. They hypothesized that there are a series of decision-making shortcuts, or **heuristics**, that are hardwired into the human brain. These heuristics are efficient and effective in certain circumstances, but in others can lead to **biases** that essentially make us poor decision makers under a wide range of conditions. Fortunately for us, those same heuristics made us good survivors in the prehistoric savanna in which our brains evolved, even if they stymie our efforts to make sense of the numerical world. They got us this far, but only this far.

One of the main biases that affect humans is referred to as the "availability" bias. People tend to ignore longer-term patterns and focus on events they have recently seen or been exposed to. Everyday life provides evidence of this bias, such as when people stock up on emergency supplies right after an earthquake (but not before and not a year after), avoid the beach after a shark attack on another continent, or keep their children home after a well-publicized abduction in another state, despite the extreme rarity of such events.

In financial markets the availability bias has people reacting to recent events and what is reported in the news, rather than broader data on the structure of the economy. In the midst of the great recession, many lost money on equities and memories of those losses made them reluctant to buy subsequently at historically low prices.[33] When house prices were going up, people forgot about longer-term trends that show housing bubbles forming and bursting with regularity. Instead, there was the repetition of the fundamentally untrue mantra that house prices never go down. A long period of low interest rates in the mid-2010s may be contributing to availability bias among investors. Any time there has been a run-up in asset prices, news reports on the price increases can contribute to availability biases that keep prices moving up, at least for a while. The biases then start to work on the downside as well. The availability bias may help make bubbles and corrections steeper than they otherwise would be.

Another common and related bias is anchoring, which is when a decision maker maintains a preconceived idea despite data to the contrary. The "anchor" can be picked up from the environment or can be long-standing. Common examples of anchoring include believing that one has some particular innate skill because of a success long ago and despite more recent evidence to the contrary, that square footage or proximity to a school is the best proxy for home value if the house you bought has that, or that living until seventy is great if you just lost someone close to you at age fifty-five. Data may be contrary to the anchored value, but it can be hard to budge these preconceived ideas.

In economics and finance, anchoring commonly appears in a number of forms. If an investor buys a stock at $40 a share, despite its dropping to $30 and showing no signs of recovering, they may have a hard time selling it because they have anchored on $40 as a fair and even cheap value. Similarly, people feel better about buying a car for $30,000 if the list price was $35,000, than if the list price was $28,000 and they were unable to negotiate it down. In one example from the retail sector, when retailer JC Penney got rid of coupons and went to all low prices, their sales suffered. People wanted to come down from an anchor and feel good, even if they were paying more on average.[34] If consumers or investors are buying, they also do not want to come up from an anchored value. If they are selling, the opposite holds. In negotiations, a common tactic is to get a "shill" to introduce a number that is far higher or lower than what the other side wants, just to break their anchor and try to introduce a new one.

Those are two common biases, but there are many others that are worth studying. The previous footnotes provide some sources to get started. Another major contribution to behavioral finance known as "prospect theory" also came from Kahneman and Tversky. It is also a bias in a way, but has had enough written about it to be a topic on its own. The basic premise is that people regret losses more than they value gains. Humans by and large feel that it is worse to lose $50 than it is good to gain $50. This also has been hypothesized to have an effect on investor behavior by prompting people to hold on to losing investments for longer than they should. Once they sell, the loss becomes real to them. Until they sell, the loss is "unrealized" and investors may cling to the hope of a price recovery.

In his book *Misbehaving* Richard Thaler has speculated that the behaviors implied by prospect theory may be responsible both for increasing risk at financial institutions and for deepening the severity of economic crises.[35] In experiments, as losses mount individuals are willing to take on more risk to erase losses and get back to even. This is a common sentiment observed among casino gamblers, but it also afflicts professional investors, as numerous financial institutions have unfortunately noted. So-called rogue traders who individually rack up huge losses at financial institutions exhibit behavior consistent with the theory and experiments.[36] The worse the trading position becomes, the greater the desperation and the bigger the bets and often ultimately the losses.

Prospect theory may also help link investor and manager behavior with a deepening of economic crises, though less directly than with the rogue trader case. Two factors may be at play. First, it may be that losses during crises (and so ultimately the crises themselves) can end up being worse than they need to be if institutions take on increased risk during these periods to try to pare back their losses. Second, and related to the inflation of bubbles, studies have shown that when investors are realizing gains they treat that money differently from the core capital. Specifically, there is a greater tendency to gamble with the gains than there is with the core capital. This is referred to as the "house money" effect also observed among gamblers, whereby they take on greater risk with their winnings than with the money they brought to the table. The house money effect may lead to higher risk taking during boom periods, leading to more money pouring into already overheated markets. This is also consistent with the work of Hyman Minsky, who speculated that periods of calm lead to risk taking that then leads to periods of turbulence.[37]

Certainly, not all economists agree on the relevance of the heuristics and biases research and findings to outcomes in global economics and financial markets. Some results attributable to the approach are quite speculative, anecdotal, and difficult to prove.[38] At the same time, this relatively new area of study can yield one more set of tools to be used as appropriate and seems to be gaining credibility and popularity rather than losing it.

Behavioral economics butts up against the rational expectations approach to markets, which has been dominant for some decades. Again, there are many articles and books on this rather complex topic, but the approach postulates that on average economic and financial decision making is rational in that it takes all available information into account and processes it efficiently and in accordance with the interests of the person taking the action. There is little to no room for even short- to medium-term system-wide biases that deviate from correct valuations, since those would be exploited by other actors.

Adherents to the rational expectations approach are correct in noting that at any point in time, it is hard to exploit market vagaries or inefficiencies for profit. Those opportunities have already been taken by other traders. As any investor will confess, it is in fact very hard or impossible to make money by exploiting price anomalies in markets and forecasting direction. Sometimes you get lucky, or intelligently exploit a short-term anomaly, but overall it is hard to apply that strategy again and again and keep making money. Most investors are content to go after **beta** or market-trend levels of returns, rather than **alpha**, which is excess return.

At the same time, the rational expectations approach has not been all that useful in either anticipating or explaining some of the more interesting global economic events of recent history.[39] Strict adherents would claim that bubbles and busts are "rational." If rationality can be defined that widely, the approach probably can't help much in preventing and/or navigating these major events. Even if the framework happens to be correct in some regard and at some times, others are probably more useful for analyzing and preparing for wide swings in market pricing.[40]

Like many debates in economics, the adherents to one school are normally deaf to the arguments of the others. Probably both the behavioral and rational expectations viewpoints have something to say about different markets at different periods of time. I am not as convinced as some that they are fully and diametrically opposed to each other. After looking at some strategies investors use in the global economy, this point will be revisited. In fact, many investment strategies that have worked do have some elements of trying to beat the market to them.

A fair but not very useful conclusion to this section would be that solid quantitative analysis of cash flows is good practice generally, but can be relatively useless in bubble or bust conditions. Investing based on rational analysis of asset values can be a losing strategy for long periods of time and/or can turn on you quickly even if it works for a while. Like everything in economics, it depends. It is good to be aware of what the data and models say, and also to be aware of human incentives, behaviors, where the money is, and the rules of the game.

This discussion of investor and market rationality or not ends with a quote from a successful investor referred to as "The House," interviewed in Steven Drobny's (2010) book *The Invisible Hands*: "If there had been more John Paulsons (hedge fund manager who made a fortune shorting mortgage bonds) in the market during the last few years, and fewer gullible institutional investors in subprime, the global economy would have been much better off." To paraphrase, if more investors had closely analyzed the conditions rather than going with the herd, the conditions for the global crisis would have had a lot more trouble materializing.

COMMON STRATEGIES FOR GLOBAL INVESTMENT

The strategies that investors use to move money around and seek returns can help in understanding global financial flows and the global economy. There may be as many strategies as there are investors, but a number of them stand out and fall into some broad categories. The particular strategy used depends on the investors, their incentives, and their goals. A few of the most popular categories of strategy are briefly reviewed here. Keep in mind that these are extremely simple base strategies and no successful investor would use them by themselves, or as they are presented. A real strategy for global investment involves a much greater level of sophistication than what is summarized here. Most of the strategies to be looked at are for portfolio investors. But it is worth taking a minute to look at direct investment first.

Strategic Positioning

Most direct investment is carried out by companies investing in productive or increased service capacity overseas, or by investors financing that investment on behalf of the companies.[41] Managers of companies usually make decisions in different ways than portfolio investors. Both want a return, but company managers usually have a longer-term outlook, and more often than not are taking the company's strategic needs into consideration.

A company that makes soup may set up a soup production facility in India, and their investment model may tell them to expect a 6 percent annual return on the investment over twenty years. That seems like a pretty decent return. On the other hand, the model may indicate that they should expect a 2 percent or even a negative return over a shorter period of time, but they make the investment anyway for strategic reasons. Reasons may include that competitors are also entering the same market or are already there, that trade barriers make it difficult to import into the market from other bases of production, that their other products are selling well there now and it is only a matter of time, or any number of other factors. They still want to and plan to make a return, but it may come through different channels and over a longer term than just a solid set of immediate cash flows from the investment. As seen before, another strategic reason companies invest in countries is to take advantage of lower taxes there.

A lot of traders tend to ignore this "not very hot" money. They probably should not. Strategy can drive a lot of money into different places. Composition of money matters, and this is generally the sort of stable (non-hot) money that is in for the longer term, even when other markets get volatile. It can be a stabilizer and help temper the effects of the hot money. Unfortunately, these sorts of strategic investments can also be put off or scaled back when there are hot money types of crises occurring, which can help to magnify their effects.

Following growth. Some global investment capital is seeking the next big investment opportunity and is trying to be among the first to find it. There is a radical and less radical version of this. The more radical side of it involves slogging around in what are called "frontier markets" like East African countries, or Burma, trying to figure out an angle on North Korea, and so on. There are lots of problems and a few opportunities if you do it right, and get lucky.

Unfortunately, in these frontier markets investment access is poor, pricing may not be all that great, and you may not even really own what you think you own. Lots of investors, including big ones like BP in Russia, have been fleeced and ended up without what they thought they had paid for.[42] It can also be hard to place any reasonable amount of money without the unintended consequence of your own investment funds driving up the market. Frontier markets are notoriously illiquid. Also related to liquidity, it can be hard to get out, at any valuation.

For those who stick it out, frontier markets can be a good buy, especially when growth and other investors follow and rights to the investment are secure. The author worked seeking out and analyzing investments for a group of early-stage investors in Bulgaria in the mid-1990s. Some money was lost, but some of those who stuck it out earned good returns. Lots of money was made (and lost) in early investments in what are now the main emerging markets, especially in real property. One reason a frontier market strategy may not be all that great anymore is that there are just not that many new markets opening up these days. Investors are everywhere, and the sums invested have been greatly swelled by a flood of Chinese money that seems immune to risk and is pouring into most of the previously neglected corners of the world.

The less radical side of the growth-chasing strategy focuses more on the existing emerging markets and trying to figure out where growth is likely to be highest, then taking a long-term position. This can require more patience and a lot of care in making sure the pricing is advantageous and not already high (not easy to figure out). A lot of indicators point to emerging markets as the place to be, and the next chapter looks at some of the reasons why that may or may not be the case. Wealth in many poorer countries does seem to be "converging" to the levels of wealthy countries, meaning that they should be good long-term investment holds. Again, more on this in the next section.

On the negative side, emerging markets have tended to be extremely volatile, illiquid, and they have poor track records of sustained upward market momentum. Most have gone through multiple periods of boom, bust, and even stagnation (the worst of the three) in recent decades, at least in terms of performance on traded markets. A "buy and hold" strategy may not work all that well (or at least has not historically), unless you get in very early, in which case getting out early might also be a good idea.

Again, more on this and potential investment strategies in the next chapter on economic growth.

Value investing. Value investing focuses on seeking out and investing in securities and markets that are undervalued relative to the values of similar securities and markets. The assumption is that the undervalued investments will rise in value to be more like the other investments in that same pool. Some valuation metric needs to be used for comparison. The PE is a common one, though there are many others. Value investing is a common strategy and has great intuitive appeal—everyone loves a bargain. Though his company doubtless employs other strategies, legendary investor Warren Buffett puts a value approach at the center of his strategy.

Figure 7.5 shows twenty-year returns to stocks traded on US markets, based on the purchase PE. The trend clearly shows that the lower the PE at time of purchase, the greater the returns. This pattern appears to hold for all periods looked at in the study, going all the way back to 1920. If anything the returns to value investing have increased over time. A lot of stocks trade at higher-than-average PE ratios, but they usually do that based on the assumption that they are worth it, and have more growth to go. Apparently that is less the case than is often believed. It would appear from the chart that these higher PE ratios are on average more based on misunderstanding and hype than inherent value.

Obviously, one of the problems with value investing is valuation, and as seen this can be hard to ascertain. In this case, though, simple PE ratios are used and seem to have worked quite well. With short-selling instruments available, value investing strategies could also be used to bet on the decline of assets that are thought to be overvalued. Given that nearly all the returns over the nearly one-hundred-year period

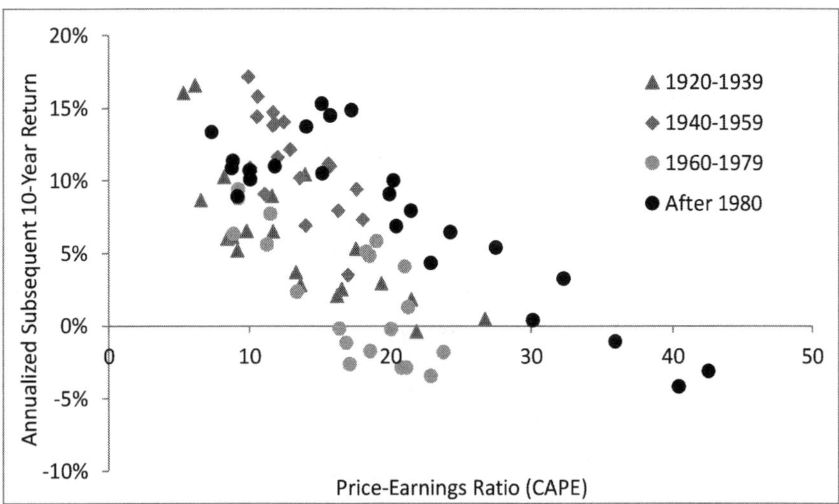

Figure 7.5. Historical PE Ratios against Subsequent Returns

Source: Data provided by Robert Shiller, originally from S&P indices, Case-Shiller data.

in the chart above are positive, this would be a risky overall strategy in "normal" market conditions.

Some version of value investing strategies brings investors in and out of global markets on a regular basis. When one market begins to look overvalued relative to another (all other things equal, of course), money will move to the "cheaper" one, the one where values are depressed or low, and where expected returns are believed to be higher. Sometimes these are markets that recently experienced a crash, but where fundamentals seem sound enough and that are now perceived to be a good value. Lots of the media talking heads either directly or indirectly advocate for value strategies, even if they tend to hype the short term. Success with a value investment strategy, like others, often requires a longer-term investment horizon.

Reversion to the mean. There is an observation and related statistical property that often applies to global markets. The observation is that some markets seem to just bounce all over the place, or bounce all over while following a secular trend. There is a lot of volatility, involving little movements up and down, but also big shocks, bubbles, and busts. The bubbles nearly always burst, and recovery nearly always follows the busts.

The related statistical property is called "reversion to the mean." When extreme events end, and when markets settle back down, at some point conditions return to a mean or average trend line. That is a pretty crude and nontechnical description, but it works to describe what has happened repeatedly in global markets.

Reversion to the mean supports a contrarian view that the best time to sell is when others are buying, and the best time to buy is when others are selling. That is a bit different from the greater fool method, which requires following market momentum. Obviously, there is a lot of market noise when bubbles and busts are happening that obscures positive identification. When bubbles are happening, everyone is saying this time is different and prices will just keep going up. Happy time, the "great moderation," when "everyone knows house prices never go down." When busts are happening, it is the opposite. Gloom prevails. This time is different, and there are ten credible-sounding reasons why recovery will never happen. But, historically, recovery has almost always happened.

That is not to say that all this talking is just noise. Sometimes prices stay high or low for a long time. As of 2016, Japanese markets have not reached the heights of the 1980s. Also, sometimes there is a fundamental shift that drives long-term price levels, upsetting the mean and putting it on a new trend line. Unfortunately, it is also extremely difficult to predict where the top and bottom will be. One nice thing about playing the reversion to the mean game is that you can both go long and short, so generally have something to do, or at least think about doing.[43]

Figure 7.6 tracks a fund that represents the Turkish stock market in USD terms. There does not appear to be a clear trend here, just a lot of bumping around, so it should be a reasonable place to consider the reversion to the mean approach. As can be seen, playing such a strategy is not for short-term investors. You need to hang in

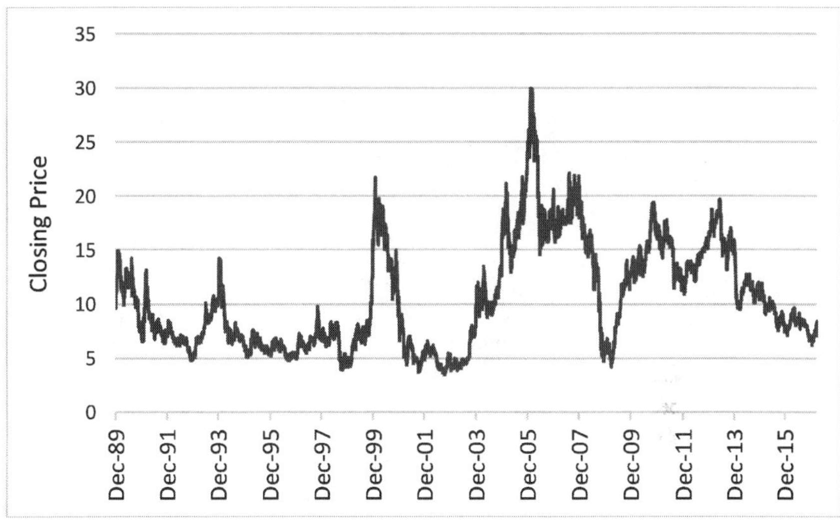

Figure 7.6. Turkish Market ETF TUR Price History
Source: Data from TD Ameritrade.

there. Both gloom and doom and exuberance can last a long time. I was in Turkey during the crash you can see on the chart that happened in 2001. I lost my job and about $10k betting on the overnight credit market, but was excited about the prospects. I called every hedge fund I could track down to get them excited about the buying opportunity. The market would recover, for sure. I encountered nothing but gloom and doom, no buyers. Emerging markets were down, Turkey was down, and risk was out of fashion. Anyone who bought in would have had to wait five years or more, but they also would have gotten a pretty clean 300 percent return without even having to time the exit very well. Some did.

Looking at charts and following a reversion to the mean strategy is not the same as technical investing, which is the belief that certain patterns in charts indicate when it is time to buy and sell. Though technical "experts" get a lot of media time, most well-conducted assessment of technical trading tools fail to conclude that standard technical methods do any better than simple guesswork.[44]

Chasing Bond Yields

This has been discussed in some detail before. Basically, investors sitting on large pools of money often seek higher returns across multiple global markets. These global fixed-income investors must take currency risk into account, given the small gains in rates they often get from moving to a new market. Keep in mind, though, that bond traders are usually doing more than looking for small gains in interest (the covered interest spread). Here are the three main returns they seek:

- Interest rate gain. What they gain in interest by moving to a new market. This is usually just a bit, especially once hedges are in place. This is the only form of gain for those who lend (buy fixed-income securities) into markets in their own currency whether through bond purchases or the extension of credit lines.
- Capital appreciation on the bond. This is from any increase in the value of the bonds, which occurs if interest rates drop in the economy they entered. Remember that bond prices and interest rates move in opposite directions. These can be significant gains. Overall, boring old bonds have given good returns on capital invested in the post–great recession period. Timing is critical, though; you need to get in as rates are dropping, which is not always easy. If rates are higher in the market the investors are moving into, some "reversion to the mean" gains may also be had if rates converge to those of other markets. Bonds can also appreciate in value if they were bought at a discount because of previous default risk, and that risk diminishes.
- Exchange appreciation. If you get into a market early and others flood in, exchange rates can go up. Appreciation of the currency in which the bond is denominated will improve returns. The opposite is also true, as a depreciating currency can lead to losses. Avoidance of depreciation risk is a major driver of the herd mentality, where investors flee markets all at one time.

The last two: capital appreciation and exchange appreciation are probably the most important for portfolio investors seeking yields in emerging markets, and where most gains and losses come from.

Program/High-Frequency Trading

As of mid-2017, upwards of 75 percent of the trades made on major, developed market exchanges were being made by machines with preprogrammed trading algorithms. The algorithms and the trading strategies behind them are normally highly confidential, so it can be hard to know what the funds behind them are really up to. Some **high-frequency trading** has been shown to be engaged in the manipulation of markets.[45]

A lot of algorithms have historically been engaged in **arbitrage**, or taking advantage of imperfections or price differences between markets. Probably, much of the high-frequency trading that is done across borders is taking advantage of minute arbitrage opportunities between markets, and between stock and options markets. Much of the arbitrage business works in small fractions of cents at high volumes. Historically, considerable effort and funds have been employed to take advantage of arbitrage opportunities. Probably, though, these movements are not a major part of global capital flows and do not affect individual economies much, at least once flows both in and out of countries are netted out.

When algorithmic trading is combined with reversion to the mean, the end result is any number of statistical arbitrage or "stat-arb" models. These seek to exploit short-term deviations from observed long-term trends in markets. Algorithms are programmed to make bets when statistically unlikely deviations occur, under the assumption that they will correct themselves. Obviously, the success of the model requires the relationships between variables to return to the longer-term mean. If there is a structural shift, the model can fail and lead to large losses.

Increasingly sophisticated versions of stat-arb models continue to be used by hedge funds. Long-Term Capital Management, whose demise has been noted a number of times in this book, used such a model. Other legendary and more successful firms such as the early adopter DE Shaw also used and probably continue to use versions of this model.

The above briefly summarizes some of the more basic strategies investors use when moving money in and out of global markets. Data is hard to come by, but in one form or another versions of such strategies are probably at the core of a significant amount of what appears on the capital and financial accounts of most countries. The key point is that global economics is finance. What appear as global economic flows are by and large just the aggregate result of a lot of people investing a lot of money and moving it in and out of markets using lots of different strategies, all for the purpose of making money.[46]

Having run through a handful of strategies, or maybe the better word is methodologies, that global investors use, it is a good time to come briefly back to the concept of efficient markets and excess returns. In its purest form, the efficient market hypothesis would indicate that the most any strategy can deliver over the longer term is a beta return consistent with the level of risk taken. That may be correct. The beta return may also not be anything to sneer at, depending on what markets the investment manager is targeting.

That said, a lot of fund managers out there are trying to do better than beta returns. Some have gotten rich (and some have done quite well on fees rather than returns). Others have not. Are differences in investment returns just normal variations around a mean, or have some people figured something out? Here are a few thoughts.

It seems that some firms that have been early to market with the right strategy have done well. In particular, certain arb and stat-arb firms have made considerable money. Algorithmic trading firms that were first in to commodity markets have also apparently done well, though perhaps to the detriment of producers and end users.[47] Arbitrage is essentially the means by which markets become efficient. Someone has to engage in the arbitrage that will drive markets toward efficiency, and there is money to be made in doing so successfully. Some of the high-frequency trading firms that make money by intervening in other people's trades may also be on to something, though the ethics are more dubious.[48]

The failure of arbitrage traders to exploit what *appear* to be longer-term cycles of boom and bust across global markets may be related to there being too few investors with the ability to lock up liquidity for the time it takes to exploit the cycles. If an investor does have that ability, perhaps there is money to be made in longer-term reversions to means. The danger of course is if something fundamental changes in the course of waiting for the cycle to revert. For example, instability in Egypt and Turkey in the mid-2010s may drive the mean down to a new, more permanent low.

These are all interesting questions that are well explored in other places. Whether or not excess returns are available to investors does not really much matter for the purposes of this book. Investors will keep trying to make money in the global economy, which will likely lead to the same broad categories of behaviors, money flows, and consequent events in the global economy seen in the past.

More important to longer-term trends in potential investment returns are the major structural changes in demographics, regulations, or technology, for example, that would drive changes in future boom-and-bust cycles. This is addressed in more detail in section two of this book.

NOTES

1. This does happen. See, for example, the fascinating story of energy hedge funds battling to control the US gas market in Dreyfuss (2013).
2. This is a reasonable working definition of FDI for the purposes here. In reality, there is debate about what qualifies. The OECD (2008) has written perhaps the definitive paper on FDI classification. The IMF and the BIS are also good sources of information on more precise classifications of FDI for national accounting purposes. See, for example, the IMF (2013) BOP manual and other resources referred to there.
3. Ibid.
4. Havranek and Irsova 2011.
5. See chapter 3 for further explanation.
6. Or as in the case of Brazil in the mid-2010s, a populace that turned a blind eye to corruption in a boom economy starts to take interest in the missing billions.
7. The IMF (2016) in its World Economic Outlook has noted that this capital of domestic origin has begun to behave more like other international capital, potentially increasing the amplitude of capital movements in and out of a given country.
8. For an overview see *The Economist* 2013a. A telling quote that parallels conclusions in chapter 3, "Exactly as emerging-market finance ministers complain, this global financial cycle is influenced by rich-world monetary policy." See Baba and Kokenyne (2011) of the IMF for an overview of the effectiveness of capital controls. See also the IMF (2012) for their official position on capital controls: *The Liberalization and Management of Capital Controls: An Institutional View*.
9. Kaplan and Rodrik 2001.
10. *The Economist* 2013a.
11. Though imports are financed almost by definition, research also shows that in less-developed market economies, remittances can increase investment and growth. See Giuliano and Ruiz-Arranz (2009).
12. There is considerable speculation on how the price of oil will affect remittances from the oil-rich Gulf States, especially as it bears on public investment and household consumption in those countries. Results as of 2016 are preliminary and unclear. See for example Ratha et al. (2015) and De et al. (2015).
13. World Bank data.

14. *The Economist* 2014a.
15. El-Erian, 2017.
16. This is from the author's own experience.
17. There are many good resources available online on how options work. The Chicago Board of Exchange has free online course materials.
18. Barbara Dreyfuss's (2013) book *Hedge Hogs: The Cowboy Traders behind Wall Street's Largest Hedge Fund Disaster* documents the commodity speculator mentality and the influence traders can have on markets.
19. Bank for International Settlements statistical database.
20. As noted before, the fall of LTCM is a story worth remembering, not only for its lessons for financial markets, but its lessons in humility for those who think they have mastered the science of economics. Lowenstein (2000) presents a very readable account.
21. Kim 2017. See also the Investment Company Institute (2016) for an overview of the ETF market.
22. See the reports from Standard and Poor's by Soe and Luo (2014) and Soe and Poirier (2016).
23. Sommer 2015.
24. *The Economist* 2016a.
25. This as well as some other related risks are discussed in a Bank for International Settlements working paper by Ramaswamy (2011).
26. See Foley and Wigglesworth (2016) and the citations therein.
27. One of the classics is the McKinsey book by Copeland et al. (2000).
28. Reference again the McKinsey book by Copeland et al. (2000).
29. Companies can make strategic investments that they may lose money on, but the investment is expected to add to the overall bottom line of their company over time.
30. The PE ratio is what it says it is. It is the current price, over the current earnings. There are lots of other similar metrics that try to get away from some of the weaknesses inherent in this ratio, such as price over forward earning, price to cash flow, and so on.
31. That said, in a prescient book *Superforecasting: The Art and Science of Prediction*, the authors lay out cases and conditions under which certain people are able to vastly outperform others and computers in determining the likelihood of world events occurring.
32. The book that set it all off was Kahneman, Slovic, and Tversky's (1982) *Judgment under Uncertainty: Heuristics and Biases*, though Kahneman's (2011) more recent book *Thinking Fast and Slow* is a bit more updated and more readable for a general audience. Others have applied these concepts to financial markets, such as Pompian (2012). Richard Thaler's (2016) book *Misbehaving* is a good introduction to the history, concepts, and methods of behavioral economics and finance.
33. A timely editorial by value investor Warren Buffett (2008) at the height of the financial crisis indicated why he was buying rather than selling at that time and highlights a number of investor biases.
34. Mourdoukoutas 2013.
35. See Thaler (2016) and especially Koppel (2011) for an assessment of how each of the heuristics and biases can affect investor behavior and markets.
36. Two of the most egregious cases are that of Bruno Iksil, the so-called London Whale who racked up $6.2 billion in trading losses for JP Morgan Chase in 2012, and Nick Leeson, who in 1995 bankrupted the two-hundred-year-old financial institution Barings after losing almost 1 billion pounds sterling.

37. See Thaler (2016), and Minsky (1986).

38. See *Animal Spirits* by George Akerlof and Robert Shiller (2009) for a readable overview of the role of psychology and human error in financial markets.

39. See *The Economist* (2015a) Buttonwood column for a short overview of behavioral economics and some of the places it clashes with the rational expectations–based neoclassical school. See also Shiller et al.'s (1984) classic article, "Stock Prices and Social Dynamics." The authors early on lay out the case for behavioral drivers of market prices.

40. I was in graduate school when and where many of the rational expectations–based dynamic models were being developed. It often struck me that rational expectations was used in modeling as much for convenience as anything. The mathematical models simply would not solve and converge to a fixed point without adopting it as an assumption. It has, though, taken on a life of its own. This is partially for political reasons, since there is not much of a role for government in rational markets.

41. Many global companies, especially in real-estate-development-related areas actually rely on outsiders to make most of their investments for them. This is particularly the case in hotel and resort development, but may be in other areas as well.

42. *The Economist* 2012a.

43. Mean reversion in stock markets was shown by De Bondt and Thaler (1985) in "Does the Stock Market Overreact?" Their work subsequently spawned a series of papers, both supporting and denying the validity of their hypotheses.

44. See Aronson (2007) for a comprehensive survey of the predictive power of technical analysis.

45. Former Solomon Brothers trader Michael Lewis writes some of the most, or maybe the only, entertaining books on finance. His 2014 book *The Flash Boys* exposed electronic front running and market manipulation in quant firms. For a more descriptive and less entertaining account, see Patterson (2010) or Narang (2013).

46. For those interested in more detail on global investment strategies actually followed by top hedge fund managers, Steven Drobny has a series of books consisting of interviews with top global money managers. Though many of those follow basic themes such as discussed here, they are much more nuanced and sophisticated, as would be expected. See the bibliography.

47. See Dreyfuss (2013).

48. Michael Lewis (2014) outlines some of these strategies in his book *Flash Boys: A Wall Street Revolt*. Though it is essentially a work of journalism, many of the strategies discussed are real.

8

Economic Growth

Whether a country is growing and how fast are both domestic and global concerns. Domestically, rate of growth is a prominent benchmark against which a government is judged. Fairly or not, governments' reelection or ouster can depend on the growth rate under their watch. For the global economy, they matter because growth rates as the building blocks of accumulated wealth drive shifts in the economic balance of power among nations. Countries with growing economies tend to attract a greater share of global capital flows, diverting flows perhaps from economies with lower anticipated growth. Growing economies also have increasing wealth, making their people and companies both better and more formidable trading partners. Countries with growing economies also in turn become important sources of global capital flows, as many emerging markets have in the past decades.

The first chapter ranked countries based on the current overall and per capita output of their economies. At the same time, knowing which economies are increasing their output over time, which are not, and which might, can help in better understanding current and future global money flows. Table 8.1 contains a selection of countries and their growth rates over a range of time periods. They are ranked top to bottom by their most recent growth performance.

A few themes stand out in the table. First, most rich countries are not growing very fast, and have not for a while. Japan is not on the list, but would come in near the bottom even of the wealthy countries. With the exception of a few countries such as South Korea, most of the richer countries got rich some time ago.

Second, emerging markets overall have been growing faster lately. It is no surprise that emerging markets investments have become popular in the past decades. This has not always been the case. Throughout much of the 1970s through to the 1990s, they were not growing much faster than the richer countries, and it was feared that they would be stuck in a poverty trap with no ability to catch up. In another rever-

Table 8.1. Selected Country GDP Growth Rates over Time

Country Name	*1980–1989*	*1990–1999*	*2000–2009*	*2010–2013*
China	10.1%	9.6%	10.2%	8.8%
Turkey	4.1%	4.0%	3.8%	6.0%
Argentina	–0.7%	4.5%	3.0%	5.4%
Costa Rica	2.3%	5.5%	4.1%	4.5%
Mexico	2.3%	3.6%	1.8%	3.6%
Brazil	3.0%	1.7%	3.3%	3.4%
Guatemala	1.0%	4.1%	3.4%	3.4%
Russian Federation	n/a	–4.9%	5.5%	3.4%
Egypt, Arab Rep.	5.9%	4.3%	4.9%	2.8%
United States	3.1%	3.2%	1.8%	2.3%
Germany	2.0%	2.2%	0.9%	2.1%
Austria	2.0%	2.8%	1.7%	1.4%
United Kingdom	2.4%	2.7%	1.9%	1.2%
Euro area	2.3%	2.1%	1.4%	0.6%
Spain	2.8%	2.7%	2.6%	–0.8%
Greece	0.8%	1.9%	3.0%	–5.7%

Source: World Bank

sal, some of these previously sluggish, but more recently faster-growing countries, such as Turkey and Brazil, saw their growth rates drop precipitously right after this 2013 data was compiled. China has been growing fast for some time, and is pretty much in a category by itself. Its growth rates were sluggish and sharply negative at times prior to the 1980s. The table leaves out a number of very poor and especially unstable countries such as Haiti, Iraq, Syria, and Ukraine that have lost ground or have not been growing very fast. It is fair to say that there is considerable volatility and variability in emerging markets growth.

GROWTH, CONVERGENCE, AND LIMITS TO GROWTH

This section introduces a number of popular frameworks used for understanding economic growth, or lack thereof. Thousands of economists have devoted their careers to this topic. Not surprisingly they argue about it incessantly and have reached little consensus. Over the past five or six decades a steady stream of frameworks has come and gone, each seeking to explain growth, a lack of growth, and what should be done to promote growth. Growth theories are commonly spawned in academia, then spread to policy institutes and development institutions where they are turned into recommendations for countries to follow.

Pinpointing sources, causes, and hindrances to growth empirically is an extremely difficult task. Long time lags between policy and response, noisy data, multiple potential causal factors, and what appear to be varied experiences with different models in different countries all make the testing of growth theories challenging. Growth is a field of economics where theory and models are widely used to substitute for empirical limitations.

Below is a summary of some of the more popular growth and development frameworks that have come and mainly gone.[1]

1. Stages of growth. Economist Walt Rostow developed this concept in the 1960s. His idea was that all countries pass through distinctive, sequential stages of growth. They would need to complete one stage before getting to the next, with the goal of reaching a final "take-off" stage characterized by rapid growth. The stages of growth model was mechanical and mainly deterministic: governments simply needed to "let it happen" and there would be success. When a lot of countries failed to "take off," the model lost credibility and more explanatory and proactive approaches took over. Economists still occasionally use Rostow's terminology, and you will hear reports of countries poised for "take-off."
2. Dependency theory. Popular among more communist-leaning and "non-aligned" countries in the 1960s and 1970s, the basic concept is that linkages to old colonial powers kept poor countries from developing. This "dependency" kept them from developing their own institutions, their own markets, and ultimately their own industries. Though still popular in university social science departments that use phrases like "cultural discourse," dependency theory ultimately spawned few workable and successful policy actions. It has made a lot of people angry, though, and has also lent legitimacy to more than one poor-country dictator who made a point of standing up to the West. Few economists think much about dependency theory anymore, though it may get attention again depending on how the incursion of Chinese investors into African countries in the 2000s works out.[2]
3. Infant industries and state intervention. Popular in the 1970s in developing countries, the infant industries argument holds that free trade with advanced companies in wealthy nations would keep domestic industry in poorer countries from developing. Since local competitors were starting with little scale, technology, or human capital, they could never achieve global competitiveness as long as they kept getting crushed by bigger, global companies. The solution was to invest state resources directly and indirectly in (sometimes carefully selected) local companies, and put up trade barriers to give them a chance to grow without foreign competition. Then when they reached maturity, they would be exposed to competition as home-grown global competitors. The **import substitution** variant of this program centered on supporting local companies that would produce goods to substitute for imports.

   This was, and to some degree continues to be, a popular argument. In reality, some countries managed to execute this well, including many Asian countries, the United States (in the nineteenth century), and some European nations. Other countries were left with weak companies in need of costly ongoing subsidies and protection. Much of Latin America, Eastern Europe, India, Africa, and some of Southern Europe had this less-positive experience with infant industries. The debates rage on, with some economists supporting the idea and others claiming it is a waste of money and potential.[3]

Two conclusions can be made. First, it seems to have worked well in some places and poorly in others. How, when, where, and why is a fascinating topic in economics. However, second, the arguments don't matter as much anymore. With trade barriers hugely reduced from successive rounds of WTO and multilateral tariff cutting and limits to subsidies, the protective conditions for spawning infant industries are harder to produce in most developing countries.[4] Whether that is part of a vast multinational conspiracy or a reasonable trade-off for the overall benefits of freer trade is yet another point that will be argued about for years to come. That said, a revival of economic nationalism may bring these concepts back to the fore. Some of the industrial policies seemingly promoted by the US president Trump have roots in infant industry and import substitution concepts. As noted, however, they will be hard to implement in the current global economic order, even for the United States.

4. Washington Consensus. At the end of the Cold War in the 1990s, it appeared that capitalism had won. The former communist countries entered the global economy with a horde of undercompetitive, overstaffed, and worn-out factories. State intervention was discredited, and a new neoliberal doctrine came from Washington, DC. The basic premise was that countries needed to reform by opening their markets, balancing their budgets and cutting subsidies, shutting loss-making companies, accepting foreign investment and know-how, and deregulating, leaving their old ways of state direction behind. The preferred way all these changes were enacted was through the "big bang" approach, or all at one time. In retrospect, like many theoretically pure ideas this turned out to be problematic in many cases.[5]

The core concepts of the Washington Consensus were spread by US diplomats and the IMF and World Bank, the two main institutions working on policy reform in Eastern Europe and the Former Soviet Union. At the same time, politicians and their advisors with free market economics training in the United States gained power in Latin America and Asia (especially at the University of Chicago and Berkeley, respectively), spreading the same ideas there.

Many of the core concepts of the Washington Consensus are still considered to be sound. The main criticisms are that they were and continue to be implemented too rigidly, too rapidly (i.e., the big bang), and in environments where they are unlikely to take hold. Many practitioners insisted on the wholesale transference of so-called best-practice ideas and institutions into places and environments where traditions and capabilities were extremely different. Some would blame the rapid opening of economies promoted by the Washington

Consensus for steep (mainly temporary) declines in living standards, political chaos, and the rise of kleptocratic and extremely corrupt governments in many countries where the policies were enacted. They would claim that old institutions were stripped away, and only a chaotic, less-than-free market was left in their place. It is fair to say that much of the theoretical work done in economics is supportive of the basic policy proscriptions of the Washington Consensus school.

5. Property rights and neoinstitutionalism. Though this area could be seen as an offshoot of the Washington Consensus concepts, it gained a life of its own. The basic precepts are that what matters most are determining and enforcing property rights, enforcing contracts, and in general establishing sound and consistent rule of law across all areas that affect the economy.[6] For this group, the exact rule that is passed is perhaps less important than competent and consistent implementation. The main phrases that are heard in these circles are "rule of law," "good governance," and "ease of doing business." The World Bank has been a major proponent, publishing its annual "Doing Business" indicators, ranking countries by how easy it is for companies to establish themselves and grow. The World Economic Forum (WEF) also publishes a similar report based on interviews with businesses called the WEF Competitiveness Report. It ranks countries' "competitiveness" as defined in their publication. There is strong, though not fully conclusive, evidence that improvements in these governance indicators are good for economic growth.[7]
6. Cluster competitiveness. Coined in Michael Porter's (1990) seminal book *The Competitive Advantage of Nations*, a **cluster** is a geographic grouping of highly globally competitive firms, their supporting industries, and facilitating physical and governmental infrastructure. Some famous clusters include the technology industry in California's Silicon Valley, the Italian digital machine tool industry, the Dutch flower business, and banking in the City of London. Cluster competitiveness advocates seek to replicate in other locations the conditions observed to exist in successful clusters, with the goal of also spawning and supporting groups of globally competitive firms. Implementation of the concept has taken many different forms, including the creation of special industrial zones, the formation of national competitiveness programs and councils to improve government support for private firms, and the ring fencing of companies in and related to certain industries into cluster groups and targeting them for support.[8] Though some infant industry arguments may work their way into cluster competitiveness programs, most programs start with a premise of engagement with rather than protection from the global economy.

Implementation along with costs and benefits has been hugely varied. Porter's term was essentially descriptive. He observed that these clusters existed, not the conditions under which they arose. Most of them likely took decades of trial and error, starts and stops, and a certain amount of serendipity to reach the point at which he observed them. Replicating that process or even putting the conditions in place for it to be replicated is a complicated effort, to say the least. Since the "real" clusters observed by Porter took decades to evolve, it is perhaps not fair to expect newer ones to do so much more quickly.

Those are (only) some of the major models for economic growth that have come and gone and worked their ways into national policies.[9] As with much else in economics, there are some problems with sorting through their relative levels of efficacy. Much partial and correlative analysis exists. However, it is practically impossible to rigorously collect and analyze the data that would be required to test and definitively prove one way or another that these concepts or the policies tied to them led to higher growth. At various points, this book has highlighted some of the data and analysis problems encountered when trying to determine policy impact over long periods of time.

A likely truth about the pros and cons of the different approaches is that each of the above concepts, and others out there, has something useful to say about how and why economies can grow. Unfortunately, as the financial author and blogger Cullen Roche has said, "Economics is mostly a policy debate masquerading as a scientific debate."[10] As such, economic growth and development fads come and everyone jumps on them when it is politically expedient. Then when the fads are gone, no one wants to go back and systematically think through what may be worth salvaging and what may be better off left in the dustbin. Broad concepts including their useful aspects are often dumped and forgotten.

Arguments on economic growth policy are frequently won and lost not on the basis of evidence, but on the ability of one arguer to claim successfully that the other arguer is a closet adherent to some debunked theory, which in all reality was never even properly debunked. "That sounds like a lot of Washington Consensus crap," or "you are just trying to repeat the failed infant industries experiment here," are the sorts of zingers often used to curtail otherwise productive policy debates. Buzzword–based attacks all too frequently replace thoughtful, data-driven analysis. A more productive approach would stem from a careful recognition of the relative strengths and weaknesses of each model and the conditions under which they would be most likely to succeed or fail.

Most of the rest of this subsection is set within the framework of economic "convergence." Economic convergence started as a theoretical construct with some very basic policy provisions attached to it, but has grown to become more than that. **Convergence** is the idea that over time poorer countries will grow more quickly than richer ones, so will catch up or "converge" in wealth. The concept came out of a paper by Robert Solow in 1956.[11] He hypothesized that capital scarcity in poor countries would lead to higher returns. This would attract more investment from countries where capital was plentiful, and cheap, and the poorer countries would then grow. At some point, different countries would "converge" to similar steady-state levels of income.

The model was nicely constructed and used some elegant math to show the dynamics. It was also pretty much wrong, in that the predicted results did not hold. Figure 8.1 shows growth rates over fifty-three years of countries against their starting GDP. There does not appear to be a clear correlation between starting wealth and

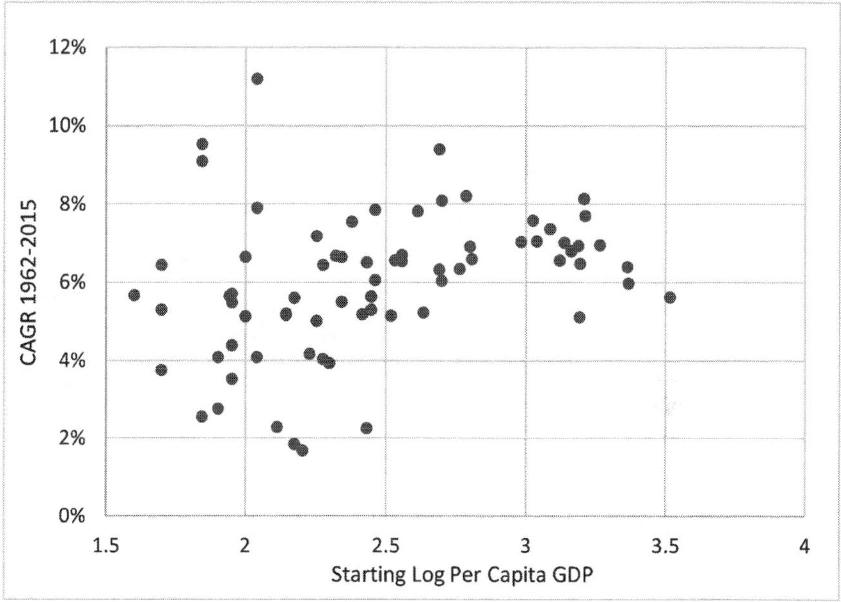

Figure 8.1. Log Starting Per Capita GDP vs. CAGR 1962–2015

Source: The data is from the World Bank database. Other sources include Durlauf et al. 2004 and Robert Barro and Xavier Sala-i-Martin 2004.

economic growth over the forty-year period captured by the data. If anything, it might be a bit negative. Other World Bank data shows a similar situation: from 1960 to 2010, the richest quintile of countries grew at 2.1 percent a year and the poorest quintile at 2.2 percent.[12] That is not a resounding case for the theory, at least when applied on a global basis.

A second limit of the theory is that convergence in the model was driven by relative capital scarcity and differential returns to capital. For that to work, the risk-adjusted return of investing in a developing country would need to be higher than in a rich country. As anyone who has invested in emerging markets knows, it is often the case that the risks are too high to compensate for the often only slightly higher expected return on capital. Capital scarcity alone does not drive higher real returns.

Though the broad results do not hold (yet, to be fair) and the reasons for convergence in the model are simplistic and probably wrong, the idea has merit: it is a decent starting framework for trying to understand why poorer countries are or are not growing. It is particularly interesting to look at where convergence has actually happened. It does seem to hold when economies are closely linked in multiple ways. Figure 8.2 shows the starting incomes of the American states, and their subsequent growth rates. For much of US history, there has been a large difference in wealth between states. Though this difference remains, the gaps have narrowed from what they were. Poorer states have grown faster than richer ones. In line with the theory, their incomes have converged over time.

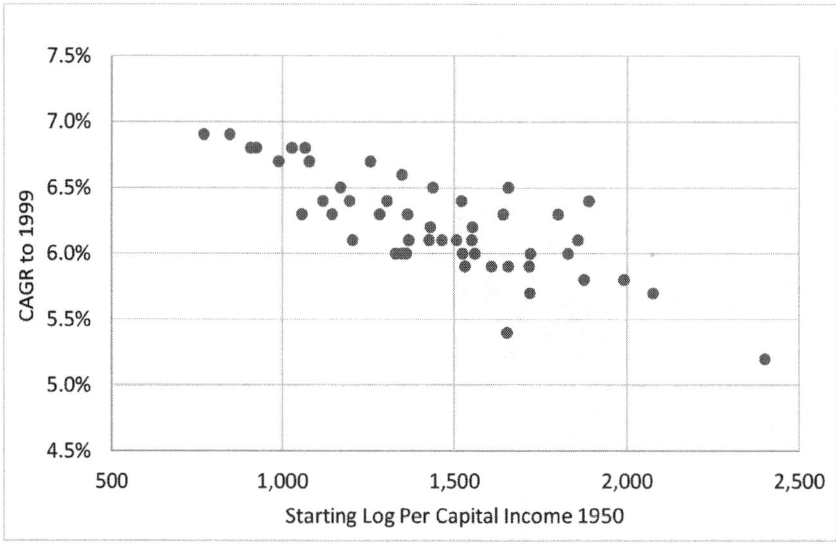

Figure 8.2. CAGR against Log Starting PC Income US States 1929–2014
Source: Data is from Brian C. Jenkins website at the University of California, Irvine.

A similar graph could be made for the countries of the European Union, where convergence also seems to hold over time.[13] Something similar can be seen with the newer EU states from Eastern Europe, at least up until the 2008 crisis. Interestingly, the crisis revealed a reversal in convergence of some of the older states of the European Union that previously had faster growth rates. Greece is the most notable example.

This conditional data can lead to a revised, more nuanced position on convergence. First, it has not held globally per the predictions of the theory. Second, economies probably do not converge for the reasons given by the theory (i.e., capital scarcity and differential returns). Third, it does seem to happen when economies are closely linked, and the more closely linked, the more convergence is seen. Fourth, and in conclusion, understanding why convergence does and does not happen in a globalized economy can help in understanding why certain economies grow or don't grow.

You could almost throw the whole convergence concept out and just talk about economic growth, but convergence is a useful basic framework. First, it seems to happen reliably when linkages between economies are tight. This is one of the clearest conclusions available on economic growth. Also, in a globalized world, countries do not develop on their own, but as part of an interconnected global economy. Myanmar, North Korea, and the former Soviet Union all tried to develop without being connected. It does not work—that much is agreed on as well. When China ditched its internally focused growth plan and embraced the global economy, it started to grow. In short, it is hard to see how growth can happen *outside* of the broader context of convergence.

If poor economies can converge to higher levels of wealth when they are closely interconnected with richer ones, and if the increasingly globalized environment presents opportunities for interconnectedness that goes beyond geography, then a useful line of thinking should be to look at what those connections are and how specifically they can drive growth. That is a starting hypothesis: that the sorts of linkages that drove convergence-related growth in US states and EU countries increasingly exist in a globalized economy.

There is a large amount of literature on this topic. Table 8.2 summarizes some of the factors that can drive or inhibit economic convergence between countries.

The above raises the question whether there may be another more global wave of convergence, similar to what was seen with the United States and the EU countries. Many of the factors that probably drove convergence in those cases were localized at the time, such as common language(s) of business, ease of communication, ease of trade due to proximity, within a couple days' travel for intermediaries, shared institutions and rules, and common educational platforms leading to a similar knowledge and cultural base.

Those same factors that drove convergence between geographically close nations are increasingly available to a wider range of economies geographically dispersed from wealthy countries and each other. Similarly, motivated policy makers in poorer nations can review a wide range of policy and institutional factors that worked in the wealthy countries, and adapt and adopt them as appropriate. The factors in the table above certainly played a role in the emergence of both China and India starting in the 1990s. Both embraced markets, technology, and at least some selected institutions.

Will wealth continue to increase, and will faster growth become the norm in an increasing number of poor countries? Like most economic questions, the answer is probably "maybe" and "it depends." There are cases where convergence would be expected, but where it did not happen, at least not to the degree one would expect. The economies of Mexico and the United States are a good case in point. Mexico's growth rate has not been exceptional, despite being next to and having strong trade and investment agreements with the largest wealthy economy in the world. Notably, it has not as of yet successfully adopted many of its northern neighbors' better institutions. Similarly, much of North Africa has not grown very quickly despite increased economic ties to the European Union, and has gone backward in many cases.

Even Greece opens up an interesting question of convergence. Did the Greek economy come further than it "should have" based on the factors in table 8.2, relying on easy credit from the European Union, and is it now returning to its "real" level of income? Maybe the case of convergence was a mirage, and absent a sufficient intensity of the factor above, a country can slip back. These are important but difficult questions. A next attempt at understanding some of the answers can be to look at some of the factors that can keep convergence-driven growth from happening or even reverse it. See table 8.3.

Table 8.2. Factors Supporting Convergence

Technology adoption	People and companies in any nearly any country can often adopt technologies and production processes that took decades to develop and take root in wealthier countries. Computers, cell phone technologies, harvesting equipment, hybrid seeds, solar panels, and CNC machine tools are only a few examples. These can in turn, in theory, yield productivity gains that took years and sometimes decades to accomplish in the countries where the technologies were developed. This is sometimes referred to as "leapfrogging."
Virtualization of knowledge	Anyone with an Internet connection and English (or many other) language skills can access information on almost any topic. This ranges from treatment of root fungus in raspberries, to optimal drill speeds for different materials and bit sizes, to classes at MIT on machine learning technology. To obtain useful, practical knowledge, it is no longer necessary to seek out a (possibly rare) knowledgeable person in the community, travel abroad, or pay for the information.
Virtualization of trade	In the past, arranging trade with a person or company in another country required going through a complicated and not very transparent process of wholesalers, shipping brokers, wire transfers, faxes, and paperwork. Now, in a few minutes it is possible to find and arrange trade with a wide range of global buyers and sellers. Sellers in any country can easily access markets abroad and then sell into them using any number of virtual tools and fulfillment services. If it is true that increased trade is good for an economy, then so is cost-saving virtualization.
Common and effective rules governing trade and investment	As global money flows have increased, rules have followed to protect that money. Companies in countries that put strong rules in place are likely get more investment at better rates (all other things being equal, of course). Investors like to see familiar rules, so countries seeking to attract investors have put similar rules in place. There may still be local risk factors, but global standards in accounting, measurement, trade paperwork, investor protection, and more can usually only help as long as they are implemented well. Poor implementation can lead to even more confusion.
Desire among populations	When exposed through media to standards of living in countries outside their own, people can get frustrated and seek change. This can put pressure on governments to adopt more progrowth policies. It can also lead to political instability and the adoption of populist policies that may not be consistent with longer-term economic growth. Contrary to popular opinion, nondemocratic states can be under at least as much pressure to appear legitimate to their populations. This can but does not always translate into progrowth policies.
Transport networks	Transportation has changed radically in the last few decades. Major changes have occurred in intermodal or container shipping, sophisticated global logistics networks that allow rapid, reliable, just-in-time shipment of goods all over the world, and instant communication between points. Tools available twenty years ago only to the most sophisticated wholesalers are now commonplace and available to small traders in all but the poorest and most isolated countries.

Table 8.3. Factors Inhibiting Convergence

Infrastructure	Convergence happened in US and EU states at least partially because of integrated market access. Despite gains from virtualization, it can be difficult to trade and invest across borders. Many roads, ports, vehicles, and railways in poorer countries are in bad condition and/or poorly managed, increasing the costs of moving goods. The real costs of importing technologically advanced products increases, because spare parts can be expensive to import and subject to considerable delays. A fancy new machine is of limited use if waiting for a spare part or technician results in weeks, or longer, of downtime.
Culture and risk aversion	People hate to talk about this topic. Likened to "blaming the victim," it can be culturally insensitive or politically incorrect to mention it. In truth, culture matters in economics. There may not be a single, identifiable element of a national culture that impedes economic activity. However, a basic threshold level of cooperative impetus and trust may be required to facilitate transactions and build companies and markets. Also, attitudes toward education, women, science, and work and leisure all factor in. When taking advantage of the forces for convergence means copying parts of societies that people may not respect, culture can impede progress. Certain ideologies may also overtly oppose technological and human progress (as commonly understood in the West).[a]
Lack of human and physical capital	Even extensive, free exposure to technologies and methods used in successful economies will mean nothing without human capital. Integration into the global market requires language skills, understanding of technology, ability to read and process complex concepts, management capability, and other skills. Grounded in a good education system, human capital is challenging to build successfully from a low starting point and takes long-term commitment. Economists tend not to worry about a lack of physical or investment capital, in part because investors are good at filling these gaps if they can make money. Building human capital is harder. If anything, the need for these skills is increasing, so populations that are behind in this area may end up even further behind (rather than converging) with time.
Weak technology supply chains	Improved access to production technology does not mean that it can be used effectively or serviced in a timely manner. Sophisticated production technology requires a fast and efficient service and spare-part supply chain to avoid prolonged outages. Technologies that are developed in wealthy countries may also be inappropriate for developing countries, and may not fit well with their mix of human capital and cost of labor versus capital.

(*continued*)

Table 8.3. *Continued*

Corruption and governance	In theory governance problems can be addressed relatively quickly. The World Bank maintains the "Doing Business" list of indicators that are used to rank country performance.[b] A clear correlation exists between countries that score well and those that are doing well economically. There is an oft-noted correlation between natural resource exporters and corruption in what has been designated the **resource curse**, or a cycle of instability, corruption, poor governance, and low growth despite high potential wealth. Corruption and poor governance are problematic for convergence because they create barriers to and increase the real costs of investment, increasing risk and lowering real returns. Corruption can be more difficult to combat than outsiders often assume. It can be intertwined with centuries-old ways of doing business, caring for family members, and supporting and maintaining peace in interest and ethnic groups.
War	There is no better way to derail an economy than a war on its own territory. Many of the worst-performing economies of any era are those in the midst of some form of political instability. Pretty much all of the ways that convergence can happen are upset by war. As Turkey, for example, experienced in the mid-2010s, even low-level forms of war such as increased terrorist activity can drive off investment and tourism inflows.

a. Two major books on this topic are by David Landes (1998) *The Wealth and Poverty of Nations* and the more controversial and blunt Culture Matters by Lawrence Harrison and Samuel Huntington (2000). Francis Fukuyama's (1995) Trust also outlines the core cultural institutions that allow markets to function.
b. See The World Bank (2016). Transparency International (2016) maintains a global corruption perception index.

Two more themes emerge from the discussion and data on convergence and growth. First, even when convergence occurs, it may have limits. If all the factors that support convergence come together, convergence may happen between economies. However, empirical evidence shows that even despite long-term growth, those countries that were once poor may still not make it into the club of wealthy industrialized countries. They can grow but may never become rich. The world has seen significant economic growth in developing countries over the past decades. What it has seen very little of is countries that are not oil-rich or microstates getting wealthy and diversified enough to be considered high-income industrial economies.

This lack of countries making the jump from middle to high income is referred to in economics as the **middle-income trap**, and economists don't really know why it occurs. A case can be made that South Korea is the only previously poor non-microstate to become a developed market economy since the middle of the twentieth century. Evidence also supports that the rate of convergence has started to slow in the middle of the 2010s, after some decades of progress. Net emerging markets' growth rates have been only slightly higher than the developed market economies since the beginning of the 2010 decade.[14] Hope that a new batch of countries would enter the ranks of high-income countries seems to be on hold yet again.

The second theme is a little scarier to citizens of wealthy countries: convergence, development, and economic progress may not be "one-way streets." There is nothing in the convergence framework to indicate that just as poor countries can become rich, rich countries cannot become poor. Argentina went from being a rich country to a poorer one in the twentieth century. The Greek economy has gone into reverse, and Japan has flirted with relative reversal for twenty years. Even the case studies of successful convergence, the states of the United States and the European Union, have seen slippage and reversal in convergence in the recent decade.[15] Such trends, though as of now short term, threaten the integrity of the European Union and the legitimacy of the US government. The foundation of modern, liberal, capitalist democracies rests on the promise of economic growth.

What could cause "backward convergence"? Perhaps any number of factors, with many resembling the flip side of those that drive convergence. It may be driven by the kinds of demographic and political shifts as populations age and older voters seek security, rather than public investment in education and infrastructure. Backward convergence may be driven by an overshooting of convergence in the first place. For example, some of the convergence observed in the European Union may have been driven by credit expansion and the illusion of increased wealth, rather than fundamental, structural change in the poorer economies. As noted, the Greek economy may be a case in point here, but others such as Italy and Spain lagged even as the rest of the European Union recovered from the great recession.

Global convergence itself may be the culprit. The entry of large, low-wage manufacturing and service powers like India and China into the global economy has taken its toll on parts of wealthy countries' economies.[16] Whole economy damage could occur if the *C* for consumption in the GDP definition drops economy-wide. Should working-class wages continue to stagnate and fall, this scenario might look more probable. Income distribution, technology plateaus, technological advances, regulation and lack of regulation, cultural shifts, deflation, and many other factors can all play into this complicated question.

Reverse convergence (or negative growth) could be a real future concern if people and governments in wealthy countries fail to take care and reinforce the tricky set of factors that make a country rich. The situation is made even more sketchy by a lack of certainty around what those factors are.

Some form of partial and possibly mixed forward and backward convergence may become more likely in the future than broad convergence of a whole economy. Current data seems to support that parts of wealthy countries will stay rich and get even richer while parts of those same, wealthy countries come to resemble poorer countries. At the emerging markets end, rather than whole economies getting rich and coming to resemble the wealthy countries at the turn of the third millennium, pockets of them will become wealthier, possibly leaving much of the country behind.[17] This is already much in evidence in emerging markets and has been for some decades.[18] That is not to say that growth has not lifted all incomes. It has. However, to take the Chinese example, the top 10 percent of earners live much like the top 10 percent of rich-world people. However, the bottom 50 percent in China despite huge progress are still economically worse off than the bottom 50 percent in the rich world. This is a topic explored later in section two on "big shifts" in the global economy.

Some economist believe that as some of the key factors that drove national growth dissipate, the period of even moderate economic growth rates in wealthy countries may be coming to an end. There is talk of a period of **secular stagnation**, or sustained low growth.[19] There is no inherent reason why if growth can slow, it cannot become negative. Both are parts of the same process with the same drivers. Wealthy economies have become poor before when looked at in a broader historical context. The horizon only needs to broaden from the last seventy-five years to the last five hundred. If the rich world does enter a period of slower growth and continuing widening income gaps, politics will increasingly govern economic outcomes as frustration builds. Some of these may lead to higher growth, and some to greater stagnation. Which prevails will depend greatly on the behaviors of interest groups, voter blocs, and the ruling elites that they elect and influence. Some scenarios will be looked at in section two when exploring the effects of demography and income distribution.

CAPITAL FLOWS AND INVESTMENT DECISIONS

Global growth rate differentials are an interesting topic by themselves, but also presage some possible shifts in the global economy. Different rates of growth in different countries will change the balance of economic power on the planet. They have before and will again. Over the longer run, the relative share of global GDP of the wealthy, developed market economies is dropping, and that of the developing countries, mainly the large emerging markets, is gaining. This trend is likely to continue. There will be variability, both within and across countries and regions, but it is hard to imagine too many longer-term scenarios where the global balance of economic power is stagnant. As such, emerging markets' international and domestic policies will increasingly affect the global economy. Related, there will be more chances for global investors to make (and lose) money in these countries, which means global investment flows of all kinds are likely to continue to trend upward. Emerging markets have also increasingly become the source rather than just the destination of these money flows.

So what now? The main emerging markets have been and should continue to grow more quickly than developed markets. The case for investing in emerging markets seems clear. They should grow more quickly, so their companies should grow more quickly. If you like fixed income instead of equities, current yields are higher. They are the future. There are lots of talking heads on the news telling people that this percentage or that of a "balanced" investment portfolio should be in emerging markets. I am not convinced that portfolio allocation should work that way in general, but am especially unconvinced in this case because oddly emerging markets portfolio investments have not generally been good long-term holds. Some may be, or more to the point, some may have been. But if you are reading this, chances are you did not get in soon enough for a long-term hold to have worked. In the past few decades if you got in and held, you mainly just got to see your portfolio bounce around.

Figures 8.3 to 8.6 below illustrate the point. They show the price trends for the main ETFs for the so-called BRIC economies, Brazil, Russia, India, and China. These are the biggest, most liquid, highest-profile emerging markets. Like the Turkish case seen in a previous section (same bouncing graph, figure 7.6), they also seem to be rather poor long-term holds. If you got in early in China, the best one of the lot, over ten years you would have slightly less than doubled your money. That is a roughly 7 percent annual return. That is actually not bad in the modern world. But that is getting into the hottest emerging market at the best time. For the rest of the BRIC lot, you would not have done so well as a portfolio investor.

EFTs or even equities are not the only way to invest in emerging markets. Bond markets have been arguably hotter, with yields higher than in the developed market economies. However, remember the big currency correction of 2013–2014 following the US Fed's quantitative easing whisper. Currencies dropped, and many nominal interest rates were raised at the same time. Both of those actions led to drops in the

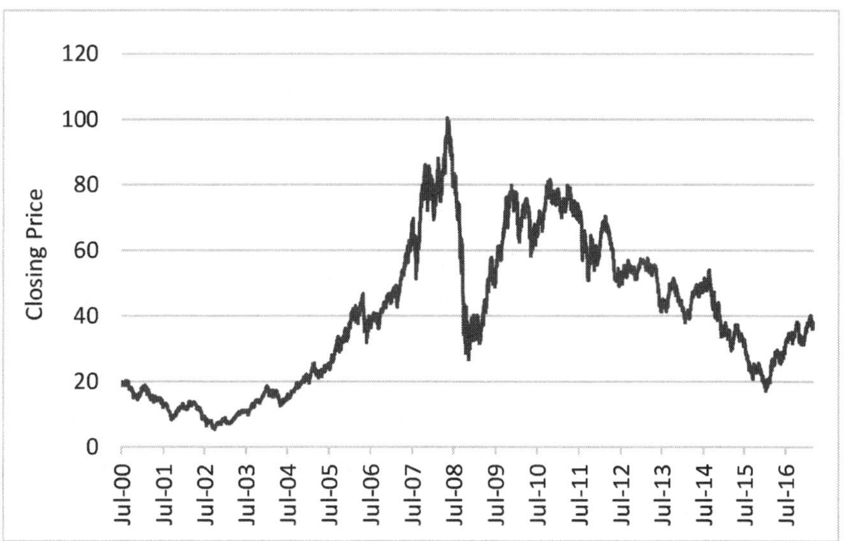

Figure 8.3. Brazilian Market ETF EWZ Price History
Source: Data from TD Ameritrade.

Figure 8.4. Russian Market ETF RSX Price History

Source: Data from TD Ameritrade.

Figure 8.5. Indian Market ETF EPI Price History

Source: Data from TD Ameritrade.

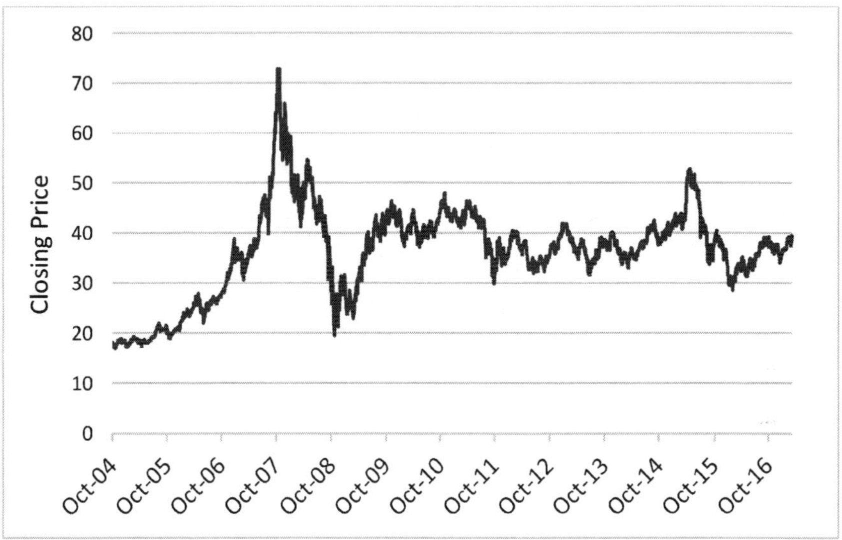

Figure 8.6. China Market ETF FXI Price History
Source: Data from TD Ameritrade.

values of bond holdings that more than erased gains from initially higher yields. This is a real risk in emerging markets bonds.

Back to equities. All of the charts shown start in relatively recent times after the ETFs were established. Certainly, there was money to be made before that. Though ETFs may have been later to the game than certain early-stage investors, they are still representative of emerging market returns. First, it is the way most people and even many investment firms access emerging markets. Low fees, diversification, and *relatively* high liquidity make them appealing. Second, the glory days before the ETFs were established were not so glorious. The various indices may have increased more before (or right as) ETFs made them accessible. However, that does not mean that people made a lot of money in these markets. They were notoriously illiquid. It was hard to buy and sell hundreds of thousands of dollars' worth of a single security in those days.

When I was working in emerging markets finance in the late 1990s, I met a partner from one of the big early emerging markets investment firms at a conference in Istanbul. The Russians had just defaulted on their bonds, called GKOs, and their firm had taken a big hit. I asked him what the appeal had been for the Russian bonds at the time. The answer: the investor had a lot of money to invest that was allocated for emerging markets and it was one of the few places he could dump $50 million or more at a time. He did not particularly like the investment. Access and liquidity drove the investment decision. That $50 million may seem like a lot of money, but for a big money manager it is not much. There was a lack of other emerging markets investment options at the time, especially in the aftermath of the Asia crisis.[20]

I had a similar experience in the Turkish repo market a few years later. Liquidity was good, and annualized real returns on the repo market had been in the range of 30 to 50 percent for years. Turkey had just reached an agreement with the IMF to continue supporting their currency (among other deal components). Then the IMF agreement fell apart and the currency cratered. Returns turned negative overnight and I lost money. When the market was dropping, liquidity dried up and it was hard to get out. That is the way it goes with liquidity, never there when you need it. In the mid-1990s I invested in the then-booming Montenegrin market. But even small trades of 1,000 euro were hard to get in and out of. Yes, the market was going up and it looked like money was being made. And some was, just not much when it came down to it. That market also gave up its gains in a pretty spectacular fall. So these early-stage "frontier" markets can seem like good places to get into pre-ETF, but it can take a lot of effort and solid nerves to do well.

Though emerging markets are experiencing high growth and potentially offer good returns, no investment is good at any price. Even high-growth and highly promising emerging markets may offer poor risk-adjusted returns at times. When working in finance in Turkey, I remember one of the top equity sales reps at the time proclaiming that he always told his clients to forget about the ups and downs. The market was a great long-term hold; just get in. That is what anyone trying to sell something says. The real estate fliers that come in the mail say that there has never been a better time to buy or sell a home. In a real market, how can that be?

It is simply not clear if the main emerging markets indices are good long-term investments, at least on a historical basis. Volatility has been more constant than returns. And with volatility comes the opportunity to play the bubble-and-bust game. That is what a lot of traders do. And ironically, that game drives capital flows through the global economy and, incidentally, drives those booms and busts. Volatility creates a game that then perpetuates more volatility.

In sum, there is considerable money moving in and out of emerging economies. The upward growth trajectory of the economies appears to have increased the quantity of that money, but as of 2017 has not led to solid, long-term upward trends in their securities markets. At least not yet.

DEVELOPMENT ASSISTANCE

Development assistance was introduced briefly in chapter 6, as a component of the balance of payments. It will be expanded on briefly here. Development assistance is when mainly wealthy-country governments or organizations donate money and/or services to poorer countries to help them improve social or economic conditions. The basic logic behind the assistance is to facilitate the types of factors that can help poorer countries take advantage of an inherent opportunity to become wealthier, or "converge." These are usually longer-term flows and are distinct from emergency disaster-type assistance. Considerable funds move across borders in this

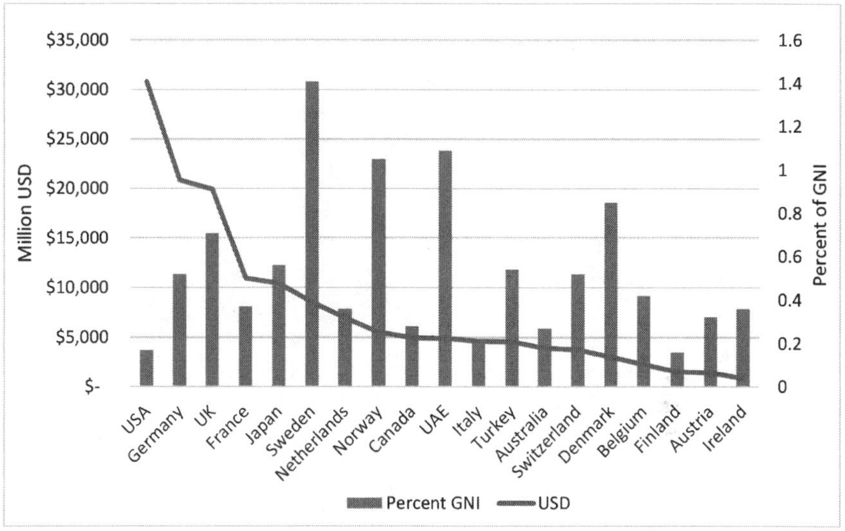

Figure 8.7. Official ODA 2015, $ and % GNI
Source: OECD 2016.

way. Figure 8.7 notes some numbers on countries of origin for official, or government, development assistance by USD and percentage of GNI.

For the recipient countries, sometimes it is a very small part of their economy. For others, it can be a significant percentage of what gets spent there on various development-related projects or even GDP. Like most of economics, there is a lot of debate about whether development assistance achieves its purported goals.[21] Other controversy surrounds whether development assistance reaches the neediest countries[22] or is allocated for political reasons, whether it primarily props up bad regimes,[23] and whether the actual benefits justify the costs of the "investment" that is ultimately made by wealthy-country taxpayers.[24] These are all important questions, upon which lives may depend. However, they are outside the scope of this book. Interested readers can refer to the resources provided in the footnotes.

The main question for the purposes of this book is how development assistance matters for the global economy. Although the flows can be significant for recipient countries, development assistance does not matter much except in cases where the countries would otherwise collapse. Most of those countries are not a major part of the global economy.

Support from the IMF is often thrown into this category, so it is probably as good a place as any to make a few comments. As noted in chapter 1, the IMF is a multilateral international financial institution set up to assist countries in overcoming short-term international payments imbalances (shortages). When hot money rushes out and reserves are drained or insufficient to finance imports, the IMF provides short-term loans.

The IMF is not a development organization despite what many believe, or believe its role should be. The IMF likes to get paid back, so it will normally impose a set of conditions on the recipient country that are designed to stabilize the situation and ensure it gets its money back. IMF conditionality commonly requires reduced government deficits (lower spending and higher taxes), and higher interest rates to attract capital back to the country. Because of an adverse effect on the immediate standard of living, IMF conditions can be unpopular in recipient countries and have led in a number of cases to anti-IMF riots. IMF conditionality is historically in line with the "Washington Consensus" line of thinking discussed above.

The IMF matters for development and global capital flows for a couple of reasons. First, it can stabilize unstable markets with its money and programs and lead to a renewed faith in the economy that brings investors back. More than one investor has made money betting on IMF programs' succeeding, buying bonds when they were at a low. Even "vulture capital" is still capital and serves a purpose in bad times, such as when capital inflow is desperately needed. Given how much bond markets swing around when there is a risk of default, this game is not for the timid. More than one investor, including the author, has been burned. When the IMF program for Turkey failed to stabilize the country in 2001, currency and bond prices plummeted and yields soared. Investors who had previously made money betting on the success of the IMF program found themselves in trouble. Similar stories abound with the Asian financial crisis.[25]

The other reason the IMF matters is that usually the World Bank follows the IMF, often with substantial (and somewhat "below market" interest rate) loans for the country. And unlike IMF loans, World Bank loans are often forgiven and/or never repaid by the recipient countries. The IMF is the bad cop, often criticized for forcing unpalatable medicine onto emerging markets (and some reemerging ones like Greece), whereas the World Bank tries to help improve the situation with low-interest loans for development purposes.

It is often unclear whether these loans have the desired outcome for recipient economies, since the World Bank, like many development organizations, is guilty of not rigorously analyzing program results. However, the loans can represent substantial inflows into a country that can be used for education, health, and infrastructure. On the flip side, these loans also increase the indebtedness of the country. I acted as an advisor to the cabinet of one emerging markets government that was being offered low-interest World Bank loans for a pilot energy program that was unlikely to have any impact whatsoever, even at the admission of the World Bank loan officer. We had a heated debate about whether that was the right thing for the country, but ultimately the country took the money. Money can be hard to resist even when it is destined for programs that make little sense.

NOTES

1. These are some of the main *policy* frameworks. Considerable additional work has been done in academia, most notably with endogenous growth models and their offspring. Some results of this work have made their way into policy frameworks, providing some supporting theoretical arguments mainly to the Washington Consensus and cluster competitiveness (through increasing returns models) frameworks.

2. Walter Rodney et al. (1981) *How Europe Underdeveloped Africa* is one of the classics of the era and puts forth many of the arguments behind dependency theory.

3. Erik Reinert (2007) maintains that all or nearly all of the successful modern economies followed some form of initial protectionist or infant industry type of policies. See Noland and Pack (2003) for a more skeptical approach.

4. As one reader of this manuscript noted, as tariff options have disappeared some countries have successfully employed nontariff, mainly regulatory, barriers to continue to protect national companies. This is much easier for large countries like China and perhaps to a lesser extent India, than for smaller developing countries.

5. The so-called big bang was a method preferred by many Washington Consensus advocates led by economist Jeffrey Sachs, though there was considerable debate about that versus the gradual approach to introducing market reforms. Ronald McKinnon (1991) wrote one of the more influential (but apparently not influential enough) books advocating for a more gradualist approach.

6. Peruvian economist Hernando de Soto's (2000) and American Douglass North's (1990, 2005) work, though quite different, are probably the most important references in this school. See also (Dixit 2004) and the work by Daron Acemoglu and he and James Robinson (2009, 2012 respectively).

7. The World Bank (2016) and the WEF (2016) publish all data and reports on their websites.

8. Michael Fairbanks's (1997) book *Plowing the Sea* is one of the main books in the cluster competitiveness canon. See also Porter 1990.

9. For a concise assessment of many of the concepts behind economic growth, see also Helpman (2004).

10. Roche 2014.

11. Solow 1956.

12. Aart and McKenzie, 2014.

13. Graphs can be found at Wunsch 2013 or in the CEPS study, "Convergence in the EU."

14. *The Economist* 2014b.

15. See Wolf (2016), for example.

16. More than one study would support this view; see Scott (2012) in the Economic Policy Institute.

17. In Tyler Cowen's (2014) book *Average Is Over*, he presents a case for the already-occurring bifurcation of the United States into wealthy areas with high taxes and levels of public services, and low-cost, poorer areas. Bolio et al. (2014) published a paper by the McKinsey Global Institute outlining the perils of what they call the "two-speed" economy in Mexico.

18. See, for example, *The Economist* (2015b) article on the African middle classes.

19. For authors following this line of thinking see Piketty (2014) or HSBC Chief Economist Stephen King (2013).

20. As reported by Deloitte Managing Director John Mennel, investors fifteen years later like the Chinese market for similar reasons. Not only is there volume, but also a preponderance of hedging opportunities that don't exist in smaller markets.

21. See *White Man's Burden* by William Easterly (2006), the former chief economist for the World Bank. He goes into an in-depth analysis of the development industry. Another book, Dambisa Moyo's (2009) *Dead Aid*, is a particularly damning account of the aid industry and its effects on poor countries. More positive perspectives can readily be found in various industry reports, such as the one from devex.com.

22. One NBER study by Qian (2014) estimates that since 1960, only 1.67 to 5.25 percent of official development assistance has gone to the poorest 20 percent of countries.

23. Bueno de Mesquita and Smith (2012).

24. See the websites of the main organizations dispersing official development assistance for material on their programs and results (e.g., usaid.gov, dfid.giv.uk, ec.europa.eu/europeaid, and others).

25. See the analysis of the IMF role in the Asian and then Russian and Latin financial crises by Paul Blustein (2001).

II

BIG SHIFT CASES AND SCENARIOS FOR THE FUTURE

Learning to forecast is probably the skill that economics graduate students most hope to learn when entering a program. Unfortunately, like all of us, economists are pretty poor forecasters.[1] It doesn't always seem that way. Reports abound of people who foresaw this or that thing that was going to happen. Hedge fund manager John Paulson made a fortune shorting mortgage bonds in 2008. Paul Krugman foresaw the Asian financial crisis of 1997. Many famous forecasters eventually fall from grace, as Paulson did with major losses in 2014. Others do not, or at least not yet. Not to discount the skilled efforts of those who really did figure something out, but with numerous people continuously making proclamations, some of them are bound to be right. As has been said, "if you must forecast, forecast often."

Forecasting success might be attributable to luck or talent and past methodologies might not apply to new conditions, making it problematic to assess what works best and when. Nicholas Taleb examined the role of luck in financial market success in his brilliant philoso-econ rant *Fooled by Randomness*, a (very entertaining) "must-read" for anyone interested in financial markets forecasting. He concludes that luck plays a great role.

In all fairness, predicting the future is hard whether it's next year's inflation rate or the next financial crisis. Humans and their forecasting tools rely almost exclusively on the known, usually near-term past. It's not our fault; past data is all we have by definition. Models can be highly sophisticated, but they are still mainly extrapolations that can't capture changes not contained in historical data.[2] Short-term predictions on stable variables can be useful and at least relatively accurate. However, the real limitation of forecasting models is that when the future swerves from its previous path, so does the forecast accuracy.

That is too bad. Fortunes, careers, and lives are won and lost with these discontinuities, when the economy veers from its previous path. Almost all the major global economic events described in this book revolved around discontinuities. This is where the real action is, and we human beings are terribly equipped to understand and prepare for them, economists or not. Mark Twain was equally right about economic history when he reportedly said, "History does not repeat itself, but it does rhyme." The question is how to get past a focus on the repeats to understand the rhymes.

Developing and analyzing scenarios is one way to dislodge our minds and models from past data and start to explore the types of discontinuities that can rattle or enrich our lives. Scenarios are also a way to apply the concepts from the first section of the book to look toward the future, rather than just at past events. The scenarios take the current state and evolution of the global economy (as much as it is known) as a starting point, and then consider the outcomes when other established shifts inside and outside the field of economics collide with that path. The collisions might create discontinuities, accelerations, or decelerations of existing trends, or might do nothing at all. Most likely, at least some of the established shifts will matter—they will collide with and change the course of the global economy. Scenario analysis gets us thinking more clearly about which shifts might matter, why, how, and how to prepare for them.

Scenario development and analysis is not the same as or a substitute for forecasting, though both can yield some of the same benefits. The goal is less to predict the future than to prepare for it, and be better positioned to manage risks or reap benefits. Scenario development and analysis can assist decision making by anyone whose future depends on the global economy, whether those decisions are in education, career choice, business strategy, investment portfolio strategy and balances, or risk hedging. In some cases, the preparation costs may be greater than the risk or potential gain. In others, it may be relatively costless to become better positioned. The scenarios and possible outcomes presented here are extremely varied in the range of their potential effects, their likelihood of coming to pass, and the costs and benefits of confronting them.

There is no pretense that the scenarios put forth are in any way exhaustive or even the most important ones. In choosing the limited scenarios that follow, many others were excluded. Some potentially influential and far-reaching scenarios were left out, partly due to lack of space and partly because of difficulties specifying them clearly and narrowly enough. The scenarios are also just starting points for deeper analysis, consisting of a series of short notes and usually specifying only a small handful of possible outcomes. The resources at www.wolandia.com is a venue for exploring these and additional scenarios and ways to position for them.

The five sections that follow start with an exposition of five major shifts that can change the path of the global economy: demographic shifts, ecological change, income and wealth distribution, virtualization and IT, and emerging markets growth.[3] The expositions are short summaries that describe the shifts, but take the evidence for them as given. There are ample outside references to access more background information, so arguments for the validity of the shifts are not repeated. Following each of these expositions is a series of potential scenarios and impacts as viewed through the lens developed in the first section of this book.

NOTES

1. A study from the International Institute of Forecasters revealed that it was not until most economies were already in recession in 2009 that economists were able to forecast a recession for the following year, Ahir and Loungani 2014.

2. A promising, human rather than machine and solely data-centric, approach is possibly developing out of the IARPA-funded work by Philip Tetlock and Dan Gardner (2015). Results are preliminary, but they have been able to vastly improve forecasts on a wide range of political and economic variables.

3. This is certainly not the first time that an author has hypothesized that big external trends will bear upon the future global economy. See, for example, Dobbs et al. 2016 for an exposition for what they call the four disruptive trends.

9

Demographic Shifts

The modern global economy was born from, shaped, and was shaped by the huge population explosion over the last two hundred years. The explosion coincided with the industrial revolution and unprecedented increases in wealth during the period. Population demographics is the study of changes in the sizes and characteristics of populations. The field is drawn from here to highlight the interplay between the global population and economy.

Figure 9.1 depicts the global population over the last two hundred years, and a forecast for the next one hundred. The population from around ten thousand to two hundred years ago was fairly small and steady, with a few dips for plagues. Almost all the real change is in the last two hundred years. Economists can feel good about the chart, in that demographers find it as hard to forecast as they do. The dotted line second from the top can probably be taken as the most probable forecast.

As the chart indicates, the structure of the world's population is in the early stages of its second major shift in two centuries. The first shift is the ongoing increase of the world's population to unprecedented levels. As of 2017, the earth's population is at an all-time high and still has 30 to 50 percent more growth left in it by most projections. The second, more recent, shift is that the population is starting to grow more slowly and growth is even going into reverse in some countries. This is indicated by the inflection points in the curves, as they bend to the right.

Not shown on the chart is how much the story varies for different countries. The European Union, Japan, and China are facing greater declines in their population growth rate. In some countries, population is already shrinking. Much of the emerging markets world outside of China is still growing and has a relatively young population. Most of the ongoing population growth will likely occur there. The United States is somewhere in between.

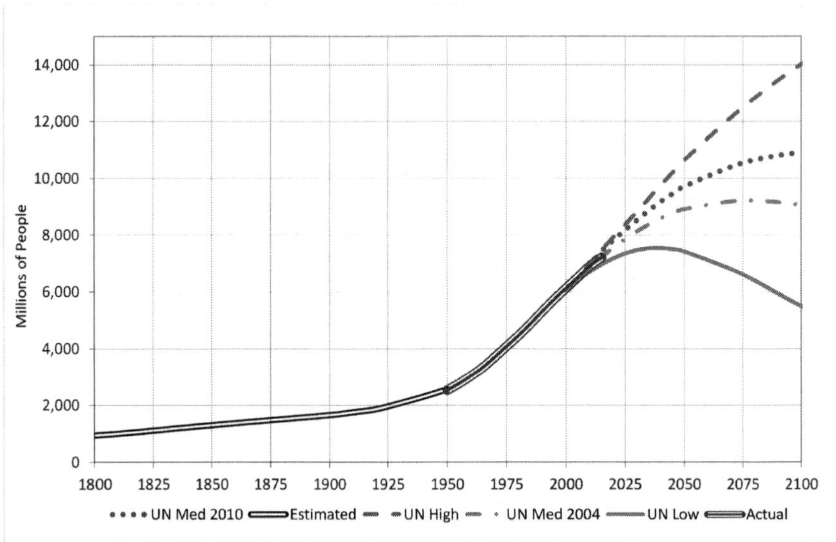

Figure 9.1. World Population, Historical and Forecast
Source: UN data compiled by Loren Cobb, UC Denver.

Just as the global economy was shaped by (and shaped) the initial population explosion, the starting hypothesis for these scenarios is that it will continue to change both as the population continues to grow *and* as the growth rate slows.[1]

The first half of the story is about the growing population. At the very least, we expect more of what we have seen in the last two centuries. Along with growth are increases in wealth and overall global consumption, especially as people are lifted out of poverty and gain disposable incomes. Implications are vast, and some will be explored in the scenarios. Areas to be considered include natural resource prices and volatility, public choices and politics, and public goods like clean air and a "normal" climate, given correlations between population growth and emissions.

The second half of the story, slowing population growth, leads inevitably to an aging population, since proportionally fewer young people are entering the world. In a modern economy, that means older and fewer workers as a percentage of the total population, especially as people live longer after they retire. The more rapid the decrease, the faster populations age. Some European countries' populations are already shrinking, as growth goes into reverse. Besides being less likely to be in the workforce, older population members make different spending, voting, and investment decisions.

The balance between workers and retirees is called the **dependency ratio**, or the percentage of the population that are "dependent" on current workers' tax payments to fund retired workers' benefits. Figure 9.2 from OECD data shows changes in the dependency ratio from 2000 to 2010, and forecasts to 2030. The dependency ratio

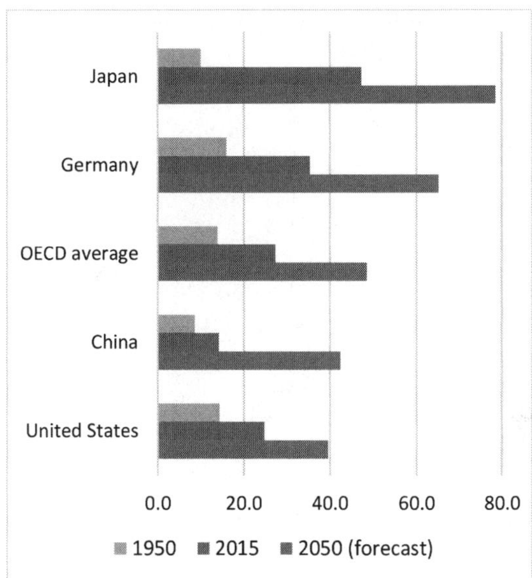

Figure 9.2. Old-Age Dependency Ratios
Source: OECD 2015b. See also *The Economist* 2014c.

is driven primarily by demographic change, and secondarily from mortality and retirement ages. People may work longer or die sooner than the projections assume, but the overall trend will continue as long as population growth slows. Shifts in the dependency ratio are not projections, but current events.

The dependency ratio is more important now than even fifty years ago. Most modern economies have social programs in place to support retirees that are paid for by current workers. People often believe their payments into pension programs support their own future retirement. In reality, in most pension systems people pay to support current retirees, and younger workers are supposed to support them when they get older. This is called a **pay-as-you-go** system and it is the global norm.[2]

An aging population also votes differently. In democracies, older people vote more frequently than the young and tend to vote more conservatively, except with regard to social services for retirees.[3] If you consider their incentives, the reliable voters of the older generation will not likely vote to reduce their benefits even if it means more debt and less investment in other public services.[4] No matter what your position on social support programs for retirees, shifts in the dependency ratio will affect the quantity and direction of global public and private spending and investment.

In most economies, government spending on retiree programs is increasing, not because benefit levels are necessarily increasing, but because more people are retiring. All other things being equal, increased spending there leaves less for investments in areas that benefit the young and help keep an economy competitive, like education and infrastructure. Dependency ratio increases will continue to exacerbate this trend. To maintain allocations to other programs, taxes will need to increase or benefits to the elderly decrease. Either option will disrupt the affected economies.[5] The analysis here is mainly a data exposition and is separate from any ideas of what to do about it. The dependency ratio itself is statistical, not political. What to do about it is political, and trying to anticipate policy decisions will help in tracking likely changes in the global economy.

The questions about slowing population growth go beyond just public pensions and health care. Other questions abound. Aging populations can directly and indirectly affect investment patterns, the attractiveness of a country for investment, interest rates, and levels of national debt between countries. Different investors from different countries may finance retirees from other countries, and those retirees may migrate as well. Slower population growth can disrupt consumption and investment patterns, with different age groups spending and investing differently. If retirees spend less on average, the consumption component of GDP, and GDP itself, may drop just from a demographic shift.

The demand for different types of domestic and international assets may shift, if different age groups prefer different risk categories. Even if they don't, most pension funds shift their asset mix as retirees age. Similarly, pension funds' drawing down assets to pay benefits may affect pricing in global markets, since pricing is just a matter of supply and demand.

That ends the short background on demographic shifts.[6] Some scenarios for consideration and discussion follow.

SCENARIOS A: INCREASING GLOBAL POPULATION TO NINE TO TEN BILLION

Given current demographic trends, global population is almost certain to reach nine billion people sometime in the middle of the twenty-first century, and peak out at around ten billion at the end of the century. At the same time, highly consuming middle-class and wealthy segments of the population are expected to continue to increase. While measuring the direct effects of population growth on the economy is problematic, such growth is correlated with other factors that can be more easily quantified.

The scenarios presented do not include any precipitated by natural disaster, war, or biological collapses. Though these may occur, the main interest is in scenarios that will unfold with only currently known endogenous driving factors.[7]

The most frequently forecast result of population growth is demand growth that leads to scarcity, especially in natural resources. This has been in the forecasts since at least the times of Malthus, who predicted impending mass starvation in the middle of the eighteenth century. Since then, various predictions of approaching scarcity have anticipated future inflation and/or deprivation.

Perhaps the most famous scarcity bet was in 1980 between Paul Ehrlich, a biologist, and Julian Simon, a professor of business administration and economist. Ehrlich bet that a group of five metals would go up in price over a ten-year period (reflecting scarcity), and Simon that they would decrease (reflecting abundance). Ehrlich ended up losing the bet.[8] Others continue to believe, with data backing up their arguments, that the global economy is on the cusp of a long-term commodity price squeeze.[9] Fortunately, other than at regional levels, major global scarcity in key resources has not come to pass, at least not with the far-reaching consequences predicted by Malthus and Ehrlich.[10]

Scarcity-related scenarios are still worth examining, though in a more contained context. Most scarcity problems resolve themselves through one of two nonexclusive means. Either prices go up and demand goes down, and/or supply goes up. This sounds simple, but the final outcomes and related nuances are not.

Scenario 1A1: Revival of Food Security Concerns in Emerging Markets Disrupts Global Agricultural Trade Markets

Overview: Food security revival

Gross forecasts for global food production, absent a biological disaster, are generally positive. Largely thanks to subsidies and modern technology, food production has historically more than kept pace with demand. There are arguments on both sides, but in general this has been and looks at least in the medium term to continue to be the case.

Adequate gross quantity does not mean, however, that food staples will always be affordable for everyone. Caloric sufficiency is not the same as distributive sufficiency. Affordability and ability to create the demand that leads to adequate distribution and caloric intake was recognized some time ago by Amartya Sen among others in their study of famines.[11] It is entirely feasible to have sufficient production, but deprivation on a large scale, even as price "solves" the overall supply and demand equation. Decreased demand can come from an inability to afford food, rather than just a lack of need for it.

Before the great recession put a damper on commodity prices, in 2007 and 2008 food prices were touching off riots in some emerging markets. Some prices spiked as late as 2011 and have been partially blamed for the fall of the Egyptian and Tunisian regimes. In recognition, the UN maintains a "civil unrest threshold" for food prices.[12] Though the relationships between food prices and civil unrest are complicated, the events revived an interest in trade disruptors such as export restrictions, increased subsidies, and the "ring fencing" of crop production in other countries by wealthy Arab states.[13] Even without real scarcity, speculation in food commodity markets can lead to price volatility and trigger policy responses from governments.[14]

Potential political responses and outcomes could include export restrictions of food staples, leading to a thinning out and spikes and volatility in spot and futures markets; purchase and stockpile of food staples, driving up prices; ongoing purchase and "ring fencing" of productive capacity for exclusive use by the purchasing country. Food security concerns can also lead to subsidies, in turn leading to more marginal land in production. Such land is more susceptible to environmental degradation and increased use of and demand for fertilizers.

Main drivers

Increased direct (as food) and indirect (for fodder and fuels) demand; indirect demand can be steady, as in the case of increased demand for meats for which each pound requires several pounds of fodder, but can also spike and be policy driven, as when food crops are diverted for biofuel production; lacking a cost-effective supply response, both increased population and/or increased wealth within a population are sufficient to drive demand and prices; climate change, freshwater stock depletion, and drops in agricultural productivity in certain geographies or crops can drive real or politically driven supply shocks from export restrictions; decreasing fishery yields can lead to more reliance on land-based sources of food and fodder.

Mitigating factors

Technology and innovation continuing to improve yields; improved logistics and storage technologies, leading to less waste; potential, but unlikely, changes in dietary habits; emerging markets growth slowdowns; changes in the operation of commodity markets, with more direct end-user to end-user contracts.

Likely time frame

Short to medium term for local and specialized markets, medium to longer term for more generalized price volatility and shocks in global food markets.

Probability

Medium for general, high for localized.

Notes on bets and risk mitigation

Long-term out-of-the-money options on key food commodities, arable and marginal farmland, and fertilizer raw materials (other than nitrogen); bets on high-density and hydroponic-type technologies; investment in storage facilities and technologies; monitoring of trends in commodity ring fencing, and analysis of effects on market liquidity and pricing; long-term, low-cost options on marginal and unexploited tracts of land.

Scenario 1A2: Increased Commodity Price Volatility in Selected Markets

Overview: Commodity price volatility

Volatility in selected commodity markets is showing signs of an upward trend, with some expecting this to continue.[15] Many factors may contribute to this and include fewer market makers and an overall increased number of centers of high demand coupled with centers of storage and supply that are less able to respond rapidly. Increased speculation, as noted earlier, can also be a driver.

Additional volatility could be touched off by unequal growth, and supply shocks such as rapid technological change and adoption rates (e.g., electric vehicles), natural disasters in supply centers (tsunami in Japan, earthquake in Chile, political upheaval in South Africa or the Middle East, etc.) or lack of free export and trade markets.

Outcomes include more active and volatile futures markets, increased investment in alternate sources, and the potential for "stranded assets" should prices swing again. Sovereign states' interest in buying and stockpiling will increase if they see either risk and potential for financial and political gain (see Scenario 1A1). Stockpiling responses will lead to less *traded* volume of actual commodities, though not necessarily *trading* volume in terms of value, and likely greater volatility there.

Contributing factors

Shifts in a wide range of supply and demand centers, some difficult to foresee, others such as technological shifts and political change may be more apparent, but difficult to time; increased volatility will feed increased speculation; new technologies can create demand by themselves, as rapidly growing markets for items such as lightweight batteries, solar cells, and highly efficient electric motors drive demand for the so-called rare earth elements; less openly traded and more "ring-fenced" markets, by both companies and sovereigns.

Mitigating factors

Volatility may decrease as formerly unstable supply centers such as in Mongolia, Central Asia, and much of Africa come online, and as technology diversifies the supply base, such as with fracking in the United States; ongoing development of substitutes or alternative extraction methods for commodities can become available as prices reach certain levels, though the supply response can lag; commodity prices of these can rapidly shift, as occurred with extraction of oil and gas from shale formations in the early twenty-first century; the mere presence of a known substitute can help mitigate price increases and volatility, especially in futures markets; slowdowns in global growth or in key consuming markets can decrease likelihood; a new global arms race or infrastructure investment push can fuel demand.

Likely time frame

Time frame varies, depending on markets, ongoing.

Probability

Nearly 100 percent in markets with more constrained supply and steady demand, lower in others.

Notes on bets and risk mitigation

Invest in actual or options in substitutes, monitor global politics, monitor demand and stock and flow rates to identify imbalances and their levels early on; focus on long-term supply and demand relationships that ignore shorter-term volatility; identify long-term, far-out-of-the-money call and put options on selected commodities with restrictive supply, or where supply conditions may be changing rapidly following innovation—the rapid rather than slow drop in oil prices long after demand slowed in Asia and fracking was booming in the United States indicates that such opportunities do occur; investment options can go both directions, with shorts/puts in areas of potential oversupply or disruption by technology-driven substitution.

Scenario 1A3: Nonsubstitutable Resource Price Inflation

Overview: Nonsubstitutable resource price inflation

As noted, betting on general resource price inflation has been a "sucker's bet." However, the immutable laws of supply and demand may drive long-term price increases in key nonsubstitutable goods and resources. Increased global wealth and inequality are contributing factors, with the very wealthy often buying multiple instances of these resources. They are inherently in limited supply and nonsubstitutable.

Three inherently scarce resources noted here are property in temperate climates; property in key wealth and cultural centers, including up-and-coming ones; and fine art. Each of these has a first and second tier, the latter of which may see lower or no increases.

There are a limited number of truly temperate climatic zones in the world, including coastal zones of California, Chile, Argentina, Australia, and the Mediterranean. Even if these areas are not currently centers of economic activity, they are centers of wealth and second and retirement homes. The first tier of these areas is already quite highly priced, but secondary areas may still be affordable. California is rife with stories about previous coastal zone backwaters becoming trendy and expensive. There are some substitution effects. Air-conditioning and heating can mimic a good climate.

Many of the key cultural centers of the world are already highly priced, though prices continue to climb. New York, London, Paris, Tokyo, and Singapore among others are all considered extremely expensive. Currently second-tier cities, especially in emerging markets, may boom, along with reviving or gentrifying developed market cities. Los Angeles is a previously scorned city that is attracting what Richard Florida calls "The Creative Class." Other cities previously devoid of cultural centers are starting to develop them. Even the previously disdained border town of Tijuana, Mexico, is developing high-rise and high-priced condos to go with its new food and arts scene.

The third area is fine art, though this lacks the inherent lack of supply, utility, and stability of preferences of the previous two examples. At the same time, certain pieces of art in certain genres have had staying power. While most investors have focused on paintings, new booms have emerged in areas including vintage vinyl, rare stamps, first-edition books, and weapons. Just beware the Beanie Babies and tulips. It is not clear whether or how increased wealth entering scarce markets will influence second-tier markets. The gulf between prices of top fine art and good but not known art is significant and only seems to be growing.

Contributing factors

Increased wealth and demand for resources with inherently limited supply; overinvestment, high prices, and/or oversupply of commodity products may drive investors into these areas as safe havens and status signals; the ability to work virtually will help in relocation to temperate climes or other cities; low-growth initiatives by wealthy residents of desirable areas keep supply low.

Mitigating factors

Some of these types of goods have a perceived rather than intrinsic value, and prices based on perception can be extremely volatile; tastes may shift and may be helped along by changes in regulations or perceptions; each of the areas with Mediterranean climates may raise concerns about safety, tax rates, earthquakes, and cultural factors; in the case of land, national interest may prevail and prevent global capital from making investments, as many countries already restrict foreign ownership of coastal and/or border land and certain natural resources; anticorruption drives can either have a dampening effect on these markets, or else an acceleration to them as titles can be opaque.

Likely time frame

Ongoing, may accelerate among key demographics in emerging markets. It could take several decades for the full effects on property markets to emerge.

Probability

Very high probability of occurrence and identification of the basic trends, lower to successfully exploit over the shorter term.

Notes on bets and risk mitigation

Seek out not yet exploited or underpriced opportunities, such as investments in temperate climates in lesser-known locations—just as land investment occurred for food security reasons (e.g., Sudanese farmland bought by GCC countries) and as prize properties (London, New York, etc.), they may occur for investment and quality of life reasons; New Zealand property markets have recently boomed, due to good climate and political stability; if long-term prospects are considered sound and the investment horizon long enough, buy after recessions and natural disasters.

SCENARIOS B: SLOWING OF THE POPULATION GROWTH RATE

With a slowing population growth rate, most of the developed market economies and China are seeing significant shifts in their populations' age distribution. The focus of these scenarios is on changing patterns of investment and consumption as populations age.

Scenario 1B1: Changes in Flows in, Compositions of, and Pricing in Asset Markets

Overview: Reversal from long-term bull to bear market with retirement drawdowns

As the largest age cohort in history, and likely ever, ages in the major market economies and China, pension and insurance funds will face increasing obligations at a time when they have been weakened by protracted low interest rates, and possibly a subsequent rout in the bond market.[16] Four potentially reinforcing effects may play out in asset markets.

First, current and near-term retirees may change the composition of the asset holdings. This cohort normally moves from riskier assets geared toward longer-term capital accumulation, toward lower-risk, income-producing assets or those that are best designed for preservation of capital. An increase in interest rates could accelerate this shift, and ironically also hold interest rates down.

Second, as the group enters retirement, most will eventually sell off at least some of their portfolio to fund retirement, leading to a corresponding decrease in demand for those assets. Many studies show underfunding of retirement, so asset drawdowns may be significant.[17]

Third, as retirees begin to draw on their private and public pensions, those funds will liquidate assets to pay obligations. Alternatively, funds may increase borrowing, but the likely state of pension fund finances at that time will negate this option. The outcome should be the same whether pensions are defined-benefit or defined-contribution types.

Fourth, as large groups of retirees begin to die, life insurance companies will also need to draw down assets to pay beneficiaries. This may follow a period of low interest rates when life insurance company balance sheets appear to be weakening.[18]

Outcomes related to this scenario depend fully on supply and demand in future asset markets. It may be that the long bull markets in the developed market economies were at least partially driven by accumulation of retirement assets by this massive cohort. If so, will there be a similar reversal into a bear market when that large age cohort does finally retire and starts to sell assets to fund retirement? Will the smaller cohort that follows behind both buy enough to counter redemptions and continue to drive markets forward?

The answer to this question lies in global, not national, capital markets and what the demand conditions are likely to be in fifteen to twenty-five years' time.

Simultaneous drawdowns and a conversion of savings to consumption may lead to lower prices and higher yields in bond markets, as long as drawdowns do not lead to a general recession and put the yields at risk. Yields would also be put at risk by monetization of retiree obligations by monetary authorities.

Contributing factors

Retirees continuing to live longer without working; continued low interest rates, forcing a liquidation of capital to fund retirement; increased interest rates, leading to an exodus from equity to bond markets; lower retirement savings and pensions of the next generation, prompting them to liquidate inherited assets; investor behavior, fleeing markets and exacerbating the effects; increases in inheritance taxes may increase current spending and pre-death asset sales, though unlikely.

Mitigating factors

Global markets and demand from outside the primary economies where this is occurring, including potential deployment of a massive savings glut from China or other emerging markets to compensate for demographically driven demand shifts;[19] increases in bond yields allowing retirees to live without liquidating capital; much wealth is held by the already wealthy and may go to inheritance, rather than being liquidated to pay for retirement; inflows from abroad if the major market economies are still seen as good investment options at the time; aggressive central bank action (e.g., extended QE-type programs).

Likely time frame

Zero to thirty years over retirement period of current "baby boomers," during which time multiple resource and budgeting battles will be fought. If medium-term demand is sufficient, the problem may go to the next generation, in the twenty-to-forty-year time frame.

Probability

Highly uncertain, and likely to unfold in a series of fits and starts that are not always easily traceable to the root causes noted above.

Notes on bets and risk mitigation

Careful monitoring of stocks and flows of assets in and out of the most affected companies and countries and net positions of retirement funds—investor sentiment is likely to be a critical driver, so perceptions of certain markets being "good bets" and others being poor can drive outcomes as much as fundamentals, especially early on; bets are long-term, out-of-the-money puts, or possibly shorts where long and slow deterioration might be more likely; targets can be the assets themselves, or the companies that provide leverage or manage the assets; should evidence of the shifts start to appear, volatility can accelerate, so some hedges may be available in stable, dividend-paying companies and prime real estate; secondary market real estate may suffer from the same sell-off as other asset classes.

Scenario 1B2: Increases in Public Health and Retirement Benefit Spending

Overview: Public benefit spending swells

Aging populations will drive changes in the level and composition of public spending. Old-age retirement benefits, mainly health care and pensions, are not discretionary items in most countries' budgets. As such, as outlays grow for a fixed level of taxation to GDP, any combination of outcomes may occur, with various consequences. This concerns both contingent public obligations (future Social Security and Medicare outlays) that are funded year to year and so-called funded programs with large pools of money (state, local, and private pension programs), but that still have large funding gaps.[20]

One outcome is an increase in debt to fund the obligations. This may well be concurrent with a shrinking labor and tax base, so could over time lead to longer-term debt payment difficulties or potentially inflationary monetization through "helicopter money."

A second outcome is a corresponding decrease in discretionary spending, on areas such as infrastructure, education, and basic research.

A third outcome is tax increases. However, under current rules capital is extremely global and able to move its tax base to alternate, lower-tax locations. The bulk of the tax burden may then fall on the middle classes, as easy-to-collect consumption taxes are implemented or increased. This is a particularly likely scenario in Europe, where citizens are already used to paying high, regressive consumption taxes.

The fourth is a decrease in benefit levels to retirees. Means testing, increased retirement age, increased copays, and other schemes could potentially offset much of the growth in obligations. These schemes are perhaps unlikely given the influence of interest groups representing retirees and their voting patterns and preferences.

Each of these outcomes, with the exception of the last, represents a deteriorating fiscal position leading to taxing and spending decisions that are arguably not in the long-term interests of the country. The ultimate outcome would be less investment to allow companies in affected countries to maintain their competitive edge. Numerous forecasts of funding gaps and outcomes are available.[21]

The focus here is on government spending, but many large companies also hold significant liabilities to their current and former employees. Similarly, many state and local governments have high unfunded pension and health care liabilities. In the United States, one estimate puts these at $3.1 trillion, for entities that have limited ability to either tax or borrow.[22]

Contributing factors

Demographic math; established, but by no means immutable voting patterns; political incentives to protect the most vocal and contributory citizens, and to avoid tax increases; a lack of long-term planning capacity on the part of governments; and a tendency to delay unpopular decision making until much later.

Mitigating factors

Increased youth political awareness; improvements in technology and delivery mechanisms to decrease medical costs; voluntary migration of retirees to lower-cost emerging markets countries and extension of medical benefits to those locations; changing of benefit payouts to decrease costs; resumption of high economic growth in developed market economies.

Likely time frame

Five to forty years over retirement period of current "baby boomers," during which time multiple resource and budgeting battles will be fought. Larger effects are expected toward the end of that period.

Probability

Nearly certain over the time frame noted above.

Notes on bets and risk mitigation

The shift could be profitable for certain providers, before it becomes problematic for governments; care facilities, device makers, home health care providers, supplemental insurance providers, and remote monitoring programs will all at least initially be growth areas; long-term interest rates may increase in the main affected economies, as investors spot additional risks; developed market economies may see diminished investment capital squeeze as investment picks up in emerging markets, many of which have sustained lower debt levels and are accustomed to paying higher interest rates; investment options may appear in long-term, out-of-the-money puts on companies (i.e., "beltway bandits") reliant on government procurement of discretionary goods and services, or in investment in disruptive technologies that can lower the need for public services reliant on discretionary spending; long-term, low-cost, out-of-the-money puts on yen and euro, the most affected currencies—the BOJ will perhaps be the first to directly monetize debt.

NOTES

1. Lee 2003.
2. A few countries such as Chile and Montenegro have implemented at least partially funded systems. Though these can relieve budgetary pressures, if pension levels are inadequate they can still become public policy issues very quickly.
3. This hypothesis is supported by survey data. See, for example, *The Economist* 2015c and Pew Research Center 2014.
4. See Parker et al. (2012) for a summary of 2012 exit poll data from the Pew Research Center.
5. See Lowenstein (2008) for a less than optimistic view of the future of pension debt.
6. For a good overview of the topic see *The Economist* (2014c), and for a summary of some of the fiscal issues facing governments, see public debt crusader Laurence Kotlikoff (2014). For a European perspective, see Guerzoni and Zuleeg (2011). A more positive spin on the impact of an aging population can be found in Sen (2013).
7. That is not to say that population pressures alone cannot lead to economic and societal disaster. See Jared Diamond (2005) for a series of case studies of overpopulation in isolated, resource-constrained environments.
8. A slightly different bet on slightly different metals would have turned out differently for Ehrlich, but that is not relevant to the bet. See a (moderately biased, since Ehrlich was at Stanford) summary from the Center for Conservation Biology (2005).
9. There is quite a lot written about the "commodity super cycle." See some of the arguments in Dobbs et al. (2016) of the McKinsey Global Institute.
10. Basic scarcity, of course, is a daily phenomenon that drives prices across every known market.

11. For example, Sen (1999).

12. Dobbs et al. 2016.

13. Plumer 2013.

14. Commodity price speculators would argue that they provide liquidity not volatility to markets, but case studies, if not broader data, call that into question. See, for example, the detailed story of wild speculation in US natural gas markets by Dreyfuss (2013). For a food-related example, see Kaufman (2011) and chapter 4 from United Nations (2011).

15. For an extensive discussion of this and accompanying data, see Dobbs et al. (2016), which charts out the increasing number of days that markets are hitting high standard deviations from the mean. See also El-Erian.

16. See OECD 2015, Business and Finance Outlook, chapter 4, entitled "Can Pension Funds and Life Insurance Companies Keep Their Promises."

17. Munnell et al. 2015.

18. See, for example, pages 5 and 6 of the US Treasury report, Office of Financial Research (2014) and Walsh 2015.

19. Given that China also has a rapidly aging population, these flows could also help to magnify the effect, rather than mitigate it. See Curran and Kearns 2015.

20. There is considerable information on funding gaps in public and private pensions. The Center for Retirement Research in the United States estimates public pensions to be only 74 percent funded even after a long boom in equity markets, with shortfalls in the trillions of USD. See, for example, Munnell and Aubrey (2014).

21. See, for example, Lowenstein (2008), Kotlikoff and Burns (2004), and pages 11 and 12 from Social Security Advisory Board (2009).

22. Collins and Rettenmaier (2010).

10

Ecological Change

Ecological change can result from any combination of climate change, natural resource overexploitation, and natural ecological cycles. The main and most pressing driver is climate change, which will also be the main subject of the scenarios.

The consensus, considered "95 percent likely" by the Intergovernmental Panel on Climate Change, is that climate change is both real and human driven. This is the starting point for the scenarios. Evidence and additional reading abounds for those interested in the topic.[1] Trends show an increase in average global temperatures, with the variation expected of any complex variable. A few degrees may seem trivial, but in a fragile ecosystem even small global increases matter. Though the warming trend is clearly documented, immediate effects may be harder to observe given normal variations in weather. Receding ice at Earth's poles, particularly in the Arctic, is immediately observable.[2]

Climate change can alter the global economy in two main ways. The first is from the direct effect of a warming planet and the consequent costs and opportunities. These are expected as the ecology of the planet changes, though will not be evenly distributed between opportunities and costs or across different demographics and economies. Assessment of final outcomes depends on the imperfect science of how much sea levels may rise and the effect on everything from expenditures in coastal cities to effects on mortgage bonds and increased arctic trade routes; which parts of the planet will get hotter (and colder); what will happen in different places with rainfall, agricultural production, and freshwater; change and adaptation in sea and fisheries; and all sorts of other important questions.[3]

Second, ecological change matters for the global economy because of how people and societies react to it. As societies implement mitigating policies, considerable resource flows are both created and diverted. Subsidies and tax credits, utility offtake agreements, carbon targets and renewable energy mandates, consumer and corporate choices, and emissions taxes and cap and trade schemes are all climate change related and continue to alter the quantity and direction of global financial flows. Mitigation programs are anticipated to continue reshaping entire industries, moving money and possibly entire industries to new locations around the globe. At the same time, consumers' daily buying decisions shift billions of dollars between companies based on perceptions of companies' "green" policies.

Whether policies are based on good science and economics or not is less important than their content. Ethanol production in the United States may not be good for either the environment or the economy, but it is at the center of a multibillion-dollar industry that receives billions of dollars in mandates and subsidies. Cloudy Germany may be one of the least likely places to efficiently produce solar energy, but subsidies to the German solar industry have fueled planet-wide investment in technology and production. Entire industries have been formed based on government and consumer decisions related to climate change. People and governments will continue to react to climate change, and understanding those reactions will shed light on ongoing changes to the global economy.

At this late stage, attempts to fully mitigate global warming are likely to be incomplete at best. The science of climate change is massively complex and fraught with uncertainty. Consequently, the mitigation task is colossal, complex, and subject to both disagreements on how to carry it out and ongoing outright resistance. It is hard to believe in complete mitigation with warming already proceeding down an increasingly well-established path, populations rising, and with global energy demand forecast to grow by 37 percent from 2014 to 2030.[4]

Global warming is one part of ecological change. Others that may bear on the global economy include fisheries exploitation, ocean water pollution, ongoing improvements in recycling and landfill use, air quality in major emerging markets' cities, and freshwater production and use. The latter is not explored in depth here but could become critical in the coming decades.

SCENARIOS A: GOVERNMENT AND INDIVIDUAL RESPONSES

Governments, companies, and citizens responding to ecological change are taking a wide variety of actions affecting incentives in the global economy. A few of these are explored below, but many remain. A potentially important omitted scenario is mass population movements in response to fears of ecological change. The small locavore and reuse movements are also left out, though they may eventually alter relative prices for finished products at least at a regional level.

Scenario 2A1: Ongoing and Increasing Spending on Technologies That Change Relative Prices

Overview: Relative price changes for technologies to combat ecological change

Direct subsidies for renewable energy reached $121 billion in 2013 and are expected to grow to $230 billion by 2030.[5] These are direct subsidies and do not include additional incentives created by regulations and requirements. The latter are undoubtedly worth many billions more in terms of their ability to change relative prices and attract investment. Renewables' contribution to electrical power generation is expected to reach 37 percent of the total in OECD countries by 2040 and subsidies will be trotting alongside that trend.[6]

Enormous funding is chasing equally enormous goals. Regardless of whether policies will mitigate climate change or not, they will change the way money is invested in energy production, distribution, and use. Currently, the bulk of subsidies go to wind and solar. Hydro is a major contributor to renewables production, but is not likely to be as subsidized going forward.

In addition to direct subsidies for renewables, which can be readily quantified, institutions may implement incentive-changing policies in other areas that have equivalent effect. For example, regulations such as those mandated by the European Union for renewables or by the United States for biofuels can radically change the relative prices of energy sources without subsidies. Carbon tax or cap and trade schemes do the same. Fuel efficiency standards, VOC limits, particle emission limits, and effluent standards are all regulatory changes that can alter incentives and relative prices.

As mitigation targets continue to be missed, technologists may devise additional investments in geoengineering solutions, such as carbon capture, light reflective schemes, filtration technologies, effluent consuming bugs, and others. Technologies that alter the effects of ecological change after the fact may see a big push some years out.

In sum, whole industries are expected to continue to emerge whose profitability and existence depend fully on climate change mitigation policies. There are as many subscenarios as there are technologies and political systems.

Contributing factors

Ongoing concern of citizens/individuals; continued, tangible revelation of the effects of ecological change; a desire by politicians to leave a legacy for the future; as green energy companies gain in size and economic power, their lobbying arms will help to perpetuate favorable subsidies and regulations; improvements in energy storage and distributed power technologies will improve the ability of renewables to take the place of baseload fossil fuel producers, removing one of the main non-cost-related obstacles to greater use.[7]

Mitigating factors

Voter fatigue and backlash especially in populist and nonglobalist movements, particularly as subsidies and energy prices climb in low-growth countries. Energy prices are a factor in commercial competitiveness, so again, low-growth developed-market economies may slow renewables growth if it appears to be hurting their economies; improvements in efficiency or geoengineering technologies may reduce the real or perceived need for additional renewables; an often-forecast movement into a "mini-ice age," as has happened many times before in the earth's history, may reduce the perceived need for a reduction in greenhouse gases.

Likely time frame

Ongoing, and likely to continue indefinitely, though with shifting emphases over a series of medium terms.

Probability

100 percent, already occurring.

Notes on bets and risk mitigation

The picture presented is extremely broad and not very useful for specific mitigation activities or to make "bets" other than in the broadest sense—at the same time, recommendations such as "invest in renewables" are not very helpful, as many companies and technologies are likely to fail badly rather than grow; rather than trying to "pick winners," a more viable strategy may be betting against targeted sunset technologies at the national or regional level(s); sunset industries may include coal in the medium term, large-scale, centralized power production and distribution in the medium to long term, out-of-the-money, LEAPS puts and possibly calls on coal anticipating populist backlash, and petrol distribution in the longer term; these and others may turn out to be the Borders Books and Blockbuster Videos of the energy world.[8]

Scenario 2A2: Ring Fencing of Dirty Industries into Limited, but Profitable Zones

Overview: Dirty industry enclaves

Through public "not in my backyard" pressure, taxes and regulations on so-called dirty industries are increasing. Outcomes are either increased cost, lack of investment in increased capacity, or outright exit.

Low transportation costs, proximity of areas with stringent controls to those with weak ones, and an ongoing industrial need for certain processes can help spur growth in unofficial "dirty" areas. Clean and dirty areas may abut, but with industrial areas outside of the regulatory purview of the highly regulated areas. Lower-cost "dirty" energy available in the alternative locations can help increase their competitiveness.

In the same way financial regulations and taxes have driven money into less-regulated havens, industry would do the same thing. Some of this type of interchange is already occurring and may intensify. Numerous processes that are essential to modern life are no longer seen as acceptable neighbors. Though the World Bank in its recent report on emissions trading schemes does not believe that relocation is an issue, a more open look at the raw economic incentives suggests otherwise.[9]

Main hubs include US-Mexico; EU–North Africa and Turkey; Japan–Southeast Asia.

Key industries might include galvanizing and plating; cement production; refining; chemicals production; painting and coating; energy production; recycling; castor bean production.

Contributing factors

Ongoing localized pressure on industry to lower emission levels or comply with energy efficiency or other standards, including uneven development of emissions taxing and trading schemes; free trade agreements can lower the cost of movement of goods back and forth across borders for processing; increases in transportation efficiency and ability to deliver goods across borders "just in time"; wage and employment pressure in emerging markets, where populations are still growing; ironically, improved environmental laws and enforcement in "dirty" markets to assure consumers in wealthy countries that they are not just exporting pollution to the poor.

Mitigating factors

Public pressure on the export of pollution and risk to poorer countries; free trade agreements, depending on the terms, as many include some provisions for mutual environmental protection; environmental movements in the receiving countries and the political sensitivity of accepting the wealthy world's environmental problems.

Likely time frame

Zero to fifteen years, until environmental standards enforcement improves globally.

Probability

Sixty to eighty percent that such activities will increase rather than decrease over time.

Notes on bets and risk mitigation

Investment in companies, industrial zones, and border areas where these activities can take place; investment in marketing and logistics companies that specialize in moving goods to existing processing plants in other countries; shorting dirty industries in developed market economies that are likely to experience pressure to relocate or become unprofitable.

SCENARIOS B: ACTUAL IMPACT

Determining the actual economic outcomes of ecological change is a massively complicated undertaking. Climate modeling is difficult even in the short term. Results of change can be highly regionalized and even localized, stymieing attempts to make general statements. Some, mainly the wealthier nations, have conducted more and better research into what the results may be. Others have not. As the effects materialize, both better tools and more funding will emerge that will allow new scenarios to be developed and older ones to be updated. This is a Bayesian exercise in the extreme.[10]

Much has been written on the potential flooding of coastal cities, the costs of preparing for flooding and consequences for cities that cannot or do not pay the price, changes in rainfall and food production, increased energy usage that creates a pernicious feedback loop, and shifts in land use in and around the polar areas. Any number of scenarios could be developed on these topics. However, specific scenario development is stunted by the challenges of moving from general to more specific locations probabilities, outcomes, and adjustments. The risks are high, and well documented in Nordhaus's (2015) book *The Climate Casino* and elsewhere, but specifics are extremely hard to quantify.[11]

While significant by itself, ecological change can also amplify the effects of other changes. For example, changes in crop and fishery yields from climatic change can drive Scenario 1A1, by making food security concerns that much more pressing in certain areas.

Scenario 2B1: Mispricing of Actuarial Risk at Extreme Ends

Overview: Risk mispricing

Humans are far better at extrapolating from the past than predicting a future that diverges from that past. People do a particularly poor job of predicting the rare, so-called black-swan events that periodically disrupt markets and the world.[12] Climate change is likely to increase the size and number of these types of events. Failure to anticipate them by using normal actuarial and extrapolatory models can lead to a severe mispricing of risk.

Correct pricing of climate risk is critical, but by most indications lacking in the business models that are responsible for the long-term management of trillions of dollars.[13]

Inherent competitiveness of the insurance business and the use of extrapolative models by both actuaries *and* regulators means that if volatility and/or future payouts reach levels that were not seen in the past, those models and the companies behind them could see their balance sheets decimated. The company that does price-in increased risk will lose business because premiums will be too high. The company that does not price it in may dominate the market, but not survive a series of previously rare events. This of course affects insurers, but perhaps more importantly, reinsurers and any direct or implied government guarantees that back them up.

Climate change–related risk mispricing can extend beyond insurance. Pricing of sea-level or storm-prone coastal property may be out of alignment. The cost of living there may change, as taxes increase to pay for preventive measures, with consequent changes in the value of underlying mortgage bonds. Clustered industries such as refineries along the shores of the Gulf of Mexico or at or near sea level in the Arabian Sea may be at risk of highly correlated events. Also, climate change could lead to geopolitical instability, as noted in a report hypothesizing a link between the Syrian civil war and the purported effects of climate change on desertification there.[14]

In reality, it is not known to what extent ecological change drives extreme weather events, though some correlations are beginning to emerge.[15]

Contributing factors

Delays in developing tools for and integrating more robust risk pricing into mortgage and insurance markets, by both regulators and investors; increased value of real estate in areas most likely to be affected, in particular coastal areas; lack of understanding of effects of freshwater shortages on high-demand residential and farming communities (exacerbated by population growth); ongoing population growth and increasing density; lack of incentive to reform regulatory models until events occur; that many ecosystems are stretched to the limits, even without extreme events.

Mitigating factors

Long-term planning and preventive measures can lower risk; increased "self-insurance" can lower risk to institutions but may increase cost of implied government guarantees especially in countries where government intervention would be expected; increased use of models that allow for extreme events; development of sound fiscal policies and reserve funds to allow for timely and sufficient intervention; better management of the high seas and other global resources.

Likely time frame

Unexpected events can happen at any time by definition. However, current evidence suggests they should become more common as populations grow and the climate changes, coinciding with an emergence of the longer-term effects of drought, excess rainfall, or shortages in freshwater. What is rare in one region may not be in another, with the lack of preparedness or mispricing of risk as problematic as the actual event.

Probability

Unknown, but the past five to ten years give some indication that the odds of permanent (in our lifetimes) shifts in weather patterns and extreme events are increasing.

Notes on bets and risk mitigation

Bets and hedges would be with similar instruments; while weather derivatives are available, as in many scenarios bets should be on extreme outliers with long maturity periods and low premiums; counterparty risk can be extreme over long time horizons so collateral should be identified carefully; insurance and reinsurance companies can be doubly affected, from mispriced risk and fluctuations in the value of underlying securities they hold; holding a series of long-term, out-of-the-money puts in institutions subject to disruptive risks from weather can help hedge a more traditional portfolio; development of better and longer-term hedging tools can perhaps be both profitable and help lower overall systemic risks.

NOTES

1. Intergovernmental Panel on Climate Change 2014. The US National Aeronautics and Space Administration (2016) GISS cites 2015 as the hottest year since records were available in 1880.
2. National Aeronautics and Space Administration (2015).
3. For an early and much-discussed analysis of impact, see the Stern Review on the Economics of Climate Change initially published in 2006, by Stern (2007). Though economists both supported and discounted the report, it touched off a wide range of additional thinking and analysis on the economics of climate change.
4. IEA/OECD 2014.
5. This is still only about 24 percent of the subsidies given currently for fossil fuels, mainly in producing countries that subsidize them to promote economic diversification and for social and political stability reasons. IEA/OECD.
6. Ibid.
7. Fuel cells and battery packs such as Tesla's Powerwall are likely only the start of technologies that can help solve the problem of the intermittent nature of most renewables.
8. See for example *The Economist* (2013b) for a report on losses at European utilities and Andresen (2013).
9. The World Bank Group (2015) report reveals the uneven progress of emissions tax and trading schemes.

10. For some of the better researched attempts to understand the effects, see Nordhaus (2015) and the work by the Paulson Institute's "Risky Business" project at the University of Chicago.

11. The difficulties are summarized in Liverman and Glasmeier (2014).

12. The term was coined and developed by Nicholas Taleb in his books *Fooled by Randomness* and the eponymously named *The Black Swan.*

13. These industries are not ignoring all potential risks. For example, see the report "ERISC Phase II: How Food Prices Link Environmental Constraints to Sovereign Credit Risk," compiled by the United Nations Environmental Program (2016) and a group of private-sector risk-assessment entities.

14. Kelley et al. (2015).

15. The climate debate is clouded by the difficult combination of scientific ambiguity and political extremism, making it difficult sometimes to find good, objective analysis. A report published in *Scientific American* perhaps comes close and does link extreme weather with climate change. See Carey (2013).

11

Income and Wealth Inequality

Economists, politicians, and the public are engaging in the inequality debate: whether it's increasing, whether it matters, and what, if anything, should be done about it.[1] Some think it is the most important problem of the current century, others a nonissue. The data itself supports two trends that at first glance might appear contradictory. The first is that inequality between countries seems to be decreasing. GDP per capita figures are slowly and erratically converging. Poorer countries are, by and large, growing more quickly than richer ones. This is the "convergence" described in chapter 7. Much of this is driven by rapid economic growth in a few countries like China and India, though some African countries are also growing fast and supporting the trend. The convergence is uneven and subject to setbacks, but seems to be happening.

At the same time, data shows inequality within countries growing. Figure 11.1 indicates the share of total income going to the top 1 percent of the population in a number of developed market economies. This trend follows many years of falling inequality after the Second World War. Note that the rich did suffer proportionally large drops in income during the 2008 crisis, but subsequently regained those losses. Another study concludes that in the United States, the top 1 percent captured over 90 percent of the income gains since the end of the 2008 recession. Other incomes stagnated or declined.[2] According to the McKinsey Global Institute, "between 2005 and 2014, real incomes in {25} advanced economies were flat or fell for 65 to 70 percent of households."[3]

Recent studies have also shown ongoing trends toward widening disparity in wealth (rather than income) with the top 1 percent expected to control over half the wealth in the world in 2016.[4] Some of the more recent data are estimates. However, it does appear that income and wealth inequality is growing, especially in most developed market

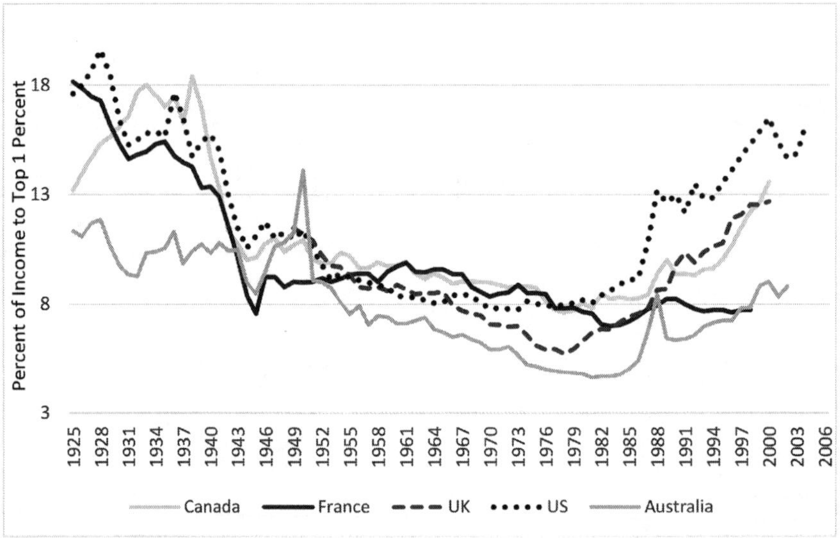

Figure 11.1. Top 1 Percent Share in National Income

Source: Data is from Daniel Waldenstrom, and available from his webpage at Uppsala University in Sweden. See also Saez and Zucman (2016). Note that though the ranks of the poor have increased, so have the ranks of the wealthy, at least in the United States. See Pew Research Center (2015).

economies. Others have included inequality of opportunity as a third area where gaps are widening, though this data is even harder to collect and interpret.[5]

Various theories seek to explain widening inequality. Evidence shows that the returns to holders of capital are increasing faster than the returns to those who provide labor.[6] Controversy surrounds why this might be, or whether it is temporary or permanent.[7] Factors that would drive it include increasing mechanization in manufacturing and service industries, and the "dumbing down" of professions where localized decision making is increasingly being subsumed by standard operating procedures.[8]

Increased trade with low-income countries, and in particular China, has also been blamed for increasing inequality. FTAs may have exacerbated the trend, but are likely not the root cause, with technology displacing far more jobs than trade.[9] A lack of workforce mobility has also been cited, with people not moving between jobs as quickly as in the past. This may be a symptom of a more important causal factor, which is the need to specialize and the lack of skills transferability between professions. You might have gone from driving a bread truck to working in a factory, but are less likely to become a software engineer. Another factor may be the globalization of meritocracy, where skilled labor is more easily identified and deployed, at least in certain technical fields. Combined with slower growth in developed market economies and technology companies' tendency to hire fewer workers per dollar of revenue, a meritocracy can flood the lower half of the job market and create more competition for those who are not at the top of their game.

What is driving the shift matters. As the chart shows, income inequality, though rising, is still below what it was only a few decades ago. That is not alarming. However, the possible culprits outlined in the paragraphs above do not show any signs of abating. More may be yet to come. Worsening inequality may itself contribute to slower growth, which can then spawn more inequality. Modern economies simply need mass consumption to grow, with the *C* part of the GDP definition upwards of 70 percent on average. This is what stimulates the *I* part and drives production. A neglect of the consuming masses could ultimately mean lower incomes for all, and a struggle for wealth in a shrinking economy.[10]

Though the evidence is perhaps not as clear-cut or permanent as with other shifts, the potential effects are serious enough to warrant consideration now. The underlying drivers of inequality and any policy measures to address it will both affect the path of the global economy. Though inequality has been growing for some time, recent surges in populism in the developed market economies may presage a sudden shift toward greater political and economic importance.[11] The World Economic Forum highlighted inequality as a major potential driver of instability in its 2017 Global Risks Report.[12]

SCENARIOS

Scenario 3A: Increased "Enclavization" and Differences More Within, Than Between, Countries

Overview: Wealthy enclaves, rather than wealthy countries

Most lower-income countries have enclaves of relatively wealthy people who are able to insulate and isolate themselves from the poor around them. Life in these enclaves is essentially identical to living in a decent neighborhood in a much wealthier country. Conditions are often superior in terms of quality of life, with an ample supply of low-cost labor for cooking, cleaning, childcare, and other services.

At the same time, public services including education in many areas, public spaces, and safety nets are either decreasing in quality or not improving in low-income areas in much of the rich world. Real-estate values have long reflected the quality of area public schools, but this also extends to police and fire protection, public parks, community activities, and overall public safety and quality of life.[13]

The scenario is one of decreasing differences between wealthy and upper-middle-class areas of the world, with richer enclaves in poor countries improving in quality, and poorer areas in rich countries falling further behind.[14] Will the time come when quality of life depends more on the city and neighborhood than the country?

If the shift accelerates, increasingly mobile global wealth will seek the location offering the best combination of safety, quality of life, and tax burden. Countries may begin (continue) to compete among themselves to offer the best terms and attract the moneyed class with low taxes. This could lead in other areas to a further gutting of social services, an acceleration of enclavization, and the proverbial "race to the bottom," barring some social upheaval. Locations that are physically safe and allow for low taxation and enclavization will be most appealing. The rise of Dubai as a global center of wealth and work is perhaps an early example. Locations with more palatable weather and political traditions may arise.

Contributing factors

Increased wealth and desire for mixing with like people, especially as an offshoot of hyper-parenting and a desire to control child peer groups; increased virtualization of work, allowing for flexibility in location; fear for safety, driving people into areas with higher property taxes funding police forces—ironically, the increased fear could come as a result of increased income disparities; developers and marketers responding to market pressures to create these enclaves; ongoing demographic change, shifting spending to entitlements from infrastructure; increasing use of virtual currencies and therefore the difficulty of tracking and taxing wealth.

Mitigating factors

Political backlashes driving improvements in public schools and neighborhoods; increased social mobility and parity improving all neighborhoods in all countries; political upheaval, making enclaves targets for disenfranchised citizens; political backlash driving increased minimum wages or increased middle-class government jobs; ongoing security issues in emerging markets—most are simply not as safe as developed market economies.

Likely time frame

Evidence of this scenario is already apparent. The question is whether social isolation accelerates or reverses. Most likely, these shifts will continue for some time, though at different rates in different places.

Probability

Extremely high for ongoing and increased enclavization. Probabilities of a backlash are a different scenario.

Notes on bets and risk mitigation

Similar to scenario 1A3, the value of prime real estate will increase as the price of entry increases with increased wealth at the top end of the range; seek out transitional and up-and-coming real-estate markets in low-cost emerging markets; if security concerns increase, those with middle incomes will spend to seek similar, but lesser enclaves; the desire, and need, for the rich to accurately signal to each other will increase the demand for certain types of events, and institutions like private schools, clubs, medical centers, and old-age-care facilities.

Scenario 3B: Electoral Backlash, Increased Transfers and Social Spending Focused on the Middle Class

Overview: Middle-class job creation programs

As has been said, the poor will always be with us. Perhaps a greater risk are ranks of educated, voting, and law-abiding citizens increasingly excluded from the benefits of economic growth. Middle-class, educated citizens are a powerful political group. With 70 to 75 percent of developed market populations seeing stagnating income over previous decades, the foundations for middle-class unrest are being built. An electoral threat may be greater than security-related threats.

It can be argued that much of the middle class in wealthy countries is already supported by well-paying government jobs that require a college education.[15] An expansion of these programs may occur across a wide range of areas, including social services, education, infrastructure, provision of professional/consulting services for the government, regulatory roles, and benefits administration.

Contributing factors

Public-sector unions seek to expand their footprint, lobbying for more such jobs; given that the middle class has high voting turnout, it is more politically sensitive to alienate them than the poor; increased student debt and lack of high-paying entry-level jobs for graduates; it is easier to absorb the educated middle class into public-sector jobs than the working class; the ongoing and increased public rhetoric around inequality makes radical measures and spending less unlikely.

Mitigating factors

Lack of resources given demographic shifts and the greater pressure to maintain and increase benefits to the elderly; the increasing mobility of capital makes tax evasion easier, increasing risks of raising taxes to fund jobs programs, especially costly middle-class ones; a greater upheaval among the poor, leading to resources diverted in that direction.

Likely time frame

Two to five years, as rates of college graduation continue to rise along with skills required for even entry-level desirable jobs.

Probability

Greater than average, especially so for some minor effects such as well-paying government jobs to help constituents of current political regimes (post 2016, military, border security, infrastructure).

Notes on bets and risk mitigation

Main risks are related to costs of funding expanded programs. Bets are on programs to help workers gain and maintain middle-class status, including government contractors to employ and train the middle class for ongoing employment; bets are also on industries likely to be stimulated to mitigate electoral risks, but could include education, infrastructure, military technology—which these are depends on whether the middle or working classes are able to better influence political outcomes.

Scenario 3C: Stability Threat, Countered by Increased Transfers and Social Spending Focused on Lower and Working Classes

Overview: Transfers to working poor

A lack of economic mobility in the working classes can lead to both electoral and security upsets. Stagnant wages and declining benefits may undermine faith in the prevailing system and lead to increased risk of dissatisfaction and upheaval. Policy makers may respond by increasing transfers and work programs. Such a scenario may follow the electoral upheaval of scenario 3B. In fact, it may be the working poor who push back against the system before the middle class. Note the 2016 US election, Brexit outcomes, and rise (though loss so far) of other populist leaders in Europe.

It may simply not be possible to combine (a) workers earning their marginal product (i.e., a salary that reflects their economic output) with (b) workers being able to meet (societally appropriate) subsistence levels of existence. Increases in minimum wages can help, as long as this does not lead to lower employment. Economic research here is mixed.

Transfers without growth or increased taxation would result in increased fiscal deficits, with an economic effect compounded by increased transfers to retirees. If income distribution evens, the greater propensity to consume of the lower-income and working class could lead to more stable growth through increased consumption.

The scenario can play out under any political system, with China perhaps being one of the prime candidates. People in many societies have historically been willing to trade direct representation for a better standard of living. Democracies are in no way immune, as they can produce system-altering demagogues under the right conditions.[16]

Contributing factors

In most European nations, a movement could be spearheaded by private-sector unions; in the United States and other countries with weaker unions, contributing factors may be populist politicians (left and right) and increased crime among ethnic majority or minority populations; the underlying contributing factor would be ongoing stagnant wages and perceived pervasive lack of opportunity where it previously existed, whether in myth or reality.

Mitigating factors

In the United States the working class has been politically conservative and against government intervention; however, the right has increasingly been involved in the rhetoric around inequality, offering politically correct solutions such as supply-side tax breaks and less politically correct ones such as protectionism;[17] in other developed market economies and emerging markets, workers are better organized and politically more powerful with a global history of working-class unrest over wages and working conditions; political intervention early on, political repression, or good political salesmanship can both increase and reduce pressure under this scenario; the main mitigating factor would be a reversal in trends toward inequality, either from a shift in the current economic forces or significant government intervention.

Likely time frame

Zero to ten years.

Probability

Greater than average, in one form or another.

Notes on bets and risk mitigation

Countries with different political and economic conditions may try a range of policies, each of which would need to be analyzed in turn; if policies tend toward drastically increased tax on the wealthy, significant shifts in capital around the world may occur, with any number of tax- and wealth-friendly countries being on the receiving end; working-class jobs can be created most readily by infrastructure and military spending, leading to opportunities in a wide range of industries and commodities; the so-called 2017 Trump Trade, leading to booming shares in infrastructure-related companies, indicates that investors are keeping a close eye on trends and possible outcomes; failure to address the issue at all may come to little, or may lead to the kinds of upheavals of the 1920s and 1930s when communism was on the rise.

Scenario 3D: Emergence of a Neofeudal Society

Overview: Emergence of a neofeudal society

Following the great recession of 2008, capital became cheap for those who could access it. Many homes vacated by those in default appear to have been purchased by wealthier buyers or institutions with access to that cheap capital.[18] The proportion of renters to buyers increased after years of decline.[19] By 2016, home prices had largely recovered to their boom-year levels, but with a different ownership structure.

An ongoing trend of high home prices and stagnant working- and middle-class wages can make homeownership increasingly elusive for citizens of all countries. A lack of disposable income also complicates obtaining the 20 to 50 percent down payment needed to purchase a house under the standard loan terms that prevail in most countries. Given the previous results from loosening loan requirements, it may be some time before homeownership rates rise again.

Interest rates available to high-net-worth and large institutional investors are also lower than those available to most homeowners, even prime borrowers. The interest rate differential serves to increase the price of the homes/assets at the margin, further pricing out those even with access to mortgages and down payments.

A possible outcome of the above may be increasingly permanent, multigenerational owner and renter subclasses. Intergenerational transfers of property wealth, of the sort Thomas Piketty identified, can help solidify the relationship.[20] Perhaps a bit overdramatically, this might be called a *neofeudal* society.

Contributing factors

Increasing house prices when mortgage eligibility is tight or tightening; stagnating real incomes, precluding down-payment accumulation, coupled with financial pressure on government first homebuyer programs; lower percentage of income earners in the population overall as housing stock grows; differences in the interest rates at which different types of borrowers can borrow; intergenerational transfers of real property, combined with a greater need for the poor to sell real estate before death to meet basic expenses, means that poorer citizens whose family had a home will have a lower chance of inheriting it and will have to start over.

Mitigating factors

Renewed efforts to improve access to both homes and business purchases; affordable housing policies; a reversal in income inequality and stagnation trends.

Likely time frame

The shift would build over the medium to long terms, though accelerated by events such as the great recession.

Probability

This scenario is one of degrees. That overall trends will continue to near-feudal proportions (to be defined) is moderately high. As a current placeholder, this is estimated at 30 to 50 percent in developed market economies, less in Europe than in the

United States, though homeownership rates are generally still higher in the United States. Probability is higher in more autocratic countries or those with a history of corruption, though in those countries preemptive unrest may also be more likely.

Notes on bets and risk mitigation

Most likely, though volatile, property values will likely continue on an upward trajectory in the most desirable places, both in terms of quality of life and employment; house prices are cyclical, but locations with low rent-to-price ratios coupled with low unemployment may be targeted for investment; as people are unable to purchase their own homes, hybrid or share ownership schemes may increase in popularity, as with REIT-like structures; government policies may range from income enhancements to allow for wider asset ownership to removing factors that lead to high home prices and benefit the wealthier such as deductibility of interest expenses.

NOTES

1. The rhetoric is sometimes couched in terms of antiglobalization, but the roots are essentially similar.

2. See Saez (2013) and Sommeiller and Price (2014).

3. Dobbs et al. 2016.

4. For a US-based analysis, see Pfeffer et al. (2013). For the global case see Oxfam (2015).

5. See El-Erian (2016).

6. Data from OECD (2012) shows that the historical relationship between productivity gains and income growth was severed in the 1970s. The gains from productivity now go disproportionately to capital, though it may be that improvements in capital are where those gains are coming from. This relationship holds across most of the major developed market economies and China. See Mishel 2012.

7. Some blame the decline of unions, for example.

8. For example, local banks and insurance companies have replaced trained professionals who are able to assess risk with "relationship" agents who pass paperwork on to algorithm-based assessments at a central office. *Rise of the Robots* by Martin Ford predicts how a wide range of skilled jobs may be taken over by machine algorithms in the coming decades. For a summary of the issues around less work see Thompson (2015).

9. Autor et al. 2015.

10. This Harvard Business School study by Rivkin (2015) highlights some of the ways inequality can lead to lower growth. See also OECD 2015.

11. Quartz and Asp 2015. It remains to be seen how far the populist revolutions of 2016 will go.

12. World Economic Forum 2017.

13. See Cowen (2017) for a glimpse of life in mass, low-income neighborhoods.

14. Such as the well-publicized case of poisoned public tap water in Flint, Michigan. *The Economist* 2016b.

15. According to the US Bureau of Labor Statistics, since 1991 more Americans have worked in government than manufacturing.

16. Germany during the Weimar Republic, Turkey in the 2010s, and Serbia at the end of Yugoslavia are three cases in point.

17. Edsall 2015.

18. See, for example, Gittelsohn 2012. There are numerous other reports, but little consolidated data.

19. See Joint Center for Housing Studies of Harvard University (2013). The report also notes that many who rent choose to do so, to maintain mobility and reduce risk.

20. Piketty (2014).

12

IT: Virtualization, Artificial Intelligence, and Robotics

Advances in technology have changed the shape of the global economy. Some of the world's biggest companies did not exist or barely existed twenty years ago. Others are extinct because they could not adapt. Money is invested in new places and pulled out of old ones, while technology drives changes in the way we work, play, interact, and invest. The scenarios will start to explore some of the where, how, and when. The broad areas examined are ongoing virtualization and the nexus between artificial intelligence, robotics, and so-called big data, or what has been referred to as the "second machine age." Most of the exposition of individual trends is left for the "scenarios" section.

Virtualization is the ability to conduct ourselves outside of physical presence.

For many tasks virtualization makes physical location or country of birth less important. Low-wage jobs can shift more easily from lesser-educated workers in expensive countries to better-educated (or just cheaper) workers in lower-cost countries. The global economy is more of a meritocracy than ever before. A motivated, capable poor person has a better chance of success in the global market than any time in history. The shift can breed instability among the poor and unemployed in wealthy countries, and perhaps greater stability among certain subsegments of the poor in less-developed countries.

The low cost and ubiquity of virtualization, however, brings on piles of junk and scams. It is easy to get work done in the global marketplace, but not always to get it done well. Economist George Akerlof introduced the idea of signaling and perverse incentives in his seminal 1970 "The Market for Lemons" paper.[1] Just as it was hard to judge used-car quality in Akerlof's paper (usually it was low), it is hard to assess quality and value of a virtual employee, manufacturer, or service provider in the global economy. Having many options is not the same as having good ones. A nice-looking, well-edited website and a few seats at a call center are commodities that anyone can buy.

The emergence and evolution of accurate signals in the global market will ultimately determine the usefulness of the virtual world and whether its growth can be sustained. Virtualization will inevitably continue to spawn whole new generations of tools for doing so.

New technologies are also changing the nature of and demand for work. The nexus between machine learning/artificial intelligence, robotics, and so-called big data is leading to a redefinition of skilled labor. Algorithms and machines can write perfectly readable news stories, parse through legal cases faster and more thoroughly than humans, scan global medical databases to diagnose diseases instantaneously and accurately assess lending risk better than loan officers, allocate investment resources, and even assemble hamburgers and tacos.

In a study published by Oxford University, the authors hypothesized that as many as 47 percent of white-collar jobs in the US economy could become obsolete with increases in technology.[2] Other authors have noted a similar potential, including Martin Ford in his ominously titled *Rise of the Robots: Technology and the Threat of a Jobless Future*. Though trade is frequently blamed for job losses in manufacturing, evidence indicates that technology has long been the main culprit.[3]

Since the industrial revolution and the Luddite movement, people have worried about technology taking their jobs. Though this often happened, additional jobs have historically appeared. Often these jobs were spawned by the very technologies that people were worried about. As the cotton gin took over cotton processing, the textile industry boomed. As washing machines took over household chores, labor was freed up for other, higher-valued uses. In the next stage, the same pattern may repeat itself. However, just assuming that the future will be like the past is never a good practice. Loss of well-paying jobs from technological advances has the potential to accelerate existing trends toward greater inequality.[4]

SCENARIOS

Scenario 4A: Fragmentation in the Structure of Companies and Work

Overview: Decentralized and fragmented work

Theories of why firms exist often revolve around the lower transaction costs of having multiple functions in-house and the need to protect intellectual capital. Though technological solutions are lowering transactions costs, protection of intellectual capital is both increasingly important on the one hand and increasingly difficult on the other.

Better communications and collaboration platforms would be expected to drive traditional firm organizational structures to a more distributed model. Even small companies or those in basic industries require a wide range of human capital to deal with the demands of competing in a complex, regulated, and globalized world. It may not be financially feasible to have all these functions in-house on a full-time basis.

At the same time, legal protections and clear task identification can keep intellectual property out of the hands of all but a core group of employees. People may work on discrete parts of confidential tasks but be unaware of how the pieces fit into the overall product or service. Storage, search, and analytic technologies can allow proprietary know-how and intellectual capital to be increasingly embedded in the technological and documentary platforms of institutions, rather than in even long-term employees.

The net outcome of these factors is hypothesized to be a continuation of trends toward either outsourcing or, more importantly, lack of permanent or full-time employment even if someone is ostensibly employed by a firm. At some juncture, whether an individual works for a company or is an outsourced source of expertise becomes difficult to ascertain. Average tenures at many companies continue to drop, and often are only a few years even at industry-leading companies.[5] Firms become large coordination factories, rather than locations for permanent, longer-term employment.[6] This can bring both costs and benefits to employees and companies.

The expected results are less long-term employment, deeper acquisition of individual expertise, greater geographical dispersion of participants, and implications for mobility, health care, taxation, and community.

Contributing factors

Cost competitiveness; market competitiveness and need for deep expertise across a wide range of topics for short intervals of time; virtual currencies or earning in multiple currencies with tax havens, allowing dispersed workers to manage their local tax systems and regulation; better corporate information, IP protection, and search platforms; cultural acceptance of the changing nature of work; portability of health care where that is the case, and increased costs of maintaining health care in the workplace; globalization backlashes that decrease international mobility and increase incentives to work virtually. Results will vary considerably across industries and firms.

Mitigating factors

Ongoing need for company-specific knowledge that cannot be divided; unwillingness to risk leaks of intellectual property with outsiders, especially those with industry expertise who are likely to be working part time or in their next gig with competitors; motivation, which is often not only about money but can be embedded in firm culture.

Likely time frame

Immediate and ongoing.

Probability

One hundred percent in certain areas, especially in more innovative industries and/or where intellectual property is not fully discernible and/or portable. More traditional industries may be even more ripe for disruption, though take longer to accept changes.

Notes on bets and risk mitigation

Outsourcing coordinating companies and collaboration platforms; software to protect IP and allow better collaboration; platforms for work and tax management for independent workers; machine learning and big data companies that can generate job descriptions and monitor performance or that can manage company intellectual property; companies that offer benefits and services specifically designed for a mobile workforce, especially in insurance, travel, and retirement.

Scenario 4B: A Future with Less Work and/or Less Skilled Work

Overview: Less work and/or skilled work

New technologies have not in the past led to the mass unemployment that people have feared. However, the scope of areas where jobs can be lost is potentially much greater in the current batch of technologies, as are firms' incentives to decrease human labor costs and content.

If pay and benefits are maintained, less work can be a utopian outcome with new jobs generated around the increased leisure time and income that people will enjoy. If it is not, and there are simply fewer jobs and/or they take less time and/or skill to complete, the scenario could lead to the dystopic emergence of an underemployed underclass of both blue- and white-collar workers.

Improved algorithms and consolidation of decision making in hubs with only a few well-paid workers have already removed most decision making from many professional services roles and entire branches (e.g., bank, wealth management, and insurance companies). Staff there act as lower-paid relationship managers whose job it is to help customers complete paperwork for decisions that are made elsewhere. Similarly, the emergence of "big box" stores in the 1990s and mass Internet shopping in the 2000s has replaced skilled, local middle-class small business owners with interchangeable, low-cost labor or almost no labor at all.[7] The hypothesis is that the trends noted here will continue and accelerate.

Contributing factors

The proliferation and acceptance of the "gig" economy; automation of many blue- and white-collar functions, leaving humans with a peripheral role such as the final editing of articles by Automated Insights' bot Wordsmith; higher minimum wages and costs of living globally may accelerate automation and selective, part-time employment; increased health care costs and employer burdens increase employers' desire to minimize traditional employment (e.g., full-time jobs with benefits).

Mitigating factors

Creation of new industries and human needs that can absorb workers at all skill levels, which has historically been the outcome; labor union resistance may lead to legislation that slows the trend, especially with unions representing white-collar workers.

Likely time frame

Three to ten years for maximum effect.

Probability

Ninety percent or greater in certain industries, probably even odds of this being a global phenomenon in the medium term.

Notes on bets and risk mitigation

Bet against dying industries in favor of those that are part of the dissolution; invest in tools that increase potential for the "gig" or "sharing" economy in areas not yet affected to take advantage of underemployed skilled labor; invest in or take options on automation/robotics/machine learning companies; personally, increase specialized skills and human-based networks; work on signaling quality over quantity.

Scenario 4C: Signaltocracy—Back to the Roots of Credibility

Overview: Emergence of the global signaltocracy

Thanks to the nearly infinite scalability of the network economy, nearly anyone anywhere can access massive open online courses (MOOCs) at elite universities like Stanford and MIT, take tests, and have their work recognized. Companies looking for programming or other quantifiable categories of talent can tap into much larger networks than any previous recruiting base.

Soft skills like management capability, work ethic, interpersonal skills, and good judgment, by contrast, are nearly impossible to test in MOOCs, or anywhere online for that matter. There are as many ways to develop false online personas as there are sound ones, with good filters few and far between. For less than the cost of the tuition, you can hire a double to get an online degree at a real university.[8] Or you can lie about the degree and probably never get caught. Services offer to get you Twitter followers, Facebook "friends," LinkedIn contacts, and favorable reviews for any good or service you can provide, on or offline.[9] It's straightforward to create a completely false virtual self or company, and difficult for others to accurately determine its validity.

However, differentiation between job candidates, business partners, and service providers remains critical, especially in fast-changing and management fields where results are harder to measure quickly and precisely. A low-risk default will continue to be to hire from prestigious universities, with risk aversion in hiring continuing to reinforce a clubby environment where people hire people like themselves.[10] This and other behavior will drive the signaltocracy, or the hierarchy driven by *achievement*-related signals.

In the midst of a technical transition and widening pool of potential colleagues (and mates), selected previrtualization signals will still reign in employment and social scenarios. But not all will prevail. Religious affiliation was a signal in ancient trade networks, with both Christian and Jewish traders trusting those of their own groups. In the modern world religion has been overused by unscrupulous types and besides is not an achievement.

However, other old-style but more selective and achievement-related networks may become more, not less, important in the global market. Those who can afford and/or get into elite schools or have the connections or can pass the personality tests to get jobs in elite companies will be the signaltocracy in the global economy. Family connections; house or business address; publications; social, sports, and intellectual clubs; and kids' schools will all hold strong in our world well into the future.

Signs of a desire to narrow the massive pool into a more traditional and manageable one abound. Applications to elite schools continue to rise while applications to less well-regarded ones are declining—sometimes putting their survival in danger. Generic college education has become commoditized, with employers aware of the startling result that "45% of American students made no gains in their first two years of university."[11] To narrow the prospect pool to a more reliable and manageable one, the dating app Hinge only presents dates in or related to those in your social networks. Expect more of the same in the future.

A virtual and physical world signaling arms race is in the early stages. On one side are the purveyors of signals, trying to short-circuit achievements to give their clients greater credibility than they would have relying on traditional and actual achievements alone. On the other are filters to determine the legitimacy of the signals. These are coupled with the traditional, offline signal types noted above. The stakes are high. Poor signals for potentially high achievers can lead to underutilization of resources and less-satisfying lives. The right signals can lead to opportunities even for individuals who lack the skills and/or work ethic to succeed in the context of the opportunities.[12]

Contributing factors

Overwhelming quantity of information and potential signaling fraud; the acute need to quickly sort through noise and determine the qualities of individuals being assessed; the habit of relying on traditional signals; the inertia of the dominant networks that contain and act as guardians of the signals and their tendency to hire like; ongoing innovation by purveyors of low-quality signals.

Mitigating factors

Difficulty verifying even high-quality signals may dilute those; better filtering options, such as search engines that accurately rank quality of source or signal as a separate category; emergence of other virtual signals that are user friendly and accurate; emergence of improved "soft skill" testing and qualification methods; advances in neuroscience and genetics can use DNA tests and brain scans to test for different types of predispositions and aptitudes.

Likely time frame

One-plus years.

Probability

Ninety percent or greater over the medium term, ongoing, but likely to accelerate.

Notes on bets and risk mitigation

Invest in higher prestige filters or access points to them (i.e., publishers, clubs, or other gatekeepers); develop new ways to create signals that appear legitimate but are difficult to verify—for example, thousands of owners linked to a particular prestige address; signaltocracy accumulation and coaching services; image-enhancing products; early accumulation and judicious management of personal signals; investment in businesses and image enhancement companies that can capitalize on consumers' frustration with problems differentiating products and services online.

Scenario 4D: Emergence of a True Virtual Currency, as a Competitor or Successor to National Fiat Currencies

Overview: Emergence of a true virtual currency

The emergence and relative success of Bitcoin has revealed the usefulness of and desire for a true virtual currency. Demand is driven by a desire to replicate the anonymity of cash on electronic exchange platforms that allow for large distances between parties to the transaction. Other demand may stem from freedom from volatility of a single currency, tax evasion, security of the block chain, or convenience.

As a "true" virtual currency, the new currency will perform the three roles of money, as a medium of exchange, a store of value, and a unit of account. The decoupling of currency values from metals (to fiat currencies) decades ago means that users' expectations are aligned to accept other "faith"-based currencies. Whatever emerges may at least temporarily circumvent or be outside the regulatory reach of the main global monetary authorities, perhaps shadowing and slipping in and out of other currencies without formal, actual exchange.

Though Bitcoin was the first serious contender, the victor may not emerge from a Bitcoin-like experiment. Its establishment may be intentional or serendipitous. Existing means of transacting goods, services, and currencies might naturally extend to issuing credits or "chits" that then become de facto currencies. For example, Amazon or eBay site credits or smartphone payment functions coupled with an active and decentralized marketplace could form a foundation for what effectively emerges as a new currency.

Contributing factors

Massive and decentralized computing power, coupled with the emergence of block-chain-like technologies; the ability of algorithms to match buyers and sellers in marketplaces without any effective middleman; a desire for anonymity in an increasingly invaded online space; an increased desire for anonymous currency movement, given increased debt levels in the rich countries and the anticipation that taxes will rise.

Mitigating factors

National and international authorities; lack of policing function and the potential for fraud and theft.

Likely time frame

One to five years.

Probability

Fifty percent in that time frame.

Notes on bets and risk mitigation

Spot investments in emerging technologies; spot investment in emerging currency markets, as many new contenders have increased rapidly in value; development of futures markets on virtual currencies; watch for abandonment of minor national currencies for virtual currency (long term).

Scenario 4E: Extension of the Sharing Economy

Overview: Extension of the sharing economy

The so-called sharing economy has led to the more intensive use of capital goods that previously had been left largely idle. The trend has been enabled by the marriage of mobile, machine learning, and "big data" technologies. This scenario imagines that the extent and effects of the sharing economy are in the early stages.

The appeal is clear. While creating new income opportunities for the owners of underused capital, the sharing economy maximizes usage per unit of capital outlay. For the users, they have access to a wide range of otherwise expensive capital goods.

The current sharing economy model can likely be extended further to airlines, luxury bus and limo transport, certain appliances and tools, housing, industrial capital equipment, and logistics and transport. As services are embedded in the sharing economy, the lines between the sharing economy and outsourcing will blur.

Perhaps more interestingly, hacks may allow groups of individuals to share goods and services that are not intended to be shared. A single virtual subscriber to a health insurance policy may be represented by several real individuals. Jobs that do not require office presence, or minimal presence, can be shared by more than one person using a single virtual persona with a particular set of qualifications and college degree. Some personas can perhaps be used for some jobs, and others for other jobs.

As the sharing economy for real assets deepens, financial services will emerge to allow for the purchase and maintenance of those assets. Though this will assist the purveyors of these services, it could also transfer more of the wealth back into the financial system, deepening rather than mitigating inequality.

Contributing factors

Improving networks, information-processing power, and mobile apps; increased need for a wide range of goods and services in both work and leisure lives; desire to avoid taxation; fragmentation of the workforce, driving part-time employees to pick up multiple "gigs" (see Scenario 4A above).

Mitigating factors

Safety concerns driven by increased contact with strangers who are hard to identify and evaluate virtually; fraud, broken equipment, and underperformance in tasks will decrease credibility of schemes; poor capital budgeting not accounting for capital depreciation and replacement options can lead to bankruptcies and a poor reputation among potential entrants; more aggressive taxation can remove some benefits of participation.

Likely time frame

Zero years to the foreseeable future.

Probability

Nearly 100 percent that the sharing economy will intensify at least in some sectors.

Notes on bets and risk mitigation

Investment in and development of financial services (investment and insurance) for the sharing economy, including development and testing of new contractual relationships; development of software applications to serve sharing economy participants; first-mover advantages in developing new sharing economy platforms; shorting of companies that will have their business damaged by the sharing economy (e.g., traditional transport and leasing companies).

NOTES

1. Akerlof (1970).
2. Frey and Osborne (2013).
3. See for example, Hicks and Devaraj (2015).
4. See the World Economic Forum, *Global Risks Report 2017*, for a discussion on the nexus between technological change, inequality, and political risk.
5. Data from Payscale.com.
6. See Gapper (2017) for a less than flattering article on the explosion of consultants and consulting services in firms.
7. See economist Tyler Cowen's (2014) work, *Average Is Over*, for his take on the bifurcation of the workforce into a highly skilled, but small, minority, and a lower-skilled mass.
8. See Newton (2015). There are numerous services such as boostmygrade.com.
9. Numerous companies pride themselves on creating good, fake TripAdvisor reviews for companies that want their rankings to improve. One claims to give all profits to charity, so you can feel good about it at the same time. Peer reviews are a favored feedback system in virtual networks. The larger a review system gets, the more useful it becomes to users. Conversely, it also gets easier to manipulate reviews, and any large site only validates a minuscule number.
10. See Cowen (2017) for a chapter on the "pairing" that has been facilitated by the digital world, and leading to declining diversity across a range of groups.
11. Arom and Roksa (2011).
12. See this article by Goldstein (2015) for one case of the right signals opening doors even after repeated failure.

13

Emerging Markets Growth

Distribution of wealth in the global economy is undergoing a major, long-term shift. Figure 13.1 shows the change in share of global GDP for developed market economies and emerging markets since 1980, forecast to 2020. Though since 2013, crises in the emerging markets have led to a reversal in gains, the longer-term trends will likely at least hold steady if not continue upward.[1]

The main gainers are India and China, which should not come as a surprise. Also gaining are some of the larger emerging markets that have seen steady growth like Vietnam, Turkey, and Egypt. Smaller countries have also gained, some of which started in particularly bad spots, like Rwanda. Other large emerging markets have done relatively well, but not well enough to keep up with India and China. Some of those countries, such as Brazil, have had their cumulative results beat down by crises they went through in the 1980s and again in the 2010s. The biggest "losers" in terms of share of global GDP are the European developed market economies.

Some observers would claim this as evidence for the decline of the West. The West may or may not be in decline, but the chart has nothing to do with that. It just shows that some subsets of countries have been doing better lately than they did in the past. The best-performing emerging market economies are still poorer than the industrial countries of Europe and North America. They have just been growing faster. That the share of the US economy in global GDP has shrunk from 50 percent to 19.1 percent (a drop of 67 percent!) since the 1950s means more than anything that others have done well. If during the same period the GDP of the United States had dropped 67 percent, that would be a different story. But that is not what happened.

Higher relative and absolute growth in the emerging markets in sum point to an increased share of global GDP. Volatility in the trend will certainly continue. Emerging markets have experienced multiple booms and busts during which growth

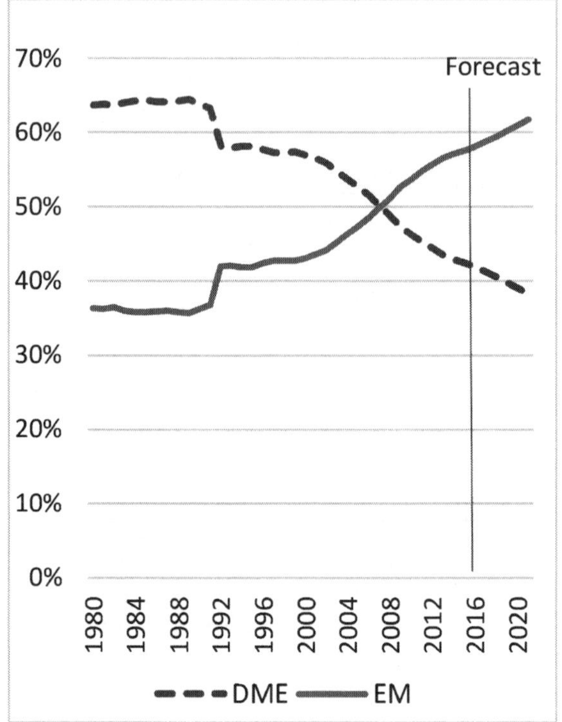

Figure 13.1. Share of Global GDP (PPP), Actual and Forecast
Source: Data and forecasts are from the IMF database.

has come and gone. However, all these headline-making booms and busts mask a consistent trend of higher growth.

There are a few big questions here with respect to emerging markets. The first is why some poorer countries are growing faster, under what circumstances that might or might not continue, and why. That was one of the main topics of chapter 8. Global capital flows will continue to shift as certain economies win and others lose.

A second question is whether emerging markets countries as a whole will develop, or whether pockets of countries will develop while leaving a lot of the country behind. Economists have usually focused on country-wide economic growth. However, national boundaries may matter progressively less in the distribution of wealth. The increasing income shares and Gini coefficients shown previously may indicate a stratification that depends less and less on national boundaries.

The third question has to do with what happens to capital flows as emerging markets grow, both in volume and volatility. Emerging markets growth can be either stabilizing or destabilizing for the global economy. Much of the answer to these questions is related to how the next question evolves.

The fourth question is, what are the implications of shifts in both economic and political power? As the emerging economies grow in wealth and power, how will they seek to change the world to reflect that new power?

SCENARIOS

Scenario 5A: Reshaping of Global Institutions

Overview: Reshaping of global institutions

The rules and institutions of the global economy were largely forged both formally and informally by the main market economies of Europe, North America, and Japan over the last two centuries, and especially since the Second World War. These rules and institutions largely reflect these economies' histories and cultural characteristics. As emerging markets grow, the larger ones and coalitions of the smaller ones can expect to reshape global political and economic institutions to better reflect their interests.

Changes may be incremental, such as the founding of a Chinese-led Asian infrastructure bank to counter the similar ones dominated by the United States. China is becoming the largest exporter of investment capital, and has reset some of the rules for investment in Africa. Along the incremental theme, a new version of the BIS could create a parallel set of banking and payments guidelines. China's $1 trillion "Belt and Road" project seeks to revamp trade infrastructure across Asia and Europe. Undoubtedly, new rules and norms will be established to govern the routes.

New institutional formations may be less incremental and more disruptive, such as dispensing with entire segments of global legal norms. For example, a bloc of Latin American and South and Central Asian countries may tire of the drug war driven by US- and European-based demand and legalize the use and/or transport of drugs and other illicit substances through their countries.

Different emerging markets' norms of competitive market behavior could spill over into the global marketplace, with collusion, barriers to entry, tax evasion, corruption (as defined by the current developed market economies, but not other countries), and other norms shifting away from developed market standards into acceptability in large, regional trading blocs. Such activities could be fueled, as in the past, by national and regional pride and the desire to stem the influence of globally dominant trading and technology companies in favor of new, more local dominant companies. Developed market economies may help the process by turning their backs on globalization themselves and reverting to more nationalist and populist lines of thinking.

As populations and wealth continue to grow, a commodity price rebound would reignite concerns about food and industrial security. Nations and regions may step back away from trading in global commodity markets, and seek to "ring-fence" key commodities to ensure sufficiency for their populations. At the extreme, the world may see Cold War types of economic zones, largely isolated from each other, at least with regard to the trading of certain goods and migratory rights. The main drivers may be economic this time, rather than political. Other countries could be on the periphery of multiple blocs, similar to the Cold War "Non-Aligned" movement.

On the extreme, but not unlikely, end of possibilities, emerging markets giants may back a new multilateral reserve currency, even partially or wholly digital, to counter USD dominance. This could be precipitated by another financial crisis in which the US Fed is unable or unwilling to work to stabilize the global economy, in the same way that it did in 2009.

Contributing factors

Increasing emerging markets' power and wealth and desire to reshape the world to their needs; global dominance of US-based companies in Internet search, e-commerce, social media, and the sharing economy will fuel the ongoing support of national and regional alternatives (e.g., Uber's experience in China); antiglobalization political rhetoric in the developed market economies leads countries and regions to take matters into their own hands, especially when representatives of the main economies talk about "tearing up" well-established agreements; increases in global terrorism may change migration patterns, with certain blocs all but prohibiting members of other blocs from visiting or immigrating; a rebound in commodity prices may lead to a decline in open-market trading volumes and liquidity.

Mitigating factors

The main economic powers, the United States and European Union, are likely to continue to offer considerable carrots (market access) and sticks (antitrust and rule enforcement) to counter the emergence of alternative institutions and rules; as emerging markets grow, some of the potential reshaping may be mitigated by their becoming more like the wealthier economies that created the institutions, and buying into them, rather than trying to change them; "emerging markets" interests are far from homogeneous, and in many areas, their interests probably differ as much among themselves as with the main developed market economies.

Likely time frames and probabilities

Some minor changes are expected to be incremental and ongoing; medium to high probability of an alternative reserve currency within a decade; high probability of accelerated commodity ring fencing within a decade; high probability of one or other current champions of the global economic system, North American or EU, abandoning one or other sets of global institutions; low to medium probability of dissolution into disparate and isolated trading blocs.

Global bets or risk mitigation

Requires careful monitoring of political directions, then long and short, out-of-the-money bets on the economic fallout of geopolitical shifts, including national industrial and service sector winners and losers across different markets; long, out-of-the-money options on commodities, anticipating trading liquidity drying up; long bets on emerging virtual currencies and related technologies, infrastructure, and enablers.

Scenario 5B: Changes in Global Economic Migration Patterns

Overview: Economic migration pattern shift

For decades, the direction of human talent has been unidirectional. The most talented students, if they had the opportunity, would go to North America or the European Union to study and then often stay to work. They were drawn by the economic opportunities, freedom of work and expression, and well-organized and relatively safe economies.

As the emerging economies grow relative to the developed market economies, the locus of opportunity can be expected to shift. Emerging economies have already seen increasing numbers of their citizens return home after gaining education and experience elsewhere. What has not happened yet is a mass semipermanent to permanent migration of professionals from developed market economies to emerging markets, seeking their fortunes there with local companies. To date, much migration is to seek employment in multinationals or global organizations, for low cost of living, or adventure, not to build a long-term life and career.

A shift could be accelerated by a long period of so-called secular stagnation in developed markets, rather than opportunities in emerging ones. However, as talent settles in and drives growth, the economies will become more attractive in their own right. At some point, talent from around the globe may flock to Hanoi or Nairobi as it has flocked to London, New York, or Palo Alto in decades past. The trend could start in enclaves and spread or may stay in enclaves, especially if enclavization solidifies as hypothesized in another scenario.

A small advance indicator of such a trend may be in Dubai, though the city has mainly attracted other emerging markets talent rather than top talent from the European Union and United States (some would differ). A more favorable climate, both physical and social, in another location could tip the scales toward a more globally originated and mobile elite.

Contributing factors

Increased opportunities versus at home, especially as the young see less social mobility than before; a "critical mass" in certain markets, much as happened in Hong Kong and Singapore in the twentieth century; terrorist violence can make locations (e.g., Latin America) that are not targets more attractive; ongoing enclavization, where areas of developing countries are as or more desirable and affordable than wealthy market alternatives; or high old-age liabilities driving higher tax rates in developed market economies.

Mitigating factors

Local biases and prejudices, with many emerging markets countries more culturally closed than their developed market counterparts even when the language of business is English; unimproved environmental and security conditions; national policies designed to keep local people in certain roles, common in many countries; a decreased culture of risk taking in developed market economies, lowering migration; biases and rules against foreign ownership, public school attendance, and eventual citizenship.

Likely time frame

Five to ten years before emerging markets become major destinations for the most talented, but state-driven efforts (like Singapore's biotechnology initiatives) will create additional incentives to relocate in certain areas

Probability

Almost inevitable over the longer term, especially if as noted in a previous scenario, emerging markets enclaves become indistinguishable from wealthy market ones.

Notes on bets and risk mitigation

At the individual and family level, language learning, in particular Spanish, Chinese, Portuguese; short developed market currencies over the long run as talent and tax revenues leave; emerging markets technology and global branding companies (i.e., fast-moving consumer goods) that will benefit from global brand acceptance; short positions on developed market companies in vulnerable areas; long-term currency speculation and hedging as competitiveness shifts; for developed market economies, work to improve economic and social standards in most desirable areas to minimize outflow, including investment in public universities and infrastructure.

Scenario 5C: Emerging Markets Global Dominance in Certain Industries

Overview: Growing EM dominance

It is accepted that emerging market companies are becoming global leaders in certain areas, and that emerging markets are as much the source as the destination for global capital. This scenario digs a bit further into possible side effects or corollaries to this general trend.

Trade treaties have largely put an end to the old state-sponsored "infant industries" of the past. However, after decades of experimentation, global competition, mandatory transfer of know-how by foreign companies, and government experience circumventing the spirit of "level playing fields" for all companies, support for local favorites may be entering a new and more successful era. Gone are the rusting hulks of industrial companies languishing behind closed borders with poorly trained management.

The new era is seeing private and quasi-private emerging market companies fully engaged in global markets and with management honed in foreign multinationals and/or at the best business schools. At the same time, state support ensures access to low-cost and even "gift" capital, more stable macro environments than in the past, loose enforcement of others' intellectual property rights, world-class infrastructure, favorable regulatory oversight in home markets, regulatory intimidation of foreign rivals, low-cost and loosely regulated land and labor markets, and concessionary tax treatments.

Turning to previous scenarios, a reshaping of global institutions, migration of talent, and enclavization can further improve the environment for these new global competitors.

A major question is which industries are likely to be affected. The case is perhaps best made for basic industries. Already there are globally dominant emerging markets companies in bakeries (Bimbo), steel (Tata), cement (Pemex), shipbuilding (Hyundai), and others. Moving up the value chain will become more complicated, though there has been success in aircraft (Embraer), telecoms equipment (Huawei), and cell phones (LG, ZTE).

Another major question is whether these companies will remain isolated, globally competitive outposts among a group of broader, more moribund local competitors. Alternatively, they could attract the talent, suppliers, and related industries (i.e., cluster), so that the economy itself becomes globally dominant in the particular industry. So far, the cases listed above have been more isolated with developed country companies still retaining strong positions overall.[2]

Potentially vulnerable industries include transport, mainstream medical devices, software, biotech, entertainment, consumer goods and brands, and basic equipment for defense. The latter is a major export industry already for Russia, Turkey, and China.

Contributing factors

Ongoing state loan and trade assistance programs (i.e., low cost of capital, high barriers and terms of entry for foreign firms); improved management training and large populations with first-rate educations, narrowing gaps between human resources in different countries; improved living standards in emerging markets, to attract the best human capital.

Mitigating factors

Legal risks in emerging markets will likely keep the (nonsubsidized) market cost of capital higher than in developed market economies; increased wages in emerging markets, reflecting a global rather than a regional cost of labor and capital; increased mechanization of developed market companies may allow them to hold on to intellectual capital while competing in manufacturing; cycles of crises in emerging markets drive changes in regulation and financing of potential global competitors; higher value-added manufacturing benefits developed market economies.

Likely time frame

Highly dependent on market; for basic industries this is ongoing.

Probability

Nearly 100 percent in certain markets.

Notes on bets and risk mitigation

Small but widespread investments in leading emerging markets firms, as they are available, either through ETFs or directly; short positions on developed market exchanges in companies and sectors likely to be most hard hit; watch for mercantilist and discriminatory responses from developed market economies.

NOTES

1. As stated previously, the term "emerging markets" is used as a taxonomical convenience, and is not meant to imply commonalities other than that the economies are not part of the wealthy group of North American or EU countries. See *The Economist* 2011a and 2015d.
2. Deloitte's 2016 Global Manufacturing Competitiveness Index gives four of the top ten spots of manufacturing competitiveness to emerging markets (China, South Korea, Taiwan, and Mexico). The United States is expected to overtake China for the number one spot by 2020, while India is expected to move to number five from eleven in 2016.

Appendix

Economics' Struggle with Methodology

Scientific method varies depending on the application, but mainly comes down to a set of basic foundations. The first is identification and description of relevant events or phenomena. The second is the creation of hypotheses about the events and phenomena, and in particular how those hypotheses can help predict how the system works. Economists are pretty good at executing these first two components of scientific method. The third foundation is the sound formulation and execution of replicable tests of the hypotheses. This allows knowledge to be created and then adjusted over time as hypotheses are fine-tuned, retested, and then fine-tuned again until a sound body of theory can be established around the validated *and* rejected hypotheses. Economics struggles greatly with this third component of the scientific method. Economists have developed a wide range of hypotheses and theories, but in truth most have not been successfully tested to the degree that science would require for validation. They usually just cannot be.

One problem is that good, relevant data can be hard to get for certain types of analysis. Economic data comes in three main forms. **Cross-section data** is data across different parts of the economy, collected all at the same time. Data on family income in March 2014 collected from one thousand families is cross-section data. **Time series data** is data on a particular variable that is collected over time. Time series data is how economic changes are tracked, and there are many examples: median family income over time, exchange rates, growth rates, stock and commodity prices, interest rates, inflation rates, and so on. The third form, panel data or **longitudinal data**, combines both types. The income of multiple families tracked from 1995 to 2015 is an example of panel data. Both time series and panel data present similar difficulties in their use in testing economic hypotheses.

Data is everything in economics, but it is rarely perfect. Sometimes there are differences in collection methods across countries, making it hard to compare figures.

Sometimes the data is incomplete and/or erroneous because it is hard to collect accurately. For example, GDP figures might include different or no estimates for the sometimes substantial gray or black market activity in an economy or externalities that come from production. Sometimes collected data is broader and has more information in it than what is needed for the analysis. The unemployment rate seems simple, but it really reflects a number of things like the number of jobs available, the skills match, how much people are willing to work for, how the workforce is defined, and the number of people actually out looking for jobs. It can be hard to compare across economies, or even regions.

For all its imperfections, data quality alone is usually not the biggest barrier to applying scientific method. Data on prices and volumes, budgets, money supply, and stocks and flows of money and other variables are detailed, accurate, widely available, and very useful for all sorts of analyses. Analysts need to be aware of where data comes from and what its weaknesses might be. Data can be a problem, but its basic availability and accuracy is not the main one that challenges economic analysis.

A more important reason sound scientific method is hard to use effectively in economics is that science advances because experiments are repeatable. That is how hypotheses and theories are validated or refined in the sciences. In economics, you cannot repeatedly conduct the same experiment to test its validity and robustness. The world is constantly evolving, and conditions that hold at one time or place may (will) not hold at another. Consequently, even if a hypothesis is validated at one place and point in time, it may never be fully valid again anywhere else, ever. Nonreplicability makes it hard to build up a good, consistent body of validated theory. It does not stop economists from trying, but conclusions are easy to attack and lack the sort of credibility that is attainable in the real or "hard" sciences.

In economics it is also hard to have a control group. When carrying out statistical analyses to test hypotheses, control groups make for good methodology. A control group in economics would be an economy where everything else is the same as in another economy, except for the policy or action whose effect is being tested for. That way you can compare the two economies, one where the policy was carried out and one where it was not. Even on a general level, it is nearly impossible to find two identical enough economies, let alone two economies where you are sure that the same things are going to happen to them over some period of time. There is too much variability in the real world and consequently too few testing opportunities to have a control group, especially for macro-level questions.[1] This lack of similarity across economies and time can also mean that hypotheses tests using economic data have a small sample size. A large sample is needed to get the best results in most types of statistical hypotheses tests.

As a result, there is inevitable ambiguity in economic conclusions. A group of economists critical of the conclusions of another group can usually fairly easily shoot down the results of their hypotheses tests by pointing out these two weaknesses. They help make economics the shouting match that it is, rather than the science everyone would like it to be. While replicability and the lack of a control group are part of the problem, the existing hypothesis-testing methods are also less than perfect when used with economic data.

Testing hypotheses with economic data usually involves statistical methods. And even without the issues above, using sound statistical methods to test hypotheses on economic data is notoriously difficult. This is especially the case when using time series data. Time series data is central to economic analysis and hypothesis testing, since a lot of important questions are about what the effect of some action will be on an economy over time.

Analyzing time series data to test an economic hypothesis means validating two separate conclusions. The first is whether an action taken is *related* to changes in a series, or the **correlation** (i.e., if they happened together or one after the other). The second is trying to figure out if the action *caused* the series to change, or proving **causation**. They are both different and necessary. Correlation can be tested for with statistical methods, though not always easily. However, just because an effect parallels or follows an action (is correlated) does not mean that the action caused the effect. Figure A1 illustrates that point in a clear (and dumb) way. So even after spending an enormous amount of effort analyzing data to arrive at a correlation, the battle is usually just beginning.

Time series data are notoriously "noisy." Noise in data is defined as everything the data might say, other than the information you are really after. The data might be accurate. The noise just means there is a lot else going on. In economics, noise makes it difficult to tell how changes in the series are related to an action taken previously and complicates establishing both correlation and causation. Noise also compounds over time. In economics, there are often long time lags between when a policy lever

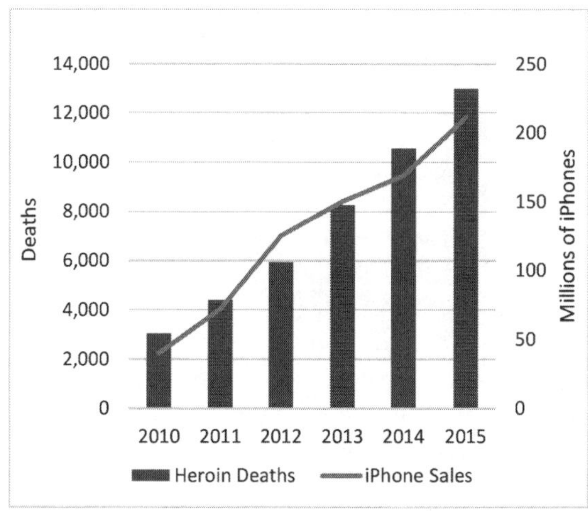

Figure A.1. Important Correlation

Source: National Institute on Drug Abuse (NIDA) database, Statista.com.

is flipped and when an effect happens, if it does at all. Because of that, there are lots and lots of other things that happen in between that can make it impossible to know what caused what.

Even when time frames are short, data can be noisy. There may be other things happening in the economy at that very moment that can also be affecting the economy in the same or totally different directions. With noisy data there can be numerous candidates for the causal factor, and it may even be one that you cannot find or include in the analysis. It may not even be in the data. The previously mentioned problem of the small sample size then comes into play, making it hard to filter effects out of the noise using statistical methods.

Noise, variability, lack of control groups, small sample size, and nonreplicability all contribute to the difficulty of effectively using a traditional scientific method in economics. Economists just cannot definitively validate the majority of the most interesting and important economic hypotheses and build these up into a consistent, validated body of theory. It is why economists don't agree. It is not that economists have not tried. The economic environment just does not support the effective use of the kinds of hypotheses testing required of sound scientific method.

Sometimes data show nothing at all happening from what might have been a significant event, like a sharp change in interest rates. Something else may be going on. Or sometimes the opposite of what is expected happens. Sometimes there are two different effects happening at the same time. An example examined in this book is the effect of the announced end in 2013 of US quantitative easing on emerging markets (a lot) and US interest rates (almost nothing and even the opposite of what many expected, including the manager of the world's largest bond fund). The policy announcement was the same, but there are good reasons why the outcome differed in different markets. Essentially, there were different people involved in each case with different incentives and ways to manage risk. There was no body of proven theory or system of equations to predict the result. As a science, economics did not come through. As a broader framework, it did, because the story could be pieced together.

Because of the inability to test hypotheses effectively, we cannot resolve endless debates over such basic and important questions like whether stimulus programs helped countries pull out of the 2008 recession. Some claim that the economy would have recovered anyway. Others claim that even if they did help a bit, the long-term damage to the economy by taking on all that debt will be too high to justify the programs. Others claim that without stimulus, more countries would have ended up in another Great Depression. The fact is, there is no way to accurately test that simple and important hypothesis in a manner that is worthy of science. That is too bad, because then policy makers don't know what to do next time. It's not even possible to use sound scientific method to test for exactly what caused the recession, which makes it hard to pass policies to avoid another one.

Economists have not really found good solutions for these problems. They are trying, though. Economics, through the subfield of econometrics, has pushed the old statistical regression analysis model to account for a wide range of common problems with economic data.[2] This research has been helpful, especially in improving the ability to work with time series, long lag times, data points that are not independent of each other, discrete data, and data that is distributed nonindependently, among other things. Unfortunately, while some problems have been solved, all these new methods have also opened up more debates about which corrections are appropriate to make under which circumstances. It does not help that effects detected by econometric models are often very small and can swing around wildly depending on which methods are used. Finally, econometric models only establish correlation, not causation. So the debates go on. This does not mean that methods are useless. They are just not definitive.

There are other methods of analyzing economic outcomes that are more based on economic theory. It is common to create large model economies using mathematical equations that are designed to mimic the structure of an economy. The models are then calibrated with data and run through simulations. These are called computable general equilibrium (CGE) models. Results are mixed, and these models are notoriously easy to rig by changing assumptions, which of course means more arguing over those assumptions. Some years ago, one model predicted that the optimal outcome for the US Midwest would be for everyone to move out of North Dakota. Fine for non–North Dakotans, but a lot of people liked it there and were doing just fine, thank you. The nice thing about these models is that they do establish causality, at least within the model. Non-data-based, purely theoretical models like dynamic general equilibrium models are also popular, though less so than they used to be. Most of the results from these hold in a narrow enough set of circumstances that they are hard to make policy from (though economists have filled many pages of journals with them).

Most economic analysis these days, and certainly the vast majority of what gets published in major journals, has a lot of math in it. The math is used to model what is happening in an economy. Lots of math makes the field of economics look and feel "sciency." To the outsider it makes economics look serious and complicated. The unspoken reality, though, is that the math is not really complicated, at least when compared to the real world. The reality is that the math used by economists is a huge simplifier. The use of these deterministic formulas rams the fluid, complex, interesting, insane world of economic events into such tight confines that it can render the results pointless, and often wrong. It makes economics look like a science, even if what really matters in a science, scientific method, is rarely able to be used.

The nature of economics is such that a unified and validated body of theory will probably never evolve. There are just too many factors changing all the time. Even if one theory is validated, by nature it will only hold in certain circumstances that may never hold again.

NOTES

1. More and more micro-level hypotheses are being tested more rigorously and with control groups in an interesting branch of economics called experimental economics. It is not uncontroversial, like everything in economics, but it is getting done and has some promise mainly at the micro level.

2. Regression analysis is a statistical method for showing the correlation between two sets of data.

Glossary

alpha Excess return on an investment, over and above the market trend return expected on the investment. Contrast with *beta*.

arbitrage Exploiting price differences between markets for gain. Arbitrage can be across physical goods, geographic, or securities markets.

balance of payments The set of accounts that shows the total flow of funds in and out of a country in a given time period.

beta The "normal" market trend return on a particular security or market. Contrast with *alpha*.

capital (currency) controls Regulations prohibiting the free flow of capital in and/or out of a country. They are normally designed with the intention of reducing volatility caused by rapid money flows.

causation That the movement of one variable causes the movement of another variable. See *correlation*.

cluster A geographic grouping of companies in a similar industry and their related support companies.

common external tariff When groups of countries in a free trade zone maintain a single tariff on imports from other countries. Not having a common external tariff can lead to confusion, cheating on the trade agreement, and considerable additional paperwork.

common shock When multiple economies with similar characteristics react similarly to a single global event.

comparative advantage A theory put forth by David Ricardo that even a country with an absolute cost disadvantage in all goods produced can gain from freer trade through specialization.

convergence The concept that over time economies will converge toward a similar level of per capita income.

correlation When two variables move together over a period of time. They may or may not actually have any effect on each other. See *causation.*

counterparty risk The risk that the other party to a contract will not be able to perform on their side. Particularly risky in noncollateralized agreements or over long periods of time. Common concern in derivatives markets.

covered interest spread The difference in interest rates between similar securities in two economies, after the costs of hedging for exchange and other risks have been accounted for. Will normally be less than the difference with a *naked trade.*

cross-section data Data from a range of variables at a single moment in time, for example 2017 per capita GDP figures for one hundred countries. See *time series* and *longitudinal data.*

currency appreciation (depreciation) When the value of a currency, or the number of units of foreign currency that can be obtained for a unit of domestic currency, is rising.

currency board An exchange regime whereby every unit of domestic currency that is issued is backed up by a unit of foreign reserve currency at the prevailing exchange rate.

currency manipulation Intervening, usually in foreign exchange markets, in order to change a domestic currency's valuation from what it would otherwise be if it were freely traded.

customs union An advanced version of a free trade area that normally lacks any barriers to movement of goods between its members and maintains a common external tariff and trade policy.

deflation A decrease in the consumer price index. The opposite of inflation.

dependency ratio The ratio of people paying into a redistributive system versus those receiving payouts from the system. Commonly used in the discussion of pension systems and the proportion of workers to retirees.

developed market economy The group of countries that have reached the highest level of economic development, generally determined by per capita GDP, total stock of wealth in the economy, depth of and liquidity in financial markets, and openness of markets.

Dutch disease The phenomenon by which capital inflows into one part of an economy drive up the exchange rate to make another, often critical, part of an economy less competitive on export markets.

emerging markets Loosely defined and very diverse group of countries with lower income and less-developed financial markets than the developed market economies.

exchange exposure The risk or potential gain an investor takes on when investing in a currency other than their own, usually due to the value of that other currency rising or falling during the period they are invested in it.

exchange regime The type of exchange rate policies that a country follows, related to how freely the currency is allowed to move as a result of market forces.

exchange-traded fund (commonly, ETF) A type of security that normally follows a particular market index, rather than being actively managed for higher returns. They are bought and sold on public exchanges and are usually made up of the basket of securities that underlie the index they track. More recent manifestations of ETFs have gotten away from simple index tracking.

exorbitant privilege The benefit the United States gains from the US dollar's being the main reserve currency, in particular the capital account financing that it receives to finance persistent trade deficits.

expectation-driven inflation Inflation that is driven by the expectation that inflation will increase. Normally, distributors and retailers will raise prices in anticipation of prices going up, creating a self-fulfilling and difficult to break inflationary pattern.

financial contagion The spreading of a financial event (normally a crisis, but need not be) from one country or group of countries to others, usually through trade and/or financial linkages.

financial flow The movement of funds from one place to another over a particular period of time.

fiscal policy The use of tax and spending decisions to carry out policy goals, often to stabilize or change the course of an economy.

foreign direct investment Investment by a foreign entity into a country that results normally in the control of that investment by the foreign entity, and that is intended as a longer-term investment.

free trade agreement Any type of agreement that results in the lowering of barriers to the movement of goods, capital, and/or people between two or more countries.

frontier markets A broad grouping of countries, with comparatively low per capita GDP, and not well-developed financial markets or legal institutions.

global savings glut The idea (not agreed on by many) that there is an excess of savings in the world chasing too few investments, leading to low returns and potentially higher risk.

gold standard When a currency is backed up by a quantity of gold that is fixed for the amount of currency in circulation; that is, it is not possible to issue more currency without obtaining more gold.

great recession The global recession that started in 2008, including many of the aftereffects.

haircut When an investor must accept a discounted value for an asset they purchased at a higher value.

hedge A type of trade that is designed to reduce risk on another trade or portfolio, rather than to pay off by itself.

helicopter money A central banking concept whereby money is introduced into consumption markets in an economy, as opposed to assets markets. No one advocates dropping money from a helicopter, but a central bank's writing checks to every citizen would be a clear example of helicopter money.

heuristics and biases A field of study that seeks to understand the shortcuts that human brains developed for problem solving in the evolutionary environment, that then can lead to biased decision making when solving problems in modern statistics, economics, and finance.

high-frequency trading A broad term for high-speed and high-volume trading that is done mainly by computers based on specific trading algorithms, rather than by humans.

high-income other A group of high-income countries that for various reasons are not considered developed market economies. Most of these are either resource-rich or small states that may not have highly developed social or financial institutions.

hot money A colloquial term for money that moves rapidly in and out of economies, often raising and lowering markets and exchange rates at the same time. Most hot money is portfolio investment, or made on public exchanges or through short-term credits.

import substitution When countries put up trade barriers and/or implement subsidies so that domestic companies begin to produce products that were previously imported.

impossible trinity The impossibility that countries encounter in maintaining control over three major, connected elements of their economies: the exchange rate, monetary policy, and capital flows.

incentive compatible When a policy successfully incentivizes economic participants to carry out activities that will achieve the goals of the policy. The goal is to make a policy as incentive compatible as possible to achieve success and minimize *unintended consequences*.

inflation An increase in prices in an economy. Consumer price and asset inflation are the two most common types.

institutional capture When a regulated body is able to influence a public regulatory institution to work in the interests of the regulated body, instead of the public.

liquidity Functionally, the ability to trade in a market at volume without undue movement in price. Liquidity is a relative term and very dependent on the types of trades and trading time frame.

long trade Buying a security with the hopes that it will increase in price over the holding period. See also *short trade*.

longitudinal data Data that has both *cross-sectional* and *time series* elements in it. Also known as panel data. An example would be the per capita GDP of forty countries over thirty years.

maturity mismatch When an investor borrows money over one time frame and invests over another. Most commonly, maturity mismatches occur when an investor borrows short term and invests over the longer term. Problems occur if they need to repay the short-term funds but cannot liquidate the longer-term investments without a loss.

mercantilism The putting up of trade barriers in the belief that trade is a "zero-sum" game, or that unequivocally exports lead to gains and imports lead to losses. Mercantilism was out of favor for much of the seventy-five post–World War II years but may be seeing signs of resurgence in the mid-2010s.

merchandise trade balance The sum of all of a country's imports and exports of goods only. Does not include services.

middle-income trap An observed phenomenon whereby countries are unable to move from emerging markets, middle-income status into that of developed market economies. Exact reasons for it are the subject of much debate.

moral hazard When regulation creates a level of publicly funded or guaranteed protection that then incentivizes others to engage in risky behavior that takes advantage of that protection. The most common cases: deposit insurance can incentivize banks to take risks with depositor funds; knowing a bank is "too big to fail" can drive managers to take excessive risk, knowing they will be bailed out; and the idea that central banks will step in to rescue financial markets means investors may not feel the full effects of the risk they are taking, and so may take on even more risk.

naked trade A trade that is not protected by any risk-reducing hedges.

nominal exchange rate The ratio of the market price of one currency versus another. Can differ from the real exchange rate.

open-market operations A conventional tool of central banking, whereby the central bank buys and sells short-term government securities on open markets, seeking to alter the supply and demand relationship and influence short-term interest rates.

pay as you go Funding for pension systems whereby current workers provide most of the funding for current retirees, and then when they retire, new workers will fund them. Funding adequacy can be affected by changes in the *dependency ratio*.

portfolio rebalancing When portfolio managers reallocate investor money from one type of instrument to another in response to perceived changes in markets. Can be responsible for large movements in global money flows.

principal-agent Concept in economics where one party (the principal) engages another party (the agent) to carry out a transaction for them, but where they will not be able to fully monitor the actions of the agent. It is a classic asymmetric information and incentives problem.

purchasing power parity (PPP) A method for adjusting income to account for differences in purchasing power that occur in different economies. Using a nominal exchange rate to compare incomes across countries can ignore that citizens of some countries can purchase much more than others using the same amount of a particular currency.

quantitative easing An unconventional monetary tool related to open market operations, whereby central banks step outside of the purchase and sale of short-term government securities and buy on the open market other types of securities with different maturities.

quantitative restriction A trade barrier whereby only certain quantities of certain goods are allowed in a country over a particular time. Not common.

quota See *quantitative restriction*.

real exchange rate An exchange rate that accounts for different rates of inflation between economies. Even if a nominal exchange rate stays steady, a higher rate of inflation in one economy will mean that its real exchange rate is appreciating as it becomes more expensive to operate there.

re-exports When goods are brought into a country and re-exported in essentially the same form in which they were imported. Can distort trade figures by over-reporting actual exports.

regulatory capture When a regulatory agency becomes less effective due to undue influence by the parties it is supposed to be regulating.

reserve currency One of a handful of currencies that dominate international exchange transactions and are usually held as official reserves. The US dollar is dominant, followed by the euro, Japanese yen, UK sterling, and Swiss franc.

resource curse The observed phenomenon whereby countries that are rich in natural resources fail to sufficiently benefit from the wealth and sustainably and consistently grow their economies.

risk premium The additional return that an investor will require to invest in an asset that is riskier than the least risky available assets.

rules of origin Rules under free trade agreements dictating the amount of local content that needs to be added to a good or service to be labeled as made in that country.

search for yield The scouring of the global economy for higher-risk adjusted returns on money than may be obtained in the home country. Responsible for considerable global money flows.

secular stagnation A long period of low economic growth.

securitization The bundling of a large number of related, but usually at least nominally diversified, income-producing assets into a single, much larger security.

short trade Sale of an asset that one does not own, with the intention of buying it back later at a lower price. Short sales are done when it is believed that the price of a security will drop.

stagflation A condition where inflation coexists with a stagnant, slow, or not-growing economy.

sterilization Various mechanisms used to reduce the effects of monetary inflows into an economy (usually inflation and a rising exchange rate). Commonly used by economies prone to *Dutch disease*.

stimulus (fiscal and monetary) The use of historically outsize levels of fiscal and/or monetary actions to increase economic growth, usually to spur growth and/or counter a recession.

stock The static value of an economic variable at a particular period of time, such as the stock of debt or assets. See also *asset flow*.

tariff A tax imposed on an import by an importing country.

tax breaks and credits When taxes are refunded or reduced from their baseline level to help achieve a policy goal.

tax havens A location where taxes are either nonexistent or lower than other places. Companies and individuals use these to reduce their overall tax obligations. Some are legal and some are not, depending on conditions and laws.

tax inversion When a company in a high-tax environment buys a company in a lower-tax environment in order to relocate their headquarters and tax base to the lower-tax environment.

terms of trade The relative price levels of key products between two countries, usually over time. If the prices of important exports are dropping faster than the prices of the main imports, a country can be said to be experiencing deteriorating terms of trade.

time series data Single variable data that is collected over time. For example, per capita GDP of a particular country for thirty years. See also *cross-section* and *longitudinal data.*

too big to fail A (fairly recent) regulatory concept whereby certain financial institutions are so important to the financial system that their failure would jeopardize the entire system.

trade barrier Any policy that restricts trade. The most well-known ones are tariffs and quotas. However, many others exist, such as subsidies, health requirements, labeling requirements, paperwork, understaffed border crossings, and cultural preferences.

trade deficit (surplus) When a country's imports are greater (less than) its exports. This may be the *merchandise trade balance*, or may include services.

trade diversion When an increase in trade due to an FTA or other policy changes is not a gross increase in trade, but a diversion from old to new trading partners.

transfer pricing When a company adjusts the pricing of its own internal trade (purchases from other divisions) so that profits are mainly made in low-tax jurisdictions, lowering the overall tax rate on a company.

transshipment The shipment of goods to an intermediate destination before being sent on to the final destination. Most reasons for transshipment are logistical, but it can be used to try to get around trade barriers in the final destination country.

unconventional monetary tools Any tool used by a central bank other than the two conventional tools of setting the rate at the discount window and using open market operations to influence short-term interest rates. Unconventional tools became very popular at central banks around the world following the great recession.

unintended consequences When incentives of a policy are not correctly understood or aligned and a policy has results that are different from or in addition to what was intended.

wealth effect The observed phenomenon that spending increases when asset values increase, even if incomes do not keep pace.

Bibliography

Abbas, S. M. Ali, and Alexander Klemm. "A Partial Race to the Bottom: Corporate Tax Developments in Emerging and Developing Economies." *IMF Working Paper WP/12/28* 20, no. 4 (January 2012). doi:10.1007/s10797-013-9286-8.

Acemoglu, Daron. *Introduction to Modern Economic Growth.* Princeton, NJ: Princeton University Press, 2009.

Acemoglu, Daron, David Autor, David Dorn, Gordon H. Hanson, and Brendan Price. "Import Competition and the Great US Employment Sag of the 2000s." *Journal of Labor Economics* 34, no. S1 (2016). doi:10.1086/682384.

Acemoglu, Daron, and James A. Robinson. *Why Nations Fail: The Origins of Power, Prosperity, and Poverty.* New York: Crown Publishers, 2012.

Actionaid International USA. "Fueling the Food Crisis: The Cost to Developing Countries of US Corn Ethanol Expansion." Report, October 2012.

Ahir, Hites, and Prakesh Loungani. "Can Economists Forecast Recessions? Some Evidence from the Great Recession." Working paper. International Institute of Forecasters, 2014.

Ahmed, Swarnali, Maximiliano Appendino, and Michele Ruta. "Depreciations without Exports? Global Value Chains and the Exchange Rate Elasticity of Exports." *World Bank Group Policy Research Working Papers*, 2015. doi:10.1596/1813-9450-7390.

Akerlof, George A. "The Market for 'Lemons': Quality Uncertainty and the Market Mechanism." *The Quarterly Journal of Economics* 84, no. 3 (1970): 488. doi:10.2307/1879431.

Akerlof, George A., and Robert J. Shiller. *Animal Spirits: How Human Psychology Drives the Economy, and Why It Matters for Global Capitalism.* Princeton, NJ: Princeton University Press, 2009.

Alexander, Klint W., and Brian J. Soukup. "Obama's First Trade War: The US-Mexico Cross-Border Trucking Dispute and the Implications of Strategic Cross-Sector Retaliation on U.S. Compliance under NAFTA." *Berkeley Journal of International Law* 28, no. 2 (2010).

Anderson, James E., and Yoto V. Yotov. "Terms of Trade and Global Efficiency Effects of Free Trade Agreements, 1990–2002." *Journal of International Economics* 99 (2016): 279–98. doi:10.1016/j.jinteco.2015.10.006.

Andolfatto, David. "'MacroMania': In Defense of Modern Macro Theory." April 12, 2015. http://andolfatto.blogspot.com/2015/04/in-defense-of-modern-macro-theory.html.

Andresen, Tino. "German Utilities Hammered in Market Favoring Renewables." Bloomberg .com. August 12, 2013.

Aronson, David R. *Evidence-Based Technical Analysis: Applying the Scientific Method and Statistical Inference to Trading Signals*. Hoboken, NJ: John Wiley & Sons, 2007.

Arum, Richard, and Josipa Roksa. *Academically Adrift: Limited Learning on College Campuses*. Chicago: University of Chicago Press, 2011.

Autor, D. H., D. Dorn, G. H. Hanson, and J. Song. "Trade Adjustment: Worker-Level Evidence." *The Quarterly Journal of Economics* 129, no. 4 (2014): 1799–860. doi:10.1093/qje/qju026.

Autor, David H., David Dorn, and Gordon H. Hanson. "The China Syndrome: Local Labor Market Effects of Import Competition in the United States." *American Economic Review* 103, no. 6 (2013): 2121–68. doi:10.1257/aer.103.6.2121.

———."Untangling Trade and Technology: Evidence from Local Labour Markets." *The Economic Journal* 125, no. 584 (2015): 621–46. doi:10.1111/ecoj.12245.

Baba, Chikako, and Annamaria Kokenyne. "Effectiveness of Capital Controls in Selected Emerging Markets in the 2000's." *IMF Working Papers* 11, no. 281 (2011): I. doi:10.5089/9781463926625.001.

Bahmani-Oskooee, Mohsen, and Massomeh Hajilee. "Exchange Rate Volatility and Its Impact on Domestic Investment." *Research in Economics* 67, no. 1 (2013): 1–12. doi:10.1016/j.rie .2012.08.002.

Baig, Taimur, and Ilan Goldfajn. "Financial Market Contagion in the Asian Crisis." *IMF Working Papers* 98, no. 155 (1998): 1. doi:10.5089/9781451857283.001.

———. "The Russian Default and the Contagion to Brazil." *IMF Working Papers* 00, no. 160 (2000): 1. doi:10.5089/9781451857733.001.

Bank for International Settlements. *Annual Report*. Basel: Bank for International Settlements, 2014.

———. "Global Liquidity: Selected Indicators." February 2015.

Barboza, David, and Charles Duhigg. "China Contractor Again Faces Labor Issue on iPhones." *The New York Times*. September 10, 2012.

Barkham, Patrick. "The Banana Wars Explained." *The Guardian*. March 5, 1999.

Barro, Robert. "Inflation and Economic Growth." *Annals of Economics and Finance* 14, no. 1 (2013). doi:10.3386/w5326.

Barro, Robert J. *Determinants of Economic Growth: A Cross-Country Empirical Study*. Cambridge, MA: MIT Press, 1997.

———. "Inflation and Economic Growth." No. W5326. National Bureau of Economic Research, 1995.

Barro, Robert J., and Xavier Sala-i-Martin. *Economic Growth*. Cambridge, MA: MIT Press, 2004.

Barroso, João Barata R. B., Luiz A. Pereira Da Silva, and Adriana Sales Soares. "Quantitative Easing and Related Capital Flows into Brazil: Measuring Its Effects and Transmission Channels through a Rigorous Counterfactual Evaluation." *Journal of International Money and Finance* 67 (2016): 102–22. doi:10.1016/j.jimonfin.2015.06.013.

Barton, John H. *The Evolution of the Trade Regime: Politics, Law, and Economics of the GATT and the WTO*. Princeton, NJ: Princeton University Press, 2006.

Basurto, Miguel Segoviano, Bradley Jones, Peter Lindner, and Johannes Blankenheim. "Securitization: The Road Ahead." *IMF Staff Discussion Note* 15, no. 1 (January 2015): 1. doi:10.5089/9781498368285.006.

Bech, Morten Linnemann, and Aytek Malkhozov. "How Have Central Banks Implemented Negative Policy Rates?" Report. Bank for International Settlements. March 6, 2016.

Bee, Charles Adam. "Geographic Concentration of Industries." *US Census Bureau ACSBR/11-23*, February 2013. doi:10.1787/871701405174.

Bernanke, Ben. Sandridge Lecture, Virginia Association of Economists, Richmond, VA, March 10, 2005.

Bianco Research LLC. *What Drives the Bond Market.* Report. Bianco Research LLC, 2011.

Blanchard, Oliver, and Daniel Leigh. "Growth Forecast Errors and Fiscal Multipliers." *IMF Working Paper WP/13/1*, 2013. doi:10.1787/eco_outlook-v2010-2-table161-en.

Blinder, Alan S. *After the Music Stopped: The Financial Crisis, the Response, and the Work Ahead.* New York: Penguin Press, 2013.

Bloom, Nicholas, Mirko Draca, and John Van Reenen. "Trade Induced Technical Change? The Impact of Chinese Imports on Innovation, IT and Productivity." *The Review of Economic Studies* 83, no. 1 (2015): 87–117. doi:10.1093/restud/rdv039.

Blustein, Paul. *The Chastening: Inside the Crisis That Rocked the Global Financial System and Humbled the IMF.* New York: Public Affairs, 2001.

Bolio, Eduardo, Jaana Remes, Tomas Lajous, James Manyika, Morten Rosse, and Eugenia Ramirez. *A Tale of Two Mexicos: Growth and Prosperity in a Two-Speed Economy.* Report. McKinsey & Company, March 2014.

Bondt, Werner F. M. De, and Richard Thaler. "Does the Stock Market Overreact?" *The Journal of Finance* 40, no. 3 (1985): 793–805. doi:10.1111/j.1540-6261.1985.tb05004.x.

Bryant, Chris, and Clair Jones. "ECB Quantitative Easing: Failure to Spark." *Financial Times* (London), September 7, 2015.

Buchholz, Todd G. "The Price of Everything and the Value of Nothing." *Finance & Development*, March 2014.

Buckland, Kevin, and Shigeki Nozawa. "Bank of Japan Stepping Up Bond Buying Pace with or without Stimulus Shift." Bloomberg.com. October 25, 2015.

Buffett, Warren E. "Buy American. I Am." *The New York Times.* October 16, 2008.

Bustos, Paula. "Trade Liberalization, Exports, and Technology Upgrading: Evidence on the Impact of MERCOSUR on Argentinian Firms." *American Economic Review* 101, no. 1 (2011): 304–40. doi:10.1257/aer.101.1.304.

Caliari, Aldo. "Where the Argentine Debt Case Stands Now, and Why It Still Matters." North American Congress on Latin America. June 4, 2015.

Call, Gregory D. "Arsenic, ASARCO, and EPA: Cost-Benefit Analysis, Public Participation, and Polluter Games in the Regulation of Hazardous Air Pollutants." *Ecology Law Quarterly* 12, no. 3 (March 1985).

Calvo, Guillermo A. "Capital Flows and Macroeconomic Management: Tequila Lessons." *International Journal of Finance & Economics* 1, no. 3 (1996): 207–23. doi:10.1002/(sici)1099-1158(199607)1:33.0.co;2-3.

Carey, John. "Special Report: Extreme Weather and Climate Change." *Scientific American.* August 30, 2013.

Caro, Felipe, and Victor Martínez-de-Albéniz. "Fast Fashion: Business Model Overview and Research Opportunities." *Retail Supply Chain Management International Series in Operations Research & Management Science*, 2015, 237–64. doi:10.1007/978-1-4899-7562-1_9.

Center for Conservation Biology. "The Two Simon Bets." Stanford University. March 16, 2005. http://web.stanford.edu/group/CCB/Pubs/Ecofablesdocs/thebet.htm.

Chang, Andrew C., and Phillip Li. "Is Economics Research Replicable? Sixty Published Papers from Thirteen Journals Say 'Usually Not.'" *SSRN Electronic Journal*, 2015. doi:10.2139/ssrn.2669564.

Cohan, William. "Plenty Deserve Blame for Greece's Woes, but Maybe Not Goldman Sachs." *The New York Times*. July 13, 2015.

Collins, Courtney, and Andrew J. Rettenmaier. *Unfunded Liabilities of State and Local Government Employee Retirement Benefit Plans*. Report. Policy Report No 329. National Center for Policy Analysis, July 2010.

Collyns, Charles, and Saacha Mohammed. "Still Looking for Better Options—Exchange Rate Regimes Since the Global Financial Crisis." The Institute of International Finance. July 30, 2014.

Cooper, George. *The Origin of Financial Crises: Central Banks, Credit Bubbles and the Efficient Market Fallacy*. New York: Vintage Books, 2008.

Copeland, Thomas E., Tim Koller, and Jack Murrin. *Valuation: Measuring and Managing the Value of Companies*. New York: Wiley, 2000.

Council on Foreign Relations. "Understanding the Libor Scandal." May 21, 2015.

Cowen, Tyler. *Average Is Over: Powering America beyond the Age of the Great Stagnation*. Plume, 2014.

———. *The Complacent Class: The Self-Defeating Quest for the American Dream*. New York: St. Martin's Press, 2017.

Coyle, Diane. *GDP: A Brief but Affectionate History*. Princeton, NJ: Princeton University Press, 2014.

Curran, Enda, and Jeff Kearns. "With $21 Trillion, China's Savers Are Set to Change the World." Bloomberg.com. June 25, 2015.

Dalton, Joe. "Eurostat Confirms EU Average Corporate Tax Rate Increases for First Time since 2001." *International Tax Review*. 2012.

Davis, Morris A., Andreas Lehnert, and Robert F. Martin. "The Rent-Price Ratio for the Aggregate Stock of Owner-Occupied Housing." *Review of Income and Wealth* 54, no. 2 (2008): 279–84. doi:10.1111/j.1475-4991.2008.00274.x.

De, Supriyo, Saad Quayyum, Kirsten Schuttler, and Seyed Yousefi Reza. "How the Oil Price Decline Might Affect Remittances from GCC." *IMF Direct*, December 21, 2015.

Deardorff, Alan V. "The General Validity of the Heckscher-Ohlin Theorem." *The American Economic Review* 72, no. 4 (September 1, 1982): 683–94.

Decreux, Yvan, Chris Milner, and Nicolas Peridy. *The Economic Impact of the Free Trade Agreement (FTA) between the European Union and Korea*. Final Report. European Commission, 2010.

Deloitte. *2016 Global Manufacturing Competitiveness Index*. Report. 2016.

Deraniyagala, Sonali, and Ben Fine. "New Trade Theory versus Old Trade Policy: A Continuing Enigma." *Cambridge Journal of Economics* 25, no. 6 (2001): 809–25. doi:10.1093/cje/25.6.809.

Diamond, Jared M. *Collapse: How Societies Choose to Fail or Succeed*. New York: Viking, 2005.

Dixit, Avinash K. *Lawlessness and Economics: Alternative Modes of Governance*. Princeton, NJ: Princeton University Press, 2004.

Dobbs, Richard, Anu Madgavkar, James Manyika, Jonathan Woetzel, Jacques Bughin, Eric Labaye, and Pranav Kashyap. "Poorer than Their Parents? A New Perspective on Income Inequality." McKinsey & Company. July 2016.

Dobbs, Richard, David Skilling, Wayne Hu, Susan Lund, James Manyika, and Charles Roxburgh. "An Exorbitant Privilege? Implications of Reserve Currencies for Competitiveness." McKinsey Global Institute. December 2009.

Dobbs, Richard, James Manyika, and Jonathan R. Woetzel. *No Ordinary Disruption: The Four Global Forces Breaking All the Trends*. New York: PublicAffairs, 2016.

Dobbs, Richard, Susan Lund, Jonathan Woetzel, and Mina Mutafchieva. "Debt and (not Much) Deleveraging." Report. McKinsey & Company. February 2015.

Dobbs, Richard, Susan Lund, Tim Koller, and Ari Shwayder. "QE and Ultra-Low Interest Rates: Distributional Effects and Risks." McKinsey & Company. November 2013.

Dornbusch, R., Stanley Fischer, and Paul Samuelson. "Comparative Advantage, Trade, and Payments in a Ricardian Model with a Continuum of Goods." *The American Economic Review* 67, no. 5 (December 1, 1977): 823–39.

Doyle, Dara, and Stephanie Bodoni. "Apple Ordered to Pay Up to $14.5 Billion in EU Tax Clampdown." Bloomberg.com. August 30, 2016.

Dreyfuss, Barbara. *Hedge Hogs: The Cowboy Traders behind Wall Street's Largest Hedge Fund Disaster*. New York: Random House, 2013.

Drobny, Steven. *Inside the House of Money: Top Hedge Fund Traders on Profiting in the Global Markets*. Hoboken, NJ: Wiley & Sons, 2006.

———. *The Invisible Hands: Hedge Funds off the Record—Rethinking Real Money*. Hoboken, NJ: Wiley, 2010.

Drutman, Lee. *The Business of America Is Lobbying: How Corporations Became Politicized and Politics Became More Corporate*. Oxford University Press, 2015.

Dunbar, Nicholas, and Elisa Martinuzzi. "Goldman Secret Greece Loan Shows Two Sinners as Client Unravels." Bloomberg.com. March 5, 2012.

Dungey, Mardi, Renée Fry, Brenda González-Hermosillo, and Vance L. Martin. "Contagion in Global Equity Markets in 1998: The Effects of the Russian and LTCM Crises." *The North American Journal of Economics and Finance* 18, no. 2 (2007): 155–74. doi:10.1016/j.najef.2007.05.003.

Durlauf, Steven N., Paul A. Johnson, and Jonathan R. W. Temple. *Growth Econometrics*. Madison, WI: Social Systems Research Institute, University of Wisconsin, 2004.

Easterly, William. *The White Man's Burden: Why the West's Efforts to Aid the Rest Have Done So Much Ill and So Little Good*. New York: Penguin Press, 2006.

The Economist. "Mancur Olson: Mancur Lloyd Olson, Scourge of Special Interests, Died on February 19th, Aged 66." March 7, 1998.

———. "Buying Farmland Abroad: Outsourcing's Third Wave." May 23, 2009a.

———. "Emerging Versus Developed Economies: Power Shift." August 4, 2011a.

———. "Russian Energy: Twilight for BP in Russia?" June 9, 2012a.

———. "Global Debt Guide." September 19, 2012b.

———. "Horns of a Trilemma: How Can Emerging Economies Protect Themselves from the Rich World's Monetary Policy?" August 31, 2013.

———. "Capital Controls: Cash Cowed." April 6, 2013a.

———. "European Utilities: How to Lose Half a Trillion Euros." October 12, 2013b.

———. "China and Africa: Little to Fear but Fear Itself." September 21, 2013c.

———. "Company Taxation: The Price Isn't Right." February 16, 2013d.

———. "Europe's Dirty Secret: The Unwelcome Renaissance." January 5, 2013e.

———. "Liquid Diet: Recent Market Turbulence May Be Only a Foretaste." October 25, 2014a.

———. "Economic Convergence: The Headwinds Return." September 13, 2014b.
———. "Demography, Growth, and Inequality: Age Invaders." April 26, 2014c.
———. "Why Argentina May Default on Its Debts." July 29, 2014d.
———. "Intel Outside." April 19, 2014e.
———. "Gross and Net Returns: The Lessons from a Star Money Manager's Exit." October 4, 2014f.
———. "What's Wrong with Finance." May 1, 2015a.
———. "Africa's Middle Class: Few and Far Between." October 24, 2015b.
———. "Lexington: Not Running, but Fleeing." May 14, 2015c.
———. "2016's Global Wealth Forecast." December 30, 2015d.
———. "Currencies: Going Cuckoo for the Swiss." January 15, 2015e.
———. "Milking Taxpayers: As Crop Prices Fall, Farmers Grow Subsidies Instead." February 14, 2015f.
———. "Free Exchange: A Weighting Game." May 30, 2015g.
———. "Thrills and Spills: America Is at the Centre of a Global Monetary Disorder." Special Report: The World Economy. October 3, 2015h.
———. "Law of Averages: Star Funds Rarely Outperform for Long." August 27, 2016a.
———. "Why the Citizens of Flint Have Poisonous Tap Water." January 25, 2016b.
———. "Old Shoes and Duckweed: Singapore's Ruling Party Plans for Its Next Half-Century in Power." February 6, 2016c.
Edsall, Thomas. "The Republican Discovery of the Poor." *The New York Times*. February 10, 2015.
Eichengreen, Barry J. *Exorbitant Privilege: The Rise and Fall of the Dollar and the Future of the International Monetary System*. Oxford: Oxford University Press, 2011.
———. *Financial Crises: And What to Do about Them*. Oxford: Oxford University Press, 2002.
El-Erian, Mohamed A. *The Only Game in Town: Central Banks, Instability, and Avoiding the Next Collapse*. New York: Random House, 2016.
EU Prosun. *Current Alarming Situation*. Report. 2013.
European Commission. *Subsidies and Costs of EU Energy*. Report. ECOFYS, 2014.
EWG. "EWG's Farm Subsidy Database." USDA Conservation Programs. https://farm.ewg.org/.
Fackler, Martin. "Japanese Housewives Sweat in Secret as Markets Reel." *The New York Times*. September 15, 2007.
Fairbanks, Michael, and Stace Lindsay. *Plowing the Sea: Nurturing the Hidden Sources of Growth in the Developing World*. Boston, MA: Harvard Business School Press, 1997.
FDIC. "The LDC Debt Crisis." In *History of the Eighties: Lessons for the Future*, 191–210. Washington, DC: Federal Deposit Insurance Corporation, 1997.
"Features." FRB: Monetary Policy. July 2016. http://www.federalreserve.gov/monetarypolicy.
Federal Reserve Bank. "Current FAQs Informing the Public about the Federal Reserve." Accessed August 6, 2016. http://www.federalreserve.gov/faqs/money_12848.htm.
———. FRB: Recent Balance Sheet Trends—September 2016. https://www.federalreserve.gov/monetarypolicy/bst_recenttrends.htm.
———. "FRB: What Are the Federal Reserve's Objectives in Conducting Monetary Policy?" June 15, 2016.
———. "FRB: What Is the Money Supply? Is It Important?" Accessed December 16, 2015.
Federal Reserve Bank. "FRB: Who Owns the Federal Reserve?" August 25, 2016.
———. "The Money Supply." July 2008.

———. "What Is the Money Supply? Is It Important?" https://www.federalreserve.gov/faqs/money_12845.htm.

———. "Who Owns the Federal Reserve?" Accessed August 6, 2016. http://www.federalreserve.gov/faqs/about_14986.htm.

Federal Reserve Bank of New York. "The Money Supply." July 2008.

Federal Reserve Bank of St. Louis. "S&P/Case-Shiller U.S. National Home Price Index©." FRED Economic Data. https://fred.stlouisfed.org/series/CSUSHPINSA.

Federal Reserve Bank of San Francisco. "What Is the Difference between a Recession and a Depression?" February 2007.

Federal Reserve Bank of the United States. FOMC. "Chair Yellen's Press Conference." News release, September 17, 2015.

Feinberg, Richard, Gary Hufbauer Clyde, and Jeffrey Schott J. "NAFTA Revisited: Achievements and Challenges." *Foreign Affairs* 85, no. 1 (2006): 156. doi:10.2307/20031874.

Foley, Stephen, and Robin Wigglesworth. "Active Managers Exposed As Most US Equity Funds Lag behind Market." *Financial Times*, September 15, 2016.

Ford, Martin R. *The Rise of the Robots: Technology and the Threat of Mass Unemployment.* London: Oneworld, 2016.

Fratzscher, Marcel, Marco Duca Lo, and Roland Straub. "On the International Spillovers of US Quantitative Easing." European Central Bank Working Paper 1557 (June 2013). doi:10.2139/ssrn.2276855.

Frey, Carl Benedikt, and Michael A. Osborne. "The Future of Employment: How Susceptible Are Jobs to Computerization." *Oxford Martin School Working Paper*, September 17, 2013.

Fry, Renee, Vance Martin, Brenda González-Hermosillo, and Mardi Dungey. "International Contagion Effects from the Russian Crisis and the LTCM Near-Collapse." *IMF Working Papers* 2, no. 74 (2002). doi:10.5089/9781451849608.001.

Fukuyama, Francis. *Trust: The Social Virtues and the Creation of Prosperity.* New York: Free Press, 1995.

Gapper, John. "The Curse of the Consultant Is Spreading Fast." *Financial Times* (London), May 9, 2017.

Gelos, R. Gaston, Ratna Sahay, and Guido Sandleris. "Sovereign Borrowing by Developing Countries: What Determines Market Access?" *Journal of International Economics* 83, no. 2 (2011): 243–54. doi:10.1016/j.jinteco.2010.11.007.

Ghosh, Atish R., Jonathan D. Ostry, and Mahvash S. Qureshi. "When Do Capital Inflow Surges End in Tears?" *American Economic Review* 106, no. 5 (2016): 581–85. doi:10.1257/aer.p20161015.

Gilens, Martin, and Benjamin I. Page. "Testing Theories of American Politics: Elites, Interest Groups, and Average Citizens." *Perspectives on Politics* 12, no. 3 (September 2014).

Gittelsohn, John. "Private Equity Bets Billions on Foreclosures." Bloomberg.com. July 26, 2012.

Giuliano, Paola, and Marta Ruiz-Arranz. "Remittances, Financial Development, and Growth." *Journal of Development Economics* 90, no. 1 (2009): 144–52. doi:10.1016/j.jdeveco.2008.10.005.

Goldstein, Itay, and Ady Pauzner. "Contagion of Self-Fulfilling Financial Crises Due to Diversification of Investment Portfolios." *Journal of Economic Theory* 119, no. 1 (2004): 151–83. doi:10.1016/j.jet.2004.03.004.

Goldstein, Matthew. "A Yale Graduate Leaves a Trail of Ventures and Debts." *The New York Times*. April 16, 2015.

Greenberg, Andy. "Silk Road Defense Says Ulbricht Was Framed by the 'Real' Dread Pirate Roberts." Wired.com. January 13, 2015.

Greenspan, Alan. *The Map and the Territory: Risk, Human Nature, and the Future of Forecasting*. New York: Penguin Press, 2013.

Guerzoni, Benedetta, and Fabien Zuleeg. *Working Away at the Cost of Ageing: The Labour Market Adjusted Dependency Ratio*. Report. EPC Issue Paper No. 64. European Policy Center, April 2011.

Haggard, Stephan. *The Political Economy of the Asian Financial Crisis*. Washington, DC: Institute for International Economics, 2000.

Haidt, Jonathan. *The Righteous Mind: Why Good People Are Divided by Politics and Religion*. London: Penguin Books, 2013.

Havranek, Tomas, and Zuzana Irsova. "Estimating Vertical Spillovers from FDI: Why Results Vary and What the True Effect Is." *Journal of International Economics* 85, no. 2 (2011): 234–44. doi:10.1016/j.jinteco.2011.07.004.

He, Dong, et al. "Digital Currencies and Financial Crime." *Financial Crime and Gambling in a Virtual World*, January 2016, 137–65. doi:10.4337/9781782545200.00012.

He, Dong, Karl Habermeier, Ross Leckow, Vikram Haksar, Yasmin Almeida, Mikari Kashima, Nadim Kyriakos-Saad, Hiroko Oura, Tahsin Saadi, Natalia Stetsenko, and Concepcion Verdugo. *Virtual Currencies and Beyond: Initial Considerations*. Report no. SDN/16/03. January 2016. IMF Staff Discussion Note.

Head, John W. "The Asian Financial Crisis: Observations on Legal and Institutional Lessons Learned after a Dozen Years." *Review Symposium on the Asian Financial Crisis* University of Pennsylvania (2010).

Hellebrandt, Tomas, and Paolo Mauro. "The Future of Worldwide Income Distribution." *SSRN Electronic Journal*, April 2015. doi:10.2139/ssrn.2593894.

Helliwell, John, Richard Layard, and Jeffrey Sachs, eds. *World Happiness Report 2013*. Report. September 2013. United Nations Sustainable Development Solutions Network

Helpman, Elhanan. "International Trade in the Presence of Product Differentiation, Economies of Scale and Monopolistic Competition." *Journal of International Economics* 11, no. 3 (1981): 305–40. doi:10.1016/0022-1996(81)90001-5.

———. *The Mystery of Economic Growth*. Cambridge, MA: Belknap Press of Harvard University Press, 2004.

Henry, James S. *The Price of Offshore Revisited*. Report. Tax Justice Network, 2012.

Herndon, Thomas, Michael Ash, and Robert Pollin. "Does High Public Debt Consistently Stifle Economic Growth? A Critique of Reinhart and Rogoff." *Cambridge Journal of Economics* 38, no. 2 (2013): 257–79.

Hicks, Michael, and Srikant Devaraj. *The Myth and Reality of Manufacturing in the United States*. Report. Ball State University Center for Business and Economic Research, 2015.

Hotten, Russell. "Volkswagen: The Scandal Explained." BBC News. December 10, 2015. http://www.bbc.com/news/business-34324772.

Huntington, Samuel P., and Lawrence Harrison E. *Culture Matters: How Values Shape Human Progress*. New York: Basic Books, 2000.

IEA/OECD. *World Energy Outlook*. Report. Paris: International Energy Agency, 2014.

IMF Independent Evaluation Office. *The IMF and Recent Capital Account Crises Indonesia, Korea, Brazil*. Report. 2003.

IMF. "Understanding the Slowdown in Capital Flows to Emerging Markets." *Too Slow for Too Long: IMF World Economic Outlook*, Chapter 2, April 2016, 63–99.

———. *Too Slow for Too Long: IMF World Economic Outlook*. April 2016.

———. *The Liberalization and Management of Capital Flows: An Institutional View*. Report, November 14, 2012.

———. *Sixth Edition of the IMF's Balance of Payments and International Investment Position Manual (BPM6)*. Technical paper. International Monetary Fund, 2013.

Intergovernmental Panel on Climate Change. *Climate Change 2014: Impacts, Adaptation, and Vulnerability*. Report. IPCC, 2014.

———. "2016 Investment Company Fact Book." 2016. http://www.icifactbook.org/.

———. "Frequently Asked Questions about the U.S. ETF Market." https://www.ici.org/etf_resources/background/faqs_etfs_market.

Ismail, Netty. "Singapore Inc.'s Bank Bet Losses Pile Up on UBS Scandal." Bloomberg.com. September 26, 2011.

Joint Center for Housing Studies of Harvard University. *America's Rental Housing Evolving Markets and Needs*. Report. President and Fellows of Harvard College, 2013.

Joyce, Michael, Ana Lasaosa, Ibrahim Stevens, and Matthew Tong. "The Financial Market Impact of Quantitative Easing." *International Journal of Central Banking*, September 2001. doi:10.2139/ssrn.1638986.

Joyce, Michael, et al. "The Financial Market Impact of Quantitative Easing in the United Kingdom." *International Journal of Central Banking*, September 2011, 113–61.

Kahneman, Daniel. *Thinking, Fast and Slow*. Macmillan, 2011.

Kahneman, Daniel, Paul Slovic, and Amos Tversky. *Judgment under Uncertainty: Heuristics and Biases*. Cambridge: Cambridge University Press, 1982.

Kaplan, Ethan, and Dani Rodrik. "Did the Malaysian Capital Controls Work?" *NBER Working Paper* 8142 (January 2001). doi:10.3386/w8142.

Karnitschnig, Matthew. "Germany's Expensive Gamble on Renewable Energy." *Wall Street Journal*. August 26, 2014.

Karolyi, G. Andrew. "Does International Financial Contagion Really Exist?" *International Finance* 6, no. 2 (2003): 179–99. doi:10.1111/1468-2362.00114.

Kaufman, Frederick. "How Goldman Sachs Created the Food Crisis." *Foreign Policy*. April 27, 2011.

Kelley, Colin P., Shahrzad Mohtadi, Mark A. Cane, Richard Seager, and Yochanan Kushnir. "Climate Change in the Fertile Crescent and Implications of the Recent Syrian Drought." *Proceedings of the National Academy of Sciences USA* 112, no. 11 (2015): 3241–246. doi:10.1073/pnas.1421533112.

Kim, Crystal. "Peak ETF Mania: Are We There Yet?" *Barrons*, April 25, 2017.

King, Stephen D. *When the Money Runs Out: The End of Western Affluence*. New Haven, CT: Yale University Press, 2013.

Kodres, Laura E., and Matthew Pritsker. "A Rational Expectations Model of Financial Contagion." *The Journal of Finance* 57, no. 2 (2002): 769–99. doi:10.1111/1540-6261.00441.

Kolhatkar, Sheelah. *BLACK EDGE: The Inside Story of the Most Wanted Man on Wall Street*. New York: Random House, 2017.

Koppel, Robert. *Investing and the Irrational Mind: Rethink Risk, Outwit Optimism, and Seize Opportunities Others Miss*. New York: McGraw-Hill, 2011.

Kothe, Emillie, Michael Gestrin, and Carly Avery. "International Investment Struggles." *FDI IN FIGURES*, February 2014. http://www.oecd.org/investment/FDI-in-Figures-Feb-2014.pdf.

Kotlikoff, Laurence J. "America's Hidden Credit Card Bill." *The New York Times*. July 31, 2014.

Kotlikoff, Laurence J., and Scott Burns. *The Coming Generational Storm: What You Need to Know about America's Economic Future*. Cambridge, MA: MIT Press, 2004.

Kraay, Aart, and David McKenzie. "Do Poverty Traps Exist? Assessing the Evidence." *Journal of Economic Perspectives* 28, no. 3 (2014): 127–48. doi:10.1257/jep.28.3.127.

Krugman, Paul R. "Increasing Returns, Monopolistic Competition, and International Trade." *Journal of International Economics* 9, no. 4 (1979): 469–79. doi:10.1016/0022-1996(79)90017-5.

Landes, David S. *The Wealth and Poverty of Nations: Why Some Are So Rich and Some So Poor*. New York: W.W. Norton, 1998.

Lavigne, Robert, Subrata Sarker, and Garima Vasishtha. "Spillover Effects of Quantitative Easing on Emerging-Market Economies." *Bank of Canada Review*, August 2014.

Lee, Ronald. "The Demographic Transition: Three Centuries of Fundamental Change." *The Journal of Economic Perspectives* 17, no. 4 (October 1, 2003): 167–90.

Leonhardt, David. "Who Will Crack the Code?" *The New York Times*. May 25, 2013.

Leontief, Wassily. "Domestic Production and Foreign Trade; The American Capital Position Re-Examined." *Proceedings of the American Philosophical Society* 97, no. 4 (September 28, 1953): 332–49.

Lewis, Michael. *Flash Boys: A Wall Street Revolt*. New York: W.W. Norton, 2014.

———. "The Secret Goldman Sachs Tapes." Bloomberg View. September 2014.

Lincoln Institute of Land Policy. "Land and Property Values in the U.S." http://datatoolkits.lincolninst.edu/subcenters/land-values/rent-price-ratio.asp.

Liverman, Diana, and Amy Glasmeier. "What Are the Economic Consequences of Climate Change?" *The Atlantic*. April 22, 2014.

Lowenstein, Roger. *When Genius Failed: The Rise and Fall of Long-Term Capital Management*. New York: Random House, 2000.

———. *While America Aged: How Pension Debts Ruined General Motors, Stopped the NYC Subways, Bankrupted San Diego, and Loom as the Next Financial Crisis*. New York: Penguin Press, 2008.

Mahbubani, Kishore. *The Great Convergence: Asia, the West, and the Logic of One World*. PublicAffairs, 2014; 86–88.

Mallaby, Sebastian. "Go for the Jugular." *The Atlantic*, June 4, 2010.

Managed Funds Association. "Institutional Investors Almost 65 Percent of Hedge Fund Assets—Managed Funds Association—MFA." January 22, 2015.

Mander, Jerry, and Edward Goldsmith. *The Case against the Global Economy: And for a Turn toward the Local*. San Francisco: Sierra Club Books, 1996.

Manyika, James, Jacques Bughin, Susan Lund, Olivia Nottebohm, David Poulter, Sebastian Jauch, and Sree Ramaswamy. "Global Flows in a Digital Age." *McKinsey Global Institute, April* (2014): 1270–85.

McBride, James, Christopher Alessi, and Mohammed Sergie. "Understanding the Libor Scandal." Council on Foreign Relations. May 2015.

McKinnon, Ronald I. *The Order of Economic Liberalization: Financial Control in the Transition to a Market Economy*. Baltimore: Johns Hopkins University Press, 1991.

Mesquita, Bruce Bueno De. *Predictioneer's Game: Using the Logic of Brazen Self-Interest to See and Shape the Future*. New York: Random House, 2009.

———. *The Dictator's Handbook: Why Bad Behavior Is Almost Always Good Politics*. New York: PublicAffairs, 2012.

Mider, Zachary, and Jesse Drucker. "Tax Inversion: How U.S. Companies Buy Tax Breaks." Bloomberg.com. April 6, 2016.

Milne, Richard. "Porsche Extends Dollar Hedge." *Financial Times* (Frankfurt), September 14, 2005.

Minsky, Hyman P. *Stabilizing an Unstable Economy*. New Haven, CT: Yale University Press, 1986.

Miroudot, Sébastien, Alexandros Ragoussis, and Rainer Lanz. "Trade in Intermediate Goods and Services." *OECD Trade Policy Papers*, 2009. doi:10.1787/5kmlcxtdlk8r-en.

Mishel, Lawrence. *The Wedges between Productivity and Median Compensation Growth*. Report. Economic Policy Institute, Issue Brief, April 26, 2012.

Mistrulli, Paolo Emilio. "Assessing Financial Contagion in the Interbank Market: Maximum Entropy versus Observed Interbank Lending Patterns." *Journal of Banking & Finance* 35, no. 5 (2011): 1114–27. doi:10.1016/j.jbankfin.2010.09.018.

Moser, Thomas. "What Is International Financial Contagion?" *International Finance* 6, no. 2 (2003): 157–78. doi:10.1111/1468-2362.00113.

Mourdoukoutas, Panos. "A Strategic Mistake That Haunts JC Penney." *Forbes*. September 27, 2013.

Moyo, Dambisa. *Dead Aid: Why Aid Is Not Working and How There Is a Better Way for Africa*. New York: Farrar, Straus and Giroux, 2009.

Munnell, Alicia H., and Jean Pierre Aubrey. *The Funding of State and Local Pensions: 2014–2018*. Technical paper. Vol. 45. Center for Retirement Research Boston College, June 2015.

Munnell, Alicia H., Wenliang Hou, and Anthony Webb. "National Retirement Risk Index (NRRI) Update Shows Half of Working-Age Americans Still Falling Short." *The Journal of Retirement* 3, no. 2 (2015): 34–42. doi:10.3905/jor.2015.3.2.034.

Naím, Moisés. *Illicit: How Smugglers, Traffickers and Copycats Are Hijacking the Global Economy*. New York: Doubleday, 2005.

Nakamura, David, and Chico Harlan. "Nuclear Plant's Panel Ignored Risk of Tsunami." *The Washington Post*, March 24, 2011.

Nakamura, Yuji, Anna Kitanaka, and Nao Sano. "The Tokyo Whale Is Quietly Buying Up Huge Stakes in Japan Inc." Bloomberg.com. April 24, 2016.

Narang, Rishi K. *Inside the Black Box: A Simple Guide to Quantitative and High Frequency Trading*, second edition. Hoboken, NJ: John Wiley and Sons, 2013.

Naroff, Joel L., and Ron Scherer. *Big Picture Economics: How to Navigate the New Global Economy*. Wiley, 2014.

National Aeronautics and Space Administration. *NASA, NOAA Analyses Reveal Record-Shattering Global Warm Temperatures in 2015*. January 20, 2016. http://www.giss.nasa.gov/research/news/20160120/.

———. "NASA Study Shows Global Sea Ice Diminishing, Despite Antarctic Gains." NASA. February 10, 2015.

Newton, Derek. "Cheating in Online Classes Is Now Big Business." *The Atlantic*. November 4, 2015.

Noland, Marcus, and Howard Pack. *Industrial Policy in an Era of Globalization: Lessons from Asia*. Washington, DC: Institute for International Economics, 2003.

Nordhaus, William D. *The Climate Casino: Risk, Uncertainty, and Economics for a Warming World*. New Haven, CT: Yale University Press, 2015.

North, Douglass C. *Institutions, Institutional Change, and Economic Performance.* Cambridge: Cambridge University Press, 1990.

———. *Understanding the Process of Economic Change.* Princeton, NJ: Princeton University Press, 2005.

OCO. The Authority on Foreign Investment. *FDI in Renewable Energy: A Promising Decade Ahead.* Report. 2012. ocoinsight.com.

OECD. *Explanatory Statement, OECD/G20 Base Erosion and Profit Shifting Project.* Paris: OECD, 2015. http://www.oecd.org/ctp/beps-explanatory-statement-2015.pdf.

———. *FDI in Figures,* February 2014.

———. *"Financial Contagion in the Era of Globalised Banking?"* Report. Vol. 14. OECD Economics Department Policy Notes, June 2012.

———. "How's Life? 2015: Measuring Well-Being." OECD Better Life Index. 2014. http://www.oecdbetterlifeindex.org/#/21111111111.

———. *In It Together: Why Less Inequality Benefits All.* Report. Paris: OECD Publishing, 2015. 10.1787/9789264235120-en.

———. "Labour Losing to Capital: What Explains the Declining Labour Share?" *OECD Employment Outlook* Chapter 3 (2012). doi:10.1787/empl_outlook-2012-en.

———. "OECD Benchmark Definition of Foreign Direct Investment: Fourth Edition." 2008. doi:10.1787/9789264045743-en.

———. *OECD Business and Finance Outlook 2015.* Paris: OECD Publishing, 2015. doi:10.1787/9789264234291-en.

———. "Official Development Assistance (ODA)—Net ODA—OECD Data." Accessed 2016. https://data.oecd.org/oda/net-oda.htm.

———. "Old-Age Dependency Ratio," in Pensions at a Glance 2015b: OECD and G20 indicators, OECD Publishing, Paris.

———. *Pension Markets in Focus.* Technical paper. 2014.

———. *Trade-Adjustment Costs in OECD Labour Markets: A Mountain or a Molehill?* Paris: OECD, 2005.

Office of Financial Research. *2014 Annual Report.* Report. 2014.

Olson, Mancur. *The Logic of Collective Action: Public Goods and the Theory of Groups.* Cambridge, MA: Harvard University Press, 1965.

O'Neill, Jim. "Building Better Global Economic BRICs." *Goldman Sachs, Global Economics Paper #66,* November 30, 2001. doi:10.1016/j.forpol.2015.10.009.

Ostry, Jonathan David, Atish R. Ghosh, and Raphael A. Espinoza. *When Should Public Debt Be Reduced?* International Monetary Fund, 2015.

"Overview." World Happiness Report. Accessed August 14, 2016. http://worldhappiness.report/.

Oxfam. *Wealth: Having It All and Wanting More. Oxfam Issue Briefing.* Report. Oxfam, 2015.

Ozkan, F. Gulcin, and D. Unsal Filiz. "Global Financial Crisis, Financial Contagion, and Emerging Markets." *IMF Working Papers* 12, no. 293 (2012): 1. doi:10.5089/9781475551167.001.

Painter, Gary, and Christian L. Redfearn. "The Role of Interest Rates in Influencing Long-Run Homeownership Rates." *The Journal of Real Estate Finance and Economics* 25, no. 2–3 (2002): 243–67.

Parker, Kim, Paul Taylor, Seth Motel, and Eileen Patten. "The Big Generation Gap at the Polls Is Echoed in Attitudes on Budget Tradeoffs." Pew Research Centers Social Demographic Trends Project RSS. December 20, 2012.

Pasadilla, Gloria O., Emmanuel San Andres, Andre Wirjo, and Rhea C. Hernando. "Do FTAs Matter for Trade?" *Asia Pacific Economic Cooperation Policy Support Unit*, May 2015.

Patterson, Scott. "Chinese Billionaire Linked to Giant Aluminum Stockpile in Mexican Desert." *Wall Street Journal.* September 8, 2016.

———. *The Quants: How a Small Band of Math Wizards Took Over Wall St. and Nearly Destroyed It.* New York: Crown, 2010.

Pear, Robert. "Soft Drink Industry Fights Proposed Food Stamp Ban." *The New York Times.* April 29, 2011. http://www.nytimes.com/2011/04/30/us/politics/30food.html?_r=0.

Perry, Guillermo, and Luis Servén. "The Anatomy of a Multiple Crisis: Why Was Argentina Special and What Can We Learn from It?" *World Bank Office of the Chief Economist: Policy Research Working Papers*, 2003. doi:10.1596/1813-9450-3081.

Pew Research Center. "Beyond Red vs. Blue: The Political Typology." June 2014.

———. "The American Middle Class Is Losing Ground." Pew Research Centers Social Demographic Trends Project RSS. December 9, 2015.

Pfeffer, F. T., S. Danziger, and R. F. Schoeni. "Wealth Disparities Before and After the Great Recession." *The Annals of the American Academy of Political and Social Science* 650, no. 1 (2013): 98–123. doi:10.1177/0002716213497452.

Piketty, Thomas, and Arthur Goldhammer. *Capital in the Twenty-First Century.* Belknap Press, 2014.

Plumer, Brad. "Chinese Firms and Gulf Sheiks Are Snatching Up Farmland Worldwide. Why?" *Washington Post.* January 26, 2013.

Pompian, Michael M. *Behavioral Finance and Wealth Management: How to Build Investment Strategies That Account for Investor Biases.* Hoboken, NJ: Wiley, 2012.

Porter, Michael E. *The Competitive Advantage of Nations.* New York: Free Press, 1990.

Qian, Nancy. "Making Progress on Foreign Aid." NBER. August 2014.

Quartz, Steven, and Anette Asp. "Unequal, Yet Happy." *The New York Times.* April 11, 2015.

Rajan, Raghuram. *Fault Lines: How Hidden Fractures Still Threaten the World Economy.* Princeton, NJ: Princeton University Press, 2010.

Ramaswamy, Srichander. "Market Structures and Systemic Risks of Exchange-Traded Funds." Bank for International Settlements. BIS Working Papers 343. April 2011.

Ratha, Dilip, Kirsten Schuettler, and Seyed Yousefi Raza. "Will Falling Oil Prices Lead to a Decline in Outward Remittances from GCC Countries?" *People Move: A Blog about Migration, Remittances and Development*, January 28, 2015.

Reed, Brian, Sean Collins, Sarah Holden, and Judy Streenstra. "What Is an ETF?" 2016 Investment Company Fact Book. 2016. Accessed August 6, 2016.

Reinert, Erik S. *How Rich Countries Got Rich—and Why Poor Countries Stay Poor.* New York: Carroll & Graf, 2007.

Reinhart, Carmen M., and Kenneth S. Rogoff. *This Time Is Different: Eight Centuries of Financial Folly.* Princeton, NJ: Princeton University Press, 2009.

Reuter, Peter H. "The Unintended Consequences of Drug Policies: Report 5." *RAND Technical Report*, 2009. doi:10.1037/e563632010-001.

Revell, Brian, John Saunders, and Caroline Saunders. "Assessing the Environmental Impact of Liberalising Agricultural Trade—With Special Reference to EU-Mercosur." Proceedings of 88th Annual Conference of the Agricultural Economics Society, Paris, France. 2014.

Rijckeghem, Caroline Van, and Beatrice Weder. "Sources of Contagion: Is It Finance or Trade?" *Journal of International Economics* 54, no. 2 (2001): 293–308. doi:10.1016/s0022-1996(00)00095-7.

Ritholtz, Barry. "222 Years of Long-Term Interest Rates." The Big Picture. January 19, 2012. http://www.ritholtz.com/blog/2012/01/222-years-of-long-term-interest-rates/.
Rivkin, Jan W. "The U.S. Economy Is Doing Only Half Its Job." *Harvard Business Review.* December 17, 2015.
Roache, Shaun, and Marina Rousset. "Unconventional Monetary Policy and Asset Price Risk." *IMF Working Paper WP/13/190*, August 2013.
Roache, Shaun K., and Marina Rousset. "Unconventional Monetary Policy and Asset Price Risk." International Monetary Fund Working Paper, 13/190 (2013).
Roche, Cullen O. "Understanding the Modern Monetary System." By Cullen O. Roche. *SSRN.* August 2011.
———. "Economics is Mostly a Policy Debate Masquerading as a Scientific Debate." Pragmatic Capitalism. 2014. http://www.pragcap.com/economics-is-mostly-a-policy-debate-masquerading-as-a-scientific-debate/.
———. "Fun with Charts—Paul Krugman Edition." Pragmatic Capitalism. May 2015. http://www.pragcap.com/fun-with-charts-paul-krugman-edition/.
———. "Reserves Do NOT Allow Banks to Make More Loans." Pragmatic Capitalism. May 2015. http://www.pragcap.com/reserves-do-not-allow-banks-to-make-more-loans.
———. "The Trade That Led to the Demise of PIMCO Total Return." Pragmatic Capitalism. September 2014. http://pragcap.com/the-trade-that-led-to-the-demise-of-pimco-total-return.
Rodney, Walter, A. M. Babu, and Vincent Harding. *How Europe Underdeveloped Africa.* Washington, DC: Howard University Press, 1981.
Rodrik, Dani. *Economics Rules: The Rights and Wrongs of the Dismal Science.* Oxford: Oxford University Press, 2015a.
———. "Economists vs. Economics." Project Syndicate RSS. September 10, 2015b.
———. *Has Globalization Gone Too Far?* Washington, DC: Institute for International Economics, 1997.
———. *In Search of Prosperity: Analytic Narratives on Economic Growth.* Princeton, NJ: Princeton University Press, 2003.
———. *The New Global Economy and Developing Countries: Making Openness Work.* Washington, DC: Overseas Development Council, 1999.
Rogoff, Kenneth, and Carmen Reinhart. "Growth in a Time of Debt." *American Economic Review* 100, no. 2 (2010): 573–78.
Rosenbloom, David H., and Deborah D. Rosenbloom. *Public Administration: Understanding Management, Politics, and Law in the Public Sector.* New York: Random House, 1986.
Roubini, Nouriel, and Stephen Mihm. *Crisis Economics: A Crash Course in the Future of Finance.* New York: Penguin Press, 2010.
Ruta, Michele, and Mika Saito. "Chained Value." Finance and Development. IMF December 2013.
Saez, Emmanuel. *Striking It Richer: The Evolution of Top Incomes in the United States.* Report. Berkeley: University of California Department of Economics, 2013.
Saez, Emmanuel, and Gabriel Zucman. "Wealth Inequality in the United States since 1913: Evidence from Capitalized Income Tax Data." *The Quarterly Journal of Economics* 131, no. 2 (2016): 519–78. doi:10.1093/qje/qjw004.
Sali-i-Martin, Javier. "Sala-i-Martin's Convergence." Accessed September 3, 2016. http://www.columbia.edu/~xs23/columbia/ec3213/convergence/convergence.htm.

Schmidt, Rachel, and Kishore G. Kulkarni. "A Partial Test of the Heckscher-Ohlin-Samuelson Model: US-Mexico Trade Relations and Labour in Mexico." *International Journal of Management* 3, no. 1 (2014). doi:10.15410/aijm/2014/v3i1/50553.

Schularick, Moritz, and Alan M. Taylor. "Credit Booms Gone Bust: Monetary Policy, Leverage Cycles and Financial Crises, 1870–2008." *NBER Working Paper* 15512. November 2009.

Schwartz, Nelson, and Charles Duhigg. "Apple's Web of Tax Shelters Saved It Billions, Panel Finds." *The New York Times*. May 20, 2013.

Schwartz, Nelson D. "As Dollar Heats Up Overseas, U.S. Manufacturers Feel a Chill." *The New York Times*. March 26, 2015.

Scott, Robert E. *The China Toll.* Report. Economic Policy Institute August 23, 2012.

Searchinger, Timothy. "Use of U.S. Croplands for Biofuels Increases Greenhouse Gases through Emissions from Land-Use Change." *Science* 319, no. 5867 (February 29, 2008): 1238–40.

"The Secret Recordings of Carmen Segarra, Transcript." Interview by Ira Glass. *This American Life*. September 26, 2014. http://www.thisamericanlife.org/radio-archives/episode/536/transcript.

Sen, Amartya. *Development as Freedom*. New York: Knopf, 1999.

Sen, Conor. "The Economy's Worst Enemy Now Is Demographics (and It's About to Be Our Best Friend)." *The Atlantic*. January 15, 2013.

Shah, Sunit N. "The Principle-Agent Problem in Finance." *The CFA Institute Research Foundation*, April 2014. http://www.cfapubs.org/doi/pdf/10.2470/rflr.v9.n1.1.

Sharma, Shalendra D. *The Asian Financial Crisis: Crisis, Reform, and Recovery*. Manchester, UK: Manchester University Press, 2003.

Sheard, Paul. "Helicopter Money and the Monetary Garden of Eden." Standard & Poor's Global Credit Portal. May 4, 2016.

———. "Repeat After Me: Banks Can Not and Do Not 'Lend Out' Reserves." S&P Global Ratings, Working Paper, 2014

Shiller, Robert J., Stanley Fischer, and Benjamin M. Friedman. "Stock Prices and Social Dynamics." *Brookings Papers on Economic Activity* 1984, no. 2 (1984): 457. doi:10.2307/2534436.

Slovik, Patrick. "Systemically Important Banks and Capital Regulation Challenges." *OECD Economics Department Working Papers*, 2012. doi:10.1787/5kg0ps8cq8q6-en.

Smick, David M. *The World Is Curved: Hidden Dangers to the Global Economy*. New York: Portfolio, 2008.

Social Security Advisory Board. *The Unsustainable Cost of Healthcare*. Report. September 2009.

Soe, Aye M., and Frank Luo. "Does Past Performance Matter? S&P Persistence Scorecard." *S&P Dow Jones Indices McGraw Hill Financial*, June 2014. doi:10.2139/ssrn.2079822.

Soe, Aye M., and Ryan Poirier. "SPIVA US Scorecard, Summary." *S&P Dow Jones Indices McGraw Hill Financial*, Mid-Year 2016.

Solow, Robert M. "A Contribution to the Theory of Economic Growth." *The Quarterly Journal of Economics* 70, no. 1 (1956): 65. doi:10.2307/1884513.

Sommeiller, Estelle, and Mark Price. "The Increasingly Unequal States of America: Income Inequality by State, 1917 to 2011." Economic Policy Institute. February 19, 2014.

Sommer, Jeff. "How Many Mutual Funds Routinely Rout the Market? Zero." *The New York Times*. March 14, 2015.

Soto, Hernando de. *The Mystery of Capital: Why Capitalism Triumphs in the West and Fails Everywhere Else*. New York: Basic Books, 2000.

"Source on Sovereign Wealth Funds, Pensions, Endowments, Superannuation Funds, Central Banks and Public Funds." SWFI. Accessed August 14, 2016. http://www.swfinstitute.org/fund-rankings/.

Sovereign Wealth Fund Institute. "Fund Rankings." 2016. http://www.swfinstitute.org/fund-rankings/.

Stahl, Ashley. "The Promise and Perils of Sovereign Wealth Funds." *Forbes*. December 19, 2013.

Statistical Office of the European Communities. *Eurostat-OECD Methodological Manual on Purchasing Power Parities*. OECD Publishing, 2012.

Stern, N. H. *The Economics of Climate Change: The Stern Review*. Cambridge, UK: Cambridge University Press, 2007.

Stevenson, Alexandra, and Michael Corkery. "Calpers, Nation's Biggest Pension Fund, to End Hedge Fund Investments." DealBook. *The New York Times*. September 2014.

Stevis, Matina. "Foreign Investment in Africa Seen at Record $80 Billion in 2014, Report Shows." *Wall Street Journal* (New York), May 19, 2014.

Stiglitz, Joseph E., and Andrew Charlton. *Fair Trade for All: How Trade Can Promote Development*. Oxford: Oxford University Press, 2005.

———. *Globalization and Its Discontents*. New York: W.W. Norton, 2002.

———. *Making Globalization Work*. New York: W.W. Norton, 2006.

Stokes, Bruce. "Is Europe on Board for a New Trade Deal with the U.S.?" Pew Research Center RSS. January 29, 2015.

Story, Louise, and Stephanie Saul. "Jho Low, Well Connected in Malaysia, Has an Appetite for New York." *The New York Times*. February 8, 2015.

Story, Louise, Landon Thomas, and Nelson Schwartz. "Wall St. Helped to Mask Debt Fueling Europe's Crisis." *The New York Times*. February 13, 2010.

Taibbi, Matt. "The Great American Bubble Machine." *Rolling Stone*. April 5, 2010.

Taleb, Nassim Nicholas. *The Black Swan: The Impact of the Highly Improbable*. New York: Random House, 2007.

———. *Fooled by Randomness: The Hidden Role of Chance in Life and in the Markets*. New York: Random House, 2005.

Taylor, Alan. "Bhopal: The World's Worst Industrial Disaster, 30 Years Later." *The Atlantic*. December 2014.

Tetlock, Philip E., and Dan Gardner. *Superforecasting: The Art and Science of Prediction*. London: Rh Books, 2015.

Thaler, Richard H. *Misbehaving: The Making of Behavioral Economics*. W.W. Norton, 2016.

Thompson, Derek. "A World without Work." *The Atlantic*. July/August 2015.

Tirole, Jean. *Financial Crises, Liquidity, and the International Monetary System*.

Transparency International. Corruption Perceptions Index. 2016.

Tressel, Thierry. "Financial Contagion through Bank Deleveraging: Stylized Facts and Simulations Applied to the Financial Crisis." *IMF Working Papers* 10, no. 236 (2010): 1. doi:10.5089/9781455209361.001.

United Nations. *The Global Social Crisis: Report on the World Social Situation 2011*. New York: United Nations Publications, 2011.

———. *Practical Manual on Transfer Pricing for Developing Countries*. Report. ST/ESA/347. New York, 2013.

———. *World Happiness Report 2013*. Publication.

United Nations Commission on Trade and Development *Global Investment Trends Monitor* No. 25, February 1, 2017.

United Nations Environmental Program. *ERISC PHASE II: How Food Prices Link Environmental Constraints to Sovereign Credit Risk.* Report. UNEP, May 2016.

"United States International Trade Commission." 2015 HTSA Revision 2 Edition. Accessed September 18, 2016. https://www.usitc.gov/tata/hts/bychapter/index.htm.

Urbina, Ian. "The Outlaw Ocean." *The New York Times.* July 23, 2015. http://www.nytimes.com/interactive/2015/07/24/world/the-outlaw-ocean.html.

US Energy Information Administration. "United States Remains Largest Producer of Petroleum and Natural Gas Hydrocarbons." May 23, 2016.

Vernon, Raymond. "The Product Cycle Hypothesis in a New International Environment." *Oxford Bulletin of Economics and Statistics* 41, no. 4 (1979): 255–67. doi:10.1111/j.1468-0084.1979.mp41004002.x.

Vonnegut, Andrew. "Real Option Theories and Investment in Emerging Economies." *Emerging Markets Review* 1, no. 1 (2000): 82–100. doi:10.1016/s1566-0141(00)00005-4.

Wacziarg, R., and K. H. Welch. "Trade Liberalization and Growth: New Evidence." *The World Bank Economic Review* 22, no. 2 (2007): 187–231. doi:10.1093/wber/lhn007.

Walsh, Mary Williams. "Risky Moves in the Game of Life Insurance." *The New York Times.* April 11, 2015.

Wildau, Gabriel, and Tom Mitchell, "China: Renminbi stalls on road to being a global currency" *The Financial Times*, December 11, 2016.

Willis Towers Watson. *Global Pension Assets Study 2017.* Report. 2017.

Wolf, Martin. *Why Globalization Works.* New Haven, CT: Yale Nota Bene, 2005.

———. "More Perils Lie in Wait for the Eurozone." *Financial Tmes* (London), December 6, 2016.

World Bank. Doing Business—Measuring Business Regulations—World Bank Group. 2016. http://www.doingbusiness.org/.

World Bank Group/ECOFYS. *State and Trends in Carbon Pricing 2015.* Report. Washington, DC: World Bank, 2015.

World Economic Forum. Global Competitiveness Report 2015–2016. 2016.

———. *The Global Risks Report 2017.* Report. 12th ed.

World Trade Organization. "United States—Measures Affecting Trade in Large Civil Aircraft—Second Complaint." WTO. October 2012.

Wunsch, Pierre. *Is the European Integration Machine Broken?* Technical paper. 2nd ed. Vol. 48. Forum: Convergence in the EU. Intereconomics, 2013.

Xing, Yuqing. "Measuring Value Added in the People's Republic of China's Exports: A Direct Approach." *ADBI Working Paper Series* 494 (2013). doi:10.1142/9789814656368_0004.

Index

About the Author

With a career spanning academia, finance, consulting, and business, **Andrew Vonnegut** currently teaches global economics at the University of California, Santa Barbara; advises on economics and finance; and owns a small manufacturing company based in Southern California. Before returning to his home state, Andrew worked abroad for sixteen years in international finance and management consulting. He has advised governments and companies on economic policy and finance in the United Arab Emirates, Qatar, Turkey, Oman, Egypt, Montenegro, and Serbia, among other countries.

Andrew earned his PhD in applied economics and statistics from the University of Minnesota, after graduating Phi Beta Kappa from the University of California, Santa Barbara, with degrees in international relations and English literature. He was a Fulbright fellow and MacArthur scholar. His experience includes working at three of the largest investment banks in Turkey, as a senior economist for the US Agency for International Development, and for the international consulting firms Booz Allen Hamilton and Booz and Co.